RSS'S TRYST WITH POLITICS

From Hedgewar to Sudarshan

RSS's Tryst with Politics

From Hedgewar to Sudarshan

PRALAY KANUNGO

MANOHAR
2026

First published 2002
Reprinted 2017, 2024, 2025, 2026

ISBN 978-81-7304-398-7 (hardbound)
ISBN 978-81-7304-506-6 (paperback)

Published by
Ajay Kumar Jain *for*
Manohar Publishers & Distributors
4753/23 Ansari Road, Daryaganj
New Delhi 110 002

Printed and bound in India

Contents

Acknowledgements

The present work is based on my doctoral dissertation which I undertook in the Department of Political Science, University of Delhi. I thank all the teachers of the Department for their kind cooperation. Special thanks to my supervisor Dr. Bidyut Chakrabarty for his generous suggestions and Professor Manoranjan Mohanty for his constant encouragement. I am grateful to all my examiners for their valuable comments that I have tried to incorporate while revising the thesis. I am particularly indebted to Professor Ashis Nandy for sharpening my ideas through his provocative queries during the viva-voce and inspiring me to explore the possibility of writing a book. I thank the University Grants Commission for providing me financial assistance under the Minor Research Projects Scheme to buy books and undertake field trips. Thanks also to all my friends for their suggestions and critical comments.

My sincere thanks are reserved for those leaders and workers of the Rashtriya Swayamsevak Sangh and its affiliates of Orissa who spared their valuable time and passed on some invaluable information. I shall specially remember the way they have extended their hospitality at various places. I thank the staff of the Nehru Memorial Museum & Library, National Archives of India Library, Orissa State Archives Library for their kind cooperation. Sincere thanks to the gentleman publisher of Manohar for kindly agreeing to publish this work and the erudite editor B.N. Varma for his painstaking efforts. Finally, lots of thanks to my wife Nina and daughter Tripti for their patience and support without which this book could not have been written.

New Delhi
August 2000

PRALAY KANUNGO

Abbreviations

ABPS	Akhil Bharatiya Pratinidhi Sabha
ABVKA	Akhil Bharatiya Vanavasi Kalyan Ashram
ABVP	Akhil Bharatiya Vidyarthi Parishad
BD	Bajrang Dal
BJP	Bharatiya Janata Party
BJS	Bharatiya Jana Sangh
BKS	Bharatiya Kisan Sangh
BMS	Bharatiya Mazdoor Sangh
CSS	Chhatra Sangharsh Samiti
DRI	Deendayal Research Institute
JP	Jayaprakash Narayan
KKM	Kendriya Karyakari Mandal
MISA	Maintenance of Internal Security Act
NAI	National Archives of India
NMML	Nehru Memorial Museum & Library
OTC	Officers' Training Camp
RSS	Rashtriya Swayamsevak Sangh
SJM	Swadeshi Jagaran Manch
TNA	Tamil Nadu Archives
VHP	Vishwa Hindu Parishad

Glossary

akhara	Gymnasium.
Bhagabata toongi	A village hutment where the people assemble every evening to listen *Bhagabat Purana* and other religious texts/discourses, usually found in coastal Orissa.
charitra	Character.
Dalit	'Downtrodden'. Militant term for Scheduled Castes.
darshan	Audience with deity.
dhangda dhangdi	Tribal practice of selecting the life partners in Phulbani (Orissa).
ekatmata	Creating a single soul, attempt of unification.
hat[a]	Open-air village market, usually held once a week.
kar sevak	A volunteer who participated in the movement to build Ram temple.
param vaibhav	Pinnacle of Glory of Hindu Nation, the objective of the RSS.
paravartan	Reconversion.
pracharak	Full-time RSS worker entrusted in organizational and ideological expansion but does not receive any remuneration except his living expenses.
Purana	A form of historical/genealogical legend text derived from Sanskrit classics collectively called Puranas.
Ramshila Pujan	Worshipping of the bricks with which the Ram Temple was to be built.
sangathan	Organization, also a movement aimed at the unity and the knowledge of self-defence among the Hindus during the 1920s.
Sangh Parivar	The family of the RSS.
Sangh	Organization; the *swayamsevaks* usually refer to the RSS as Sangh.
sankirtan	Hindu procession of devotional singing and music.

sarsanghchalak	Chief of the RSS.
satyagraha	Non-violent means of protest, particularly used by Mahatma Gandhi.
shakha	Branch of the RSS, bottom in the organizational hierarchy.
shastras	Hindu sacred scriptures.
shuddhi	The movement started by the Arya Samaj during 1920s to reconvert to Hinduism those who had embraced other faiths.
swayamsevak	Member of the RSS.
tabligh	The Muslim conversion movement.
Thakurani ghara	Place of worship of goddess found in tribal villages. This room is also a centre of activity of tribal cultural life.
yajna	Sacrificial fire in which offerings are made to different gods.

CHAPTER I

Introduction

If New Delhi's familiar Ring Road is known as Mahatma Gandhi Marg, the upcoming parallel Outer Ring Road has been named after Keshav Baliram Hedgewar, the founder of the Rashtriya Swayamsevak Sangh (RSS). Hedgewar, a marginal Congress activist, perhaps never imagined that his *swayamsevaks* would one day become so powerful as to assign place to him parallel to Gandhi. The naming of a road is perhaps inconsequential and may easily be dismissed as a purely symbolic gesture. But this is certainly not symbolic when the Bharatiya Janata Party (BJP), the carrier of Hedgewar's legacy, has occupied the seat of power at Delhi for the third time, though the first and the second times were only for thirteen days and thirteen months respectively. The Congress, which supposedly inherited the Gandhian legacy, has been convincingly defeated in the race to control state power.

This is not to make any comparison between Gandhi and Hedgewar, but to recognize that an organization, which started with only five persons in 1925, has spread its tentacles into every possible sphere of India's civil society, including the political. Hedgewar may be unknown to the Indian masses, but his creation—the RSS—has become a household name. Its ideology—*Hindu Rashtra*—which remained peripheral during India's freedom struggle, has come to occupy the centrestage.

The RSS is perhaps the most talked about and probably the most controversial organization in contemporary India. It is equally revered and feared, applauded and attacked. While its proponents incessantly chant the hymn of *Hindutva* and *Hindu Rashtra*, the opponents unequivocally condemn its 'communalism', 'fascism' and 'fundamentalism'. Interestingly, it preaches an exclusivist ideology, which simultaneously segregates and integrates, divides and unites. Thus, any discussion on RSS generates strong reactions and opinions swinging from one extreme to the other. And accordingly, most of the contemporary literature on the RSS exhibits either a blind defence or an uncharitable offence. In order to have a better idea about the mission, motive, method and messengers of the RSS, it would be useful to examine some of the literature associated with the RSS.

MISSION

What is the RSS's mission? Its ideologues explain that Keshav Baliram Hedgewar founded the organization with the objective to unify and revitalize the Hindu community and to establish India as a *Hindu Rashtra.* M.S. Golwalkar, the second chief of the RSS, thus announces that the supreme goal of his organization is to achieve 'the all-round glory and greatness of our Hindu Rashtra'.[1] What is *Hindu Rashtra*? What sort of ideology and politics does it represent?

Revivalist?

The commitment of the RSS to the *Hindu Rashtra* creates an impression that it is revivalist in nature. Craig Baxter, an American State Department official, describes the RSS as 'a virile organization dedicated to the revival of Hinduism and to the setting up of a Hindu Rashtra in India'.[2] K.K. Gangadharan[3] observes that the RSS inherits and represents the strong and militant Hindu revivalist ideologies, which sprang up in Maharashtra. Andersen and Damle[4] also characterize the RSS as 'Hindu revivalist', which seeks to define the national identity by taking inspiration from 'Hindu antiquity'. Without providing an adequate explanation, they believe that the RSS represents the 'reformist' variety of revivalism.

What type of revivalism does the RSS represent? The revivalist usually upholds the tradition and confronts the modern. How successful has been the RSS's role towards this end? Does it really espouse traditional Hinduism? Ashis Nandy's answer is in the negative. To him the RSS idea of a *Hindu Rashtra* is 'only an edited version of the modern nation-state'[5] which it wants to capture in the name of ancient Hindu traditions. *Hindutva,* in his opinion, not only comically mimics nineteenth century European nationalism, it also carries a deep hostility towards everyday Hinduism and ordinary Hindus. Further, the RSS has scant reverence for the plural culture of traditional Hinduism. Nor does it criticize modern science and technology, except for a vague commitment to some selected indigenous systems 'that are relatively more Brahmanic and happen to be peripheral to the pursuit of power'.[6] Despite its occasional testimonials to Ayurveda it never advocates any 'romantic' adventure with denuclearization and anti-militarism. The RSS will certainly not give up on Western nuclear and missile technology.[7] Nandy thus concludes that Hindu nationalism has always been an illegitimate child of modern India, not of Hindu traditions.

Hindu nationalism is not the remainder of a pre-modern religious conception, suggests Partha Chatterjee: it is an entirely modern, rationalist and historicist idea. Like other modern ideologies, it allows for a central role of the State in the modernization of the society and strongly defends the State's unity and sovereignty. Its reason is not religious but political, and the framework of its reasoning is entirely secular.[8]

True, the RSS employs tradition, but it is only for the sake of the modern. As Ainslie Embree[9] suggests, the main objective of the RSS is to define the modern Hindu nation. Peter van der Veer[10] has shown that the Vishwa Hindu Parishad (VHP), an important member of the *Sangh Parivar,* does not revolt against modernity but in fact is an expression of it. In this light it becomes difficult to label the RSS as revivalist as its proclamations do not actually speak of its revivalist commitments. At the same time, the impact of its revivalist rhetoric and rituals in the identity-building process can not be ignored and needs to be studied carefully.

Fundamentalist?

Revivalism promises a return to an earlier, better age. People succumb to the temptations of fundamentalism under conditions of disruptive modernization.[11] It needs to be explored whether the RSS could be characterized as fundamentalist.[12] Martin E. Marty, the director of the Fundamentalism Project of the American Academy of Arts and Sciences and R. Scott Appleby, treat the RSS as one of the fundamentalist movements.[13] The project noted three general findings. First, fundamentalisms are inevitably political. Secondly, fundamentalist movements are also genuinely religious: 'We will fail to understand these movements if we neglect their irreducible religious dimension.' Thirdly, religious fundamentalisms are hegemonic, anti-pluralist movements that are constrained in their impact by the conflicting demands made upon them by their dual identity as inherently religious and inherently political entities.[14]

Disagreeing with the inclusion of the RSS under the banner of fundamentalism, Dipankar Gupta[15] observes that the term 'fundamentalism', as employed in *Fundamentalisms Observed* is often synonymous with orthodoxy, traditionalism and communalism or even nationalism. The RSS is a communal rather than a fundamentalist organization, Gupta argues. As he explains, communalism and fundamentalism are, in some respects, close to each other: for example, both have activism in common and the activists in both cases are generally urban, educated, middle and lower members of the petty bourgeois and bureaucratic class. Despite these similarities, there remains a major distinction: whereas the communalists have a 'particular other', for the fundamentalists it is rather a case of 'us' versus the 'rest'. Gupta, therefore, pleads that had the RSS been a fundamentalist organization, Hindu disenchantment would not be limited to teaching the Muslims a lesson, but would extend to the other religions as well. He further argues that this could only happen if Hindus in India had been a deprived community, or if there had been a great cultural gulf between a closed set of Hindus and the rest. In his opinion, India's vast middle class reach out to classes both above and below to take the wind out of any fundamentalist sail.[16]

Gupta's analysis does not consider whether 'us' versus 'them' has the potential to become 'us' versus the 'rest'. His assertion that the Hindu antagonism of the RSS is restricted to the Muslims alone has been proved wrong, as Christians have also become recent targets of the *Sangh Parivar*.[17] Further, he dispels the fear of fundamentalism, as Hindus are not a deprived community and the presence of a huge middle class acts as a buffer against fundamentalism. This proposition could also be questioned, as the RSS, through its professional propaganda machinery, could successfully create an imaginary deprivation among the Hindus. Moreover, the middle class could hardly be relied upon in the light of some past experiences.[18]

Mark Juergensmeyer[19] thinks that 'fundamentalist' is an inadequate expression to describe the RSS. First, the term is pejorative, less descriptive and more accusatory; it reflects our attitude towards other people than it describes them. Secondly, fundamentalism is an imprecise category for making comparisons across cultures. Finally, the term suggests only religious motivation and does not carry any political meaning. Juergensmeyer, therefore, prefers to describe the RSS as 'religious nationalist' as it has both religious and political interests. However, Susana B.C. Devalle[20] argues that *Hindutva* has become a key concept in Hindu fundamentalist ideologies. Both Hans Bakker[21] and Susan Bayly[22] also highlight the fundamentalist features of the RSS-sponsored Ayodhya movement.

The RSS has time and again denied the charge of fundamentalism. Balasaheb Deoras, the third chief of the RSS, argues that while the fundamentalists accept the holy book as the 'literal truth', the RSS does not have such a book. Moreover, unlike the former, the RSS never insists on a particular form of worship. The RSS, he mentions, has never suggested that the government should be run as per the dictates of the Shankaracharya. Deoras observes that though the RSS is proud of the past and would never forget it, at the same time it would 'not walk towards the past'; it is not 'a stagnant pond of traditions and beliefs'.[23]

Could the RSS then be exonerated from the charges of fundamentalism just because it is not a revivalist organization? As Moin Shakir[24] observes, fundamentalism should not be mistaken with the tendency of reviving religion and adhering to pre-modern ideology, though it certainly utilizes religion and tradition to respond to the contemporary needs and to meet the challenge of a secular democratic polity. He finds the origin of fundamentalism in economic and political factors rather than religious ones.

Fundamentalism, first of all, has faith in the authority and infallibility of the scriptures or other sacred traditions; and accordingly, it prescribes the ordering of the family, civil society and the state. With regard to the first aspect, the denial of the RSS about its commitment to any sacred scripture needs a thorough examination. The RSS does not rule out the possibility that certain 'fundamentals' laid down by V.D. Savarkar's *Hindutva* and M.S. Golwalkar's *We or Our Nationhood Defined* will not be imposed on the citizens of *Hindu Rashtra*; these treatises, though not holy in the conventional sense, are no less sacred to the champions of *Hindutva*. Secondly, the RSS has developed a model of man, family, civil society and state on the basis of the 'fundamentals' laid down by its ideologues.

Communal and Fascist?

Despite the controversial nature of the term 'communalism', in its common Indian usage the word refers to 'a condition of suspicion, fear and hostility between members of different religious communities'.[25] The common charge against the RSS is that it is communal.[26] Most of the critics stretch their arguments further to describe it as fascist as well.

In Jawaharlal Nehru's opinion, the RSS is communal as well as fascist. K.K. Gangadharan finds a striking similarity of ideas between Hitler and Golwalkar, the main ideologue of the RSS. However, he is not sure whether this was a mere coincidence or an imitation. Comparing 'Hitlerism' with 'Golwalkarism', he concludes that the ideology of the RSS is 'Hitlerism under Hindu garb'.[27] D.R. Goyal,[28] a former *swayamsevak* and a staunch critic of the RSS, describes the RSS as communal, anti-democratic, totalitarian, authoritarian and fascist. Ram Lall Dhooria,[29] another former *swayamsevak*, is no less bitter. Characterizing the RSS as a 'rank communal outfit' with an antediluvian way of thinking, Dhooria believes that it is not different from its 'nazi cater-cousin'. He finds similarity between the *swayamsevaks* of the RSS and the German Youth of Hitler, as both believe in the ideology of hatred and body culture and have a blind unreasoning faith on their respective leaders. Marzia Casolari[30] claims that there existed direct contacts between the representatives of the fascist regime, including Mussolini and Hindu nationalists, especially B.S. Moonje—the mentor of Hedgewar. Casolari thus concludes: 'No doubt, beginning with the early 1920s, and up to the Second World War, Hindu nationalists looked at the political reality of fascist Italy, and subsequently of Nazi Germany, as a source of inspiration . . . such influence is still alive in today's militant Hinduism.'[31]

The authors of *Khaki Shorts and Saffron Flags*[32] brand the RSS as the 'fountainhead of aggressive Hindu communalism', which aspires to change the nature of Indian polity, subverting the basic principles of democracy and secularism. Sumit Sarkar[33] compares 'Hindu communalism' of the *Sangh Parivar* with the traits of Nazism of Hitler. Sarkar concludes that the RSS is fascist to the core. He further asserts, the agenda of the *Sangh Parivar* is nothing less than to remove the secular foundations of the Indian state and usher in a fascistic authoritarian polity.

Not all communalism as such is fascism, argues Aijaz Ahmed.[34] But with reference to the destruction of the Babri Masjid, he observes that the very nature of the event, the modes of mobilization and the very structure of the *Sangh Parivar* and the specific ideological form in which the RSS practices and propagates its communalism demonstrate the fundamentally fascist character of the organization and the event. He concludes convincingly that the true object of its desire is not mere Muslim submission but state power and re-making of India as a whole—politically, ideologically, historically.

The RSS hates to be called communal and fascist. Nanaji Deshmukh, RSS *pracharak* and leader of the erstwhile Bharatiya Jana Sangh and the Janata Party, points out the following dissimilarities between fascism and the ideology of the RSS.[35] Unlike fascism, the RSS does not advocate a totalitarian state; it believes in democracy and encourages independent spirit. Its cultural nationalism is not chauvinistic, but tempered with Hindu traditions. Moreover, whereas the fascist discipline is terrifying, the RSS commands a purely spontaneous and voluntary discipline. Deshmukh further argues that while fascism thrives on propaganda, the RSS shuns publicity. Finally, the RSS believes in non-violence. He however adds that the RSS does not run away from a fight if it is imposed on it. Deshmukh dismisses the charges of fascism as 'slander' and 'communist propaganda'.

Some scholars also defend the RSS against the charge of fascism and caution that the comparison with the European expression of fascism needs a careful handling as there exist significant differences between the two.[36] They argue that in the European manifestation of fascism the 'National Will' is embodied in a 'leader'. To a certain extent this applies to the RSS also; yet the RSS leader is supposed to be austere and detached, untainted by worldly temptations. Secondly, while the European fascism sought to destroy or seek control of all existing centres of socio-political and economic power, the RSS does not have either totalitarian or revolutionary objective. Finally, while the former bestows all power to the political leader, the RSS displays a marked distrust of political leadership. In the ideal society envisaged by the RSS, political power is held to be illegitimately exercised unless guided by constitutional sages who interpret *dharma*. Despite this defence, the charge of fascism can not be merely dismissed as 'slander' or 'communist propaganda'. The authoritarian organizational structure and functioning of the RSS, its vicious propaganda against the 'enemy' and violent mobilization certainly share some of the main characteristics of fascism.

At the same time, there exists some important dissimilarities as well. Christophe Jaffrelot points out: 'As distinct from Nazism, the RSS's ideology treats society as an organism with a secular spirit, which is implanted not so much in the race as in a socio-cultural system and which will be regenerated over the course of time by patient work at the grassroots. Finally, in contrast to both Italian fascism and Nazism the RSS does not rely on the central figure of the leader.'[37] Achin Vanaik also mentions some of the dissimilarities: the absence in the

Sangh combine of any truly charismatic leader; the absence of an explicitly anti-liberal/anti-democratic and anti-working class themes in its campaigning; the absence of any verbal anti-capitalist demagogy; the absence of any orientation to the theme of a 'general revolt'; and so on.[38] Hence, it seems problematic to situate the RSS in a fascist paradigm, suggests Achin Vanaik. He perhaps rightly argues that in post-colonial societies, religious fundamentalism or religion-based nationalism are not so much the fascist formations as, at most, potential fascist formations where that potential may or may not be realized. Thus, he argues, while the fascist state in India would necessarily be Hindu nationalist, the Hindu nationalist state would not necessarily be fascist.[39] In this light the charge of fascism against the RSS needs a cautious scrutiny.

Hindu Nationalist?

The term Hindu nationalism, at times, creates confusion. For instance, *Webster's New World Dictionary* (1984), quite erroneously, describes Mahatma Gandhi as a 'Hindu nationalist leader'. *Webster's* reinforces the very political identification of India with Hindu that Gandhi opposed.[40] It is not Gandhi, but the RSS, which represents Hindu nationalism by claiming India as Hindu. Of late, more and more scholars have started describing the ideology of the RSS as Hindu nationalist; for example, Bruce Graham,[41] Mark Juergensmeyer,[42] Malik and Singh,[43] Christophe Jaffrelot,[44] and Thomas Blom Hansen.[45] Certain sympathetic writings on the RSS also accept this classification.[46]

As Bruce Graham explains, on the eve of Indian independence, those who favoured a Hindu-oriented State were split into three main groups: the Congress, the Hindu Mahasabha and the RSS. While the Congress had Hindu traditionalists in its fold, the Hindu Mahasabha was comprised of a mixture of Hindu traditionalists and Hindu nationalists; the RSS was constituted by a contingent of militant Hindu nationalists. Graham argues that while the Hindu traditionalists were essentially backward-looking, the Hindu nationalists, though revivalists, were forward-looking; whereas the former were conservative and emphasized on time-honoured values to justify the continuation of a hierarchical social order, the Hindu nationalists wanted to remould Hindu society on corporate lines and to fashion the State accordingly.[47]

Such characterization of the RSS is rejected by Bipin Chandra, who makes a distinction between the communalism and the religion-based nationalism as witnessed in Indonesia or Iran or some Arab countries. Though the political struggle in these countries was defined in religious terms, it was directed against colonialism. In contrast, communal politics in India was directed against fellow Indians and not against colonialism; the fight was against the other 'community'. Therefore, argues Chandra, the RSS is communal rather than Hindu nationalist.[48] It is true that colonialism remains the main enemy of nationalism in a colonial era. But the RSS identified Muslims rather than the British as the primary enemy of *Hindu Rashtra* and refrained itself from anti-colonial struggle. As its ideal is an 'imagined' Hindu nation, a nation exclusively for the Hindus, it attempts to construct a Hindu identity by projecting the Muslims as the principal enemy of the Hindu nation.

Moreover, as the Hindus are in a majority in India, Hindu nationalism becomes a majoritarian movement. The RSS defines the Indian nation as a whole and does not claim to represent one community fighting others in India, but rather the real India trying to assert itself. Therefore, though the RSS represents the main protagonists in majoritarian Hindu communalism, its Hindu nationalism 'does not espouse communal conflict in principle'.[49] But in practice, it certainly does. The RSS, however, rejects the charge of communalism arguing that communal conflict is an unintended by-product of Hindu nationalist self-assertion that results from adverse reactions from minority communities and from the Indian State.[50] Hence, the complex relationship between Hindu nationalism and communalism needs to be understood.

MOTIVE

'Culture' or 'Politics'?

The constitution of the RSS claims that 'the Sangh as such, has no politics and is devoted to purely cultural work'.[51] The RSS leaders frequently deny that its motive is either religious or political and instead assert that it is a cultural organization that eschews political involvement. Refuting the claim of the RSS as a 'cultural' organization, J.A. Curran,[52] as early as 1951, described the RSS as 'an extremist Hindu organization that strives for political power in the Republic of India'.[53] Though the RSS was not a contender for political power at that time, Curran understood its political ambition. Its advocacy of a 'Hindu State', the 'militant' nature of organization, the 'rightist' orientation and sharp 'anti-Congressism' convinced Curran that the RSS aspired to acquire political power.

Balraj Madhok, a former RSS *pracharak* and former President of the Bharatiya Jana Sangh (BJS), also spells out the political motive of the RSS. He argues that Hedgewar was a political man having a political vision and political objective. To define India as a Hindu Nation, to organize the Hindus for assertion of their identity was surely a political objective, writes Madhok.[54]

Strongly rejecting the 'cultural' argument of the RSS, D.R. Goyal emphasizes that the RSS is nothing if not political. He argues, 'the culture which is fostered through the *shakha* drill is political, not only in essence, but in its entirety. If the political content be taken out, nothing would be left behind. Even the denial of political character is deeply political.'[55] Goyal observes that the political role of the RSS could be properly understood only if the process of culturization, which the *swayamsevaks* go through, is correctly grasped.

This analysis is shared by Sumit Sarkar, Tapan Basu and others—the authors of *Khaki Shorts*. As they suggest, the RSS insistence that its domain lies in the propagation of Hindu culture alone without any political overtones, is just a play with words. The notion of Hindu culture that is propagated in its *shakhas* is a definition of a majoritarian and authoritarian *rashtra* where Hindus, under RSS direction, will lay down the rules by which the minorities must abide. They argue that the RSS version of Hindu culture is actually political as it is inextricably mingled with antagonism against the non-Hindu. Golwalkar's distrust of conventional politics and the 'culture'/'politics' conflict within the RSS came to an end with the formation of the BJS; with the emergence of this affiliate, the RSS 'came to have a frankly political extension, open to a considerable measure of pragmatism and flexibility – while retaining for itself the advantage of a claim to be purer and "above" politics'.[56]

While the RSS takes a broad view of culture, its interpretation of politics seems to be very narrow. H.V. Seshadri, a veteran RSS leader, explains that the achievement of *param vaibhav*—the pinnacle of national glory—is the supreme goal of the Sangh. This requires 'the resuscitation of every single field of people's endeavour in the cause of the nation—including the political'.[57] As Seshadri writes, though the political power is a potent instrument which can shape the destiny of the nation, the RSS 'feels that the crucial problem confronting the nation is not political.

It is something more basic and concerns the very psyche of the people.'[58] Therefore, the RSS is engaged in awakening and organizing the Hindu people by instilling in them intense national consciousness and character as also a spirit of discipline and dedication to high national values, explains Seshadri.

As the RSS defines its concept of nation as cultural, its definition of culture is all-comprehensive, all-embracing and all-absorbing. Political, economic, social and religious activities are various manifestations of culture. Hence, in the RSS framework, culture is not just one aspect, but it encompasses every aspect of a nation's life observes Curran. This version of culture provides the RSS with the prerogative to intervene in every sphere, including political, as politics is an integral part of the life of a nation.

Long Term 'Cultural Hegemony' vs. *Short Term Electoral Politics*

Analysing the definition of culture and politics offered by the RSS, one hardly misses the long term as well as short term objectives of the organization. Taking note of its long-term objective, Curran writes that the 'cultural' objective of the RSS is 'to achieve the acceptance of its outlook as the framework for the Hindu community'.[59] Once this is attained, the basic elements will exist for the creation of a strong Hindu 'Nation'. After the merger of the RSS and the Hindu community, 'the hard core of the Sangh—its full-time members—will continue to be responsible for maintaining the "cultural" health of society'.[60]

Bruce Graham observes that the RSS is determined 'to convert politics from disputes about party programmes into a great battle for the cultural heart of the nation', a battle in which those who believed in the corporate integrity of the Hindu community 'would be aligned against the forces of Islam on the one side and the forces of communism on the other'.[61] As such a conception of political reality has more in common with religious revivalism than with party competition, this implies that the people have the potential 'not only to respond to an appeal to their basic spiritual values but also to organize themselves as a huge popular rally capable of converting India into a truly Hindu state'.[62]

Keeping this long-term objective in mind, the RSS, so far, has not directly entered the electoral arena as a political party. Curran offers two possible explanations: First, the RSS feared that it would weaken its efforts by diverting the attention of its members towards 'superficial' objectives. Second, it apprehended that the electoral participation would stimulate personal ambitions within the organization and encourage rivalry and disunity.[63] Analysing the reasons for which the RSS preferred to stay away from the electoral politics, Daniel Gold comments that the RSS leadership perhaps 'would prefer to play the role of institutional guru to the nation, keeping their own sanctity as an institution pure and unstained by the tough and sometimes dirty business that electoral politics in India often entails'.[64]

Besides the long term objective to control civil society and establish a Hindu hegemony, the RSS has also pursued its short term political objective. Craig Baxter, in his study of the Bharatiya Jana Sangh, reveals its close connection with the RSS, both in terms of ideology as well as organization. The RSS not only supplied manpower to this political party, it soon controlled its organizational apparatus through some trusted *pracharaks.* Baxter also brings out the factional fights between the RSS and the non-RSS factions within the party. He particularly notes the contribution of the RSS in consolidating the party and making it possible for its members to share power in some north Indian states in 1967.

After revealing all this, Baxter surprisingly concludes that the RSS did not try to achieve its political objective through the Jana Sangh. Despite his description of the Jana Sangh as 'heir to the spirit of nationalism infused in the workers of the RSS', he strongly denies that the RSS has ever controlled it. Baxter, however, admits that the party leaders only informally inform about their political activities to the RSS.[65]

The RSS leadership felt the need to have a political party which would defend its interest and champion the ideal of *Hindu Rashtra,* discloses Balraj Madhok.[66] He gives the details of the RSS interference in the affairs of the BJS and highlights the factional fights not only between the RSS and non-RSS elements of the party, but also between the leaders from the same RSS background. Madhok was expelled from the party in 1973, despite his strong RSS background.

Bruce Graham, in his study of Jana Sangh, traces its doctrinal and organizational dependence on the RSS. He describes how the young RSS workers took control of the party after the death of Syama Prasad Mookerjee and gave it a militant Hindu nationalist orientation.[67] H.T. Davey[68] finds a great deal of influence of the RSS had over Jana Sangh because of its control over party leaders and cadres at all levels. Geeta

Puri's study also establishes the ideological and organizational connection between the RSS and the BJS.[69] The studies undertaken by Malik and Singh,[70] Partha S. Ghosh[71] reveal that the BJP, the incarnation of the BJS, is also intimately linked with the parent body in a similar manner.

All these explanations, thus clearly suggest, though the RSS resisted the temptation of direct electoral participation officially, it was very much on its agenda since the emergence of Bharatiya Jana Sangh. Its role in electoral politics increased further during the *sarsanghchalakship* of Balasaheb Deoras. Therefore, it is hard to accept that 'the Sangh's programme is above politics', even in a limited sense.

It would be fair to argue that the RSS tries to pursue simultaneously both the short-term political and the long-term cultural objectives. It aspires not just power, but 'power above power'.[72] This power above power implies that its objective is not just limited to control the government and the state, but to define and specify the terms and directions of the state as well as the civil society. This latter aspect demands a cultural perspective, thus keeping it engaged in a 'struggle for cultural hegemony'.[73] When the RSS was a marginal political force, by and large, both political and cultural had supplemented each other and it could resolve the occasional conflicts that occurred between these two objectives. But with its emergence as an important political player, the RSS increasingly finds it difficult to manage the conflicts and contradictions between political and cultural.

METHOD

The choice of a proper method is the key to the success of any cherished mission. As the RSS aimed at long-term 'cultural hegemony', it chose a method which would be political in content but cultural in form. Knowing that the attainment of *Hindu Rashtra* and Hindu *Sangathan* would be long and torturous, the RSS preferred to opt for building a hardcore cadre by 'man-moulding' and 'character-building' through a carefully crafted organization.[74] Therefore, for the RSS, the organization became inextricably linked to its ideology.

Brotherhood

The *shakha* is the basic unit of the organization where the 'character-building' takes place. The training process imparts physical as well as ideological training. But more importantly, it also makes the bond among the members quite strong. Andersen and Damle believe that the RSS family is closely knit because of the friendships and personal relations among its members brought up under a common socialization process. Thus they argue that the ***brotherhood in saffron*** is based more on personal relations, than on ideological commitments. However, the ideology plays a crucial role in the socialization process cementing this brotherhood.

Authoritarian Structure

What is the nature of the organizational structure of the RSS? One of the most conspicuous characteristics of the RSS 'has always been its strong hierarchical organization, with an apex in charismatic leaders who have by and large maintained practical control. Like its vision of the ideal Indian society, the RSS would consistently appear as a coherent, organic body, with a recognized head guiding firm limbs.'[75] Centralization of authority is the most obvious feature of the RSS. Most of the *swayamsevaks* do not have any role in the formulation and direction of the Sangh's policy, nor do they think that they should have this prerogative. They have complete faith in the ability of their leaders to guide the organization towards the desired goal, which they consider too fundamental to permit dispute.[76] The rare disagreements that do arise are successfully settled in the local *shakha*. The centralization of authority, therefore, not only ensures discipline, but also effectively implements a uniform politico-ideological line. This type of authority is perhaps instrumental in establishing a close coordination among the members of the *Sangh Parivar*.

Formal Democratic Features

The representational features were introduced in the RSS constitution. But they are only formal in nature or 'a facade'; they do not have any real meaning.[77] RSS leaders believe that too much democracy in the organization would be dangerous as it would lead to the formation of cliques and scrambles for power resulting in disunity. Moreover, too much democracy would waste unnecessary energy on minor issues. Therefore, the RSS emphasizes the creation of a group mind, eliminating as far as possible, the individual point of view among its members. RSS preaches that an office of responsibility affords an opportunity to serve silently, not power *per se*. The implications of this argument are not dangerous as long as the RSS does not seek political power, observes Curran. But it is not so.

MESSENGERS

To whom does the ideology of the RSS appeal? From what social groups does it draw its membership? J.A. Curran identifies three[78] social groups: First, the college and university students; second, the middle and lower socio-economic groups, such as shopkeepers, clerks, labourers and the like; and third, the well-to-do businessmen, and professional men, such as doctors and lawyers. The RSS has been concentrating on educational institutions since the early 1930s and thus ensured support from this group. The second segment gets attracted to the RSS for a number of reasons. Perhaps they find in the RSS activities a partial release from the frustrations of their daily lives; the public restlessness, the limited economic opportunities and anti-Muslim propaganda also drive a large section of the poorer classes towards the well-organized agitation of the RSS. As Curran mentions, the militant Hinduism of the RSS also fascinates the lower classes as they are 'quite Hindu-minded'. The third segment comprising of businessmen and professionals are numerically small and they rarely participate in the daily activities. However, as Curran finds, their social prestige and financial aid is of strategic importance to the RSS.

Bruce Graham[79] argues that being the political extension of the Brahminic tradition, Hindu nationalism began from a restricted intellectual base. It drew support mainly from upper-caste Hindus, familiar with its background and assured of its implicit acceptance of their status and their privileges. Besides, Hindu nationalism was also restricted in a geographical sense. 'Its historical mythology, based on the notion of that Hinduism had begun in the north amongst the original Aryan tribes . . . was much less likely to appeal to Hindu elites in the south and the east.'[80] Though the RSS was careful not to associate itself with any one regional tradition of Hindu nationalism, its literature frequently refers to the coming of the Aryans, the wars of Mahabharata and northern heroes such as Shivaji, Maharana Pratap and the Rani of Jhansi. Its 'myths were a synthesis of earlier regional myths, but they nevertheless expressed a northern view of Hindu origins'.[81] In the context of its nationwide expansion, the RSS had perhaps strategically modified this 'northern view' to accommodate different regional traditions and to appeal both the elites as well as non-elites of other parts of India.

D.R. Goyal observes that the class character and composition of the RSS membership is overwhelmingly middle class, who ordinarily harbour fear about other classes and communities and seek security in group life offered by the RSS. The authors of *Khaki Shorts* interpret the emergence of organized *Hindutva* as an upper-caste reaction to self-assertion by downtrodden groups within the Hindu fold. They further argue, the RSS, since its inception, has retained an overwhelming middle class Brahmin-Bania composition, being directed against other social groups like Muslims and lower caste Hindus. This analysis fails to explain how this narrow Brahmin-Bania alliance could make *Hindutva* such a dominant wave. It seems that *Hindutva* has made a conscious attempt to break through class, caste and regional barriers.

After analysing the literature on the mission, motive, method and the messengers of the RSS, the present work will focus on its tryst with politics—from Hedgewar, the founder, to Sudarshan, the present *sarsanghchalak* (chief). It will demonstrate that the core of the RSS ideology—*Hindu Rashtra*—is political, contesting the RSS contention that its content is cultural. However, it is also true that the RSS has been espousing its political agenda of *Hindu Rashtra* under the guise of the cultural. Hedgewar's objective was political and he understood the importance of organizing the Hindus to reach his destination. He successfully built up the RSS by his innovative use of culture for political training. Golwalkar, his successor, amplified and reinforced the ideology of *Hindu Rashtra* and expanded the organization all over the country. With his saintly appearance and overt distaste for 'politics', he created a 'cultural' aura, though the RSS remained political deep down. The third chief, Balasaheb Deoras, not having much fancy for 'culture', daringly intervened in politics on the solid organizational and ideological foundation laid by his predecessors. However, he intelligently and successfully used powerful cultural symbols for political mobilizations. Deoras enlarged and energized the *Sangh Parivar* and seriously pursued its homogenizing agenda to integrate different sections like the Dalits, tribals and women into the framework of *Hindu Rashtra*. Due to his pragmatic and flexible strategy the RSS emerged as an indispensable political player in mainstream politics. Rajendra Singh, the successor of Deoras, consolidated the political mission further by getting control over State power and also by trying to reach out to civil society more effectively. K.S. Sudarshan, has given enough indication that he would like to have tight control over State power and at the same time reinforce *Hindutva*. Like all his predecessors, he also frequently swears by culture while talking of the issues, which are fundamentally political. The mission and motive of the RSS is nothing but political though it employs various cultural methods and techniques to forge a monolithic Hindu identity. Thus, the RSS continues its tryst with politics to convert India into a *Hindu Rashtra*.

Chapter II discusses the historical context in which the RSS was born, evolved and flourished. The RSS was born in 1925 at Nagpur. While discussing its origin, both the all-India context of competitive communalism and the regional socio-political environment of Central Provinces and Berar (hereafter C.P. & Berar) are taken into consideration. The political ideas and experience of K.B. Hedgewar are also highlighted to understand the ideological and political roots of the RSS. Then the growth of the RSS under the guidance of M.S. Golwalkar is discussed.

Chapter III draws the outline of the organizational structure and training process of the RSS and proposes to examine how they are carefully designed to promote its politics and ideology of *Hindu Rashtra*. As the RSS has adopted a uniform organizational structure and method of training throughout the country, this chapter takes illustrative instances from the Orissa unit of the RSS.

Chapter IV attempts to understand the ideology of *Hindu Rashtra* through the RSS discourse on community, history and nation. The RSS arguments are mainly taken from M.S. Golwalkar's *We or Our Nationhood Defined*, *Bunch of Thoughts*, Deendayal Upadhyaya's *Integral Humanism* and certain contemporary writings.

Chapter V seeks to explain how the RSS has been homogenizing the Hindus as they are not a monolith. Recognizing the political importance of certain identities, such as Dalits, tribals and women, the RSS has made some strategic shifts to integrate them into the *Hindutva* agenda. However, this strategic compromise, has only achieved a limited success.

Chapter VI highlights how Balasaheb Deoras has established the RSS as an important political player in national politics. It is shown, how the RSS, under his leadership, has responded to the changing dynamics of Indian politics and chartered various courses of its political journey—from moderate, pragmatic, and accommodative to militant, rigid, and intolerant.

Chapter VII discusses how Rajendra Singh has continued with the Deoras experiment and facilitated the BJP to control Delhi. It examines to what extent the RSS controls the state apparatus and handles the emerging contradictions between ideological purity and political pragmatism. It probes if the RSS really dilutes its ideological core for political compulsions. An attempt is also made to understand the implications of the take over by K.S. Sudarshan as the new chief.

NOTES AND REFERENCES

1. M.S. Golwalkar, *Bunch of Thoughts* [1966] (Bangalore: Jagarana Prakashana, 1980), p. 57.
2. Craig Baxter, *The Jana Sangh: A Biography of an Indian Political Party* (Bombay: Oxford University Press, 1967), p. 53. Baxter takes a sympathetic view of the RSS.
3. K.K. Gangadharan, *Sociology of Revivalism: A Study of Indianisation, Sanskritisation and Golwalkarism* (Delhi: Kalamkar, 1970).
4. Walter K. Andersen and Shridhar D. Damle, *The Brotherhood in Saffron: The Rashtriya Swayamsevak Sangh and Hindu Revivalism* (Delhi: Vistaar Publications, 1987).
5. Ashis Nandy, 'The Fear of Gandhi: Nathuram Godse & His Successors', *The Times of India*, 27 April 1994.
6. Ashis Nandy et al., *Creating a Nationality: The Ramjanmabhoomi Movement and Fear of the Self* (Delhi: Oxford University Press, 1995), p. 62.
7. Nandy's analysis has been substantiated when the BJP government implemented the nuclear agenda of the RSS. It would be pertinent to remember that while K.B. Hedgewar, the founder of the RSS, was a doctor, the second chief M.S. Golwalkar was a biologist, the fourth chief Rajendra Singh was a nuclear physicist and the present chief K.S. Sudarshan is trained as a telecommunication engineer.
8. Partha Chatterjee, *The Nation and Its Fragments: Colonial and Postcolonial Histories* (Delhi: Oxford University Press, 1995), p. 111.
9. Ainslie T. Embree, 'The Function of the Rashtriya Swayamsevak Sangh: To Define Hindu Nation', in Martin E. Marty and R. Scott Appleby, eds., *Accounting for Fundamentalisms: The Dynamic Character of Movements*, Vol. 4 (Chicago: University of Chicago Press, 1994), pp. 617-52.
10. Peter van der Veer, 'Hindu Nationalism and the Discourse of Modernity: The Vishwa Hindu Parishad', ibid., pp. 653-68.
11. J.W. Bjorkman, 'The Dark side of the Force: Notes on Religion and Politics' in J.W. Bjorkman, ed., *Fundamentalism, Revivalists and Violence in South Asia* (Delhi: Manohar, 1988).
12. The term fundamentalism was first used in early 1920s by certain conservative Protestant groups in North America, who set out to define the 'fundamentals'

of Christianity. These included, for example, the divinity of Christ and the infallibility of the scripture.

13. See Martin E. Marty and R. Scott Appleby, eds., *Fundamentalisms Observed*, Vol. 1 (Chicago: University of Chicago Press, 1991); *Fundamentalisms and Society*, Vol. 2 (Chicago: University of Chicago Press, 1992); *Fundamentalisms and the State: Remaking Polities, Economies and Militance*, Vol. 3 (Chicago: University of Chicago Press, 1993); *Accounting for Fundamentalisms: The Dynamic Character of Movements*, Vol. 4 (Chicago: University of Chicago Press, 1994); *Fundamentalisms Comprehended*, Vol. 5 (Chicago: University of Chicago Press, 1995).
14. Gabriel A. Almond, Emmanuel Sivan, and R. Scott Appleby, 'Politics, Ethnicity, and Fundamentalism' in Martin E. Marty and R. Scott Appleby, eds., *Fundamentalisms Comprehended*, op. cit., p. 503.
15. Dipankar Gupta, *The Context of Ethnicity: Sikh Identity in a Comparative Perspective* (Delhi: Oxford University Press, 1996).
16. Ibid., p. 209.
17. The role of the *Sangh Parivar*, particularly the VHP and the Bajrang Dal, in the recent attacks on Christians, suggest that this antagonism is also directed against other religions like Christianity.
18. For example, the attitude of the middle class towards the issue of reservation, demolition of Babri Masjid and even to the attacks on minorities does not guarantee at all that it would act as a buffer against fundamentalism.
19. Mark Juergensmeyer, *Religious Nationalism Confronts the Secular State* (Delhi: Oxford University Press, 1995), Introduction, pp. 1-8.
20. Susana B.C. Devalle, 'Social Identities, Hindu Fundamentalism, and Politics in India', in David N. Lorenzen, ed., *Bhakti Religion in North India: Community Identity and Political Action* (Albany: State University of New York Press, 1995), pp. 306-22.
21. Hans Bakker, 'Ayodhya: A Hindu Jerusalem: An Investigation of "Holy War" as a Religious Idea in the Light of Communal Unrest in India', *Numen*, 38 (1), June 1991, pp. 80-109.
22. Susan Bayly, 'Fundamentalism: A Historian's View of India after Ayodhya', *The Cambridge Review*, 114 (2322), October 1993, pp. 99-106.
23. *Organiser*, XLII (10), 14 October 1990.
24. Moin Shakir, 'Rise of Fundamentalism: An Enquiry into Its Causes', *Radical Humanist*, 50 (5), August 1986, p. 27.
25. See Gyanendra Pandey, *The Construction of Communalism in Colonial North India* (Delhi: Oxford University Press, 1992), p. 6.
26. Some of the important works include, Govind Sahai, *R.S.S. Ideology, Technique, Propaganda* (Allahabad, 1948); Subhadra Joshi, ed., *RSS: A Danger to Democracy* (Delhi: Sampradayikta Virodhi Committee, 1967); K.K. Gangadharan, *Sociology of Revivalism: A Study of Indianisation, Sanskritisation and Golwalkarism* (Delhi: Kalamkar, 1970); D.R. Goyal, *Rashtriya Swayamsevak Sangh* (Delhi: Radha Krishna Prakashan, 1979); Ram Lall Dhooria, *I was a Swayamsevak: An Inside*

View of the RSS (Delhi: Sampradayikta Virodhi Committee, n.d.); Bipin Chandra, *Communalism in Modern India* (Delhi: Vikas Publishing House, 1987); K.N. Panikkar, ed., *Communalism in India: History, Politics and Culture* (Delhi: Manohar, 1991); Tapan Basu, Pradip Datta, Sumit Sarkar, Tanika Sarkar and Sambuddha Sen, *Khaki Shorts and Saffron Flags: A Critique of the Hindu Right* (Delhi: Orient Longman, 1993); Gyanendra Pandey, ed., *Hindus and Others: The Question of Identity in India Today* (Delhi: Viking, 1993); Mehdi Arslan and Janaki Rajan, eds., *Communalism in India: Challenge and Response* (Delhi: Manohar, 1994); David Ludden, ed., *Making India Hindu: Religion, Community and the Politics of Democracy in India* (Delhi: Oxford University Press, 1996).

27. K.K. Gangadharan, *Sociology of Revivalism*, op. cit., pp. 99-102.
28. D.R. Goyal, *Rashtriya Swayamsevak Sangh*, op. cit.
29. Ram Lall Dhooria, *I was a Swayamsevak*, op. cit.
30. Marzia Casolari, 'Hindutva's Foreign Tie-up in the 1930s: Archival Evidence', *Economic and Political Weekly*, XXXV (4), 22 January 2000, pp. 218-28.
31. Ibid., p. 227
32. Tapan Basu et al., *Khaki Shorts and Saffron Flags*, op. cit.
33. See Sumit Sarkar, 'The Fascism of the Sangh Parivar', *Economic and Political Weekly*, XXVIII (5), 30 January 1993, pp. 163-7.
34. See Aijaz Ahmed, 'Culture, Community, Nation: On the Ruins of Ayodhya', *Social Scientist*, 21(7-8), July-August 1993, pp. 17-48.
35. Nana Deshmukh, *RSS Victim of Slander: A Multidimensional Study of RSS, Jana Sangh, Janata Party and the Present Political Crisis* (Delhi: Vision Books, 1979), p. 12.
36. Andersen and Damle, *The Brotherhood in Saffron*, op. cit., pp. 82-3.
37. Christophe Jaffrelot, *The Hindu Nationalist Movement and Indian Politics 1925 to the 1990s: Strategies of Identity-Building, Implantation and Mobilisation [with special reference to Central India]* (Delhi: Viking Penguin India, 1996), pp. 63-4.
38. Achin Vanaik, 'Situating Threat of Hindu Nationalism: Problems with Fascist Paradigm', *Economic and Political Weekly*, XXIX (28), 9 July 1994, pp. 1729-48.
39. Ibid., p. 1740. Also see his book, *Communalism Contested: Religion, Modernity and Secularization* (Delhi: Vistaar Publications, 1997), Part III.
40. See David Ludden, *Making India Hindu*, op. cit., p. 7.
41. Bruce D. Graham, *Hindu Nationalism and Indian Politics: The Origins and Development of the Bharatiya Jana Sangh* (Cambridge: Cambridge University Press, 1990).
42. Mark Juergensmeyer, *Religious Nationalism Confronts the Secular State*, op. cit.
43. Yogendra K. Malik and V.B. Singh, *Hindu Nationalists in India: The Rise of the Bharatiya Janata Party* (Delhi: Vistaar Publications, 1995).
44. See Christophe Jaffrelot, *The Hindu Nationalist Movement and Indian Politics 1925 to the 1990s*, op. cit.; also see his article, 'Hindu Nationalism: Strategic Syncretism in Ideology Building', *Economic and Political Weekly*, XXVIII (12-13), 20-7 March 1993, pp. 517-24.

45. Thomas Blom Hansen, *The Saffron Wave: Democracy and Hindu Nationalism in Modern India* (Delhi: Oxford University Press, 1999).
46. See K. Jayaprasad, *R.S.S. and Hindu Nationalism: Inroads in a Leftist Stronghold* (Delhi: Deep & Deep, 1991).
47. Bruce D. Graham, *Hindu Nationalism and Indian Politics*, op. cit., p. 6.
48. Bipin Chandra, *Communalism in Modern India*, op. cit., p. 99.
49. David Ludden, ed., *Making India Hindu*, op. cit., p. 15.
50. Ibid., p. 16.
51. See Article 4, Constitution of the RSS.
52. J.A. Curran, Jr., *Militant Hinduism in Indian Politics: A Study of the RSS* (New York: Institute of Pacific Relations, 1951). He was the first scholar to attempt a comprehensive and authentic study of the RSS in 1951. Though the study was conducted long ego, the analysis seems to be remarkably fresh and relevant.
53. Ibid., Preface.
54. Balraj Madhok, *RSS and Politics* (Delhi: Hindu World Publications, 1986), Chap. II.
55. D.R. Goyal, *Rashtriya Swayamsevak Sangh*, op. cit., p. 186.
56. Tapan Basu et al., *Khaki Shorts and Saffron Flags*, op. cit., p. 47.
57. H.V. Seshadri, *The Way* (New Delhi: Suruchi Prakashan, 1991), p. 67.
58. Ibid.
59. J.A. Curran, *Militant Hinduism in Indian Politics*, op. cit., p. 26.
60. Ibid.
61. Bruce D. Graham, *Hindu Nationalism and Indian Politics*, op. cit., p. 48.
62. Ibid.
63. The first explanation proved to be wrong. The organization 'that strives for political power' certainly could not treat electoral participation as 'superficial'. Curran failed to anticipate the creation of BJS, the political affiliate of the RSS. The second reason, however, seems to be more appropriate in the context of development of factionalism among the RSS cadre within the BJP in Gujarat, UP, Rajasthan, Delhi and other provinces.
64. Daniel Gold, 'Organized Hinduisms: From Vedic Truth to Hindu Nation', in Martin E. Marty and R. Scott Appleby, eds., *Fundamentalisms Observed*, op. cit., p. 571. The RSS literature often praises the role of traditional *Rajarshi*. Plato is one of the favourite thinkers of the RSS; the *sarsanghchalak* would perhaps prefer to be Plato's Philosopher King rather than a mere *Rajarshi*.
65. Leaders of the BJP, the incarnation of the BJS, never concede that their organization is controlled by the RSS. However, they admit that they consult the RSS leadership at times.
66. Balraj Madhok, *RSS and Politics*, op. cit.
67. Bruce D. Graham, *Hindu Nationalism and Indian Politics*, op. cit.
68. Hampton Thompson Davey, Jr., 'The Transformation of an Ideological Movement into an Aggregative Party: A Case Study of the Bharatiya Jana Sangh', unpublished Ph.D. Thesis, University of California, Los Angeles, 1969, p. 2.

69. Geeta Puri, *Bharatiya Jana Sangh Organisation and Ideology, Delhi: A Case Study* (Delhi: Sterling Publishers, 1980).
70. Yogendra K. Malik and V.B. Singh, *Hindu Nationalists in India*, op. cit.
71. Partha S. Ghosh, *BJP and the Evolution of Hindu Nationalism: From Periphery to Centre* (Delhi: Manohar, 1999).
72. Clifford Geertz, *The Interpretation of Cultures* (New York: Basic Books, 1973), p. 320.
73. See Shashi Joshi and Bhagwan Josh, *Struggle for Hegemony in India 1920-47: Culture, Community and Power*, Vol. III, *1941-47* (Delhi: Sage Publications, 1994).
74. Chapter III makes a discussion on the organizational structure and training.
75. Daniel Gold, 'Organized Hinduisms: From Vedic Truth to Hindu Nation', op. cit., p. 555.
76. J.A. Curran, *Militant Hinduism in Indian Politics*, op. cit., p. 53.
77. See Ainslie T. Embree, 'The Function of the Rashtriya Swayamsevak Sangh: To Define Hindu Nation', op. cit., p. 625. Also see Barbara Wilmot Flynn, 'Communalization of Politics: National Political Activity in India, 1926-30', unpublished Ph.D. Thesis, Duke University, 1974, p. 101.
78. J.A. Curran, *Militant Hinduism in Indian Politics*, op. cit., pp. 50-1.
79. Bruce Graham believes, popular Hinduism, in contrast, has much greater scope for political expression as it has strong appeal among the so-called backward and middle castes. Gandhi used the language and imagery of Bhakti movements to build up support for the Congress. See Bruce Graham, *Hindu Nationalism and Indian Politics*, op. cit., p. 51.
80. Ibid., pp. 51-2.
81. Ibid., p. 52.

CHAPTER II

Origin and Evolution of the RSS: Hedgewar and Golwalkar (1925-1973)

A study of the origin and evolution of the RSS is essential to understand the historical context of its ideology and politics. First, this chapter attempts to analyse the socio-political environment in which its foundation was laid and then it shows the evolutionary process of the RSS under the first two *sarsanghchalaks*—K.B. Hedgewar and M.S. Golwalkar.

COMMUNAL CLIMATE

The Montague-Chelmsford reforms of 1919 brought religion more pervasively and passionately into Indian politics and exacerbated communal animosity. While a section of Hindus began to characterize themselves as 'the dying race',[1] their Muslim counterparts saw a grave danger for the Muslim community. Mahatma Gandhi, however, always emphasized Hindu-Muslim cooperation and successfully mobilized them in his Non-Cooperation movement against the British.[2] But soon after he withdrew this movement, Hindu-Muslim relations soured and communal riots broke out with alarming frequency and intensity. Now communal suspicion and clashes replaced inter-communal cooperation. Competitive communal mobilizations like *shuddhi* and *sangathan* among the Hindus, *tabligh* and *tanzim* among the Muslims further deteriorated Hindu-Muslim relations.

Shuddhi *vs.* Tabligh

The period from 1923 to 1928 has been described as 'an era of Hindu communal resurgence' in North India in which Arya Samaj played an important role.[3] *Shuddhi* had been a part of Arya Samaj activities during the late ninteenth century.[4] But now under the leadership of

Swami Shraddhanand,[5] the campaign became intense. His proselytizing mission was aimed at those Hindus who were converted to Islam or other groups of borderline Muslims who had retained many Hindu customs.[6] These attempts undoubtedly provoked the Muslim leadership, particularly the *ulemas*. Their response to *shuddhi* was *tabligh*. This effort was initiated by a number of *ulemas* and *sufis* including Khwaja Hasan Nizami and Maulana Bari. Muslim preachers worked on the same Muslims who were targets of *shuddhi*, thus obviously leading to a course of collision. Both these movements used provocative methods in their campaigns, which further vitiated Hindu-Muslim relations and led to communal clashes.

Analysing the causes of communal clashes, Basant Kumar Basu, an advocate from Calcutta, wrote in 1926 that the reasons could be traced 'partly to the reconversion of Mahomedans into Hinduism started by the Arya Samaj'.[7] He added that though Hinduism has every legal and moral right to seek converts, the Koran considered apostasy as a capital offence. Therefore, Hindu-Muslim confrontation became inevitable when the promoters of *shuddhi* encouraged apostasy.

Sangathan *vs.* Tanzim

Strengthening of community through militant mobilizations became the major concern of the leaders of different communities during the 1920s. *Sangathan* meant the acquisition of strength through the consolidation of the community, and this became the rallying cry of the Hindus who believed themselves to be lagging behind the Muslims in mobilization and militancy.[8] The *sangathanists* sought to obliterate the image of the Hindu as a 'dhoti-wearing coward' and supplant it with that of a militant Hindu who would be willing 'to use whatever means' to maintain his honour and that of his community.[9]

R.B. Lal Chand outlined the *sangathan* ideology in his speech delivered at the 1909 Punjab Hindu Conference. He highlighted the plight of the Hindus during that period 'characteristic of communal struggle', in which 'survival of the fittest' was the 'all-predominant and universal law'. He identified three crucial factors which could shape the destiny of a community and ought to form the watchword of any community that wished to survive: 'self-consciousness, fitness, and consolidation'.[10] The Hindu Mahasabha vigorously took up the cause of *sangathan* under the leadership of Lajpat Rai (Punjab), Madan Mohan Malaviya (United Provinces) and B.S. Moonje (Maharashtra).

The 1923 Benaras session of Hindu Mahasabha gave a boost to

the *sangathan* movement by bringing together a cross section of Hindu groups including some prominent Congress leaders on this common Hindu platform. In his presidential address, Madan Mohan Malaviya stated: 'Friendship could exist between equals. If the Hindus made themselves strong and the rowdy section among the Mahomedans were convinced they could not safely rob and dishonour Hindus, unity would be established on a stable basis.'[11] His prescription was to educate all boys and girls, establish *akharas* (gymnasiums), establish a volunteer crops to persuade people to comply with decisions of the Hindu Mahasabha, to accept untouchables as Hindus and grant them the right to use wells, enter temples and get education. Swami Shraddhanand, in his pamphlet *Hindu Sangathan* suggested that one *Hindu Rashtra Mandir* should be built in every city and important town of India, as the first step towards the organization of Hindus. Unlike most of the Hindu temples, this 'Catholic Hindu Temple' was to be devoted to the worship of 'the three mother-spirits'—*Gau-mata* (or Mother Cow), *Saraswati-mata* (Mother Saraswati, the Goddess of Learning) and *Bhoomi-mata* (Mother Earth).

The *sangathanists* were keen to prevent Malabar-type riots, in which many Hindus were reportedly killed and a large number were forcibly converted to Islam.[12] Analyzing the causes of the Malabar riots, the 1923 report of B.S. Moonje, blamed the upper-caste Hindus for alienating the low-caste ones.[13] One of Moonje's explicit aims was to remove the 'docility' and the 'mildness' from the temper of the Hindus and make them imbibe the 'aggressiveness' of their neighbours. He claimed that *ahimsa* or non-violence emasculated the Hindus. Moonje mooted the idea of providing the settlement of 'our war-like races, such as the Marathas, Rajputs, Sikhs, etc., in Malabar which alone, I think can solve the Mophlah terrorism over the meek and helpless Hindus'.[14] Expressing great concern on the conversion of the Hindus, Moonje said that during the last 900 years India had lost 7 crore of her men to another religion. He emphasized that the challenge before the Hindu movement was 'to keep together all Hindus and to extend the Hindu religion, so that India might again be called Hindustan, the land of the Hindus'.[15]

The Muslim response to *sangathan* was *tanzim.* Dr. S. Kitchlew started the *tanzim* (organization) movement in late 1923. He called for the organization of Muslim volunteer corps, schools, charitable bodies, and even banks, and the collection of an all-India Muslim fund for this purpose. He started an Urdu daily, *Tanzim,* which published anti-Hindu articles. However, the *tanzim* was much less effective than the *sangathan* movement.

FOUNDATION OF THE RSS

Initially, Punjab was an ideal ground for the *sangathan* movement[16] because the Hindus were in a minority in this province. As communal conflict increased during the early 1920s, its message and organization spread to other provinces, including the C.P. & Berar. As one Government Report of 1925 mentions, a *sangathan* leader Swami Satyadeo completed his tour of the province in that year and 'succeeded in offending the Muhammadans at some centres by remarking that they were almost all converted Hindus'. Contrasting these activities with the activities of the Congress, the Report proceeds, 'Sunderlal, the leader of the no-change party, continues to lecture to apathetic audiences on Hindu-Muslim unity and the virtues of the charkha.'[17] Thus, it was evident that while the Congress efforts on Hindu-Muslim unity could not generate much enthusiasm in C.P. & Berar, the Hindu *sangathan* leaders were able to antagonize the Muslims.[18]

In this charged atmosphere of communal confrontation, a new organization of the Hindus was established at Nagpur on the Vijaya Dashmi day of 1925, upholding the spirit of *sangathan* ideology. The founder was Dr. Keshav Baliram Hedgewar. The four other persons present on the occasion were Dr. B.S. Moonje, Dr. L.V. Paranjape, Dr. B.B. Thalkar and Babarao Savarkar. The name given subsequently to this organization was Rashtriya Swayamsevak Sangh (RSS). To understand the origin of this organization, one has to grasp the dynamics of politics of Nagpur, which was the power-centre of C.P. & Berar as well as the socio-political background of the founder of the RSS.

Socio-political Dynamics of C.P. & Berar

Dominance of the Maratha Brahmins

The C.P. & Berar[19] consisted of not only two distinct administrative units, its population was divided into two linguistic groups—one speaking Hindi or its dialect Chhattisgarhi, and the other Marathi. The Marathi region, being more developed than its Hindi counterpart, experienced more social tension. Among the Marathi population the Brahmins enjoyed a dominant position. These Maratha Brahmins were formed of two sub-castes: *Konkanasthas* from coastal Maharashtra and *Deshasthas*[20] from the *desh* or plateau.

The Bhonslas of Nagpur concretized the dominance of Brahmins by granting them lands and appointing them in administrative services. The Brahmins felt threatened when the British incorporated the Bhonsla kingdom under the pretext of the 'Doctrine of Lapse'. They got further enraged when the British introduced certain reforms such as the abolition of *sati*, the Hindu Widows Remarriage Act of 1850s and carried on intense missionary activities. The Maratha Brahmins perceived all these developments not only as threats to their privileged position but also to their religion.

Ironically, British intrusion, which these Brahmins resented, further enhanced their dominance by opening up new educational and economic opportunities. Initially the *Deshasthas* were less enthusiastic than the *Konkanasthas* about these opportunities. This was mainly because of their close association with the Bhonsla kingdom. The *Deshasthas* carried on their traditional vocation a little longer. However, during the later part of the nineteenth century, they also entered the educational institutions in large number and begun to dominate the Maratha society and politics alongwith their *Konkanastha* brothers. Thus, these Maratha Brahmins maintained their earlier socio-economic dominance under the British rule.

Brahmin–non-Brahmin Dichotomy

Unlike Punjab and Bengal, the Muslim population in Maharashtra was not significant and its immediate political past was free of Muslim domination. Here the Brahmin–non-Brahmin dichotomy was crucial.[21] The emergence of non-Brahmin consciousness posed a challenge to the supremacy of Brahmins. The most important non-Brahmin castes which raised protest against the Brahmin dominance, were Marathas and Kumbis. Gopal Hari Deshmukh (known as *Lokhitwadi*), published his famous letters in 1848, in which he wrote against priestly obscurantism. Tukaram Tatriya Padval attacked the caste system in *Jatibhed Viveskar* in 1861. Jyotiba Phule founded schools for girls (1851) and untouchables (1852), both first of their kind. The orthodox Brahmins asserted their position with the publication of *Nibandhmala* (Garland of Essays) by Vishnu Shastri Chiplunkar in 1874, which violently attacked Phule and Lokhitwadi. Bal Gangadhar Tilak, the emerging leader, subscribed to many of the orthodox ideas of Chiplunkar.

Importance of Nagpur

Nagpur, as the capital of the province, was naturally well-placed to stimulate intellectual and political activities including the Brahmin–non-Brahmin controversy. Prominent newspapers like *Hitavada* and

Maharashtra were published from here. Apart from possessing prestigious educational establishments like Hislop and Morris College, it also played host to medical, engineering and agricultural institutions. Therefore, the city produced a substantial educated community; one-fourth of the graduates of the province were from Nagpur, most of them being Maharashtrian Brahmins.[22] Nagpur was the seat of political power under the Bhonslas in which these Brahmins had a dominant position. They continued to maintain their superiority vis-a-vis the non-Brahmins even under the British. But their dominance was challenged by the non-Brahmins. Nagpur was emerging as a site of non-Brahmin assertion and consolidation.[23] In this backdrop, K.B. Hedgewar, a Maharashtrian Brahmin, founded the RSS at Nagpur.

FOUNDER OF THE RSS: K.B. HEDGEWAR

Hedgewar's Early Life

Keshav Baliram Hedgewar[24] lost his parents in his childhood and was looked after by his uncle who was not well off. As Keshav did not show much inclination towards the study of the traditional Shastras and Vedas, his uncle sent him to a school imparting modern education. There he came in close contact with a group of young associates of B.S. Moonje. Keshav was reportedly rusticated from the school for leading the *Vande Mataram* movement.[25] After completing school education, he was inspired by B.S. Moonje, his political guru,[26] to join the National Medical College, Calcutta. Hedgewar reportedly got associated with the Anushilan Samiti and participated in revolutionary activities during his stay at Calcutta though he never went to jail during that period.[27] However, K.R. Malkani claims that his movements were closely watched by the British spies.[28] Hedgewar returned to Nagpur after completing his medical education and started to practice, but soon abandoned it for full-time political activities.

Political Ideas Shaped Up

Hedgewar shared the political values of many of the *Deshasthas* of his time. They never forgot the British intrusion of the kingdom of their patron, the Bhonslas, and always nurtured an anti-British psychology. Moreover, the poverty in which many *Deshasthas* including Hedgewar were born and brought up, hardened this attitude. Their orthodox upbringing gave them a conspicuous Hindu perspective, which was further crystallized with an anti-Muslim bearing because of their reverence to Shivaji, the famous Maratha fighter who had perpetual enemity with the Mughals. In this background, the political ideas of Hedgewar took shape, particularly during early 1920s.

After his return from Calcutta, he participated in Congress politics as a staunch follower of Tilak and joined the National Council in the Central Provinces. Like other Tilakites, he had reservations on the Khilafat issue. However, he joined the Non-Cooperation movement and was sentenced to rigorous imprisonment for a year.[29] The consequences of the movement profoundly disillusioned him. Hedgewar regretted that Indian Muslims had proved themselves 'Muslims first and Indians only secondarily'; when the Khilafat demand was given up in Turkey, they withdrew from the allied movement for national independence and displayed 'Muslim fanaticism'.[30] Thus, Hedgewar argued that Indian Muslims were more concerned with the fate of the Turkish Caliph than with Indian Independence and was convinced that the Non-Cooperation movement failed due to its association with the Khilafat issue. He accused the Muslims of withdrawing the movement. But it was Mahatma Gandhi who decided to withdraw.

The post-Non-Cooperation period witnessed a volcanic eruption of Hindu-Muslim riots from Kohat to Kanpur and from Multan to Malabar. Hedgewar argued that these were not Hindu-Muslim riots but only 'Muslim riots' because 'in every single case it is they who start them and go on the offensive'.[31] He warned that the 'yavana-snakes' reared on the milk of Non-Cooperation 'were provoking riots in the nation with their poisonous hissing'.[32]

Nagpur Riots: A Watershed

However, Hindu-Muslim riots at Nagpur became a watershed in Hedgewar's thinking and greatly influenced him to start the RSS. One of the major causes of the Hindu-Muslim confrontation at Nagpur, like any other place, was the issue of music before the Mosque. On 30 October 1923, the collector banned a '*Dindi*' procession of the Hindus. Influential Hindu leaders called for a march defying the ban in which 20,000 Hindus joined.[33] Hedgewar and other Hindu leaders were quick to appreciate the potential power of an organized mobilization. This experience established a precedent to the riots next year. Hindu leaders, this time, applied a new strategy—boycott of Muslim-owned businesses. This demanded further cohesion and consolidation of the Hindus. A Hindu Sabha was organized under the presidentship of Raja Laxmanrao Bhonsle of Nagpur's royal family. Moonje was its vice-president and Hedgewar, the secretary. The Hindu Sabha tried to arouse their com-munity by arguing that it was a matter of shame that the population of 1.3 lakh Hindus against only 20,000 Muslims at Nagpur should feel insecure.[34] It squarely blamed the Muslim community for forcing the Hindus to adopt a tough posture.

The successful mobilizations of the Hindus at Nagpur sharpened and crystallized the anti-Muslim ideas of Hedgewar. Hedgewar argued that the Muslims ('Yavana Snakes') were 'anti-national' and that Hindu-Muslim fraternity was a misnomer and 'only Hindu strength could save the country'.[35] He questioned the rationality of those who thought of binding the Muslims into a common national chord as they did not believe in common interests, common aspirations, common ideals and common traditions.[36] He considered the Muslims as the enemy of the Hindus and prescribed that the Hindus needed to be organized to counter their threat. The Nagpur experience certainly provided him the clue to organize and mobilize the Hindus on a large-scale by projecting the Muslims as the main enemy.

Hedgewar's Hindu Rashtra

Thus, the Nagpur happenings moulded Hedgewar's ideological perception of the *Hindu Rashtra*.[37] He claimed that the Hindus were a mighty and prosperous nation long before recorded history, and their benign influence 'extended over vast regions of the earth and our flag flew over many lands. . . .'[38] Then how did the Hindus 'succumb first to a handful of Muslims and then again to a handful of British merchants'? He further questioned: 'What did we lack that the Muslims and English possessed? Man-power? Wealth? Weapons? Physical prowess? Intellectual acumen?' Hedgewar argued that though the Hindus did not lack in any of these things, yet they lost; they were 'helplessly weak in one vital aspect on which nation's survival or death depends. And that is national consciousness and cohesion.'[39] Therefore, in Hedgewar's diagnosis, the basic weakness was the absence of 'national consciousness' and 'utter lack of feeling of being the organic limbs of a single national life and the resultant hatred, discord, jealousy and internecine quarrel to gain selfish ends'.[40]

Hedgewar was convinced that this 'malady' could not be cured by merely raising an anti-British struggle. He argued that if nothing was wrong with our national life before the British came, then how did the nation lose to them at all? Even earlier, why was the nation enslaved by the Muslims? Therefore, he concluded that an anti-British struggle would not be enough; the real solution remained with the arousal of 'national consciousness' and building up of 'national solidarity'.[41]

In his paradigm, the 'Nation' was a Hindu Nation '*Hindu Rashtra*' and the 'National' consciousness and solidarity were Hindu consciousness and Hindu solidarity. He is credited with the idea of founding the RSS to propagate India as a *Hindu Rashtra.* The Hindu Mahasabha, till then, had not moved beyond claiming the 'legitimate rights' of the Hindus as a majority community. Hedgewar made a significant shift from the Mahasabha's *Hindu Raj* (Hindu Rule) to *Hindu Rashtra* (Hindu Nation).

Contemporary Influences: Savarkar and Moonje

Hedgewar's ideas were almost similar to the philosophy and prescription of the Hindu *sangathanists,* though the RSS does not properly spell out the influences of these leaders on its founder.[42] V.D. Savarkar's *Hindutva* (1923) was undoubtedly a major influence in Hedgewar's formulation of *Hindu Rashtra.*[43] Prior to the formation of the RSS, Hedgewar sought the advice of Savarkar and stayed with him for two days in March 1925.[44] Though there is no evidence to establish V.D. Savarkar's hand in the formation of the RSS, his brother Babarao was one of the five participants present in the inaugural meeting.

Another key Hindu leader of Maharashtra, B.S. Moonje, was the political guru of Hedgewar. He was a constant source of inspiration to Hedgewar since his school days and was instrumental in sending him to Calcutta to study medicine. After his return to Nagpur, Hedgewar remained his close associate. Surprisingly, the RSS portrays Moonje as a protege rather than a patron of Hedgewar.[45] Though the RSS leaders refer to Moonje as a father figure to Hedgewar, they however emphasize that their leader 'did not totally agree' with Moonje.[46] Hedgewar might have differed with him occasionally with regard to the participation of RSS cadres in the Hindu Mahasabha activities, but Moonje's influence on his pupil was unmistakably clear. For instance, Moonje wrote, 'the Hindus were living under two dominations, the political domination of the British based on their strongest of Machine guns and the domination of Mahomedans based on their aggressive mentality'.[47] Hedgewar shared this analysis. How were these dominations to be fought? Moonje advised Hindus of all castes to see that their youths got proper training and particularly in *lathi* play for their defence.[48] The RSS also trained its *swayamsevaks* to master the wielding of the *lathi*. The intention was not obviously to match the machine gun, but the *lathi* would certainly be handy against the Muslims for 'self protection'. The RSS was not prepared to counter the British but the Muslims, who were identified by Hedgewar as the principal enemy of the Hindus. Thus, Moonje's ideas had a direct bearing on Hedgewar. Moonje was also a source of inspiration to the new organization. He was one of five founder members of the RSS and participated in its important functions.

Despite Hedgewar's ideological and organizational indebtedness to Savarkar and Moonje, the RSS put him on a higher pedestal. To show Hedgewar's distinct position from the four other leading figures including Moonje, who were present at the inaugural meeting of 1925, the RSS sources mention that while only Hedgewar was the *swayamsevak*, others were promoters.[49] To his followers, Hedgewar is obviously above the rest. And the entire credit of the RSS project should go to him alone and is not to be shared.

Real Innovation: Organizational Technique

The originality of Hedgewar's ideas may be contested,[50] but his original contribution lies in innovative organizational techniques and methods to organize the Hindus. More importantly, he simply did not prescribe, but dedicated his life to the cause. He found a tremendous potential in Sister Nivedita's suggestion to Hindus to congregate daily and pray together for fifteen minutes to become an invincible force. This was developed into a uniform programme of rituals-cum-physical training, to be performed by the RSS *shakhas*.[51]

Evolution of the RSS: Early Years

Hedgewar's attempt was modest to start with. At the outset, his activities were confined only to Nagpur district. Quality rather than quantity was his major theme; he was selective in admitting the new members after questioning the aspiring ones intensively. Therefore, the recruitment to the RSS in the initial years was not impressive. He followed the policy of 'Catch them Young'—targeting the school boys from twelve to fifteen year age group, as it would be easy to mould their mind. These boys were imparted both physical as well as ideological training. He continually tested the reasoning capacities of the *swayamsevaks.* An extremely close relationship developed between Hedgewar and his first group of recruits. Hedgewar was thus nurturing a group of young boys who would be loyal to him personally as well as to the ideal of the RSS. His boys were special to him; he did not allow them to do petty jobs for other organizations and individuals, thus developing a sense of self-respect among them. His recruits obviously felt superior to the volunteers of other organizations. After all they would be the future missionaries of the RSS and carry Hedgewar's message of *Hindu Rashtra.*

The *shakha* programme started in 1926. Along with physical training the solid core of the RSS went through intellectual and political training by the 'preparation of minds'. The boys were attending an *akhara* in the city. On Tuesdays and Thursdays, a political class was held which later developed into *baudhik* (intellectual discourses). Therefore, the *shakha* represented 'an ideological *akhara*'.[52] Yet the organization did not have a name, flag, funds and hierarchy. On the *Ram Navami* day of 1926, the name[53] Rashtriya Swayamsevak Sangh was selected after considerable discussion.[54] Hedgewar preferred *rashtriya* to Hindu as he wanted to assert that Hindu and *rashtriya* are synonymous. A flag was later chosen that supposedly belonged to Ram, and was said to have been used by Shivaji. A prayer was composed in mixed Hindi and Marathi (perhaps reflecting the bilingual composition of C.P. & Berar) to be sung at every *shakha* meeting, along with the utterance of a few slogans like *Rashtra Guru Samarth Ramdas ki jai* and *Bharat Mata ki jai.* The prominence of Shivaji, his flag, and his guru Ramdas in the rituals of the RSS suggested a strong Maharashtrian influence on this infant organization. The RSS was also commonly accused to be an organization of Maharashtrian Brahmins. This was because Hedgewar's recruitment was confined only to Maharashtra and most of these schoolboys were Brahmins. They became the core of the RSS and later occupied the organizational positions, thus creating this impression.[55]

To reinforce the *shakha* training further, Hedgewar organized the first training camp of the RSS in 1927. The boys were trained in the use of *lathi,* sword, javelin and dagger-weapons.[56] They were also indoctrinated with the idea of Hindu nationalism. Hedgewar invited prominent Hindu leaders to these camps to impress them through a display of discipline of his boys. The practice of life oaths of members, reminiscent of revolutionary-terrorist traditions,[57] began in 1928 to intensify their commitment to the organization and its ideology. A batch consisting of

99 *swayamsevaks* took oath in front of the *bhagwa dhwaj* (saffron flag) in a forest near Nagpur. Metaphysically, the flag was considered the 'Guru' (Chief) of the RSS. Hedgewar thought that too much honour to any individual was dangerous and therefore *swayamsevaks* were to pledge primary allegiance to this flag. The present form of the RSS slowly began to emerge. The political class became a regular feature of daily *shakhas* under the name of *boudhik.* Prayers and the use of bugles for marches were instituted. Six regular festivals[58] were selected to be observed at each *shakha.* Military training was also imparted.[59]

Finance was vital for the new organization. Initially, it depended on the contributions of Hedgewar and his friends. Different suggestions were considered, including selling of drama tickets and organizing a lottery. Finally, Hedgewar borrowed a novel method from the Hindu tradition, the concept of *Guru Dakshina*—donation being voluntarily offered by the disciple to the *Guru* (Teacher), out of gratitude. Accordingly, each *swayamsevak* would make his offering to their *Guru,* the *bhagwa dhwaj,* according to his capacity. This system 'would neither glorify the giver nor make the RSS dependent on any particular person'.[60] The first *Guru Dakshina* function was held in 1928 and the total collection was Rs. 84.[61]

The RSS leaders, in a meeting on November 1929, adopted the principle of *ek chalak anuvartita* (to follow one leader). Appaji Joshi proposed Hedgewar's name as *sarsanghchalak,*[62] the supreme director, on a life-time basis. It was quite clear that *sarsanghchalak* would exercise absolute power in the organization. Hedgewar categorically stated that a *swayamsevak* had to obey the orders of the *sarsanghchalak* at any stage, under any circumstances and without any hesitation.[63] The RSS thus became a centralized command structure under *sarsanghchalak,* who would exercise enormous power in the organization. The principle of *ek chalak anuvartita,* according to the RSS sources, is very much on the lines of the traditional Hindu joint family system, and hence, the most appropriate for an organization committed to Hindu way of life.

Hedgewar's Political Links: Congress and Hindu Mahasabha

Hedgewar continued his association with the Congress despite his total involvement with his new organization. He remained on the Executive Committee of the Central Province Congress Committee. His associate in the RSS project, Appaji Joshi, was its secretary. Hedgewar attended the 1928 Congress session in Calcutta. In 1930 Mahatma Gandhi launched Salt Satyagraha, undertaking the Dandi March. Hedgewar was initially reluctant to participate in the 1930 *satyagraha* for he thought that the RSS work would suffer. 'Information was given that the Sangh will not participate in the satyagraha.'[64] A delegation met Hedgewar and tried to convince him that this movement would give independence and the Sangh should not lag behind. At that time, when a gentleman told Hedgewar that he was ready to go to jail, Hedgewar said, 'Definitely go. But who will take care of your family then?'[65] Finally, Appaji Joshi persuaded him to join the movement. Hedgewar was arrested and remained in prison for nine months. He 'established close relations with leaders and activists in the prison, explained the work of the Sangh to them and obtained promise of cooperation for work in future. He came out of the prison only after making plans for a big leap for work expansion.'[66] Thus, his association with the Congress helped him to expand the RSS in the later years.

The relationship between the Hindu Mahasabha and the RSS creates some confusion. It appeared that both the organizations shared the same ideology—*Hindu Rashtra.* Undoubtedly, Mahasabha leaders like V.D. Savarkar and B.S. Moonje were a source of inspiration to Hedgewar. He continued to invite them to the important RSS functions and especially when he had to make significant public pronouncements regarding the Sangh. Hedgewar provided volunteers for Hindu Mahasabha sessions, though his boys were never at the command of the Hindu Mahasabha. His primary objective of sending the volunteers was to demonstrate the potential of a trained and disciplined cadre in front of the prominent Hindu leaders and to earn their goodwill to be encashed in future. Lacking trained youth power, the Mahasabha leaders also found potential with the RSS. The 1932 Delhi session of Mahasabha passed a resolution commending the activities of the RSS and expressed the urgent need to spread its network all over the country. In the same year, Bhai Parmanand extended a special invitation to Hedgewar to attend the Karachi session of Hind Yuvak Parishad. Hedgewar utilized his visit in establishing contacts with prominent Hindu leaders in Sindh and Punjab, who not only opened the door for the RSS but worked zealously to promote it in their areas. Babarao Savarkar brought the RSS in touch with Mahasabha activists in Delhi and Benaras, the areas of future expansion. Thus the RSS was able to penetrate the north-west and northern areas with the help of the Hindu Mahasabha.

Organizationally, however, the RSS was independent of the Hindu Mahasabha. In fact the Mahasabha leadership was unhappy because RSS refused to become a subsidiary of their organization. Hedgewar also did not extend support to a major Hindu Mahasabha campaign in 1938-9, when it was trying to project itself as a full-fledged political party. Thus the relationship between the Mahasabha and the RSS soured; in 1939, the Mahasabha established its own uniformed youth corps, the *Ram Sena* (Ram's Army). Despite these developments, in 1938, Savarkar suggested the name of Hedgewar 'than whom no other person can be more entitled to open the Hindu Youth Conference'.[67] It is also significant to note that when Hedgewar died in 1940, V.D. Savarkar, as the president of Hindu Mahasabha, instructed Hindu Sabhas throughout India to observe 30 June as a day of mourning for him.

Growth of the RSS under Hedgewar

Hedgewar started the RSS with only five persons in 1925 at Nagpur. By 1931, the RSS started moving beyond Nagpur and Wardha to Vidarbha region and the Hindi-speaking areas of Central Provinces. The Sangh could muster the active sympathy and support of numerous prominent Hindus of these provinces including Raja Laxmanrao Bhonsle of Nagpur, Raja Raghoji Rao Bhonsle, Sir Chitnivis, Hon. Tambe (former Governor of C.P. & Berar), Sir Morpant Joshi, Rao Bahadur Kelkar (former Minister of C.P. & Berar). With the patronage of these notables, the RSS increased its membership to 30,000 by 1937 in C.P. & Berar alone.[68]

As early as 1932, the government was getting alarmed over the expansion and programmes of the RSS, whose leaders were 'definitely associated with anti-Government agitation' and it was felt by the authorities that 'this movement will require close attention'.[69] In one confidential reports,[70] the celebration of the Dussehra festival by the RSS at Nagpur in 1932 has been characterized as 'the most important political feature' in the south of C.P. & Berar. On this occasion 1,000 uniformed volunteers headed by Moonje marched past. The important personalities present included the Bhonsla king, G.D. Savarkar, Hedgewar and others. In 'an objectionable and provocative address', Hedgewar mentioned that 'the settlement of the political future of India was for the Hindus alone to decide. No interference either by foreigners or by non-Hindu residents of India should be brooked.'[71] On the basis of his speech the government was considering to take action against Hedgewar.

On December 1932, the Central Provinces Government had issued orders forbidding government employees to join or take part in the activities of the RSS. Another circular instructed the teachers in District Council schools not to join the RSS. The government's decision was based on two reasons: first, the RSS was considered to be communal and secondly, it was aiding anti-government political movements. Thus the British Government objected to the communal and political nature of the RSS. The Congress also viewed it as communal and restrained its members from joining in its activities.

On the occasion of 'Til Sankrant' celebrations on 10 January 1933, Hedgewar asserted that the government had acted on base insinuations made against the Sangh and denied that it was either political or communal. On the other hand, M.V. Joshi, who presided over the same meeting, admitted that 'the Sangh was a communal organization although he justified its existence on the ground that the Hindus should be able to defend themselves in times of stress. He further remarked that the Sangh was opposed to the idea of non-violence.'[72] B.S. Moonje, speaking in the same function, favoured offence rather than defence and advocated a policy of 'strike first'.[73] This suggested that the RSS continued as a communal organization.

Hedgewar adopted two major strategies for the expansion of the RSS in the 1930s. First, he focussed his attention on the universities outside Maharashtra and dispatched his trained volunteers to recruit students in the campuses. The RSS started a *shakha* in the Benaras Hindu University campus with the help of Madan Mohan Malaviya.[74] M.S. Golwalkar, the successor of Hedgewar, was recruited here. Second, Hedgewar requested the prominent members of the Hindu Mahasabha to introduce the RSS *pracharaks* to the notables of their respective areas and arrange for their stay. The Hindu Mahasabha channel proved to be very useful in the initial stage when the RSS was looking for an entry outside C.P. & Berar.

Between 1937 and 1940, the RSS expanded feverishly amidst deteriorating Hindu-Muslim relations in northern India. The *pracharaks* were active in Punjab, Delhi, United Provinces and Bihar. In 1939, the RSS entered the southern states of Tamil Nadu and Karnataka. The first attempt to form a Madras branch of the RSS was made in April 1939 when C.S. Paramarth of Nagpur, 'the Chief Organizer of the Madras Province', visited Madras and recruited about 40 members.[75]

The expansion was steady and impressive. There were only 60 *shakhas* in 1931. In 1936, the RSS claimed to have 200 branches and 25,000 members. By 1939, there were 500 branches and 40,000 members; in

1940, the RSS had 700 branches and 80,000 members.[76] Hedgewar also made his organization financially sound. The income of the Sangh came from subscriptions and donations from volunteers, supporters and well-wishers, usually collected at the annual Guru Purnima festival as *Guru Dakshina*. A 1939 report stated that Rs. 20,000 was kept as a fixed deposit with two Nagpur money-lenders, Chitnavis and Ghatate. Strict control was maintained over the finances of the Sangh and each branch was normally permitted to retain only a Rs. 200 deposit.

Alongwith the expansion and a sound financial position, its character also underwent a transformation from being a regional to an all-India organization. Hedgewar was quite pragmatic; he decided to dilute the Maharashtrian emphasis of the RSS to make it acceptable to other regional Hindu traditions. Initially, it did not find an easy acceptance in northern India because of the opposition of the Arya Samaj to the idolatrous rituals and practices of the RSS. Therefore, the worship of Hanuman[77] was given up and insistence on Hindu rituals was less emphasized. The prayer was changed to Sanskrit to break the regional barrier.

Thus, Hedgewar's innovative organizational skill, missionary zeal and perseverance helped the RSS to grow considerably in a short time. By 1940, when Hedgewar died, the RSS had a nationwide presence except Assam, Orissa, and Kashmir. 'I see before my eyes today a miniature *Hindu Rashtra*', Hedgewar reportedly said in his last speech to the trainees of the 1940 Nagpur Officers' Training Camp (OTC).

THE SUCCESSOR: M.S. GOLWALKAR

Why Madhav Sadashiv Golwalkar was Chosen?

Before his death on 21 June 1940, Hedgewar had nominated Madhav Sadashiv Golwalkar[78] as the next *sarsanghchalak*, thereby setting the precedent that the top leadership position would not be open to democratic election. The choice of Golwalkar surprised many of the RSS members as senior and experienced stalwarts like Appaji Joshi, Keshav Apte and Dadarao Parmarth were bypassed. The RSS members had speculated that Appaji Joshi, the senior most leader, would be the likely successor. However, according to the RSS sources, there was no dispute over the issue of succession.

Why was Golwalkar preferred to others? What was his special

quality? Was he more committed to the *Hindu Rashtra*? In fact Golwalkar had greater inclination towards personal salvation than national resurrection. In contrast to Hedgewar, who was an extrovert and an outright political activist, Golwalkar was more inward-looking and inclined to spiritualism. Then why did Hedgewar choose such a person as his successor? The reason for this choice remains in the sphere of speculation. One possible explanation is that Hedgewar was frustrated by the endless bickering among Hindu Mahasabha stalwarts—between Moonje and Savarkar, Bhai Parmanand and Savarkar. Therefore, he was keen to detach the RSS from the Hindu Mahasabha despite their ideological proximity and wanted a successor who would effectively keep his organization away from the influence of these Mahasabha leaders.[79] Golwalkar ideally fitted into this criterion as he was not close to any of the Mahasabha leaders. Moreover, he had other advantages vis-a-vis his competitors: educational and intellectual background, young age and above all, his short but intense relationship with Hedgewar.[80]

Golwalkar's Ideology and Strategy

Golwalkar's intellectual potential was evident in his translation of the speeches of Vivekananda into Marathi. But with the publication of *We or Our Nationhood Defined* (1939),[81] he established himself as the ideologue of the RSS. Hedgewar's treatment of ideology was not piercing. Golwalkar provided rigour to the concept of *Hindu Rashtra* and made an ideological distinction between 'we' and 'others' in this work. Obviously, 'we' did not include all the inhabitants of this land; non-Hindus were kept outside its pale. Golwalkar rejected territorial nationalism and defined his ideology as cultural nationalism.

Golwalkar took over when the Second World War was looming large. The new leadership got preoccupied with two major considerations: first, the protection of the Hindu community against a possible Japanese invasion of India, and second, the handling of communal conflicts at the end of the War. Keeping this perspective, Golwalkar was shrewd enough to understand the disadvantage of an open conflict with the government. Therefore, the RSS withdrew from the political arena. Accordingly, it did not support the Hindu Mahasabha's call to the Hindus to get enrolled in the British army. Golwalkar also refused Moonje's invitation to the Sangh volunteers to attend the guerilla warfare classes at Bhonsle Military School, Nasik.[82] He instructed all the RSS branches to comply with the government order of 5 August 1940, which prohibited military drill and wearing of military uniform. He also stopped the military training and abolished the Military Department of the Sangh. Some militant *swayamsevaks*, including Nathuram Godse, disagreed with this policy and deserted the RSS to join the Mahasabha.

Golwalkar apparently changed the orientation of the RSS from its paramilitary and militant profile toward a more 'brahminical strategy' of cultivating a high moral culture that would gradually transform Hindu society. His adoption of a 'cultural path', which shunned public, high-profile activities and discouraged agitation, confrontation and mass action, created a culture/politics schism within the organization. But Golwalkar was determined to adopt this strategy in order to avoid British ire and expand the organization quietly avoiding any public controversy.

RSS and Quit India

Unlike his predecessor, Golwalkar never participated in the anti-British struggle. Therefore, he could conveniently ignore whatever little anti-British legacy Hedgewar left behind. The RSS neither joined the individual Civil Disobedience of 1940-1, nor the Quit India movement of 1942. The Bombay Home Department reported, ' . . . the Sangh has scrupulously kept itself within the law and, in particular, has refrained from taking any part in the disturbances that broke out in August 1942. . . .'[83] A Report from the Deputy Commissioner, Jubbulpore, mentioned: 'The organization as a whole remained aloof from the present subversive activities indulged in by the Congressmen.'[84] The RSS defends that it 'viewed the movement sympathetically' but did not participate in it on the organizational level; it felt that 'it was the time to organize and strengthen the people, and not to land ourselves in jail and remain immobilized for years. . . . All the same time a few RSS workers participated in the 1942 movement in their individual capacity.'[85] However, the RSS does not provide any evidence to substantiate its claims: it neither looked at the 1942 movement sympathetically, nor did its members join the movement in their individual capacity. On the contrary, Leeladhar Bajpai, a freedom fighter, alleges that during Quit India movement Atal Behari Vajpayee made a 'confession' to the British police on the basis of which he was jailed for five years.[86] He accuses Atal Behari Vajpayee of betraying the Quit India movement.[87] There were rare instances, however, when the RSS activists joined the 1942 movement.[88]

Quiet Expansion

The RSS, during the period, consciously adopted a policy of aloofness from the mainstream national struggle for independence.[89] A Home Department Report, comparing Inayatullah, the leader of the militant Muslim Khaksars, to Golwalkar, stated that while 'Inayatullah is an unbalanced and blustering megalomaniac, Golwalkar is a wary, astute and, therefore, by far the most capable leader'.[90] In the perception of the government, the RSS did not pose an immediate menace to law and order. Thus positioning itself outside the scrutiny of the British, the RSS expanded quite considerably during these years. In a speech on 25 October 1942, Golwalkar claimed that the Sangh all over India had 1,500 branches and 2,00,000 members.[91] However, as per the government estimate, by 1943, the membership of the Sangh in British India reached 76,000 (excluding the figures of the Indian states).[92]

Golwalkar adopted the method of infiltration of the RSS members in all the key services, both civil and military. The RSS not only enrolled reliable government servants, teachers and clerks, it also set up new branches in the Gun Carriage Factory, Jubbulpore and the Ordnance Factory, Khamaria to attract military personnel.[93] Like Hedgewar, he also realized the importance of students in the expansion of Sangh work. In April 1943, he sent 175 student volunteers from Nagpur districts to all over India to organize new branches.[94] Golwalkar also pursued a policy of expansion in the villages. Hedgewar laid down that 3 per cent of town-dwelling Hindus and 1 per cent of villagers should belong to the Sangh.

Communal and Secret

Golwalkar's outward compliance with government orders was 'no more than a smoke-screen behind which to carry on secretly or in a modified form the very activities that he has renounced'.[95] The Government of Central Provinces at Nagpur printed a confidential pamphlet containing detailed information regarding the strength, organization and activities of the RSS from all the districts of the province. A summary of the District Reports concluded: 'Their policy is to wait until they themselves are better prepared and the state of the country offers better opportunities for intervention . . . the Sangh, though not now dangerous, might become a menace later in times of serious communal disturbances, etc.'[96] G.S. Parmarth, an important RSS leader, asked the volunteers to be ready 'to meet Muslim goondaism during the impending pandemonium due to war conditions'.[97] Thus the RSS was quietly increasing its strength and reserving it for the future battle with the Muslims.

The RSS organized periodic camps to impart rigorous ideological and physical training to its members and then assign them responsibilities to expand the organization. In these camps, the Sangh leaders were expressing their real motive. Addressing a camp, Golwalkar rejected the non-violent method adopted by the Congress for India's independence and believed that freedom could be achieved only by blood sacrifice and 'the main object of the organization was to organize and strengthen the Hindus generally, first to overcome Mohammedans and finally to oust the British'.[98] He reportedly asked the *swayamsevaks* 'not to indulge in politics but quietly and secretly to carry on Sangh activity so that after 2 or 3 years, when their strength would be about 25 lakhs, they would be able to fight their way to India's independence'.[99]

The Rashtriya Swayamsevak Sangh maintained 'a very rigid secrecy' and took pains 'to avoid the attention of the authorities'. Its 'ultimate aim is an India ruled over by the Hindus and its [*sic*] has been quietly preparing for this for years'.[100] The Government of Punjab warned New Delhi on 21 January 1944 that the RSS 'is communal in character and is becoming increasingly popular among Hindus. Its leaders feel that it is necessary to exercise the greatest caution in working for the Hindu domination of India and the activities of the organization are conducted with great secrecy.'[101] The reports from other provinces were not different. The British responded with promulgating the Camps and Parades (Control) Order, 1944 to deal alike with the RSS, the Khaksars and the Muslim League's National Guard.

Communal Riots and Partition

The increasing communal tension and demand for Pakistan helped its expansion drive as more and more Hindus started believing that the RSS would be able to defend and counter the Muslim aggression. The 'finest hour' of the RSS came when Jinnah gave a call for Direct Action in 1946 leading to the Great Calcutta Killings of August in the same year.[102] These events further strengthened the RSS argument that the Muslim menace was clear and threatening and Hindus and Muslims could not live together. In the chaotic communal climate preceding partition, the RSS activists swung into action by taking part in communal violence, 'though this was never officially sanctioned by the leadership.

Yet in the logic of RSS ideology this was "just" violence, acts of self-defense against the cruel enemy.'[103] According to a RSS source, '. . . there was the consideration of protecting Hindu life and honour throughout Northern Bharat. Muslim riots were going on all over. Who would save the Hindus in Pakistan areas—including Congress ministers—from annihilation?'[104] Thus the RSS got actively involved in these riots in the pretext of saving the Hindus. Even Sardar Patel, who was sympathetic to the RSS, did not approve its role during these riots. In his letter[105] to Golwalkar, Patel mentions: 'Organizing the Hindus and helping them is one thing, but going in for revenge for sufferings on innocent and helpless men, women and children is another thing.'

Amidst the breakdown of the administrative machinery during the period, the RSS organized the evacuation of Hindus from West Pakistan. Punjab Relief Committee, which was under the RSS control, undertook relief work among Hindu refugees coming from Pakistan, who instantly started identifying with the RSS ideology. Thus the demonstrative dedication, sacrifice and organizational capacity during the riots enabled the RSS to establish its image as the 'Saviour of the Hindus'. This image helped the RSS to expand rapidly in Punjab, Jammu & Kashmir, Delhi and other places of north India.

The RSS leadership failed to anticipate that the British were about to quit and the country would be partitioned. Golwalkar even stated in an OTC camp in August 1947 that the British were not going to quit.[106] Balasaheb Deoras admitted that the then leadership was unable to foresee these events. Therefore, it could not take any step to prevent partition. The RSS felt that partition was a result of a mistaken softline towards the Muslims. 'The RSS view was (and remains) that all those who believed in the good will of Muslims (including Gandhi), were dangerously naive and therefore responsible for the mass killings and the expulsion of millions of people.'[107]

Mahatma Gandhi's Murder and the First RSS Ban

The communal situation further worsened with the expansion and consolidation of communal organizations. Communal suspicion and propaganda gathered momentum and Mahatma Gandhi became its victim. He was killed on 30 January 1948 by Nathuram Godse, who had deserted the RSS and joined the Hindu Mahasabha.[108] After Gandhi's murder, the RSS faced wrath from the public as well as the government. On 4 February 1948, it was declared unlawful. There was a large scale arrest of RSS functionaries including Golwalkar.

The RSS decided not to resist the ban orders and suspended its public activities for sometime. The regular *shakhbas* were not conducted. The RSS approached some prominent personalities to persuade the government to lift the ban. Golwalkar started a correspondence with Nehru and Patel after his release on August 1948 to get the ban lifted. He pleaded that his organization was innocent and the charges were unfounded. When this failed, Golwalkar, in his letter to Nehru[109] on 24 September 1948, raised the bogey of communist danger and requested Nehru to ensure an atmosphere in which the RSS will be able to help the government to fight the menace. In another letter to Patel,[110] he reiterated that since the ban on the RSS, the youths had begun 'to lean more and more towards communism. . . . I for one feel that if you with government power and we with organized cultural force combine, we can soon eliminate this menace.' Nehru was not prepared to trust, and an even more sympathetic Patel, insisted that the RSS had to mend its ways.

Besides the appeal, the RSS adopted other methods to pressurize the government to lift the ban. It carried out a signature campaign and mustered the support of 9 lakh people and formed a Janadhikar Samiti (People's Rights Committee) to mobilize public opinion, under the chairmanship of J.B. Kripalani.[111] And finally, the RSS launched a *satyagraha*[112] in December 1948, in which 60,000 *swayamsevaks* were arrested. Golwalkar called off the *satyagraha* in January 1949 and resumed negotiations with the government. G.D. Birla was one of the mediators. The ban was lifted on 12 July 1949, only when the RSS agreed to adopt a written constitution, function in openness and confine itself only to the cultural field.

Political Front Launched: Bharatiya Jana Sangh

In these trying days of wilderness, some of the young RSS *pracharaks* felt the urgent need of a political party which would defend and promote the interests of the RSS. After the lifting of the ban, the *Organiser* published a series of articles by C. Parameswaran,[113] Balraj Madhok[114] and K.R. Malkani[115] advocating RSS entry into politics, despite the fact that the new constitution denied any such role. Obviously, these articles could not have been published 'without the virtual imprimatur of the RSS leadership'.[116] Golwalkar reportedly sent secret instructions to the provincial *sanghachalaks* to 'make preparations to contest the coming general elections', though the *Organiser*[117] vehemently denied this. However, Dada Parmarth,[118] dismissed each of the major political parties and clarified that though the elections were beyond the purview of the RSS, it might heed a call from the nation if the parties failed.

There were two view-points within the RSS on its entry into politics; while the 'activists', consisting of the young members felt such a need, the 'traditionalists' of older generation of *swayamsevaks* did not approve of the move. Golwalkar also did not seem to be very enthusiastic on the steps taken by these young *pracharaks*. This led to occasional contradictions in the statements of the leaders.[119] The confusion in the RSS leadership was obvious in the context of the new atmosphere of independence, parliamentary democracy and a secular constitution. Thus the culture/politics schism came to the fore. Golwalkar and other traditionalists were not keen on a direct participation in politics. The younger *pracharaks* favoured direct intervention.

Finally, the RSS leadership decided to go ahead with the plan of setting up a new political party. Among the younger activists, Madhok and Malkani in particular, prepared the draft for the new political party. Thus emerged the Bharatiya Jana Sangh (BJS) from a combination of a partyless leader, S.P. Mookerjee, and a leaderless party, the RSS.[120] Mookerjee asked Golwalkar to bring the RSS into the new party. Golwalkar refused but deputed some of his 'staunch and tried workers' to work for the new party.[121]

Expanding Sangh Parivar

Golwalkar did not remain complacent with the opening of this new political front—BJS. He knew well that the RSS could achieve its objective only by sharpening its ideology and expanding its organization. While he recharged the ideological arsenal of the RSS through a long speech in March 1954, his organizational innovations included the decision to shape the *Sangh Parivar*—creating a series of affiliates or 'family' members to spread the RSS world-view among specific social groups. Thus, in 1955, emerged Bharatiya Mazdoor Sangh (BMS) to organize the workers under the leadership of a trusted *pracharak*, Dattopant Thengadi. The student wing, the Akhil Bharatiya Vidyarthi Parishad (ABVP), was already established in 1948. The RSS continued to provide the training to the cadre through regular *shakha* programmes and periodic camps and then sent the tried and trusted *pracharaks* to work in these affiliates. With the emergence of the *Sangh Parivar*, the history of the RSS took a decisive turn.

Major Programmes

Golwalkar allowed the RSS to participate in various public activities. It was at the forefront of relief operation among East Bengal refugees and 1950 Assam earthquake victims. It started a campaign against cow-slaughter in 1952. *Pracharaks* were dispatched to participate in the *Bhoodan* campaign of Vinoba Bhave. In 1954, the *swayamsevaks* joined the *satyagraha* to liberate the Portuguese enclaves of Dadra and Nagar Haveli. The RSS constituted an important element of Goa Vimochan Sahayak Samiti (Goa Liberation Committee). The 1955 Goa agitation further established the Hindu nationalist credentials of the RSS. Along with these public activities, the RSS, by and large, remained preoccupied with its focus on traditional 'character-building' through regular activities at its *shakhas*. Golwalkar even temporarily stopped the practice of sending the *pracharaks* to the affiliates in order to highlight his 'non-political' inclination. This move was however reportedly resented by Balasaheb Deoras and his brother Bhaurao.

The Sino-Indian war of 1962 provided an opportunity to the RSS to demonstrate its patriotic credentials to the public. Its public image became so commendable that the Nehru government permitted the RSS to participate as a separate contingent in the Republic Day parade of 1963. Subsequently, during the Indo-Pak war of 1965, its traditional anti-Muslim propaganda got a boost and it was able to further consolidate its patriotic image.

Meanwhile the Vishwa Hindu Parishad (VHP) was floated in 1964 and All-India Goraksha Sammelan (Cow-Protection Conference) was held at Vrindavan, in the Mathura district of Uttar Pradesh. Golwalkar inaugurated the sammelan in August 1964 and a deadline was given to the central government to pass legislation to ban cow-slaughter. Although the parliament did not concede this request, many state legislatures, by 1966, adopted appropriate legislations in this direction. However, the RSS organized a massive demonstration outside the parliament on November 1966, demanding a total and comprehensive ban on cow-slaughter. The demonstration turned violent.

The year 1967 ushered in a new era in the political scenario. The monopoly of the Congress was challenged effectively by non-Congress opposition parties. In the Lok Sabha elections, the BJS, the political affiliate of the RSS, polled 9.35 per cent of votes and won 35 seats. Its performance in the assembly elections in the northern Indian states was quite impressive. In U.P., it won 98 seats with 23 per cent of votes; in M.P., 78 seats with 31.77 per cent of votes; in Rajasthan, 22 seats with 34.84 per cent of votes; in Punjab, 9 seats with 21.19 per cent of votes; in Haryana, 12 seats with 28.49 per cent of votes; in Himachal Pradesh, 7 seats with 25.25 per cent of votes; and in Bihar, 26 seats with 12.43 per cent of votes. The RSS became flexible to allow the BJS to share power with the opposition parties as part of the SVD governments in some of these states, in which even the Communists participated. Akhil Bharatiya Pratinidhi Sabha of the RSS noted the 'changed political picture of the country' and hoped that 'the present coming together of several parties will help understanding one another' and 'wipe out animosity'.[122] Though the experiment was short-lived, the RSS, for the first time, got the taste of political power.

In 1971, the RSS supported the call of the Prime Minister Indira Gandhi to sink political differences and meet the Pakistani challenge unitedly. The Kendriya Karyakari Mandal of the RSS urged the people to cooperate with the government and the armed forces whole heartedly in the event of an aggression by Pakistan. It also asked the *swayamsevaks* to remain in the vanguard of the people's efforts in the cause of the nation's defence.[123] After India's victory, the Akhil Bharatiya Pratinidhi Sabha of the RSS praised 'the unparalleled heroism and acumen of the armed forces and the firm leadership of the Prime Minister'.[124] The RSS thus established its strong patriotic credentials.

With the death of Golwalkar in 1973, an era came to an end. During his long reign of 33 years, he not only sharpened the ideology of *Hindu Rashtra*, but also consolidated the organization and made it formidable. His focus on the *pracharak* system and the creation of the *Sangh Parivar* were innovative strategies for the expansion of the saffron brotherhood.

NOTES AND REFERENCES

1. Swami Shraddhanand raised the alarm in his pamphlet, *Hindu Sangathan: Saviour of the Dying Race* (1924). He drew inspiration from Col. U.N. Mookerjee, who wrote a series of articles entitled 'A Dying Race' in the newspaper *Bengalee* in 1909. Using the Census data from 1872 to 1901, Mookerjee argued that the Hindus would disappear within a few years. See Pradip Kumar Datta, ' "Dying Hindus": Production of Hindu Communal Common Sense in Early 20th Century

Bengal', *Economic and Political Weekly*, XXVIII (25), 19 June 1993, pp. 1305-19.

2. For a detailed discussion, see Gail Minault, *The Khilafat Movement: Religious Symbolism and Political Mobilization in India* (Delhi: Oxford University Press, 1982), pp. 192-3.
3. G.R. Thursby, *Hindu-Muslim Relations in British India: A Study of Controversy, Conflict and Communal Movements in Northern India 1923-1928* (Leiden: E.J. Brill, 1975), p. 6. The author provides a detailed account of communal politics in north India during 1923-8.
4. Kenneth W. Jones, *Arya Dharm: Hindu Consciousness in Nineteenth Century Punjab* (Delhi: Manohar, 1976).
5. For a discussion on Shraddhanand's life and mission, see J.T.F. Jordens, *Swami Shradhanand: His Life and Causes* (Delhi: Oxford University Press, 1981).
6. *Shuddhi* also intended at abolishing untouchability by converting outcastes and securing for them access to wells and temples.
7. *Government of India* (hereafter *GOI*), *Home Department (Political)*, File No. 179/1, 1926, NAI, Delhi.
8. Jaffrelot characterizes this as a strategy of 'stigmatising and emulating the threatening others'. See Christophe Jaffrelot, *The Hindu Nationalist Movement and Indian Politics 1925 to the 1990s: Strategies of Identity-Building, Implantation and Mobilisation [with special reference to Central India]* (Delhi: Viking Penguin India, 1996), Chap. I.
9. G.R. Thursby, *Hindu-Muslim Relations in British India*, op. cit., p. 158.
10. See Bhai Parmanand's foreword to Indra Prakash, *A Review of the History and Work of the Hindu Mahasabha and Hindu Sangathan Movement* (Delhi: Akhil Bharat Hindu Mahasabha, 1952).
11. *Leader*, 22 August 1923. Quoted by Walter Andersen, 'The Rashtriya Swayamsevak Sangh–I: Early Concerns', *Economic and Political Weekly*, VII (11), 11 March 1972, p. 592.
12. Some historians argue that Peasant Uprisings in Malabar are wrongly portrayed as an expression of Muslim fanaticism against the Hindus. See K.N. Panikkar, *Against Lord and State: Religion and Peasant Uprisings in Malabar, 1836-1921* (Delhi: Oxford University Press, 1989). Also see C. Wood, *The Moplah Rebellion and its Genesis* (Delhi: People's Publishing House, 1987).
13. For the *shuddhi* and *sangathan* leaders, 'the question of the place of untouchables and tribal groups that were only loosely attached to Hindu society, now acquired a new importance'. See Gyanendra Pandey, 'Hindus and Others: The Militant Hindu Construction', *Economic and Political Weekly*, XXVI (52), 28 December 1991, p. 2998.
14. 'Forcible Conversions in Malabar', *Moonje Papers* (13), Nehru Memorial Museum & Library, Delhi.
15. Moonje's speech at the Annual Meeting of the Burrabazar Hindu Sabha, Calcutta. See *Swarajya* (Madras), 27 July 1926, in *GOI, Home Department (Political)*, File No. 187/1926, NAI, Delhi.

16. For an understanding of the *Sangathanist* ideology and movement, see Bhai Paramanand, *Hindu Sangathan* (Lahore: The Hindu Yuvak Sabha, 1936) and R.B. Lal Chand, *Self Abnegation in Politics* (Lahore: The Central Hindu Yuvak Sabha, 1938).
17. *GOI, Home Department (Political)*, File No. 112/1925, NAI, Delhi.
18. A public meeting of the Muslims was held in Bombay 'in furtherance of the Tanzim campaign. Shaukat Ali spoke at length.' Ibid.
19. For a comprehensive account of the socio-political dynamics of the province, see D.E.U. Baker, *Changing Political Leadership in an Indian Province: The Central Provinces and Berar 1919-1939* (Delhi: Oxford University Press, 1979).
20. K.B. Hedgewar was a *Deshastha* Brahmin. His ancestors migrated from Khandakurti in Andhra plateau to Nagpur in early nineteenth century due to 'Muslim persecution'. See C.P. Bhishikar, *Keshavah Sangha-Nirmata* (Delhi: Suruchi Prakashan, 1991) [Trans. from Marathi to Hindi by Moreshwar Tapasvi], p. 3.
21. For a well-researched account of the non-Brahmin challenge to Brahmin dominance, see Gail Omvedt, *Cultural Revolt in a Colonial Society: The Non-Brahman Movement in Western India 1873-1930* (Bombay: Scientific Socialist Education Trust, 1976).
22. *Interview* with Baburao Paldhikar, the first *Prant Pracharak* and founder of the RSS in Orissa. Paldhikar was a student of Morris College, Nagpur.
23. The All India Depressed Classes Conference was organized at Nagpur on 30-1 May 1920 and Ambedkar emerged as a militant leader of the community challenging the moderate leadership of V.R. Shinde, an upper-caste social worker, who was dedicated to the cause of the depressed classes. For details on Ambedkar's differences with Sindhe, see Gail Omvedt, *Dalits and the Democratic Revolution: Dr. Ambedkar and the Dalit Movement in Colonial India* (Delhi: Sage Publications, 1994), pp. 142-50; M.S. Gore, *The Social Context of an Ideology: Ambedkar's Political and Social Thought* (Delhi: Sage Publications, 1993), pp. 74-80.
24. A number of RSS writings describe the life and activities of Hedgewar. See Narayan Hari Palkar, *Dr. Hedgewar* [in Hindi] (Prayag: Dr. Surendra Mital, 1962); Narayan Hari Palkar, ed., *Dr. Hedgewar: Patraroop Vyaktidarshan* [trans. from Marathi to Hindi by Mukund Hambarde] (Indore: Archana Prakashan, 1989); C.P. Bhishikar, *Keshavah Sangha Nirmata*, op. cit.; C.P. Bhishikar, *Sangh Vriksh Ke Beej: Dr. Keshavrao Hedgewar* [in Hindi] (Delhi: Suruchi Prakashan, 1994); Vachnesh Tripathi and Kaushelendra Kumar, eds., *Dr. Hedgewar: Prerak Jivan Prasang* [in Hindi] (Lucknow: Lokhit Prakashan, 1992); Ramashankar Agnihotri, *Dr. Hedgewar: Ek Chamatkar* [in Hindi] (Jaipur: Gyan Ganga Prakashan, n.d.).
25. Golwalkar writes that Hedgewar 'had imbibed the spirit of undiluted patriotism right from his mother's womb'. See M.S. Golwalkar, *Bunch of Thoughts* (Bangalore: Jagarana Prakashana, 1980), p. 611.
26. Walter Andersen, 'The Rashtriya Swayamsevak Sangh–I: Early Concerns', op. cit., p. 591.

27. J.A. Curran, Jr., *Militant Hinduism in Indian Politics: A Study of the RSS* (New York: Institute of Pacific Relations, 1951), p. 9.
28. K.R. Malkani, *The RSS Story* (Delhi: Impex India, 1980).
29. A public meeting was held in the honour of Hedgewar after his release. Distinguished leaders like Motilal Nehru, Vithalbhai Patel, C. Rajagopalachari, K.R. Ieyangar, Hakim Ajmal Khan and others reportedly welcomed him. See *Organiser*, XXV (51), 29 July 1972, p. 10.
30. C.P. Bhishikar, *Keshavah Sangha Nirmata*, op. cit., p. 25.
31. Ibid.
32. Ibid., p. 7.
33. The Hindu leaders were impressed not only by this massive response but also by the positive response of the various segments of the Hindu population. Hedgewar realized that the fight against the Muslims could bring unity among the Brahmins and the non-Brahmins.
34. The spirit of the time was well described in a Nagpur newspaper when it observed: 'If both communities love each other, there will be settlement. If both of them fear each other, there will be settlement too.' The RSS believed in the second option. See *The Hitavada*, Nagpur, 1 October 1925.
35. C.P. Bhishikar, *Keshavah Sangha Nirmata*, op. cit., p. 25.
36. Ibid., p. 31.
37. Though Hedgewar left hardly any ideological writings, the RSS makes an effort to construct the ideology of its founder. Hedgewar's arguments are taken from RSS literature.
38. *Sangha Darshan* (Bangalore: Prakashan Vibhag, RSS Karnatak, 1964), p. 5.
39. Ibid., p. 6.
40. Ibid., p. 8.
41. Ibid.
42. Critics suggest that the RSS literature tends to exaggerate the role, greatness and originality of Hedgewar. Savarkar's *Hindutva* does not find even a casual mention. See D.R. Goyal, *Rashtriya Swayamsevak Sangh*, op. cit., p. 50. The *Sangathanists* actively considered floating an RSS-type of organization for quite sometime. The idea of the RSS 'did not simply float down from heaven into Hedgewar's head'. See Tapan Basu et al., *Khaki Shorts and Saffron Flags: A Critique of the Hindu Right* (Delhi: Orient Longman, 1993), p. 16.
43. Walter K. Andersen and Shridhar D. Damle, *The Brotherhood in Saffron: The Rashtriya Swayamsevak Sangh and Hindu Revivalism* (Delhi: Vistaar Publications, 1987), p. 33.
44. Palkar, the biographer of Hedgewar, mentions about this meeting. See Narayan Hari Palkar, *Dr. Hedgewar* [in Hindi], op. cit., pp. 139-40.
45. Goyal sees it as a deliberate attempt on part of the RSS leadership to keep the *swayamsevaks* in the dark about the sources of inspiration which may divide the loyalty for the founder. See D.R. Goyal, *Rashtriya Swayamsevak Sangh*, op. cit., p. 50.
46. Appa Joshi, a close associate of Hedgewar, revealed that Moonje wanted to use

the RSS for election purposes to strengthen the Hindu Mahasabha which was not permitted by Hedgewar. See *Organiser*, XXIV (1), 15 August 1970, p. 15.

47. *Swarajya* (Madras), 27 July 1926, in *GOI, Home Department (Political)*, File No. 187/1926, NAI, Delhi.
48. Ibid.
49. The RSS literature rarely mentions the names of four other members. As all of them were connected with the Hindu Mahasabha, the RSS perhaps deliberately underplayed their role as it wanted to have its independent identity.
50. Even Balasaheb Deoras admits that Hedgewar was 'not an intellectual giant'. See *Organiser*, XXII (33), 29 March 1969, p. 2.
51. 'The notion of a spiritual energy generated by universal time-bound prayer and ritual draws its inspiration from a concept of an invisible congregation.' See Tapan Basu et al., *Khaki Shorts and Saffron Flags*, op. cit., p. 16.
52. Christophe Jaffrelot, *The Hindu Nationalist Movement and Indian Politics*, op. cit., p. 35.
53. As Palkar informs, in April 1926, Hedgewar took the *swayamsevaks* to Ramtek village which was celebrating the Ram Navami. These volunteers organized queues and provided drinking water to the pilgrims. They also prevented unscrupulous Muslim *fakirs* and Brahmins from taking money from the villagers. The name and the uniform were chosen for the occasion. The uniform included *khaki* shirt, *khaki* shorts, a black cap, long socks, and boots and it resembled the uniform worn at the 1920 Congress session at Nagpur. See Narayan Hari Palkar, *Dr. Hedgewar* [in Hindi], op. cit., pp. 138-9.
54. A few names like Jari Patka Mandal (after Shivaji's 'gold bordered flag'), Bharat Udharak Mandal, Hindu Sevak Sangh and Rashtriya Swayamsevak Sangh were suggested. See K.R. Malkani, *The RSS Story*, op. cit., p. 16.
55. However, these initial recruits have been gradually getting extinct and the preponderance of Maharashtrian Brahmins in the RSS leadership has come down considerably.
56. These weapons were more likely to be used against fellow Indians rather than the British soldiers or policemen. See Tapan Basu et al., *Khaki Shorts and Saffron Flags*, op. cit., p. 18.
57. Hedgewar's Calcutta experience undoubtedly proved to be very useful in his future project. He incorporated various characteristics of Anushilan Samiti into his organization: secrecy, oath, discipline, military training, etc.
58. They were: (1) Varsha Pratipada (new year of the Hindus); (2) Shivarajyarohano-ttsava (coronation of Shivaji); (3) Shri Guru Poornima (tribute to the Guru, giving money to honour the Guru—*bhagwa* flag); (4) Raksha Bandhan (a north Indian festival in which sisters tie ribbons round the wrists of their brothers; on this occasion the leader of the *shakha* ties the ribbon round the pole of the *bhagwa* flag, after which the *swayamsevaks* perform this ritual among one another as a mark of brotherhood); (5) Vijayadashmi (i.e. Dussehra, when *swayamsevaks* pay homage to arms) and (6) Makarasankraman (when the Sun enters Capricorn, a festival symbolising prosperity).

59. Military training was dropped during World War II and the department was scrapped.
60. Walter Andersen, 'The Rashtriya Swayamsevak Sangh: Early Concerns', op. cit., p. 593.
61. K.R. Malkani, *The RSS Story*, op. cit., p. 16.
62. Malkani informs that Appaji Joshi suddenly called the *shakha* to attention, when Hedgewar was coming to *sanghsthan*, and said aloud: 'Sarsanghchalak Pranam–ek . . . do!' Two other posts were also created: Balaji Huddar and Martand Rao Jog were appointed as *sarkaryavah* and *sar senapati* respectively. Ibid., p. 20.
63. Walter Andersen, 'The Rashtriya Swayamsevak Sangh: Early Concerns', op. cit., p. 593.
64. C.P. Bhishikar, *Sanghvraksh ke beej—Dr. Keshavrao Hedgewar*, op. cit., p. 20.
65. *Shri Guruji: Samagra Darshana*, Vol. IV (Nagpur: Bharatiya Vichar Sadhana, 1974-81), pp. 39-40.
66. C.P. Bhishikar, *Sanghvraksh ke beej—Dr. Keshavrao Hedgewar*, op. cit., p. 21.
67. *Savarkar Papers*, File No. 4 (March-December 1938), Letter from J.D. Malekar to Phadnis, dt. 7/11/1938, Nehru Memorial Museum & Library, Delhi.
68. Dada Naik of Mumbai Prantik Sabha of the RSS, in his letter to Jayakar, dated the 1 February 1937, mentions this in his note on the RSS. See *Jayakar Papers*, File No. 65 (67), NAI, Delhi.
69. *GOI, Home Department (Political)*, File No. 18/10, 1932, NAI, Delhi.
70. Ibid.
71. Ibid.
72. *Memorandum of Government of India, Home Department Intelligence Bureau, No. 60-D, G-42, Dated New Delhi, the 18th May 1942*, in Partha Sarathi Gupta, ed., *Towards Freedom: Documents on the Movement for Independence in India 1943-1944*, Part III (Delhi: Oxford University Press, 1997), p. 3047.
73. Ibid.
74. The critics point out that though the RSS boasts of the patronage of Malaviya, it could not grow in the university during his life-time. See Girish Mishra, *RSS Shadow over Benaras Hindu University* (Delhi: Sampradayikta Virodhi Committee, n.d.).
75. Note on RSS by Police Chief, Madras, Government of Madras, U.S. Files—File No. 56/1943, TNA, in Partha Sarathi Gupta, ed., *Towards Freedom*, op. cit., p. 2977.
76. Memorandum of Government of India, Home Department Intelligence Bureau, No. 60-D, G-42, Delhi, 18 May 1942, ibid., p. 3048.
77. Hedgewar was a devotee of Hanuman and always carried an idol of Hanuman wherever he went.
78. Madhav Sadashiv Golwalkar was born in 1906 into a Brahmin family of Nagpur. His father was a school teacher. Madhav passed his matriculation in 1922 and joined the missionary college in Nagpur. Here he reportedly got 'incensed' at the 'open advocacy' of Christianity. Much of his concern for the defence of Hinduism may be traced to this experience. Golwalkar went to Benaras Hindu

University and finished an M.Sc. in Biology in 1927. He studied and practised Yoga between 1927 and 1930. Golwalkar showed interest in religious philosophy and was attracted to asceticism. In 1931, he was appointed a lecturer at the Benaras Hindu University (he is popularly known as 'Guruji' since those days). He came in contact with Hedgewar during the latter's visit to Benaras Hindu University. In 1931, he was appointed as *sanghachalak* of Kashi. Returned to Nagpur in 1932. Enrolled as a student in Law and simultaneously took up the secretaryship (*karyavah*) of the central branch of RSS in Nagpur. He was also given the charge of the Officers' Training Camp in Akola. At Nagpur, Golwalkar was a regular visitor to the Ramkrishna Mission Ashram. He left for Bengal in 1937 to become a disciple of Swami Akhandananda (one of the eleven disciples of Ramakrishna Paramahansa) and accomplish *sadhana* as a *yogi*. The Swami died after a short period. Golwalkar soon returned to Nagpur to shoulder the responsibilities of the RSS.

79. Hedgewar, 'sick of pulls and pressures exerted by his political patrons and seniors, wanted to hand over the reins of the organization to a person who was under no obligation to them'. See D.R. Goyal, *Rashtriya Swayamsevak Sangh*, op. cit., p. 79.
80. *Guruji Doctorji ke atma thay* (Golwalkar was the soul of Hedgewar). Interview with Baburao Paldhikar, one of the recruits of Hedgewar.
81. The authorship is controversial. Golwalkar disclosed only in 1963 that this was not his original work, but a translation of Baba Rao Savarkar's Marathi treatise *Rashtra Mimansa*. This controversial work was later withdrawn from circulation because it contained many laudatory references to Hitler and his theory of racial superiority, which became embarrassing for the organization. A detailed analysis of this ideological work will be made in Chap. IV.
82. Note on RSS dt. 30.11.1943 (Intelligence Bureau), File No. 28/3/43– Home Poll (I), in Partha Sarathi Gupta, ed., *Towards Freedom*, op. cit., p. 3065.
83. *Government of Bombay to Government of India*, File No. 28/3/43, Home Poll (I), NAI, Delhi.
84. D.O. No. C.–Pol., dated Jubbulpore, the 21st December 1942, from the Deputy Commissioner, Jubbulpore, in Partha Sarathi Gupta, ed., *Towards Freedom*, op. cit., p. 2996.
85. *Shri Guruji, the Man and His Mission: On the Occasion of His 51st Birthday* (Delhi: Bharat Prakashan, 1957), p. 33.
86. Leeladhar Bajpai reportedly took out a procession at Bateshwar (Vajpayee's village) in Agra district on 27 August 1942 and hoisted the Congress flag on two government buildings, one of which was the Forest Department office. Atal Behari and his brother were part of the procession. Though the procession was non-violent, British police attempted to create a 'false' story that they had damaged the wall of the Forest Department building. In his statement to the police, Vajpayee reportedly said, 'I did not cause any damage. I did not render any assistance in demolishing the government building . . .' Naming Leeladhar Bajpai and Mahuan, Vajpayee told the police that they had delivered a speech in

the Bateshwar bazar and 'persuaded the people to break the forest laws'. Vajpayee's deposition stated that when about 200 people went to the forest office, 'I and my brother stayed below and all other people went up. I do not know the names of any other person except Mahuan and Kakua (Leeladhar Bajpai), who were there. It appeared to me that bricks were falling. I could not know who was demolishing the wall but the bricks of the wall were certainly falling. . . .' See Leeladhar's Press Statement in *The Hindu*, 19 September 1999.

87. Ibid. In the absence of Vajpayee's rejoinder to Leeladhar's allegations, to be fair enough, it needs to be mentioned that Vajpayee was barely 16 and had joined the RSS only in 1941, hardly a few months before this incident. His deposition may also be interpreted as a simple statement of facts, not necessarily a sort of 'betrayal' of Quit India or part of a planned strategy. In any case, the RSS decided to remain aloof from the movement.
88. For instance, in Jubbulpore district, K.B. Agnihotri, organizer of Sihora RSS and Lattu alias Suraj Chandra Bani, an instructor of Shahpura RSS, were detained under Defence India Rules 'because of their pro-Congress activities'. See D.O. No. C.–Pol., dated Jubbulpore, the 21 December 1942, from the Deputy Commissioner, Jubbulpore, in Partha Sarathi Gupta, ed., *Towards Freedom*, op. cit., p. 2996.
89. Both *Hindutva* and Muslim Nationalism tended to subordinate anti-colonial perspectives to the requirements of communal rivalry and conflict. See Sumit Sarkar, *Writing Social History* (Delhi: Oxford University Press, 1997), Chap. IX.
90. Official Notings on RSS dt. 13.12.1943, (Intelligence Bureau), File No. 28/3/43–Home Poll (I), NAI, Delhi, in Partha Sarathi Gupta, ed., *Towards freedom*, op. cit., p. 3068.
91. Minutes of the Fourth Security Conference Held at Nagpur on 8 and 9 March 1943 Extract, ibid., p. 3037.
92. Note on RSS dt. 30.11.1943 (Intelligence Bureau), File No. 28/3/43–Home Poll (I), NAI, Delhi, ibid., p. 3067.
93. Note on RSS dt. 30.11.1943 (Intelligence Bureau), File No. 28/3/43–Home Poll (I), NAI, Delhi, ibid., p. 3063.
94. Official Notings on RSS dt. 13.12.1943 (extracts), File No. 28/3/43–Home Poll (I), ibid., p. 3068.
95. However, the government could not take any action against the RSS as it generally took care to keep itself on the right side of the law and avoided any clash with the authorities.
96. See Partha Sarathi Gupta, ed., *Towards Freedom*, op. cit., p. 3038.
97. Ibid., p. 3041.
98. Note on the Rashtriya Swayamsevak Sangh training camps held in various provinces during the months of May and June 1944—followed by Official Comments (dt. 29.7.1944), File No. 28/3/43–Home Poll (I), NAI, Delhi, in Partha Sarathi Gupta, ed., *Towards Freedom*, op. cit., p. 3219.
99. Ibid.

100. Minutes—Security Officers Conference—8/9 March 1943, File No. 111/43–Home Poll (I), NAI, ibid., p. 2877.
101. Government of Punjab to the Government of India, File No. 28/3/43–Home Poll (I), NAI, Delhi, ibid., p. 3093.
102. On 1946 Calcutta riots, see Suranjan Das, *Communal Riots in Bengal: 1905-1947* (Delhi: Oxford University Press, 1993), Chap. VI.
103. See Thomas Blom Hansen, *The Saffron Wave: Democracy and Hindu Nationalism in Modern India*, op. cit., p. 95. Communal carnage of Partition was seen by RSS men as a kind of patriotic baptism, an initiation through blood and sacrifice to the nationalist cause, for the individuals involved as well as for the corporate body. Ibid.
104. *Shri Guruji, the Man and His Mission*, op. cit., p. 34.
105. Patel's letter to Golwalkar, dated the 11 September 1948, reproduced in *Justice On Trial: Historic Document of Guruji–Government Correspondence* (Bangalore: Sharada Press, 1968), pp. 26-8.
106. D.R. Goyal was present in that meeting. For details, see D.R. Goyal, *Rashtriya Swayamsevak Sangh*, op. cit., p. 96.
107. Thomas Blom Hansen, *The Saffron Wave*, op. cit., p. 95.
108. A brilliant psycho-analysis of Gandhi–Godse encounter can be found in Ashis Nandy, *At the Edge of Psychology* (Delhi: Oxford University Press, 1980 [1993 Reprint]), pp. 70-98.
109. See *Justice On Trial*, op. cit., pp. 8-9.
110. Ibid., pp. 23-6.
111. Kripalani was a veteran Gandhian and a prominent leader of the Congress Socialist Party. He was a staunch critic of Nehru. Kripalani's service was again sought by the RSS during the anti-Emergency struggle against Indira Gandhi.
112. It is interesting to note that despite their rejection of the Gandhian concept of Hindu-Muslim unity, the RSS has been using the Gandhian method of *satyagraha* quite frequently.
113. *Organiser*, III (1 and 2), 22 and 30 August 1949.
114. *Organiser*, III (3), 6 September 1949.
115. *Organiser*, III (14), 23 November 1949.
116. Craig Baxter, *The Jana Sangh: A Biography of an Indian Political Party*, op. cit., p. 55.
117. *Organiser*, III (19), 28 December 1949.
118. *Organiser*, III (22), 23 January 1950.
119. Craig Baxter, *The Jana Sangh*, op. cit., pp. 58-9.
120. Ibid., p. 54.
121. Ibid., p. 65.
122. *Organiser*, XX (34), 9 April 1967.
123. *Organiser*, XXV (11), 23 October 1971.
124. *Organiser*, XXV (35), 8 April 1972.

CHAPTER III

Organization and Training: Reinforcing Politics and Ideology

Hedgewar observes: 'Strength, it should be remembered, comes only through organization. It is therefore the duty of every Hindu to do his best to consolidate the Hindu society. The Sangh is carrying out this supreme task.'[1] The RSS thus aims at *Hindu Sangathan*—organization of the Hindus. Since its inception, erecting a mighty organization has always remained at the top of its agenda. Though the RSS constitution of 1949 spells out the intricate organizational structure and functions, it still leaves out certain important aspects. Moreover, the changes, both formal and informal, which were introduced since then, have not been incorporated in the written constitution. For instance, the RSS opened its *prachar vibhag* (publicity wing) in 1994 though it earlier discouraged publicity. In August 2000, it created another new office of official spokesperson 'to represent the RSS view correctly to the media'.[2] M.G. Vaidya, a RSS veteran, who earlier set up the publicity wing, has been appointed to this new office. Therefore, any analysis of the organization, has to go beyond the text.

This chapter analyses the organizational structure and training procedure of the RSS and seeks to explain how they are carefully designed to reinforce its politics and ideology. As the RSS has spread its influence to various spheres of civil society through a number of 'affiliates', the study will also focus on the interconnection among the members of the *Sangh Parivar* (RSS family).

The organizational structure of the RSS is like a pyramid. At the top of the hierarchy, there is *sarsanghchalak* (supreme director) who is assisted by Akhil Bharatiya Pratinidhi Sabha (an all-India assembly). Then the country is divided into geographical units: *kshetras* (zones), *prantas* (states), *vibhags* (divisions), *zillas* (districts), *nagaras* (cities) and *mandalas* (blocks), having a clearly defined leadership at every level. The *shakhas* remain at the bottom of the organizational hierarchy.

SHAKHA STRUCTURE

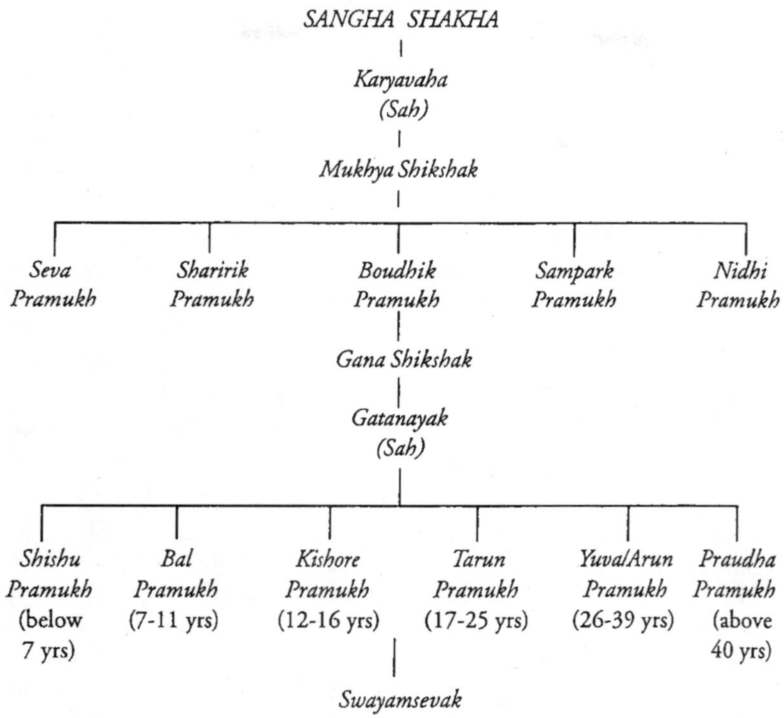

Source: Chart displayed at the 1st Year all-Orissa RSS OTC (1995), Cuttack.

As Golwalkar mentions, 'the real spirit of our work will be understood when one comes in contact with the shakha'.[3] The basic unit of the RSS is the *shakha*; it is considered to be the chief instrument to organize Hindus. Membership in a *shakha* is small, usually not exceeding 100 male members (*swayamsevaks*). These *swayamsevaks* of each *shakha* are divided into six[4] age groups: *shishu* (below 7 years), *bal* (7-11 years), *kishore* (12-16 years), *tarun* (17-25 years), *yuva/arun* (26-39 years) and *praudha* (above 40 years). The *shakha* is held everyday, usually in the morning (*pratah shakha*). It is also conducted in the early evening (*sayam shakha*), and even at night (*ratri shakha*) taking into consideration the convenience of the *swayamsevaks*. For those who cannot afford to attend it daily, there is a provision for weekly or monthly *shakhas*. In 1994, the RSS reportedly conducted more than 30,000 daily *shakhas*, about 10,000 weekly gatherings and another 11,000 on monthly basis.[5] In 1998, the RSS was running 28,000 daily *shakhas*, 39,000 weekly and monthly gatherings.[6]

The *swayamsevaks* of a *shakha* are divided into *gatas* (groups); the strength of a *gata* does not usually exceed 20. A *gata* is usually composed of a common age group, and the participants live in a particular locality. Each *gata* has a *gatanayak* (group leader) and a *shikshak* (teacher). These two first level officials in the RSS hierarchy are appointed by the *mukhya shikshak* (chief teacher) of the *shakha*. A *gatanayak* is like an 'elder brother' to the *swayamsevaks* in his group and is expected to be a model of ideal behaviour. The *shikshak* teaches the games and exercises to the *swayamsevaks* and acts as the group leader of his *gata* during the discussion (*charcha*) in the *shakha*. *Gatanayaks* and *shikshaks* usually meet with the local *pracharak* (full-time preacher) every fortnight to discuss several questions related to the functioning of the *shakha* such as attendance, programmes, strategies of expansion and also RSS policy regarding various socio-political issues. Every *shakha* has a *karyavah* (secretary). He is invariably a well-known person of the locality and only has a nominal authority. The *mukhya shikshak*, who is elevated to this post from the rank of *gatanayak* and *shikshak*, exercises the real power. Besides these functionaries, each *shakha* has the following departments, each looked after by one *pramukh* (head): *sharirik* (physical) *pramukh* and *boudhik* (intellectual) *pramukh*, *nidhi* (finance) *pramukh*, *sampark* (liaison) *pramukh* and *seva* (service) *pramukh*.

In most of the areas where *shakhas* are conducted, the RSS maintains an office (*Sangh karyalay*). It is like a 'clubhouse'; but unlike the club, here everything is quiet, disciplined, organized and in order. Its clean and simple environment impresses the visitor. Each *karyalay* usually adorns the photographs of Bharat Mata, prominent Hindu religious and political leaders like Shivaji, Rana Pratap, Vivekananda, Tilak, Hedgewar, Golwalkar, and other RSS leaders. *Swayamsevaks* come to the office to meet the *pracharak*, who usually resides there. Sometimes the visiting *swayamsevaks* from other cities stay there as guests. When the *swayamsevaks* from the small places come to the cities for higher education or jobs, they are permitted to stay in the *karyalay* for a temporary period. This provides them a lot of security and confidence in an unknown place. Here they come in contact with the RSS leaders and gradually take up the organizational responsibilities in the colleges and work places.

Recruiting the Young Boys

The recruitment procedure is very crucial. The boys are recruited at a very tender age. The RSS leaders prefer not to invest time and energy on the higher age-groups, who already have well-formed opinions. Therefore, they concentrate on the teenage boys as it is easy to inculcate political messages of fairly simple basic themes in their minds.[7]

What attracts these boys to the RSS? Most of the *swayamsevaks* and leaders stated during the interview that they were initially attracted towards the RSS because of their love for games and sports. They were also influenced by the impressive personality of the *pracharak*,[8] his emotional oratory and his appealing storytelling powers. Further, in a small town milieu, where the youth looks forward to an alternative culture, the *shakha* fills in the void as a source of recreation, socialization, and intellectual education.

Many recruits desert the RSS because of its demand of time and increasing commitment. Therefore, it becomes a challenge to the RSS to ensure the loyalties of its members to the organization on a permanent basis. It is the *shakha* which plays an important role in this effort. Because of its size, structure, neighbourhood orientation, and perhaps the similar social backgrounds of the members, the *shakha* is able to maintain an intense social solidarity among the *swayamsevaks*.[9]

Shakha *Schedule: Cultivating Continuity, Conviction and Conformity*

Golwalkar's lucid description of a *shakha* schedule is worth quoting:

> There is an open playground. Under a saffron flag groups of youths and boys are absorbed in a variety of Bharatiya games. Resounding shouts of joyous enthusiasm fill the air. The sight of the daring young men pressing forward with the cry 'Kabaddi Kabaddi' on their lips thrills the heart. The leader's whistle or order has a magical effect on them; there is instant perfect order or silence. Then exercises follow—wielding the lathi, Suryanamaskar, marching, etc. The spirit of collective effort and spontaneous discipline pervades every programme. Then they sit down and sing in chorus songs charged with patriotism. Discussions follow. They delve deep into the problems affecting the national life. And finally, they stand in rows before the flag and recite the prayer: . . . (*Many salutations to Thee, O loving Motherland*!) whose echoes fill the air and stir the soul. 'Bharat Mataki jai' uttered in utmost earnest furnishes the finishing and inspiring touch to the entire programme.[10]

Golwalkar's description could be corroborated at any *shakha*. The boys assemble in an open ground. The programme begins with the standing of the *swayamsevaks* in rows before a flagstaff, each row limited to a single age group. The rows may have up to twenty people or a *gata*. While the *agresar* (leader), usually the *gatanayak*, takes position in the front, the *shikshak* stands at the back. When the rows are assembled, the *bhagwa dhwaj*[11] is hoisted. Then *swayamsevaks* offer *pranam* (salute) to the flag by raising the right hand to the chest, palm parallel to the ground, head down. After the roll call, the *swayamsevaks* assemble in different areas of the field in *gatas* or groups. Then starts the *sharirik* (physical training); the *shikshak*, assisted by the *gatanayak*, teach games, *Surya pranam*, *asanas* and other *yogic* exercises. The *swayamsevaks* play a number of Indian games,[12] the most popular being *kabaddi*. They also learn 'defensive' skills in the use of the *lathi*.[13] The *mukhya shikshak* blows a whistle after about an hour, to mark the end of the *sharirik* programme.[14]

The games are just not meant to build a spirit of cooperation, they also intend to make the *swayamsevaks* more brave and courageous vis-a-vis opponents. The psychological[15] aspect is no less important than the physical. It is also interesting to note that the leader efficiently integrates both play on the one hand and authority and discipline on the other.[16]

After the session of physical exercise the members sit in a circle for discussion. As the RSS claims to aim at 'character-building' and 'man-moulding', the themes of the topics relate to the attributes of 'good' character, e.g., fidelity, fortitude, honesty, hard work, obedience and respect to superiors, personal discipline, etc. But the main thrust is on the ideology of the RSS; the themes of the discussion focus on various aspects of *Hindu Rashtra*—the plight of Hindus in India and the need for unity among Hindus, etc. The *swayamsevaks* are also repeatedly reminded of 'Muslim oppression' and 'Muslim atrocities' on the Hindu community for centuries. The anti-Muslim obsession is evident in the '*boudhiks*'. The stories on some hero or heroic event in the history of Hindu India are narrated to the *swayamsevaks*. Occasionally, patriotic songs are sung glorifying Hindu warriors and heroes or venerating *Bharat Mata*.

Finally, the *swayamsevaks* again assemble in rows before the flag to recite the Sangh prayer (*prarthana*)—*Namaste sada vatsale Matribhume* (Salutations to thee oh loving Motherland!). This is followed by the shouting of slogans like *Bharat Mata ki Jai* (Victory to Mother India) and the *shakha* comes to an end (*bikir*). Then the members disperse and have an informal chat. Later some of them visit the sick and those absent.

A few special *baudhiks* are arranged every month, usually in the evenings. These are mainly the background sessions to acquaint the teachers with issues to be discussed at the *shakhas*. Occasionally, these meetings are utilized to explain policy-decisions made at central and state levels, to seek opinions on political and social issues, or to draw the attention of the *swayamsevaks* to major organizational and ideological problems of the RSS.

Golwalkar refers to the activities of a *shakha* as *sadhana*. An ideal *swayamsevak* is expected to practice *sadhana* in the *shakha* every day. The purpose of the *shakha*, as explained by one RSS leader, is two-fold: continuity and conviction.[17] Regular attendance is a sacred routine of the ideal *swayamsevak*. He is excused only if he is either ill or has gone out. It gradually becomes a habit for the member to come to the *shakha* daily. Golwalkar describes a parable on the techniques of habit formation. A rich man, seeing a beautiful peacock in his garden one day, gave it some opium mixed with food. The peacock started coming everyday, and eventually got so habituated that it used to come regularly at that hour, even without the opium. Golwalkar identified three factors in this technique of habit formation: first, constant meditation of the ideal that is to be formed into a *samskar*; second, constant company of persons devoted to the same ideal; and third, engaging the body in activities congenial to that ideal. *Shakhas*, therefore, orient the body, the mind and the immediate surroundings on identical lines.

Golwalkar rightly mentions that the *shakha* is the 'living practice of principles' and not a bundle of dry preaching.[18] It is described as a process of *loka sangraha* (collecting the people), *loka samparka* (mass communication), *loka samskara* (inculcation of a new spirit) and *loka niyojan* (deployment of the people).[19] The main purpose of the *shakha* is to instill in its members the spirit of cohesion, discipline, reverence to organizational authority and ideological conformity.[20]

Unique Brotherhood

The *shakhas* create and cultivate a unique brotherhood among the *swayamsevaks*. The common observation of rituals and common participation in the physical activities and discussions, a common uniform, the choice of a common set of vocabulary are all designed to enhance a sense of community and brotherhood. The success of the *shakhas* largely depends on the extent of brotherhood and kinship they create and sustain among the *swayamsevaks*. If a *swayamsevak* does not attend the *shakha*, the *adhikaris* (office-bearers) and other members visit his house to find out the reason. In case a *swayamsevak* is ill, his fellow members of the *shakha* show necessary concern and care.[21] Even in case of the illness of the family members of a *swayamsevak*, the organization extends possible help.[22] This humane approach has strengthened the RSS kinship further. While concern for fellow-beings has become a casualty under the pressure of modernization, the RSS has successfully maintained a unique brotherhood among its members. This is one of the main reasons for the growing popularity of the RSS.

THE HIERARCHICAL ORDER

Local

The RSS is organized in a hierarchical order: local, district, provincial and all-India bodies. Above the *shakha* in the pyramid of authority is the *mandal* committee, which is composed of representatives from the *shakhas* of the given locality. Representatives from *mandals* form a *nagar* (city) committee. The city committee is very important as most of the day-to-day work takes place at this level. The city committee consists of a *sanghchalak*, a *karyavah* and heads of the departments of physical training (*sharirik*), intellectual training (*boudhik*), recruitment (*sampark*), finance (*nidhi*) and service (*seva*). The committee meets weekly. The decisions taken along with the orders received from above are transmitted down to the *mandal* through the *karyavah* (secretary). The *mukhya shikshak* and the local *pracharak* pass on orders and information to the *swayamsevaks*, the lowest level of the communications circuit. Next to the city committees there may be *zilla* (district) and *vibhag* (regional) committees. Above this structure are state and national assemblies.

Provincial

The Prantiya Pratinidhi Sabhas (state assemblies) are deliberative bodies, but exercise no real power. According to the RSS constitution,[23] the *sabha* consists of one elected delegate for every fifty *swayamsevaks* entitled to vote. The *prant sanghchalak* is elected by the state assembly, and he, in consultation with the *prant pracharak* appoints lower level office bearers. In fact, the *sanghchalak*, who is the constitutional head at each level, with few exceptions, enjoys little power over the day-to-day activities of the RSS. He is usually an older influential notable, whose participation gives the RSS an aura of respectability as well as important contacts. It is not uncommon for a *sanghchalak* to have no prior personal experience in RSS activities.

National

The Akhil Bharatiya Pratinidhi Sabha (ABPS) meets at least once a year and is presided over by the *sarkaryavah* (general secretary). It includes the delegates chosen by the Prantiya Pratinidhi Sabhas, *prant sanghchalakhs* and *prant pracharaks*, and members of the central executive. About 1,000 *pratinidhis* and 50 observers from 30 countries took part in the annual session of the Akhil Bharatiya Pratinidhi Sabha of the RSS which was held on March 1998 near Bangalore.[24] This body has no effective power, though the RSS constitution empowers it to 'review the work and lay down the policy and programme of the Sangh'.[25] The administrative power is actually exercised by the *sarkaryavah* and Kendriya Karyakari Mandal (central working committee). The general secretary enjoys considerable power and is generally acknowledged to be the *sarsanghchalak*-in-waiting. Golwalkar, Deoras and Rajendra Singh were all general secretaries.

The 1949 constitution of the RSS promised to make the organization more democratic and representative in character and accordingly it has been conducting periodic organizational elections. However, these elected office-bearers and representative bodies are a facade because of two reasons: First, the highly disciplined and dedicated *swayamsevaks* are simply required to ratify the choices of the RSS leadership; an ideal member should not think of defying it. Secondly, the *pracharaks* (full-time officers), who have complete control over the organization, are accountable only to the RSS headquarters, not to any other body.

SARSANGHCHALAK

At the apex of the organizational hierarchy, there is a *sarsanghchalak*, referred to in the RSS constitution as the supreme 'Guide and Philosopher'. Each of the *sarsanghchalaks* has chosen his own successor. Hedgewar, before his death, chose Golwalkar bypassing many experienced and senior leaders. Golwalkar chose Balasaheb Deoras as his successor. The constitutional provision requires that the *sarsanghchalak* shall nominate his successor only 'with the consent of the . . . Kendriya Karyakari Mandal'. But in practice, the KKM simply acquiesced. No RSS leader ever questioned the legitimacy of the selection process. This is not surprising as the RSS leaders believe that competitive election to this supreme post would be an irony as the organization shuns power politics publicly. Contesting elections would demean the '*Rajarshi*' image of the chief. Moreover, this could turn into a disruptive catalyst, resulting in factionalism that would undermine the unity of the organization. Deoras, though chose Rajendra Singh as his successor, made significant changes. While his predecessors allowed their successors to take over only after their deaths, Deoras handed over the reign during his life-time. Moreover, for the first time, the RSS was to be headed by a non-Maharashtrian and a non-Brahmin.[26] Rajendra Singh followed the footsteps of Deoras and nominated K.S. Sudarshan, a Kannada Brahmin, for this top post

The *sarsanghchalak* enjoys complete authority. This prompts the critics to describe the RSS as authoritarian and fascist. But the RSS does not agree to have been inspired from 'a perverted foreign model'; it rather claims being modelled 'on an ideal Hindu family',[27] in which the *sarsanghchalak* is the ideal head of the family and the *swayamsevaks* are his children. Hedgewar is unambiguous about his authority when he says that it is essential for the *swayamsevaks* to obey the commands of the *sarsanghchalak* in all the circumstances. His decisions cannot be challenged. H.V. Seshadri, an ideologue of the RSS, thus emphasizes: 'The tail should not wag the body. That is the secret of the success of the Sangh.'[28]

Despite his unambiguous authority, the *sarsanghchalak* does not keep all the powers in his hands. He has a Kendriya Karyakari Mandal consisting of senior and experienced leaders to carry out the day-to-day business of the organization. The decisions taken by the central working committee are passed on to the various regional branches, which then get transmitted downwards. The *sarsanghchalak* assigns the administrative functions to the *sarkaryavah* (general secretary), who is assisted by a *sah-sarkaryavah* (joint-general secretary).

Dilution of Authority?

Has there been any dilution of authority of the *sarsanghchalaks* over the years? A careful examination would find that the headship has passed on from 'Doctorji' to 'Guruji' to Mananiya Deoras Ji to Rajju Bhaiya to Sudarshan Ji. These are not simply changes in nomenclatures of different *sarsanghchalaks*; they also suggest the changes that have taken place in the position of his office.

Hedgewar, the founder, personally picked up the young boys and trained them to become the future missionaries of the RSS. His close personal relationship with these young recruits made them deeply loyal to him as well as to the ideal. The first generation *swayamsevaks* almost revered 'Doctorji' and never doubted the sanctity of the office of *sarsanghchalak*.

Golwalkar was junior to many of the RSS leaders in terms of age and experience when he succeeded Hedgewar. But he had certain invaluable assets: his title of 'Guruji', his saintly appearance, his distaste for the 'political', and above all, his intellectual acumen, further glorified the office of *sarsanghchalak*. Golwalkar's charismatic personality and ideological clarity mesmerized the *swayamsevaks*. Despite the rapid expansion of the RSS and creation of various affiliates during his tenure, Golwalkar's control over the organization was total and his command was supreme. However, an apparent distance was noticed between the leader and the followers, perhaps because of the overbearing stature of 'Guruji'. In fact the ordinary *swayamsevak* was so overwhelmed by his personality that he always preferred to revere the office from a distance.

When Deoras became the head, he had neither the toughness of Hedgewar nor the intellectual brilliance and personal charisma of Golwalkar. But he was unique in his own way, being an organizational wizard, and a management genius. Deoras was 'truly a child of the organization', by growing with it since his childhood as an early recruit of Hedgewar. He understood well that the organization would be the real testing ground for the ideology and politics in the coming years; the *sarsanghchalak* had to intervene in the organizational affairs more actively to motivate the cadre for greater participation in the socio-political affairs. Hence, an effective communication had to be established between the leader and the cadre. Accordingly, he allowed the highest office to shed its earlier mysticism and become more down to earth. Further, the organization had grown up so big and multi-dimensional that the concentration of power at a single source would be detrimental to its functioning. Deoras, therefore, decided to grant more 'autonomy' to the members of the *Sangh Parivar* (affiliates).[29] Under his regime, various affiliates like the BJS (later the BJP), the ABVP, the BMS and the VHP emerged as key players in Indian socio-political life; many of their leaders achieved national prominence and had a taste of political power. Though 'Mananiya' Deoras still enjoyed a unique position as the head of the *Sangh Parivar*, the leaders of various affiliates, nonetheless, carved their status within the *Parivar*.

When the mantle fell on Rajendra Singh, the organization had not only become gigantic, it had also been transformed into a movement during the *Ramjanmabhoomi* agitation.[30] The RSS was at the threshold of political power; and Rajendra Singh had all the qualities to hit the bull's eye. For this mission, an intimate relationship had to be developed between the supreme leader and the common *swayamsevak*. The image of the fourth *sarsanghchalak* was ideally Rajju Bhaiya, the elder brother, with whom the ordinary *swayamsevak* was at ease. Thus, the *sarsanghchalak* had to perform this new role along with his traditional role of a 'guide and philosopher'. Further, during the last years of Deoras, the character of top leadership was turning from individual to collective. The failing health of Deoras may have been a contributing factor in this orientation, but also important was the enormous growth of the RSS and their affiliates. H.V. Seshadri, denying that he was in the 'race' for this top post, said: 'There is no claimant nor any contestant for the post. It is a team work in our organization.'[31] He also described Rajendra Singh as a 'friend, philosopher and guide'.[32] As per the RSS constitution, *sarsanghchalak* is only 'the guide and philosopher', and not 'friend'. In the changing context, Rajendra Singh was perhaps expected to act more of a 'friend', as the leader of a 'team', rather than the supreme leader. Rajendra Singh performed this role well and to his credit, the BJP succeeded in capturing the political power in Delhi, thereby making it possible for the RSS to have control over the state apparatus—a long cherished desire. The compulsion of alliance restricted its power however.

Sudarshan takes over at a time when the RSS needs to consolidate the political power further and move forward to hegemonize civil society through the ideological and organizational network of the *Sangh Parivar*. This is a tough job; it not only demands an effective control over the political affiliate, but also a tight grip over the burgeoning *Sangh Parivar*. Moreover, *Hindutva* must be ideologically asserted. Accordingly, Sudarshan expects that the new millennium will usher an 'explosion of *Hindutva*'. As he predicts, there will be an imminent polarization of pro-*Hindutva* and anti-*Hindutva* forces in which the former will triumph. Thus, Sudarshan seems very keen to see an ideological assertion of *Hindutva*. Sudarshan has limitations, however. He can hardly afford to ignore the political compulsions of the BJP. He also finds difficult to dictate terms to Atal Behari Vajpayee because of the latter's seniority and stature. Further, senior leaders like Rajendra Singh and Seshadri remain in the National Executive of the RSS. As Sudarshan himself admits: 'Decision-making in the RSS is through a process of collective thinking'. He describes Rajju Bhaiya as *paramacharya* (great teacher) and seeks Seshadri's blessings. He also talks of 'consensus'.

Thus, there has been a dilution in the authority of the *sarsanghchalaks* since Golwalkar's departure. True, *ek chalak anuvartita* still exists; *sarsanghchalak* remains the supreme leader and his authority is unquestioned. But the dynamics of power politics and expansion of the RSS into a mammoth *Sangh Parivar* have compelled the RSS to encourage collective decision-making and permitted limited decentralization.

PRACHARAKS: LINKING LOCAL, PROVINCIAL AND NATIONAL

The *pracharak* system 'is the bedrock on which the Sangh stands'.[33] The *pracharaks* are the links between the various levels of the RSS, whom the constitution defines as unpaid, full-time workers of high integrity whose 'mission is to serve the society through the Sangh, and who, of their own free will, dedicate themselves to the Cause'.[34] The *pracharaks* form a communication network outside the 'constitutional' system. Golwalkar reinforced this tradition for the expansion as well as to ensure ideological cohesion of the organization. The *pracharaks* not only act as catalysts to the growth of the RSS, they also bind the entire organization in a particular ideological mould.

The *pracharaks* are sometimes referred to as whole-timers.[35] In fact, they are different from each other. The RSS constitution stipulates that the *pracharaks* will receive no remuneration. The unit to which they are assigned, provide them with living expenses (maintenance), and travel expenses connected with their duties. On the other hand the whole-timers receive some honorarium (*mandhan*). The whole-timers mostly work for the affiliates.

Recruitment

The *Akhil Bharatiya Prachar Pramukh* appoints *prant pracharaks* with the consent of the *sarkaryavaha* and in consultations with the concerned *sanghchalaks*. The *prant pracharak* recruits the *pracharaks* in consultation with local officials. Despite the fact that the state units assess their own manpower needs and have considerable discretion in assigning their own *pracharaks*, the ultimate power for their appointment, transfer and discontinuance of the service resides with the *sarkaryavaha* (national general secretary). He may shift them to other states and affiliates if needed.[36] *Pracharaks* during their probation period, which usually lasts for one or two years, are called *vistaraks*. The potential of the probationer is assessed during this period, and his future tenure and placement is decided.

Most of the *pracharaks* are recruited in their early twenties. They are usually college-educated and have been associated with the RSS activities since their early adolescence. Before getting this assignment, they should have attended at least two Officers' Training Camps (OTCs) as well as a number of other RSS camps. They usually know Hindi, English and the language of the area in which they work. They also have a flair for travelling.

For a long time, the *pracharaks* were recruited from an urban middle class, upper-caste background. However, in recent time, a good number of them come from the rural peasantry background.[37] Some also belong to those families who have had close association with the RSS for a long period. As these families are committed to the ideal of the RSS, they do not oppose their kith and kin to take up the assignments.

Life Style

The *pracharaks* remain bachelors during their tenures, though the constitution does not demand so.[38] The RSS does not really denigrate family life; rather it exalts family values. However, it feels that a *pracharak* cannot completely devote himself to the cause of the organization if he has to fulfill family obligations.

The *pracharaks* lead a very simple life. The senior Maharashtrian *pracharaks* like Babu Rao Paldhikar, Babu Rao Deshpande (the seniormost *pracharaks* in Orissa), who were recruits of Hedgewar, lead a very austere lifestyle. Even the Oriya *pracharaks* like Harihar Nanda (former *prant prachar pramukh*, Orissa) and Raghunath Sethi (*pracharak*) are persons having minimum needs. They sleep either on the floor or on a hard bed, eat simple vegetarian food with fellow *swayamsevaks* and wear simple Indian clothes (cotton *dhoti* and *kurta*).

In a territory like Orissa, where the communication system was very poor, some of the *pracharaks* had to walk miles in the difficult terrain to establish the *shakhas* during the initial years. Sometimes they had to sleep in the *hata* (rural market place) and managed only with a handful of *channa* (horse-grams). The credit for expansion of the RSS goes mainly to these types of *pracharaks*, who have become symbols of hard work and sacrifice. Their simple dedicated life-style has attracted many young men to the RSS fold and always remained a source of inspiration to many *swayamsevaks*.

Changing Tradition: 'Old' vs. *'Young'*

Is there any shift in this *pracharak* tradition? How do the young *pracharaks* differ from their older counterparts? Some changes have crept in, observes a senior *pracharak*, particularly with regard to the outward characteristics. The young *pracharaks* now wear western clothes. As the organization has expanded and the sphere of work extended, many of them prefer to travel by motorcycles for easy and quick mobility. Despite this, he argues, the younger generation has undergone hardly any substantial change; both the old and the young *pracharaks* are guided by the same ideology. However, another senior *pracharak* thinks that the younger counterparts now look for more comforts and privileges. Perhaps, this assessment is more correct in the context of RSS's tryst with political power. Therefore, the real difference between these two categories is with regard to their attitude vis-a-vis political power. While the older ones imbibing the traditions of Hedgewar and Golwalkar are found to be more concerned with the ideal and consider political power as its derivative, the young *pracharaks* trained in the traditions of Deoras and Rajendra Singh show a significant inclination towards political power.

The *pracharaks* actually bind the RSS structure together. It is argued that they possess few of the symbols of power, are given no independent authority and have no control over funds and have no say in their placement.[39] This seems to be partly true because the *pracharaks* command tremendous respect from the *swayamsevaks* for their devoted and dedicated service. In fact they are asked to do their job quietly, away from the centrestage. The *sanghachalaks* know it well that their own prestige and position depends largely on the *pracharaks*, who tirelessly operate in the background. The total devotion and dedication to a cause certainly enhances their power and prestige; the high regard they are held in by the common *swayamsevaks* reinforces their missionary zeal further.

Withering Away of Tradition?

The job of a *pracharak* is very hard. Though he has to become an ascetic mentally (*sanyasi*), yet he has to work within the physical and material space of society. He has to remain a bachelor and lead an austere, self-denying life resisting various material temptations. Thus, a *pracharak* passes through a continuous mental struggle (*manasika sangharsh*).[40]

The RSS is conscious of this problem and takes various steps to keep their morale high. It puts the *pracharaks* under continuous and rigorous ideological training. Every month a meeting of the *vibhag* is organized to reassure them about the purpose of their mission. In the discussion, the examples of the dedicated old *pracharaks* and *karyakartas* are generously cited to inspire the young *pracharaks*.

Despite these efforts, one could still notice an element of introspection, apprehension, uncertainty and sense of guilt among some of the young *pracharaks*. At times they regret their decision. As many of them have taken up this assignment against the wishes of their family, they feel guilty of hurting the sentiments of their kith and kin. The *pracharaks* from middle class and lower middle-class background never really forget their family responsibilities and obligations. They invariably get apprehensive about their future as the prime of their lives is dedicated to the cause of the RSS. A sense of uncertainty grips them when they think of going back and starting a family life. A senior *pracharak* hopes that this 'unusual system' will come to an end when the RSS becomes '*sarvavyapi*' (all pervading) and '*sarvasparshi*' (all embracing). And that will take a long time.

PERIODIC TRAINING: RSS CAMPS

Besides daily *shakhas*, the RSS conducts a large number of camps for the continuous indoctrination of *swayamsevaks*, to teach them *samskars*, and to consolidate the sense of community and brotherhood. The camps are of the following three categories. The first, the Instructors' Training Camps (ITC), are usually managed by *nagar* committees. These camps are intended primarily for older members, and the emphasis is on the intellectual aspects. They are usually held during the winter months for duration of about fifteen days. A number of three-day camps, which are organized throughout the year, belong to the second category. Some of these camps cater to specific groups, such as school students, college students, businessmen, etc. These camps are particularly attractive to the younger members of the RSS.

The third category covers the most important of all the camps—*Sangh Shiksha Vargas*—the Officers' Training Camps (OTCs).[41] There are three stages of OTCs: the highest stage of training for outstanding *swayamsevaks* who have completed the first and second stages is the third stage, which is conducted at Nagpur. As reported, details of the *Sangh Shiksha Vargas* conducted during the year 1999-2000 are as follows: the number of centres and *swayamsevaks*: I year 44/9815, II year 222/4187, III year 1/1993. The RSS also conducted *Proudha Vargas*: I year 5/523 and II year 4/206.[42]

The purpose of these camps is two-fold.[43] First, the trainees receive a much more concentrated dose of Sangh ideology than is imparted in the *shakhas*. They also go through an intensive physical training. Secondly, these camps provide the opportunity to the *swayamsevaks* of a particular locality and social group to come in contact with members of other localities and social groups, thereby removing parochialism and developing a broader outlook. The trainees also gain the privilege of meeting senior provincial and national leaders of the RSS.

The duration of these camps is about a month. Planning and the selection process of the trainees commence much earlier. The timing of these camps are properly arranged by the central executive of the RSS to enable the senior leaders including the *sarsanghchalak* to visit all these camps. Only the promising *swayamsevaks* are recommended for the OTCs by the *mukhya shikshak* of the *shakha* and the local *pracharak*. While it is mandatory for teachers and other office bearers to attend at least one camp, for the *pracharaks*, the requirement is at least two.

These camps are held in some large vacant places, usually in college or high school premises, during the summer holidays. They remain isolated from the outside world, and are totally self-sufficient, containing residential blocks, community kitchen, clinic, bookstore and laundry.[44] Everyone is dressed identically in the RSS uniform. *Swayamsevaks* pay for their own expenses at these camps.

Most of the trainees at these camps are between fifteen and twenty-five. The participants of OTC are assigned to *ganas* (groups of between fifteen and thirty) which are directed by *gana pramukhs* (instructors). The instructor stays with his group throughout the camp period. He is responsible for teaching the physical (*sharirik*) and intellectual (*baudhik*) classes which form the camp curriculum. The RSS leadership makes a deliberate effort to combine the *swayamsevaks* of different age groups and different regions of the district/province to overcome their feelings of exclusiveness.

ORGANIZATION OR MOVEMENT?

Is the RSS an organization or a movement?[45] The RSS does not consider itself as a mere organization, as it is engaged in organizing the entire society along Hindu lines. It does not remain a *sanstha* (institution) any more; it is transformed into a *vyavastha* (system).[46] The RSS has become a gigantic system, particularly with the emergence of a large number of 'affiliates' or 'off-spring' or 'off-shoots' or 'branches' to organize different sections and groups of Hindu society and become a huge family, commonly known as the *Sangh Parivar*.[47] The RSS cannot be called a movement just because of its burgeoning growth. However, the superb coordination among its various affiliates for mass mobilizations during the *Ram Janmabhoomi* agitation, and the response it generated, has perhaps transformed the RSS into a movement.

Notwithstanding the controversy on its acquiring the status of a movement, it is true that no discussion on the RSS is complete without considering the role of its affiliates and their interconnections.[48] What is the interconnection between the RSS and the its affiliates? How does it control such a huge system? What is the secret key of the organizational management of the *Sangh Parivar*?

The basic objective of the RSS behind the creation of affiliates is to spread its activity to various spheres of society and to propagate its worldview among different social groups. After creating an affiliate, the RSS appoints a few trusted *pracharaks* in key posts of the new organization. Almost every affiliate has the post of a general-secretary and an organizing secretary (*sangathan mantri*), which are usually occupied by the RSS *pracharaks*. While the strategic organizational positions in an affiliate are controlled by the RSS *pracharaks* and whole-timers (*poornkalin karyakartas*), the ceremonial ones are reserved for its trusted sympathizers and notables.

The RSS not only appoints these functionaries, it also reserves the right to transfer them from one affiliate to the other. For example, *pracharaks* like Acharya Giriraj Kishore, the present general-secretary of the VHP, and Madan Das, the *sah-sarkaryavaha* of the RSS, previously worked as secretary and organizing secretary of the ABVP respectively.

Present BJP leaders like K.N. Govindacharya, Narendra Modi, Sushil Kumar Modi, were all office-bearers of the ABVP.

Thus the RSS ensures organizational harmony and coordination by manning crucial organizational positions of various affiliates with its committed *pracharaks.* This is not to suggest that factionalism does not crop up among its cadre or conflict does not occur between one affiliate and the other. But the RSS, by and large, has remained successful in controlling these conflicts through sustained ideological training and a long cultivated brotherhood.

As the *Sangh Parivar* gets access to political power in a few states and subsequently at the national level, the dynamics of power politics has started threatening the long cultivated brotherhood. Shankersinh Vaghela and Kalyan Singh are two examples. Moreover, as the affiliates expand, they attract to their fold a large section of people from a non-RSS background as well. Sometimes this creates tension between the RSS and the non-RSS section. To acquaint the newcomers with its family culture, the RSS organizes various training programmes imparting them with a soft dosage of ideology. Despite these emerging problems, the RSS has so far maintained its firm control over the *Parivar.*

The RSS, therefore, is just not a simple cohesive organization, but also a well-integrated system of organizations. The key to the efficient management of this huge system lies in identical ideological training and cultivated brotherhood in the *shakhas.* The hierarchical line of command further ensures uniformity in the entire structure. The members are taught not to ask questions but simply to follow the instructions (*suchna ke elawa sochna nahin hai*). The periodic camps further consolidate the ideological commitment and bring uniformity, breaking the local and regional barriers among the *swayamsevaks.* The RSS knows that its mission of *Hindu Rashtra* depends largely on its organizational expansion and efficiency. It has accordingly designed the organization and training schedule to reinforce its politics and ideology.

NOTES AND REFERENCES

1. *http://rss.org/mission.htm.*
2. *The Times of India,* 8 August 2000.
3. M.S. Golwalkar, *Bunch of Thoughts* [1966] (Bangalore: Jagarana Prakashana, 1980), p. 512.
4. This six-fold division is based on the above chart. However, in practice, the com-

mon division consists of four age-groups: *shishu* (6-10 years), *bal* (10-14 years), *taruna* (14-28 years) and *praudha* (28 years or above). See Walter K. Andersen and Shridhar D. Damle, *The Brotherhood in Saffron: The Rashtriya Swayamsevak Sangh and Hindu Revivalism* (Delhi: Vistaar Publications, 1987), p. 84.

5. This figure is quoted from Rajendra Singh's statement in his first press conference as the *sarsanghchalak*. See *Frontline*, 8 April 1994, p. 131.
6. Madan Das, the *sah-sarkaryavah* of the RSS, gave this figure to the press. See *Organiser*, XLIX (36), 5 April 1998. This shows that while the number of daily *shakhas* has come down, the weekly and monthly gatherings have increased considerably.
7. Critics point out that the RSS believes in an 'non-dialogic', 'non-argumentative' mode of learning. See Tapan Basu et al., *Khaki Shorts and Saffron Flags: A Critique of the Hindu Right* (Delhi: Orient Longman, 1993), p. 35.
8. A detailed discussion on *pracharak* will follow in this chapter.
9. Andersen and Damle, *The Brotherhood in Saffron*, op. cit., p. 84.
10. M.S. Golwalkar, *Bunch of Thoughts*, op. cit., pp. 511-12.
11. For more discussion on the origin, development and meaning of the saffron flag, see Narayan Hari Palkar, *Bhagwa Dhwaj* [in Hindi] (Lucknow: Lokhit Prakashan, 1992).
12. Some *shakhas* have introduced certain changes. *Judo* and *karate*, though not Indian games, have been included in the *sharirik* programme because of their increasing popularity among Indian youth.
13. Dhooria mentions that the training also stresses the use of sword, dagger, spear, etc. He also informs that the *shakhas* sometimes conduct 'sham warfare' to instill courage among the *swayamsevaks*. See Ram Lall Dhooria, *I was a Swayamsevak: An Inside View of the RSS* (Delhi: Sampradayikta Virodhi Committee, n.d.), p. 38.
14. Embree argues that the focus on the physical culture of young men is in a way reminiscent of General Baden-Powell's Boy Scouts or the fascist youth movement of pre-war Germany. See Ainslie T. Embree, 'The Function of the Rashtriya Swayamsevak Sangh: To Define the Hindu Nation', in Martin E. Marty and R. Scott Appleby, eds., *Accounting for Fundamentalisms: The Dynamic Character of Movements*, Vol. 4 (Chicago: University of Chicago Press, 1994), p. 627.
15. My observation on 9 October 1991 at the *Shri Ram Prabhat Shakha*, Keonjhar city of Orissa (the same district in which Graham Staines and his two sons were murdered) substantiates this point. When the *swayamsevaks* were playing *kabaddi*, a *bal swayamsevak* went inside the territory of the tougher adult opponents. The *gatanayak* was repeatedly commanding '*daro nahin*', '*daro nahin*' (don't be afraid) and '*maara nahele mard*' (do or die) to prepare him psychologically to face the strong opponents. The *gatanayak* incidentally belonged to the Mahanta community, among whom Dara Singh, the main accused in the Staines murder case, is very popular.
16. 'Physical training in the RSS is only the means to the end of a psychological drill leading to a total surrender of individuality to what the RSS likes to call the "ideal".' Tapan Basu et al., *Khaki Shorts and Saffron Flags*, op. cit., p. 34.

17. Interview with Bhupendra Kumar Basu, *prant sanghchalak* of Orissa.
18. M.S. Golwalkar, *Bunch of Thoughts*, op. cit., p. 513.
19. For a discussion on these concepts, see Dina Nath Mishra, *RSS: Myth and Reality* (Delhi: Vikas Publishing House, 1980), pp. 55-7.
20. The *shakha* trains the member to answer the question 'Who am I'? with the affirmation, 'I am Hindu'. It also asserts that to say 'I am an Indian' is also to say 'I am a Hindu'. See Ainslie T. Embree, 'The Function of the Rashtriya Swayamsevak Sangh . . .', op. cit., p. 628.
21. Dhooria, an ex-*swayamsevak* writes that it is erroneous to assume that all the *shakha* members are compassionate like Buddha; they act thus it is their 'duty', not that it is a spontaneous call from within. 'It was enjoined on us to treat all other *swayamsevaks* as our blood-brothers and to come, rather rush to their help or succor if they were in difficulty or distress.' See Ram Lall Dhooria, *I was a Swayamsevak*, op. cit., p. 38. Whether spontaneous or otherwise, in case of any crisis situation like death in the family of a *swayamsevak*, the *shakha* members reach in no time. In marriages and other occasions, they extend both physical as well as emotional support which an individual needs at this hour. In these occasions, the needy *swayamsevaks* sometimes receive clothes, groceries, etc., in credit, from the trader-members of the RSS.
22. Kamal Dutta, a *pracharak*, disclosed that the RSS has started a new project called *Rugna Prakalpa* (Project for the Sick) in Orissa. As the in-charge of the Orissa unit, his job is to liaison with the hospitals and the doctors. When any *swayamsevak* or his family member comes for treatment, this wing of the RSS facilitates his/her admission to the hospital and treatment.
23. See Article 19 of the RSS Constitution.
24. *Organiser*, XLIX (36), 5 April 1998.
25. See Article 15(e) of the RSS Constitution.
26. Though the RSS leaders deny that any casteism was involved in the choice of leadership, political observers looked at the accession of a *kshatriya* from UP having significance with caste emerging as a major political factor in the Hindi belt.
27. On 11 June 1995, in a *boudhik* session at 1st year Officers' Training Camp (OTC) of Orissa, the speaker was explaining to the members that no criticism is entertained in the RSS as in the case of a family. However, there is always scope for introspection.
28. H.V. Seshadri, ed., *Dr. Hedgewar: The Epoch Maker* (Bangalore: Sahitya Sindhu, 1981), pp. 112-13.
29. All the leaders of the RSS affiliates claimed during the interviews that their respective organizations enjoy autonomy vis-a-vis the RSS. They deny the charge of being dictated by the RSS. However, they admit that they consult the parent organization at times. It may be true that these affiliates manage their day-to-day functioning themselves, but their broad polices and guidelines are laid down by the RSS. Further, the organizational control remains in the hands of trained *pracharaks*. Under the leadership of Deoras, the affiliates expanded their work

quite considerably even within this limited autonomy. Deoras also made clear to the affiliates that they should be financially self-reliant. They may be given some loan in the teething years, but they have to pay back within a short period and generate enough resources to manage their own affairs. This has worked quite well for the affiliates.

30. The RSS writings describe their organization as a movement.
31. *Organiser*, XLV (33), 20 March 1994.
32. Seshadri's speech to ABPS of the RSS on 11 March 1994. Ibid.
33. Dina Nath Mishra, *RSS: Myth and Reality*, op. cit., p. 63.
34. See Article 17 of the RSS Constitution.
35. An interesting comparison could be made between the *pracharak* of the RSS and the whole-timer of the Communist Parties. Both have intense dedication and ideological commitment to their respective causes. But they differ in their personalities. The former is always a cool customer, usually avoids arguments and demonstrates his power in a subtle way. On the other hand, the latter, invariably enjoys arguments and tries to score points through debate.
36. The capable *pracharaks* are shifted out of their home territory for strategic reasons. First, the RSS demonstrates its national character when a south Indian *pracharak* works in the north and *vice versa*. Second, these *pracharaks* display a remarkable adaptability, e.g. they speak the local dialect, wear local costume, eat local food, and observe local customs and mannerisms, thus influencing the potential recruits of the region quite considerably. Third, they take these assignments as a challenge and give their best performance to move up in the organizational hierarchy.
37. This trend is noticed in Orissa.
38. 'With the tremendous value placed on marriage and family in India, and by all religious communities, not just by Hindus, self-chosen celibacy is as dramatic a statement of commitment to a cause as one can make.' See Ainslie T. Embree, 'The Function of the Rashtriya Swayamsevak Sangh . . .', op. cit., p. 626.
39. 'The glitter belongs to the *sanghchalaks*, and the *pracharaks* are expected to behave differently towards them. There is an analogous situation in all the affiliates of the RSS.' See Andersen and Damle, *The Brotherhood in Saffron*, op. cit., p. 87.
40. Interview with Harihar Nanda, former *prant pracharak*, Orissa.
41. See Appendix, Visit to a RSS Camp.
42. See the Annual Report of the RSS for the year 1999-2000. *Organiser*, LI (35), 26 March 2000.
43. J.A. Curran, Jr., *Militant Hinduism in Indian Politics: A Study of the RSS* (New York: Institute of Pacific Relations, 1951), p. 50.
44. The *swayamsevaks* do all the jobs to keep the camps in running order, 'including those of sanitation, which most Hindus would shudder at the thought of doing'. Ibid., p. 50.
45. Embree argues that the RSS has become a movement. See Ainslie T. Embree, 'The Function of the Rashtriya Swayamsevak Sangh . . .', op. cit.

46. See Appendix, Visit to a RSS Camp.
47. Seshadri lists over 150 affiliates. See H.V. Seshadri, *RSS: A Vision in Action* (Bangalore: Jagarana Prakashana, 1988). The RSS does not accept the above terminologies for its family members; instead of *Sangh Parivar*, it would prefer to use *Sangha Shristi*.
48. Though the focus of the present research is RSS and not the affiliates, still a few dynamic members of the *Parivar* would be mentioned off and on in the context of politics and ideology of the RSS. Prominent members among them are: the ABVP, the BJS/BJP, the BMS, the VHP, the VKA, the SJM and the Rashtra Sevika Samiti.

CHAPTER IV

Constructing *Hindu Rashtra*: Community, History and Nation

There has been a massive upsurge of community consciousness and identity politics all over the world in recent years. As the pace of modernization accelerates, the individuals are increasingly seeking to escape from individualism towards a more community-based identity.[1] Every major philosophy of the present time considers individual alienation and cultural dislocation as important problems of man and society.[2] The RSS, which has been championing the cause of a Hindu community since the 1920s, has also intensified its ideological propaganda during the last decade on the themes of 'Hindu identity', *Hindutva* (Hinduness) and *Hindu Rashtra* (Hindu Nation).

Hindu Rashtra constitutes the ideological core of the RSS. The purpose of this chapter is to discern and demystify the political and ideological content of *Hindu Rashtra* through the RSS discourse on Hindu community, Hindu history and Hindu nation, with special reference to the writings of M.S. Golwalkar, Deendayal Upadhyaya and other RSS ideologues.

SEEKING A HINDU IDENTITY

Community[3] is a symbolic construction; it is a system of values, norms, moral codes, which provides a sense of identity to its members within a bounded whole.[4] This concept thus carries both the notions of similarity and difference; the members of a group not only share certain commonalities with each other, they also possess certain characteristics which distinguish them from the other groups in a significant way. Individual identity is not just one's relationship with other members of the community; it is essentially a matter of being and it is this consciousness of belongingness to a particular community that determines his identity.

Therefore, identity formation, generally a cultural construct, is a process of inclusion and exclusion of values and symbols defining 'we' and 'others'. In the process, boundaries between the two take shape whose forms keep changing from time to time. Relationships between 'we' and 'others' are not necessarily always conflicting or competitive; commonality and overlapping between the two in various social spheres often blur the boundaries.[5] Further, the ascriptive identities, be they ethnic or communal, are products of changing historical contexts, and are not culturally fixed. However, this does not suggest that collective identities are undeveloped without clear boundaries. They are neither fuzzy[6] nor determinate though at any given point of time they may appear to have been always there in exactly the same form.[7]

A community's awareness of its identity crystallizes when it finds a whetstone in another community, which is different from it. Cultural identity takes a political form and differentiation between 'we' and 'they' gets sharper and more concrete. Cultural identity is transformed into communal identity and community consciousness becomes communal consciousness. Now it is not just a question of one's belongingness to a community but also the intensity of this belongingness. In a 'communalized' situation, the intensity of communal consciousness is related to one's perception about 'others' who are considered enemies. The campaign against the 'other' is carried out through hostile propaganda, which completely ignores the commonality between 'us' and 'them' and only magnifies the differences. In the process, the meanings of 'we' and 'they' transcend the cultural mould and prejudices become pronounced. All these changes lead to communal violence.

Violence becomes inevitable when the individual identity of a substantial number of population gets submerged in the communal identity, championing love for 'us' and the hatred against the 'other' who is 'homogenized, depersonalized, and increasingly dehumanized'. Rumors and rival mobilizations fuel a persecution mania. The slightest spark leads to violence.[8] This communal violence, in turn, further reinforces communal identity.[9]

The RSS discourse on Hindu identity needs to be examined in the above light. For the RSS, identity is given or fixed rather than a construction.[10] However, neither the 'primordialist' nor the 'instrumentalist' approach fully explains the concept of identity though both are not without justification; both complement each other and need not be necessarily viewed in either/or terms.[11] Therefore, despite the RSS denial that it is engaged in constructing a Hindu identity, it really does so. At the same time, it does not construct such an identity simply in a vacuum.

The RSS construction of a Hindu identity has two different, but interrelated aspects: first, it seeks to create a homogenized 'we'—the Hindus—ignoring and underplaying the internal social, economic, and cultural differentiations; and second, it attempts to project and sustain the antagonistic 'other' for the purpose of organization, mobilization and consolidation of the Hindus. The RSS tries to achieve this not only by reinterpreting history, inventing legends and invoking symbols, but also by undertaking several mobilization programmes.

Hindu Identity in pre-Modern India

To understand the RSS arguments on Hindu identity and *Hindu Rashtra*, the term 'Hindu' has to be understood in a proper perspective. Probing the etymology of 'Hindu', one surprisingly does not find this word in Sanskrit, the language in which most of the texts of Hinduism have been written. Even the Vedas, the Upanishads and *Bhagavadgita* are silent on this word. Then how did this word originate? The term, it is argued, emerged as a geographical nomenclature and implied a geographical identity to the people living across the Sindhu or Indus river.[12]

Then how does one explain 'Hinduism'? Ever since the term has been in vogue, scholars have been looking for an acceptable definition of it. However, the religious diversity of India has made it really difficult to find one. It is described as a false conceptualization, which is conspicuously incompatible with any adequate understanding of the religious outlook of Hindus; even the term 'Hindu' was unknown to the classical Hindus and 'Hinduism' as a concept they certainly did not have.[13]

Did the people of this geographical area really identify themselves with an inclusive Hinduism? It is observed that multiple communities based on various identities, rather than some sort of inclusive Hinduism, existed in pre-modern India—Hinduism was a 'mosaic of distinct cults, deities, and ideas' adjusting to and distancing themselves from each other.[14] The term 'Hindu' which emerged as a geographical nomenclature gradually came to be used not only for those who were living across the Indus river but also for those who professed a religion other than Islam or Christianity. This all-inclusive term 'was doubtless a new and bewildering feature for the multiple sects and castes who generally saw themselves as separate entities'.[15] Since Hinduism was a cluster of distinctive sects and cults, the people identified themselves with region, language and caste rather than with an inclusive Hinduism.[16] Unless by 'Hindu' one means 'nothing more, nor less, than "Indian"(something native to, or found within the continent of India), there has never been any such thing as a single "Hinduism" or "Hindu Community" for all of India'.[17] Furthermore, there has never been any one religion nor even one system of religions—to which the term 'Hindu' can be accurately applied.[18]

It may be true that self-contained religious constellations existed in pre-modern India, which identified themselves with much more immediate and obvious domains of religious commitment rather than with the wider field of 'the Hindu tradition'. Yet the manner in which the representatives of these theistic formations relate and refer to one another, indicates the presence of this wider field.[19] Thus, 'it represents a sense of identity, a sense of coherence in a shared context and of inclusion in a common framework and horizon, and it refers us to some fundamental implications of the elusive reality of "Hinduism"'.[20] It may be further argued that that just because the term 'Hindu' was first used only in Arab texts does not make the application of the term Hinduism to earlier periods invalid. Despite the existence of a wide range of beliefs, from animism to atheism, the term Hinduism could still be applicable to the belief system of pre-modern India as one could see some of its features in the Hinduism of the later period.[21]

Modern Indian Search for a Definition of 'Hindu'

At the turn of the twentieth century when community politics was in the ascendant, Hindu leaders began searching for a definition of the term 'Hindu', which would justify a separate Hindu identity. Different definitions were attempted, but each contradicted and turned down. Some defined Hindus as the people who burn their dead. Even this definition, based on the least common denominator, was found faulty, as a *sanyasi's* dead body is never burnt. Bal Gangadhar Tilak tried to end this uncertainty by proposing something different: A Hindu is he who believes that the Vedas contain self-evident and axiomatic truths. But this definition was also found to be incomprehensive and defective in as much as it excluded the Jains and Sikhs from the fold of Hinduism.[22] Thus, to the Hindu leaders, all such attempted definitions were partial and incomprehensive.

V.D. Savarkar's definition of 'Hindu' in his work *Hindutva* (1923) was a departure from the earlier Hindu leaders. He provided a clear and precise definition, which apparently resolved the dilemma of the Hindu leaders once and for all. Savarkar defined Hindu as 'a person who regards the land of Bharatvarsha from Indus to the Seas as his Fatherland as well as his Holyland—that is the cradle land of his religion'.[23] This definition got applause and acceptance from the Hindu leaders and was heralded as 'a message given at the dawn of a new age' (Swami Shraddhananda).

RSS Definition of 'Hindu'

K.B. Hedgewar subscribed to Savarkar's definition of 'Hindu' and founded the RSS to propound India as a *Hindu Rashtra*. However, his successor, M.S. Golwalkar, who consolidated and amplified the ideology of *Hindu Rashtra*, seemed to have reservation on Savarkar's formulation.[24] As he explains: 'Of course, many attempts at definition have been made from time to time, but all such definitions have proved to be incomplete. They do not express the whole truth and it is natural in the case of a people who have been growing and evolving for the last so many scores of centuries.'[25] Thus Golwalkar did not accept the finality of Savarkar's definition of Hindu by projecting the Hindus as a 'growing and evolving' people. He understood that flexibility of the definition could be used to the advantage of the RSS.

Golwalkar admits the difficulty in defining the term 'Hindu'. For him, it is a paradox that though the Sun and the Moon could be defined easily, it seems impossible to define their creator, God. But does it imply that God does not exist, questions Golwalkar. The origin of the Hindus is unknown to the historians: 'In a way we are *anadi*, without a beginning.'[26] Thus Golwalkar tries to keep the origin of the Hindus out of historical scrutiny by the mystic expression of *anadi*, the Hindu concept of timelessness.

The Hindus were the enlightened people and knew the laws of nature and the laws of spirit, boasts Golwalkar. 'Then the rest of humanity were just bipeds and so no distinctive name was given to us. Sometimes in trying to distinguish our people from others, we were called "the enlightened"—the Aryans, and the rest—the *Mlechhas*.'[27] Thus the Hindus existed when there was no need for any name; the necessity for naming was felt only when the Hindus came in contact with alien faiths.

Golwalkar arrogantly projects the Hindus as learned and enlightened and the 'Others' as uncivilized and barbaric. For him, it is not correct that no man is born Hindu or Muslim or Christian but a simple human being; while Hindus are born as Hindus, others are born as unnamed human beings and become Muslims or Christians only after being either circumcised or baptized. Golwalkar thus makes every attempt to prove the superiority of the Hindus vis-a-vis other communities.

Why does Golwalkar prefer 'Hindu' to 'Aryan' and 'Bharatiya', which were much more ancient than the former? As he thinks, the use of the term 'Arya' would be self-defeating because of the following reasons: first, it has been out of use for the last thousand years; secondly, some historians have spread the 'venom of Aryan-Dravidan controversy'.[28] He also discards the term 'Bharatiya', as it would include Muslims, Christians and others. Instead, he prefers 'Hindu', as this word 'alone connotes correctly and completely the meaning that we want to convey'.[29]

Despite having a bewildering variety of phases and forms, Golwalkar notices one thread of unification running inherently through the multitude of its expressions and manifestations—a single way of life called 'Hindu'. He cites the example of a tree that has many heterogeneous parts, but the same sap running through and nourishing all those parts. Hindu society[30] is depicted as 'a living reality'. Thus, Golwalkar takes a wide assimilationist view of the term 'Hindu' comprising all sects and castes.

CONSTRUCTING A 'HINDU' HISTORY

Interpreting the past by harnessing selective memories is crucial to any identity formation. The existing dominant interpretations of Indian history, the RSS argues, dilute the Hindu identity. Therefore, its objective is to contest these 'distorted' interpretations[31] and construct an alternate 'Hindu historiography' to promote and consolidate a Hindu identity.[32]

The RSS historiography rejects the Aryan Invasion thesis as a myth. It treats the prevalent Indian historiography as a biased exercise, as it projects *Ramayana* and the *Mahabharata* as mythologies and the pre-Muslim period as the dark age. This interpretation, the RSS believes, has deprived many well-educated Indians of the chance to learn about the glorious achievements of the Hindus, for example, the establishment of a vast cultural empire in the Far East.[33] It resents the fact that this historiography treats India as a mere geographical unit and denies due place to Hindu/national heroes like Maharana Pratap and Chhatrapati Shivaji.

The RSS, therefore, takes up 'a factual re-writing of Indian history' not only to demolish various existing 'myths', but also to analyse the causes behind several 'historic' events and formulate current policies accordingly. For example, it is keen to understand why the Hindus failed to assimilate the Muslims, while they were successful vis-a-vis the Greeks, the Sakas and the Huns.[34] History is exercised by the RSS to act as a cohesive force to morally recover from defeats and humiliations inflicted by 'outsiders'.

'Hindu Historiography' asserts that it is only the history of the 'Hindus' that constitutes the sum total of Indian history. Anything other than the achievements of the Hindus is an intrusion in the Indian past: 'aberration, distortion, it is no part of the real history of Bharatvars'.[35] Thus the RSS historiography differs fundamentally from the nineteenth century Hindu nationalist leaders. Though these nationalists considered India as primarily Hindu, they never contended that communities other than 'the Hindus' were an excrescence, which had no place in the land.

Periodization of Indian History: A Long Hindu Period

The RSS rejects the European notion of periodization of Indian history into the Hindu, Muslim and British. Despite fluctuating fortunes, the history of Bharat is 'one long Hindu period', argues Golwalkar. His logic is interesting; that the periods of history 'are known after nationals and not after foreign usurpers and dictators masquerading as kings. . . .'[36] Therefore, there is only one period of history—the Hindu period—and the latter two are considered as aberrations which have to be extirpated so that Hindu society can once again attain its continuity with its past history. Ironically, while analysing historical events, the RSS historians follow the pattern of the European periodization when they glamorize the glorious 'golden age' of ancient Hindu India, decry the 'dark age' of the medieval Muslim India and show indifference towards the colonial British India.

The RSS gives priority to the reinterpretation of ancient India as during that period its imagined ideal Hindu society flourished. While emphasizing the indigenous origin of the Hindus, Golwalkar uses 'Hindu' and 'Aryan' interchangeably, thus implying that the Aryans did not immigrate from outside but originated in India and then spread towards Western Europe from here; the Indian civilization and culture started with the Aryans.[37] RSS historians insist that the Harappan culture was created by the Vedic people despite the striking contrast between the pastoral life of the *Rig Veda* and the urban life of the Harappans. They also stress that the Harappan script was alphabetical and that it represents examples of proto-Sanskrit—a claim contrary to the archeological evidence.

The attempt to prove India as the indigenous home of the Aryans is essentially an attempt to bolster a false sense of national pride.[38] The theory of indigenous origin of the Aryans serves a dual purpose: first, it refutes the claim of the Dravidians as the original inhabitants of India who were pushed beyond the Vindhyas by the Aryan aggressors; and, second, it highlights that Central Asian Muslim migrants alone were foreigners.[39] The objective of the RSS is to stress that those people whose ancestors were not indigenous to India are not truly Indian and those whose culture is different from the ancient Hindu culture are foreigners.[40] Any historical scholarship which provides the opposite version is dismissed as the 'shady testimony of Western scholars'. It is obvious that the rationale of *Hindu Rashtra* would never accept the foreign origin of the Aryans.

Since, for the RSS the origin of the Aryans is indigenous, they logically proceed to the claim that Indian culture is synonymous with Hindu culture. Muslim culture is different from Hindu culture/Indian culture, as its origin is foreign. This viewpoint draws its sustenance from the writings of some leading ancient Indian historians like K.P. Jayaswal, H.C. Raychaudhuri and K.A. Nilkanta Sastri, who, 'sometimes overstepped the limits of scientific reconstruction'.[41] The relevance of the foreign origin of the Indian Muslims is questioned on the ground that most of them have indigenous origins, mainly being converts from the lower castes. Moreover, those who came from outside made this country their home and adopted its culture.

Golwalkar presents 'the glory of Hindu Civilization' till the time of Mahabharata. Since then the nation had lived its usual life without any serious occurrence for thousand years. 'Then came Buddha and the great Emperors of the Gupta dynasty, Asoka, Harshavardhan, Vikramaditya, Pulakeshi, and others of whose rule of peace, power and plenty, we obtain incontrovertible evidence. The invasion of the "world-conqueror" Alexander was a mere scratch. In fact he cannot be said to have invaded the country at all, so hasty was his retreat.'[42] Buddhism, to Golwalkar, is merely a variant of Hinduism.

Golwalkar's account of history is obviously limited in its scope as its prime motive is to emphasize the glorious record of the Hindus. He has ignored the recorded evidence available and 'straitjackets these centuries into a static time-frame whose only denominator is "Hindu Kings"...'[43] The treatment of Buddhism by Golwalkar aims at assimilating it within the Hindu fold. Buddhism is certainly more than a variant of Hinduism.

The other pet theme of the RSS account of history is Hindu tolerance.[44] This has been strongly rejected by the historians. *Divyavadana* depicts Pushyamitra Sunga, a powerful Hindu king, as a great persecutor of Buddhists. In the early medieval period, south India witnessed conflicts between Jains and Shaivites in which the Jains were impaled. The period also experienced violent confrontations between the Buddhists and followers of the Brahmanical religion. One of the reasons for the disappearance of Buddhism could be attributed to the intolerant attitude of medieval Hindu rulers.[45]

Even for Vivekananda, the apostle of modern Hinduism, Hindu tolerance did not include tolerance of hostile criticism of Hinduism. His conceptualization of Hindu religious tolerance included 'intolerance of intolerance',[46] thus imparting a combative edge to Hinduism vis-a-vis Christianity and Islam. The claim of tolerance sounds even more hollow if one scrutinizes the hierarchical caste system within Hinduism. It leaves no doubt that despite the doctrinal flexibility of Hindu philosophy, the Hindu social order is quite inflexible and intolerant.

The Hindu-Muslim Encounter: Medieval India

For RSS historians, the Muslim medieval period was a dark age. These historians are inspired by some leading historians like R.C. Mazumdar,[47] who trace the 'dusk' of the Indian civilization to the tenth century and the 'long night' to the establishment of the Delhi Sultanate. Mazumdar observes that at the establishment of the sultanate, India was permanently divided into two distinct communities and cultures, each with marked individuality of its own, which ruled out any fusion or even coordination. He also talks of wholesale destruction of temples and monasteries by the Muslim invaders and rulers who very nearly extinguished the Hindu culture. RSS historians echo the same when they point out that the Muslim period was one of the unmitigated savagery that 'brought a near standstill in scientific progress, and the destruction and loss of numerous cultural treasures'.[48]

On the other hand, Marxist historians observe that Islam did not appear as a monolithic religion to the inhabitants of India when it arrived in her soil. They argue that the term 'Muslim' does not appear in the records of early contacts. The terms used frequently were *turuska*, *yavana* and *mlechha*, which implied ethnic, geographical and cultural dimensions rather than religious ones.[49] The court chronicles of Sultans refer to Hindus sometimes in the sense of the indigenous population, sometimes as a geographical entity and sometimes as followers of a non-Islamic religion. 'Possibly the germ of a Hindu community begins when people start referring to themselves as Hindus, perhaps initially as a concession to being regarded as "the other". Such usage in non-Islamic sources is known from the fifteenth century.'[50] Therefore, these scholars find that the germination of a Hindu community started much after the encounter.

As the RSS argument runs, the Muslim invaders were not only plunderers, they were also religious fanatics. Marxist historians, on the contrary, argue that though these invaders were plunderers, their sole obsession was loot and plunder of the invaded land, irrespective of the faith of those who inhabited it; for example, Mahmud of Ghazni, Muhammad of Ghor and Timur of Samarkand massacred the Muslim masses and rulers in Central Asia. These historians find the main reason behind the destruction of the Hindu temples was the vast amount of wealth they had accumulated. In contrast, the architecture of mosques being such as to comprise an open structure meant for prayers, left hardly any space for the storage of wealth.

Hindu apologists interpret the Bhakti movement in their own right. In their analysis, though this was Hindu response to Muslim rule, it was a form of resistance rather than an attempt at synthesis or compromise.[51] It was an attempt to disarm Islam with the help of a popular movement with a clear message that equality before God was as much part of Hinduism as it was of Islam. The RSS rejects the view that the medieval period symbolized an efflorescence of a composite culture and cultural synthesis.[52]

The RSS portrays the medieval period as a rule of the Muslims. How far is it correct to depict the medieval period as a period of Muslim rule? It is certainly true that Muslim kings, mostly of foreign origin, ruled India for six or seven centuries. But the mass of the Muslims belonged to the lower middle class and working class. However, while the Muslim upper classes controlled the administrative machinery, the economic system was dominated by the Hindu upper class. Social and economic history of the period has shown that there was no Muslim rule under the Sultans or the Mughals. It needs to be emphasized that all Muslims did not form the ruling class. Marxist historians argue that political moves were made under economic and political considerations and not out of religious interests. The fact remains that the upper class Muslims had cultural commonalties with upper class Hindus and the same is true about the lower class Muslims and their Hindu counterparts.

The RSS builds up an anti-Muslim mindset of the Hindus on the basis of the negative image of the Mughal Emperor Aurangzeb.[53] He has been described as a butcher of Hindus, destroyer of Hindu temples and an anti-Hindu zealot. However, some scholars provide a different interpretation of Aurangzeb. Though Aurangzeb destroyed some temples, he also gave grants to other Hindu religious bodies and employed more Hindus as *mansabdars* than Akbar.[54] Despite these interpretations, by and large, most of the Hindus are obsessed with the negative image of Aurangzeb. RSS historians find it most convenient to focus on him in order to intensify the anti-Muslim attitude amongst Hindus.

Legend as History?

Keeping in tune with their interpretation of Muslim India, the RSS argued that Babur, a fanatic invader, in order to humiliate the Hindus, willfully demolished a temple commemorating the birthplace of Lord Ram at Ayodhya and erected a mosque at the site. For the settlement of this long-standing dispute the RSS pleaded for the restoration of the status quo ante, which meant demolition of the mosque and construction of the temple. Marxist and secular historians ridicule this Hindu claim on the basis of 'objective factual evidence' and describe the RSS version of Ayodhya's history as reconstruction of 'imagined history' based on faith.[55]

During the last decade Ayodhya and Ram have occupied the centre-stage of Indian politics. 'Ram' remains no more a metaphor in the Gandhian sense. The *Sangh Parivar* has presented an alternate account of the history of Ayodhya and its association with Ram. This new mode of history-writing is criticized on the following grounds: 'The first is that it claims to be a history—in a way that popular Hindu tradition (and Gandhi) would never have bothered to do. The second is that this history is fundamentally ahistorical—in that it allows for no change or development in the character, position, interests, behaviour (shall we say, the history) of its several protagonists.'[56]

The claims about the historicity of the event, namely the destruction of the temple and the building of a mosque, have been severely challenged by several historians. Though most of these scholars dismiss the claims of the RSS as the mythical construction of the past, a few among them recognize that in popular perceptions myths are a way of constructing the past: 'We cannot dismiss such myths. We cannot counterpoise history to myth as truth to falsehood. These are different modes of knowledge, varying ways of understanding the world. . . . The facts, the events, and the social actors referred to in myths often have no "real" historical existence. Yet myths do refer to reality. They talk about the world symbolically, metaphorically.'[57] Hence, it seems relevant to understand that the critical task of history here may be not what 'really happened' but how people came to believe what happened.[58]

Beyond a 'Propagandist' and 'Defensive' Approach

Thus, the perception of the RSS on the issue of Hinduism's encounter with Islam varies greatly from the Marxist and secular historians. While the RSS historians magnify the religious divide out of proportion, Marxist and secular historians excessively emphasize the ethnic, racial and cultural aspects of the encounter, ignoring the religious part. The RSS harps on the loot and intolerance of Muslim rule; the secular historian underscores only the Hindu-Muslim cooperation.

The RSS is right when it claims that many temples have been either demolished to build a mosque, or looted to increase the coffers of plunderers. But it is also true that the Hindus and Muslims had enough goodwill for each other during medieval times and they lived in harmony for long periods. Hindus enjoyed prestigious positions as generals and ministers in Muslim courts. Under the patronage of Muslim rulers, the Ayurveda and Unani school collaborated and flourished. Further, most surprisingly, many Hindus even had Muslim names. But 'one tendentious history, no matter how well meaning, cannot correct the other: it in fact serves as grist to the mill'.[59] Therefore, the complexities of Hindu-Muslim interaction in the pre-colonial period needs to be 'studied beyond the propagandist or defensive approaches'.[60]

The emphasis only on ethnic, racial and cultural aspects of the encounter does not fully explain the interaction or confrontation between Hinduism and Islam. The religious dimension can not be simply wished away. For a proper evaluation, a few questions need to be answered. First, what was the nature of the state in medieval times? Did it play any role in religious affairs? Richard Eaton's[61] study on early encounters in Bengal highlights the following important points. First, though Muslim conquest was neither a necessary nor a sufficient condition for widespread Islamization, nevertheless, most of the pre-colonial rulers adhered to a faith, and this affected public policies to greater or lesser degrees. Secondly, many rulers did patronize several faiths; in no case was the patronage even-handed.[62] Thirdly, the notion of separation between state and religion was introduced to India by the British. Some individual officials might have helped missionary activity but this was not the rule. Fourthly, while both Hindu and Muslim rulers accepted it as their duty to uphold their religion, there were very important differences in

Islamic and Hindu political theory. First, the Islamic texts, in comparison to classical Hindu texts, clearly assigned the state to safeguard the religion and extend its message. Secondly, the two differed with regard to their treatment of non-believers. 'Although the Hindu king may well have regarded other religions or sects as inferior to his own, it is still possible to assert of Hindus, as one cannot of Islamic rulers,' that 'the king was charged with the duty to protect *all* religions in his kingdom'.[63] This speaks of religious tolerance as a mark of the Hindu group of religions.

Keeping these arguments in mind, a mere dismissal of the religious and cultural divergence and a strong belief in a 'composite culture' cannot be accepted without qualification. Hindu-Muslim religio-cultural tensions are an integral part of medieval and modern Indian history, though there were examples of individual and collective efforts at understanding, and even composite development. Though the achievements in architecture, music and literature are undoubtedly glorious, in some respects, this composite culture is an aspect of the myth that all was well before the British arrived. This so-called composite culture was just the 'north-Indian courtly culture', which neither spread all over India nor encompassed the lifestyle of a large number of population even in north India.[64]

The champions of composite culture strongly believe that syncretic practice excludes the possibility of communal riots. Citing the increasing communal conflicts in modern India these scholars contend that the consolidation of social identities is a recent development. They believe that pre-modern India witnessed no such conflicts, as identities were 'fuzzy' with uncertain boundary markers. On the other hand, Christopher Bayly attempts to identify 'the pre-history of communalism' in religious conflicts of the eighteenth and early nineteenth centuries. He also rejects the observation that riots of the late colonial period were markedly different from earlier ones.[65] Though Bayly rightly identifies the existence of defined religious identities in medieval India, he fails to recognize the complexities of modern day ascriptive rivalries. It is only in modern times that ascriptive ideologies have become sharper and combative by using history as a source of symbolic and ideological sustenance. This is precisely what distinguishes ascriptive animosities of today from those of the past. Therefore, Bayly's position could not be accepted in toto: 'We must, therefore, investigate into the nature of this historical consciousness, as well as into the social forces that brought it into being, if we are to overcome both Bayly's ahistoricism and the impasses that tendentious histories have come to.'[66]

All this suggests that in pre-modern India identities were never blurred despite the fact that they were less organized and cohesive. The Hindu community of India became much more conscious of its identity as a community under the stimulus of its contact with the Islam of the Turks, Afghans and Mughals who invaded India during the medieval period. The religious dimension was no less important than the racial, cultural and ethnic dimensions of the encounter. Sheldon Pollock[67] has forcefully argued that the rise of the worship of the avatar Rama in this same period was in large part a response to Muslim presence and the Hindu search for a cohesive oppositional identity.

Colonialism Crystallizes Hindu Identity

After analysing the question of Hindu identity in pre-modern India it remains to be seen how colonialism exacerbated and sharpened communal identities. Some scholars argue that the search for a monolithic Hindu community is a recent development. The all-India Hindu community was a colonial creation, as also the all-India Muslim community, to a large extent.[68] As the argument runs, the social and economic changes brought by colonialism, Indian efforts to defend the indigenous religions and culture against western missionary attacks and the unifying drive of the colonial state tended to promote the idea of an all-India Hindu community and an all-India Muslim community who were supposedly ranged against one another for much of the time. The notion of a single Hindu community became necessary in a colonial situation. The competition for economic and political resources between various groups demanded a change from a segmented identity to one based on community.

As Robert Eric Frykenberg [69] comments, the 'Hindu community' is the twin of 'India' as a state, both were constructed about the same time. He mentions three parallel processes—institutional, ideological and socio-political—which significantly contributed to the shaping of the modern religious community known as Hinduism.

The institutional processes started with the government fiat in 1810, just when the term 'Hindu' came into vogue as a tool to describe all things indigenous to India. The other significant institutional innovation was the all-India Census of 1871. The Census introduced a vocabulary of communal, social and religious categorizations. It gave a concrete meaning to the term 'Hindu' which was a vague label till then. It also demonstrated that the 'high born' constituted roughly 15 per cent of the total population which made them apprehensive about their future role in a representative democracy.[70] The Census helped to change the very concept of Hindu from a religion to that of a community.[71] 'Perhaps its most fundamental impact rested with its influence on conceptualizations of religion, of community, and of self, plus the relation of all of these to the state.'[72]

The ideological process, inspired by Warren Hastings and many Orientalists like William Jones, H.T. Colebrooke, William Carey, H.H. Wilson, and James Princep, made valuable contributions to the fields of Indian philology, archaeology, and history.[73] Orientalism provided an aura of intellectual and philosophical respectability to the emerging notion of Hinduism and linked it with certain powerful elements, which were doctrinally very attractive, such as tolerance and non-violence. For the Orientalists, India was an ancient Hindu civilization in which Brahmanical authority was paramount. Orientalist discourse found its way 'into religious reform movements and into religious nationalism'.[74]

The third important process was mobilization of local resistance to conversion movements initiated by Christian missionaries in the eighteenth century. These radical conversion movements became potent and contagious. Reinforced by the two parallel process described above, radical conversion 'inspired the first glimmerings of a fundamentalistic reaction and marked the emergence of a more fully self-conscious "Hinduism" distinct from other religions'.[75]

Therefore, it would be fair to conclude that though the seed of the Hindu community germinated much before the colonial conquest, it was fragile. Although colonialism certainly did not create the Hindu community, it did act as a powerful catalyst in its consolidation. Colonial intervention certainly facilitated the emergence of an all-India Hindu community. In this context, it would be useful to observe how various socio-religious movements and various Hindu thinkers and activists, whom the RSS claims to be its ideological predecessors, responded to colonial intervention and helped the Hindu communal consolidation.

MAKING A *HINDU RASHTRA*

Ideological Lineage

The RSS admits that though *Hindu Rashtra* is the core of its ideology, it did not create this concept; it has only inherited this legacy from various Hindu thinkers of the nineteenth century, such as Vivekananda, Bankim, Aurobindo, Dayananda, Tilak, Savarkar and others.[76] The nineteenth century was predominantly a period of cultural protest and adjustment in India. This produced new forms of community consciousness, particularly in three regions: Bengal, Punjab and Maharashtra. Hindu tradition was not immune to this development. A number of socio-religious reform movements like Brahmo Samaj[77] and Arya Samaj[78] emerged mainly 'as a reaction to the threat of Western domination and especially to a two-fold cultural challenge, the utilitarian reformism and Christian proselytism'.[79]

These socio-religious reform movements attempted to defend, redefine and recreate Hinduism on the model of Christianity. They sought for the equivalent of a monotheistic God, a book, a prophet or a founder and congregational worship with an institutional organization supporting it.[80] The ideology of these movements was of 'strategic syncretism': syncretism because there is a strong intention to reform one's society through the assimilation of Western values consistent with the Hindu cultural equilibrium, and strategic syncretism since the equilibrium in question remains the prime concern.[81]

The nineteenth century 'cultural counter-offensive' against the colonial rule has great variety and range, from emancipatory to divisive. It was a conscious effort to overcome the marks of subordination and humiliation inflicted by colonial rule. However, at times, this feeling of subordination extended back before the beginning of colonial rule, into the period of Muslim rule as well. For example, Dayananda tempered his Hindu reformist zeal with a growing emphasis on Hindu unity, foregrounding cow protection[82] and the replacement of Urdu by Hindi in the Devanagari script; these two issues aggravated communal conflicts in north India during the last decades of the nineteenth century.[83] With Dayananda 'rationalism gave way to faith, equivalence to superiority, and tolerance to militancy'.[84] Thus, as nationalist thought took shape, the Muslims increasingly displaced the British in the category termed 'foreigner'. And this gave rise to the construction of the Other in Indian society and engagement with this Other became necessary for making a Hindu identity.[85]

When the RSS claims to be the ideological heir of Vivekananda, Bankim and Aurobindo, it is important to note that it subscribes to their ideas only on a selective basis. It emphasizes only those aspects which would support and strengthen its ideological and political arguments and does not refer to the context of these writings. Further the RSS prefers to remain silent on the higher philosophical aspects of the ideas of these Hindu thinkers.

For instance, without referring to the context, the RSS highlights Vivekananda's concern for the physical strength of Hindus. It is true that Vivekananda appealed to the Hindus to get back their manliness, bravery and courage and prescribed beef and football as ready means for their regeneration.[86] But the context of this appeal was different; as Vivekananda believed in an integration of body and mind, he felt that a strong body was a precondition for a healthy mind. Though all *sangathanists* including the RSS stress body culture, their notion of physical power is not aimed so much at the spiritual regeneration of self but at countering the 'other' effectively. Further, the RSS swears by Vivekananda's *Advaita Vedanta*. This philosophy has ethical, social and political relevance for the future of all mankind; it has been invoked against poverty, injustice and has been associated with such concepts as tolerance, equality, peaceful co-existence, brotherhood, democracy, and social justice as well as nationalism and anarchy.[87] Does the RSS really believe all these implications of this philosophy? Perhaps not.

Similarly, the RSS swears by Bankim's *Vande Mataram* (Salutation to the Mother) which became a powerful slogan of the nationalist struggle, and was also used by the Hindus each time they had a confrontation with Muslims.[88] Bankim's thought, of course, was the product of Bengal which was subjected to 'alien rule over long centuries'.[89] He depicted the Muslims as irrational, bigoted, devious, sensual, immoral. However, Bankim's target was not the upright Muslim but the decadent tyrant: 'It is not so much Moslem qua Moslem who was disliked by Bankim.'[90] He was also severe on decadent Hindus. His last phase can be seen 'more as constituting the link between nineteenth century Hindu revivalism in Bengal whose Hindu supremacist agenda was not primarily turned against the Muslim or Islam'.[91] Obviously the RSS does not give due consideration to this dimension of Bankim's ideas.

Sri Aurobindo, whom the RSS reveres, had seen the history of Muslim rule in India in a different light. In *The Spirit and Form of Indian Polity*, he wrote: 'The Mussulman domination ceased very rapidly to be a foreign rule. . . . The Mogul empire was a great and magnificent construction and an immense amount of political genius and talent was employed in its creation and maintenance. It was as splendid, powerful and beneficent and, it may be added, in spite of Aurangzeb's fanatical zeal. Infinitely more liberal and tolerant in religion than any medieval or contemporary European kingdom or empire.'[92] The RSS would perhaps never agree on this.

Though it is true that the dream of these nineteenth century Hindu thinkers from Bengal was essentially Hindu, they did not have any particular prejudice against the Muslim *other*. However, the cultural and political traditions of Maharashtra, rather than Bengal, played a predominant role in the ideological construct of the RSS. Bal Gangadhar Tilak and V.D. Savarkar decisively influenced its formulation of *Hindu Rashtra*.

Tilak and the Hindu Nation

Bal Gangadhar Tilak needs a special discussion for the following reasons: first, he not only attempted to draw the outline of a Hindu nation, he also actively and effectively mobilized the Hindus to crystallize Hindu identity; secondly, Hedgewar and his political guru Moonje were ardent followers of Tilak. The ideology of the RSS undoubtedly took its cue from Tilak.

In his writings—*The Orion* and *The Arctic Home in the Vedas*, Tilak attempted to prove that his Aryan ancestors had actually planted the seed of civilization. Though Tilak's thesis did not have strong scholarly foundation, his conclusion certainly generated a sense of psychological superiority among the Hindus. 'In a land where antiquity was generally equated with superiority, few contributions to the inflation to the national ego were of greater significance.'[93] Golwalkar claims a similar superior status by defining the Hindus as *anadi*.

Tilak had developed his thinking in terms of a Hindu nation: 'The common factor in Indian society is the feeling of Hindutva (Hinduness).' When he talked of Indian society, he meant Hindu society. He considered the Hindus of different regions as one, all of them believing in a Hindu *dharma*. He observed, 'there may be different doctrines in the Hindu dharma, but certain principles can be found in common, and because of this alone a sort of feeling that we belong to one religion has remained among people speaking different languages in such a vast country'.[94] And this feeling of oneness among the Hindus was further strengthened by different institutions of the Hindu religion like temples and places of pilgrimage, he analysed.

Tilak believed that religion was a vital element in nationality and argued that India was a self-contained nation during Vedic times. He observed: 'A Hindu of this place is as much as a Hindu as the one from Madras or Bombay . . . the inner sentiments which move you all are the same. The study of *Gita*, *Ramayana* and *Mahabharat* produce the same ideas throughout the country. Are not these -common allegiance to the Vedas, *Gita* and *Ramayana*—our common heritage?'[95] Tilak believed that the divergent sects of India could converge to form a 'mighty Hindu nation' if they would only follow the original principles of the Hindu tradition as set forth in such texts as the *Ramayana* and the *Bhagavadgita*. And this convergence should be the goal of all Hindus.[96] The writings of the RSS very much reflect these ideas.

Mobilizing Hindus: Asserting Communal Identity

Tilak not only recognized *Hindutva*, he made an innovative attempt to mobilize the Hindus on the basis of this common denominator. During the 1893 Bombay communal riots [97] he wrote that though the Hindus did not of their own accord attack others, the Marathas were not cowards to suffer meekly without retaliation.[98] He emphasized that the only way for continued goodwill amongst the two communities was the consciousness of each other's strength.

The 1893 Bombay riots certainly soured Hindu-Muslim relations. Hindu leaders of Poona decided to boycott the Muharram festival, which had been celebrated jointly by both the communities till then. In 1893 a separate Hindu festival started. From being a purely private religious function, the Ganapati celebration became a public festival. Tilak and his followers not only tried to organize Hindu nationalism around Ganapati, they also used it 'as a vehicle for anti-British, anti-Muslim and anti-social reform propaganda'.[99] This festival was also designed to wean away the Hindu lower classes from the ritual of another religion by promising them an equally attractive alternative.

The Ganapati festival was followed by a Shivaji one. Shivaji was another symbolic choice. In developing the myth of Shivaji as protector of orthodox Hinduism—*go-brahman-pratipalak*—the Hindu leaders not only gave it an anti-Muslim bias but also a pro-Brahmin one. In emphasizing the role of Ramdas as guru of Shivaji, 'they implied that any Maratha king needed Brahman advice to succeed'.[100] If the Ganapati festival imparted to Hinduism a congregational character, the Shivaji festival went a step further by deifying the father of the Maratha nation, 'and thereby sanctifying its political history, thus providing Indian nationalism with a precept from its own past'.[101] The RSS has certainly borrowed from Tilak the technique of militant mobilization to assert and consolidate Hindu identity. It also emphasizes, like Tilak, the importance of demonstrating one's strength in a charged communal atmosphere.

Tilak observed that the central thrust of the *Gita* was *karma-yoga* (philosophy of activism) rather than *sanyasa* (renunciation) and *loka-samgraha* (the highest good for all people) was the best end of such action. Therefore, his political activism became a religious activity, nay obligation (*dharma*), for all Hindus. Universal salvation was to be achieved by striving for the highest good for the people (*lokasamgraha*). In effect, Tilak 'made Lokasamgraha the equivalent of Moksadharma in this world (society)'.[102] The RSS subscribes to Tilak's understanding of *karma-yoga* and *lokasamgraha* and the *swayamsevaks* are advised to read the *Gita* regularly.

V.D. Savarkar: Defining Hindutva *and* Hindu Rashtra

Savarkar's definition of Hindu was a decisive step in Hindu communal politics. As discussed earlier in this chapter, he defines 'Hindu' as a person who regards Hindustan as his *pitrubhoomi* (fatherland) and *punya-bhoomi* (holyland). In Savarkar's *Hindutva,* two catch phrases were stressed: *Hindu Rashtra* (Hindu Nation) and *Hindutva* (Hinduness). He clearly distinguished *Hindutva* from Hinduism. To him, *Hindutva* is not a word but a history, not only the spiritual or religious history of the people but a history in full. 'Hinduism is only a derivative, a fraction, a part of Hindutva.'[103] Savarkar was clear: the Hindus have to profess *Hindutva* rather than Hinduism as the first defining characteristics of themselves.

Savarkar listed three criteria for confirming the *Hindutva* or Hinduness of a person—geographical, racial and cultural—'a common *Rashtra,* a common *Jati,* and a common *Sanskriti.* For the first two essentials of *Hindutva—Rashtra* and *Jati*—are clearly denoted and connoted by the word *Pitrubhu;*[104] while the third essential of *Sanskriti* is pre-eminently implied by the word *Punyabhu,* as it is precisely *Sanskriti* including *sanskars,* i.e. rites and rituals, ceremonies and sacraments, that makes a land a Holyland.'[105] In essence, this emphasizes that a Hindu is one who follows a religion which had originated in India. Savarkar's idea of Hinduness, then, explicitly differentiates the Hindu Nation from the orthodox Hindu religion that acknowledges the authority of the Vedas. In other words Sikhs, Buddhists, Jains, etc. were thus in this sense Hindu. At the same time Muslims and Christians were obviously not. This suggested that the primordial loyalties of the Muslims and Christians were not towards India since their religions originated in a foreign land.

Thus this definition carries with it exclusion as well as catholicity. Since in the case of Muslims and Christians, the *pitrubhoomi* is not identical with the *punyabhoomi*, their patriotism is always in suspect. At the same time the monists, monotheists, polytheists, atheists, Sikhs, Arya Samajists, Satanamis are clubbed together under the canopy of *Hindutva* despite their serious differences in beliefs and practices.[106] The logic of Savarkar is that all these sects originated in Bharatvarsha.

In his discourse, no particular Hindu symbol or rite is indispensable. However, these could be taken up in a pragmatic manner and resanctified since *Hindutva* involves a 'common culture', a 'common civilization', and a 'common history' and so Diwali, Rakhi, and Hindu pilgrimages are discovered to be essential 'from a national and racial point of view'. Particularly significant in today's context is Savarkar's discussion of Ram's symbolic significance: 'some of us worship Ram as an incarnation, some admire him as a hero and warrior, all love him as the most illustrious representative monarch of our race'.[107]

Bankim and Aurobindo elevated nationalism to the status of a religion. For them 'Hindu' was basically a religious rather than a cultural or racial unit.[108] Savarkar viewed nationalism and nationality not as a religious or a theological category. For Savarkar the term signified the cultural and the racial rather than the religious. In his discourse, 'religion if it entered at all was important only for its cultural connotations'.[109]

The idea of a Hindu Nation stood in contrast to the idea of a composite, territorially defined political entity. The modern Western idea of a nation, as Savarkar explained, could not be applied to India as it ignores the ancient glory of the Hindu people, the indigenous and numerically dominant population. The people whose culture evolved and developed in greater India—from the Himalayas to the southern seas, by some accounts from Iran to Singapore—this, for Savarkar, was the Hindu Nation.

Though Savarkar did not reject the territorial concept of nationhood, he modified it substantially. He asserted that in the formation of nations—religious, racial, cultural and historical affinities count immensely more than their territorial unity. Savarkar's position was that 'in Hindusthan the Hindus were a nation, and other people were communities and numerically, therefore, minorities'.[110]

RSS CONCEPT OF *HINDU RASHTRA*

Hedgewar agreed on Savarkar's formulation of *Hindutva* and founded the RSS on the conviction that India is a *Hindu Rashtra.*[111] It needs to be kept in mind that the founder of the RSS was a competent organizer rather than a brilliant ideologue. That is why he did not leave many ideological writings on the *Hindu Rashtra.* It was left to his successor M.S. Golwalkar to fill this gap. Golwalkar came out with a clear exposition of the ideology of *Hindu Rashtra* in his controversial work, *We or Our Nationhood Defined* (1939), the Bible of the RSS. This work was later replaced by *Bunch of Thoughts* (1966). Another ideologue, who further enriched the concept of *Hindu Rashtra,* was Deendayal Upadhyaya.[112] The present RSS ideologues like H.V. Seshadri and Dattopant Thengadi, by and large, conform to their predecessors. Therefore, an understanding of the works of Golwalkar and Deendayal and others would be helpful to grasp the ideological content of *Hindu Rashtra.*

M.S. Golwalkar

In *We or Our Nationhood Defined* Golwalkar proposes that 'the idea contained in the word Nation is a compound of five distinct factors fused into one indissoluble whole the famous five "Unities"—Geographical (Country), Racial (Race), Religious (Religion), Cultural (Culture) and Linguistic (Language)'.[113] All these five components are 'indispensable ingredients' for the Nation to exist and that the loss or destruction of any one of these means the end of the Nation as a Nation. Golwalkar gives the examples of England, Germany and Russia[114] in which the five 'unities' exist.

Applying this 'Nation principle' to India, he first takes up geography, race and religion:

> Here is our vast country, Hindusthan, the land of the Hindus, their home country, hereditary territory, a definite geographical unity, fulfilling all that the word should imply in the Nation idea. Living in this Country since prehistoric times, is the ancient Race—the Hindu Race, united together by common traditions, by memories of common glory and disaster, by similar historical, political, social, religious and other experiences, living and evolving, under the same influences, a common culture, a common mother language, common customs, common aspirations. This great Hindu Race professes its illustrious Hindu Religion, the only Religion in the world worth of being so denominated.... Guided by this Religion in all walks of life, individual, social, political, the Race evolved a culture, which despite the degenerating contact with the debased 'civilizations' of the Mussalmans and the Europeans, for the last ten centuries, is still the noblest in the world.[115]

Golwalkar then discusses the two remaining characteristics of a nation: culture and language. He highlights the 'glorious fruits' of Hindu culture—the Hindu artists, scientists, sculptors, politicians, diplomats, soldiers, philosophers and others, past and present. He compares these luminaries with their Western counterparts and attempts to prove the superiority of the former. 'No race is endowed with a nobler and more fruitful culture surely. No race is more fortunate in being given a Religion, which could produce such a culture.'[116] Then he clarifies the misunderstanding regarding language:

> The last component of the nation, language, seems to present some difficulties, for in this country every province has its own language. It appears as if the Linguistic unity is wanting, and there are not one but many 'Nations', separated from each other by linguistic differences. But in fact that is not so. There is but one language, Sanskrit, of which these many 'languages' are mere offshoots, the children of the mother language. Sanskrit, the dialect of the Gods, is common to all from the Himalayas to the ocean in the South, from East to West and all the modern sister languages are through it so much inter-related as to be practically one. . . . There is thus no doubt regarding the existence in us of the fifth component of the Nation idea—language.[117]

He thus asserts: 'We repeat; in Hindusthan, the land of the Hindus, lives and should live the Hindu Nation—satisfying all the five essential requirements of the scientific nation concept of the modern world. Consequently only those movements are truly "National" as aim at re-building, re-vitalizing, and emancipating from its present stupor, the Hindu Nation.'[118]

'We' and 'Others'

Golwalkar begins *We or Our Nationhood Defined* with an attempt to understand the word 'Swaraj'. It originates from 'swa' meaning 'we'. Who are 'we'? The central argument of this work is that 'we' means Hindus and 'Swaraj' means 'Our Kingdom' or India is a *Hindu Rashtra.* To substantiate his thesis, Golwalkar argues that Hindus alone are the original inhabitants of India: 'We—Hindus—have been in undisputed and undisturbed possession of this land for over 8 or even 10 thousand years before the land was invaded by any foreign race' and therefore, this land, 'came to be known as Hindusthan, the land of the Hindus'.[119]

Golwalkar takes Savarkar's *Hindutva* as his starting point. Savarkar clearly identified Muslims and Christians as the other. But he did not provide any solution to the problem. Golwalkar attempts to provide an extreme solution. He makes it clear that as far as the concept of nation is concerned, all those who fall outside the five-fold limits of that idea can have no place in the national life, 'unless they abandon their differences, adopt the religion, culture and language of the nation and completely merge themselves in the National Race. So long, however, as they maintain their racial, religious and cultural differences, they cannot but be only foreigners.'[120] He categorically provides two options to these 'foreigners'—'either to merge themselves in the national race and adopt its culture, or to live at its mercy so long as the national race may allow them to do so. . . . That is the only logical and correct solution.'[121]

Elaborating the parameters of these courses, Golwalkar writes, '. . . the foreign races in Hindusthan must either adopt the Hindu culture and language, must learn to respect and hold in reverence Hindu religion, must entertain no idea but those of the glorification of the Hindu race and culture, i.e. of the Hindu nation and must lose their separate existence to merge in the Hindu race, or may stay in the country, wholly subordinated to the Hindu nation, claiming nothing, deserving no privileges, far less any preferential treatment—not even citizen's rights. There is, at least should be, no other course for them to adopt.'[122] To strengthen his argument, he cites the example of Czechoslovakia, where the unabsorbed minorities hastened the disruption of the state in 1938. He appreciates Hitler's role in resolving this 'five unity' theory.[123]

Extending Boundary of the Other

While the RSS, since its inception, has been treating the Muslims as the primary other of the Hindus, Golwalkar extends the boundary of the other in his *Bunch of Thoughts.* In a section entitled 'The Nation and its Problems', he introduces a Chapter[124]—'Internal Threats' extending the boundary of the other. Christians and Communists are clubbed with Muslims. Despite his mellowness in *Bunch of Thoughts,* his hostility towards the other is very much evident.

Christians

The RSS focused its propaganda and action against the Muslims during the period of India's freedom struggle and partition. The secessionist activities in some of the North-Eastern states with substantial Christian populations and the proselytization activities of Christian missionaries in tribal areas provided an excuse to Golwalkar to elaborate an anti-Christian ideology and add Christians to the list of the other.

'So far as Christians are concerned,' observes Golwalkar, 'to a superficial observer they appear not only harmless but as the very embodiment of compassion and love for humanity! Their speeches abound in words like "service" and "human salvation" as though they are specially deputed by the Almighty to uplift humanity! They run schools and colleges, hospitals and orphanages.'[125] But this is all supposed to be deceptive and 'the real and ulterior motive' behind all this is 'to increase the number of followers of Jesus Christ.[126] Christian missionaries have often declared unequivocally that their one single aim is to make this country a province of the Kingdom of Christ', writes Golwalkar.[127]

Golwalkar alleges that Christian missionaries are only trying to further their political ambition in the name of God and religion, and that their activities are not merely irreligious but also anti-national. Golwalkar further accuses the Christian missionaries of engineering a secessionist movement in Nagaland and spearheading the demand for another separate hill state in Assam and a Jharkhand in Bihar.

The other serious charge of Golwalkar against the missionaries is that they are working 'as the agents of a world strategy': the first stage was to make the Southern peninsula Christian-dominated, with the whole of the Himalayan belt being captured in the second sweep.[128] He also cites the pledge taken in the all-India Conference of Christians 'to establish Christian Empire in Bharat'.[129] The history of Christian missionaries in America, Australia and Africa is deemed atrocious and they have proved to be not 'blood-givers' but 'bloodsuckers', declares Golwalkar. In India also, 'they carried sword and fire' in Goa and other places.[130]

Golwalkar warns: 'So long as the Christians here indulge in such activities as agents of the international movement for the spread of Christianity, and refuse to offer their first loyalty to the land of their birth and behave as the true children of the heritage and culture of their ancestors, they will remain here as hostiles and will have to be treated as such.'[131] Golwalkar created the VHP and deputed trusted *pracharaks* to work in the tribal areas to counter the proselytization activities of the Christian missionaries.

Golwalkar thus accuses that though the Christians, like the Muslims, are born in this country they do not feel that they belong to this land. Moreover they also look to some foreign land as their holy place. Golwalkar argues that it is not merely a case of change of faith, but a change of national identity. Therefore, like Muslims, the Christians are also anti-national as their first loyalty remains not with their *janmabhoomi*, i.e. India, but with their foreign holy land. He advises them to merge themselves in the national life and respect its culture, or face the consequences. However, he refrains himself from applauding Hitler's method of handling the minorities, as he did in 'We or our Nationhood Defined'.

Communists

The inclusion of communists in the list of others appears interesting. Golwalkar's anti-Communist stance was not new. When he was imprisoned after Gandhi's assassination, he offered to Nehru and Patel that the government and the RSS should jointly fight the growing menace of communism. The Sino-Indian war of 1962 provided the immediate context to Golwalkar to club communists with Muslims and Christians. He uses socialism and communism interchangeably and charges communism with being a 'foreign ideology'. . . . 'Socialism is not a product of this soil. It is not in our blood and tradition. . . . It is a thought alien to crores of our people here. . . . Thus we see that it does not possess even the primary qualification to serve as an ideal for our national life.'[132] Being a 'foreign ideology', communism and, by implication, any communist Indian becomes 'anti-national' by definition.

The two other charges levelled against communism are: first, it is 'against religion' and secondly, 'anti-democratic'. Golwalkar observes that communism appears when faith goes and warns that any attempt to uproot the ancient faith of Hindus would bring national disaster. He further writes that 'socialism and democracy are mutually contradictory' as individual freedom is the 'first victim' of socialism.[133]

Golwalkar cites the example of China, which under the garb of socialism, has come to acquire absolute power. Here old nobles, chiefs and industrialists were liquidated and all industries were nationalized.[134] Golwalkar seems to have been concerned over the communist threat to landlordism and the right to property: 'To deny that is to deny all social distinctions and the very basis of good nationhood.'[135]

There are also other implicit exclusions in the scheme of Golwalkar, thus extending the boundary of the other; 'the Hindu appears also as *male, upper-caste* and, . . . possibly *north-Indian* as well'. Golwalkar's vision of *mlechhas*[136] often include not only Muslims, Christians and communists, but also 'the insufficiently "reclaimed" untouchables and tribals, Kabirpanthis and Satnamis, on occasion "women", "south Indians", the people of north-eastern states of India, and indeed any other group or sect that challenges "the social laws" of the Hindus as defined by the upper castes and classes of Hindu society'.[137]

Denationalization: Real Curse

Golwalkar attributes the reasons for the decline and defeat of the powerful Hindu Nation to what he calls 'denationalization'. He states that over the centuries the nation allowed itself to slip into attitudes of laxity and sloth, and the cohesive spirit of the Hindus gradually disappeared. As a result a number of small kingdoms arose, each trying to be independent of the others. The idea of a nation was lost. The dormant national spirit awakened under Shivaji and others, but it was not strong enough to repel the British. The calumniation of Hindu religion started by the Muslims continued under the British. Under British patronage, India's history was distorted and the Hindus were taught that they were never a nation.

Golwalkar argues that this denationalization has reached a point at which the Hindu is almost unable to think for himself and too readily ascribes real wisdom and greatness to alien ideas and achievements. The tradition has developed that everything Western '. . . was gospel of truth; everything Hindu by contrast was naturally false and foolish'.[138] Pointing to westernized Hindus, he states, 'this "Educated" class of Hindus became in truth . . . slaves of the English. . . . They had cut their moorings, lost their footing in the National past, and become de-culturized, denationalized People.'[139] This was also the conclusion of Hedgewar.

Golwalkar's Cultural Nationalism

Golwalkar points out that the climax in the process of denationalization was the propagation by the foreign ruler '. . . of the amazing doctrine that the Nation is composed of all those who, for one reason or the other happen to live at the time in the country'.[140] He completely rejects the idea of territorial nationalism, which, according to him, had deprived us of the positive and inspiring content of our real nationhood. He regrets that in the early days of our 'so-called freedom struggle', the leaders used to propagate falsely that we were a nation in the making, thus ignoring the fact that 'there was a full-fledged ancient nation of the Hindus, and the various communities which were living in the country were here either as guests, the Jews and Parsis, or invaders, the Muslims and Christians'.[141] Savarkar had kept a certain link with territorial nationalism through his concept of *pitrubhoomi*, but had then shifted his emphasis towards Hindu 'sentiments' or 'culture' by arguing that *pitrubhoomi* and *punyabhoomi* could be identical only among the Hindus. But Golwalkar brought out the implications, in all their totalitarian fullness.[142]

Golwalkar prefers to call his theory of nationalism 'cultural nationalism'.[143] The cultural nationalist sees the nation as inherent in the group of people who possess certain common cultural traits. While the territorial nationalist gives priority to the direct relationship of the individual to the territorial defined nation-state, the cultural nationalist gives priority to collective cultural realization through nationalism. Golwalkar argues that the concept of a Hindu Nation is not a mere bundle of political and economic rights. 'It is essentially cultural. Our ancient and sublime cultural values of life form its lifebreath. And it is only an intense rejuvenation of the spirit of our culture that can give us the true vision of our national life, . . .'[144]

Then how does he define culture? Cultural values are not something mysterious and out-worldly as perceived by the Western-influenced elite, writes Golwalkar. He regrets that sometimes culture becomes another name for cheap entertainment; the so-called men of culture associate themselves with 'Miss India' beauty contests.[145] Golwalkar admits that though the term 'culture' defies definition, it has left an indelible stamp on all walks of life. Giving the example of Jawaharlal Nehru's decision to offer the sacred relics of his wife in the bosom of *Gangamata*, Golwalkar states: 'This is *samskar*, the imprint of culture.'[146]

What role does culture play in the national life? For Golwalkar the most fundamental aspect of life is the urge 'to realise God'. As he observes, God is neither *Nirakar* (without form) nor *Nirguna* (without attributes). His conception of God is a living God, who would respond rather than only hear: 'Our People are our God'. Golwalkar contends that though both Ramakrishna and Vivekananda advised to 'Serve Man', their concept of man was too broad to be seen and felt as one solid entity. Therefore, the idea of serving humanity ended in inanity and inaction, argues Golwalkar. To overcome this drawback, he suggests that the Hindu People, rather than the Humanity, should be treated as the *Virat Purusha*, the Almighty manifesting Himself.'[147] Thus, Golwalkar's vision of Godhood is not extended to humanity but limited to the Hindu people alone.

Golwalkar's cultural nationalism is a nationalism exclusively of the Hindus, whereas territorial nationalism is by definition secular in the sense that it includes non-Hindus as well and does not demand their submission to a 'Hindu culture'. Golwalkar's assumption of Hindus as a homogenous cultural community ignores the fact that culture has many dimensions: material, social and ideational. Moreover, Hindus of different regions of the country have shared regional modes of living, traditions and values. A wider all-India identity 'seems to be so far only a fugitive one for any community'.[148] Further, different regions have historically negotiated certain modes of coexistence between communities. Therefore culture has to be understood in a wider framework than Golwalkar's organic model of cultural community.

DEENDAYAL UPADHYAYA

Deendayal Upadhyaya supplements Golwalkar's cultural nationalism with his theory of integral humanism (*Ekatma Manavavad*).[149] This new theory adds some sophistication to the RSS concept of *Hindu Rashtra* and enriches its ideological underpinnings. Upadhyaya avoids the crude, aggressive, and offensive formulations of Golwalkar's *We or Our Nationhood Defined* and offers a sober, logical and refined version of nation and culture.

Though essentially he shares Golwalkar's formulations, Deendayal adds some innovative dimensions to it. Despite Golwalkar's talk of India's spiritual mission in the world, he very rarely went beyond the confines of nation. Upadhyaya, on the contrary, talked of integration of the nation with the rest of humanity, universe and the Almighty (*Paramesthi*). But this integration is more emotional and philosophical rather than political. The central idea of integral humanism is that 'while the humanity and the entire animate and inanimate nature around man are full of almost infinite diversity, it has got a common *Atma* (nearest English rendering is Ethos or Soul). The diversity is superficial. Because of the common *Atma*, all things naturally are cooperative and complementary. This is expressed by the word *Ekatmata*.'[150]

The logic of this philosophy not only intends to obviate the conflict between various entities, but also desires the merger of the smaller into the bigger one in the process of development. Thus the individual merges into the family, the family into nation and nation-state into world state on the basis of integral humanism. In the realm of thought the highest level would be the principle of non-dualism, *Advait*.

Individual and Society

Deendayal writes that the individual is a conglomerate of body, mind, intellect and soul. These are all integrated. Confusion has arisen in the

West because 'they have treated each of the above aspects of human being separately and without any relation to the rest'.[151] But in Bharat, he proceeds, we have placed before ourselves the ideal of the four-fold responsibilities of catering to the needs of body, mind, intellect and soul with a view to achieving the integrated progress of man.[152] *Dharma, artha, kama* and *moksha* are the four kinds of *purushartha* or human efforts. *Purushartha* means, efforts which befit a man. These four efforts are thought to be integrated.

Elaborating the relation of this integrated individual with the society, Deendayal explains that the individual is not limited to a singular 'I' but is also inseparably related to the plural 'We', i.e. the society. He categorically rejects the social contract theory[153] and believes that society is an organic entity with its own self and life. Society too has its body, mind, intellect and soul. It also has four *purusharthas* (objectives) in its life. But since the individual and the society are *ekatma,* there is no conflict in their interests; they are mutually complementary.

He admits that classes and castes do exist in society. But the conflict is not fundamental. He explains that the entire Western-thought stream has presumed a conflict between the individual and society. The main theme round which the conflict is woven is the concept of rights. Indian thinking, on the other hand, lays emphasis on cooperation and synthesis. The emphasis is on duties, not on rights.

Nation and Culture

Deendayal explains that a nation too has a soul. There is a technical name for it—*chiti,* which is analogous to that of an individual. *Chiti* determines the direction in which the nation is to advance culturally. Whatever is in accordance with *chiti* is included in the culture. These things are to be cultivated. Whatever is against *chiti* is discarded as a perversion, undesirable and is to be avoided. He concludes that the soul of Bharat could be properly understood only from a cultural point of view. To him the nation is not a political but a cultural concept. Elaborating further, he writes, the basis of our nationalism is not simply Bharat but Bharat Mata; Bharat would remain just a piece of land if the word Mata is taken away. The first characteristic of a Bharatiya culture is that it looks upon life as an integrated whole. However, to him, 'there can be only one culture in India. The slogans of many cultures can break this country into pieces and destroy it.'[154] This very much reflects Golwalkar's ideas.

Deendayal makes a critique of both Western materialism and Marxism contrasting them with the Hindu/Bharatiya culture. Upadhyaya's integral humanism does not take into consideration the divergent social, political and philosophical cross-currents of Western countries and club them under one monolithic 'West'. Similarly, the diversities of Indian life and thinking are ignored by putting them under a monolithic Bharatiya culture. Though in his discourse he emphasizes more on the term Bharatiya than Hindu, he certainly believes that both are synonymous.

However, Upadhyaya's innovation lies in outlining a new economic blueprint that he believed 'would suit our national genius'. In his opinion both Marxism and capitalism are unsuitable; while the former denies individual freedom, the later encourages profit motives and aggrandizement. He categorically rejects the Nehruvian model of economic development as it does not conform to our cultural and spiritual heritage. He strongly believes that *swadeshi*[155] and decentralization would constitute the essence of an alternate economic system. In this respect, Upadhyaya identifies more with Gandhian economic philosophy.

POST- DEENDAYAL PERIOD

After Golwalkar and Deendayal no single ideologue dominated the *Sangh Parivar.* The ideological writings of Deoras, Thengadi, Seshadri and others conformed broadly to the concept of nation enunciated by the former ideologues. However, they have, in their limited capacity, tried to enrich the concept and fill in the gaps. Within the broad framework, these ideologues have experimented with certain innovations to keep the ideology of *Hindu Rashtra* in tune with the present requirement. For instance, in the changed socio-political context, some *Hindutva* writers have made Nehruvianism their main target. Though Golwalkar's cultural nationalism has always remained an antithesis of Nehru's concept of India, he never launched a frontal attack on Nehru as such. As the Nehruvian framework started withering, the RSS soon intensified its anti-Nehru tirade.

The present ideologues reiterated Golwalkar's position that Nehru wrongly propounded that all those who happen to reside on the soil of India together form a nation. Nehru is accused of turning the nation into a mere geographical entity and thus negating the cardinal principle of nationhood, viz. emotional unity. He is further criticized for not treating Hindus as a nation, but as a mere religious community, just like Muslims and Christians, and wrongly advocating that all these communities constitute India. *Hindutva* writers find that this Nehruvian framework led to certain serious distortions. First, the Hindus being the largest community, were conceived as potentially dangerous to the other communities. Secondly, since the Hindus posed a potential threat to the other communities, the more they could be weakened the better it would be for the health of the nation. Thirdly, the good of the other communities was also the national good because their participation constituted the crucial element of our nationhood. Fourthly, the idea of regarding alien cultures also as our own thus gained currency through the convenient slogan of *sarva dharma sama bhava.* Fifthly, since the distinctiveness of the largest community was Sanatana Dharma, a cult of denigrating the Sanatana Dharma was promoted. Finally, the vision of Indian history was distorted: we were asked to regard India's history as one of synthesis.[156]

Challenging Secularism

Secularism constitutes one of the major pillars of the Nehruvian framework. Interestingly, instead of disowning and dismissing the secularism of the Indian constitution, the RSS ideologues have given it a new nomenclature and meaning: positive secularism. The term 'secularism' as used in the Indian context has two contradictory meanings: one is *dharmanirapekshata* and the other is *sarva dharma sama bhava.*[157] While the former means indifference to religion and upholds the separation of religion and state, the later advocates an equal respect for all religions based on the principle of accommodation. Thus the debate on secularism oscillates between the two extremes of *separating* religion from politics and *accommodating* different religions through the intervention and assumed neutrality of the state.[158] Yet there is an implicit connection between the two strands despite being juxtaposed against each other.

At one extreme, there are some secularists who advocate the need to keep a distance from religious matters, both at personal and political levels. One dominant ideological trend among them represents an unadulterated secularism, which completely dismisses the complexities of religion as obscurantist or reduces it to the level of superstition, a mere remnant of pre-modern states of oppression.[159] At the other extreme, there are individuals and groups, who, despite being secular in their everyday lives, may be inclined to a certain idea of God or divinity. Though they draw a line between religion and politics, myth and history, they still believe that this dichotomy cannot be assumed on purely rationalist grounds. Neither is the scientific temper of the enlightenment to be summarily dismissed, but it need not be fetishised either.[160]

While the former category ignores the cultural matrix, the second one rejoices in it. But there is an imminent danger when the second category comes under the control of orthodox sentiments and starts imagining that a new secular order can be built on the foundations of religion-as-faith. Believers, one should acknowledge, are capable of being 'fundamentalized' though not every believer is a fundamentalist.[161]

RSS Critique of 'Pseudo-secularism'

The RSS and other Hindu nationalists have been questioning the genuineness of secularism pursued since independence. They basically share three important objections raised by other critics with regard to the doctrine of secularism and to the State guided by it. First, that the concept is alien to Indian culture by virtue of its profoundly Christian/Western character.[162] Secondly, the concept is absolutely insensitive to religious people. By propagating religion as a matter of private preference, it breaks the link between religion and community and deprives people of their sense of identity.[163] Thirdly, though a secular state claims to be neutral, in reality it favours either the non-believer or the minority community.[164]

The RSS argues that the secular state in India is far from neutral. In its view, the state, through various legislations, has hindered the growth of a Hindu identity. While the Hindus have been compelled to view themselves primarily as non-religious individuals, the Muslims are often encouraged to conceive their identity purely in terms of their religion. While the state officially professes neutrality, it is both anti-religious and pro-Muslim. Some *Sangh Parivar* members like the VHP even claim that the Indian state is anti-Hindu.[165]

Interestingly, the RSS does not attack the term 'secular'.[166] It has rather added the concept of 'positive secularism' to the existing ideological debate on secularism and branded all other practitioners of secularism as 'pseudo-secularists',[167] conceding thereby its approval of the ideal as such of the secular state.[168] But its secularism has a distinct feature: it is against any type of 'minority appeasement', particularly Muslim appeasement.

Muslims are a pampered lot in India and successive governments have pursued the policy of minority appeasement in the name of secularism, charges the RSS. But recent statistics[169] on the socio-economic index of the 140 million Muslims who constitute 14 per cent of India's population does not substantiate this charge. Obviously, in its campaign against the Muslims, the RSS ignores these statistical data conveniently. Rather it prefers to focus on issues that would arouse passion among Hindus. First, Muslims are traitors because they forced the partition of India. Since an Islamic Pakistan has been created why do Muslims continue to live in India? India is only meant for Hindus. Secondly, Muslims living in India are not loyal to this country and harbour pro-Pakistan sentiments. Muslims in India are willing pawns in the Pakistani strategy of destabilization in Kashmir. Thirdly, Muslims put their religion above nation, and the Koran above the Constitution. Fourthly, Muslims are inherently intolerant and obscurantist and do not allow even reasonable criticism of Islam. Fifthly, Muslims can have four wives while the Hindus can have only one. Moreover, *mullahs* encourage Muslims not to accept family planning and hence their population grows faster.[170] There is an imminent danger of Hindus being swamped by them very soon. Sixthly, the large scale flow of Muslim Bangladeshi illegal immigrants is jeopardizing the security of India and putting a great strain on its economy, as well as upsetting the demographic balance. Finally, India is surrounded by hostile Muslim nations, including Pakistan, Bangladesh, Malaysia, Indonesia, Afghanistan, the Middle Eastern and Gulf States, and the new Muslim States which have emerged after the breakdown of the Soviet Union. The supposed extra-territorial loyalty of Indian Muslims adds to the threat as their presence amounts to having an enemy within.

How far are these charges genuine? Are they really based on purely 'half-truths, outright lies and paranoid fantasies'?[171] If so, then how is the RSS able to convince many Hindus of these anti-Muslim charges? One possible explanation lies in the construction of a Muslim stereotype. For example, Sadhavi Rithambara, the firebrand propounder of *Hindutva* during the Ayodhya campaign of the *Sangh Parivar* focuses on a simplified Hindu-Muslim dichotomy: 'The Hindu writes from left to right, the Muslim from right to left. The Hindus prays to the rising sun, the Muslim faces the setting sun when praying. If the Hindu eats with the right hand, the Muslim with the left. If the Hindu calls India "Mother", she becomes a witch for the Muslim. The Hindu worships the cow, the Muslim attains paradise by eating beef. The Hindu keeps a mustache, the Muslims always shaves the upper lip

Whatever the Hindu does, it is the Muslim's religion to do the opposite.'[172] No doubt, stereotyping has exaggerated the uniformity among the Muslims and made a sharp distinction between the Muslims and the Hindus. But that does not fully explain the reason why the anti-Muslim pogrom of the RSS receives such a huge response from the Hindus. The suspicion of Muslim loyalty to the Indian state has two main sources.[173] First, there has been a historical tendency among upper-class Muslims (or those aspiring to a higher status in the community) to stress or invent Persian, Arab, or Turkish ancestry rather than rest content with their more humble Indian origins. The tendency, more pronounced among Muslim fundamentalists, is to see themselves as superior beings from outside India who share Indian history only as the country's erstwhile rulers. Secondly, the specific Muslim history, the community's conservative spokesmen would like to construct and exalt is the one shared with Muslims of the Middle East, especially the sacred history of early Islam and of the Dar al-Islam between the seventh and fifteenth centuries, when Islamic civilization was at its zenith and Muslims had conquered half the world.

Features of 'Positive Secularism'

The RSS calls its own brand of secularism as true or 'positive secularism'. What are its salient features? First, the RSS consistently clarifies that the *Hindu Rashtra* does not advocate a theocratic state. This could be believed, as the RSS is aware of its impracticability. Therefore it would rather prefer to have a state in which Hindus would enjoy a hegemonic role. It is very unlikely that in a *Hindu Rashtra* the laws of the state would conform to this or that *samhit.*[174] In this matter the position of the RSS can be said to have undergone a considerable shift in position from that of the Hindu Mahasabha at the time of the debate over the Hindu Code Bill (1955). Its position is also quite different from that of most contemporary Islamic fundamentalist movements, which explicitly reject the theoretical separation of state and religion as Western and un-Islamic.

The second corollary feature of this secularism is the usefulness of the modern state in the establishment of a uniform and homogenized 'national culture'. The majoritarianism of the Hindu Right 'is perfectly at peace with the institutions and procedures of the Western or modern State'.[175] In fact the RSS understands that an interventionist modernizing State could be of immense help in obliterating the presence of religious or ethnic particularisms from the domains of law or public life and to provide a homogenized content to the notion of citizenship. In this role, the Hindu Right in fact seeks to project itself as a principled modernist critic of Islamic or Sikh fundamentalism and to accuse the 'pseudo-secularists' of preaching tolerance for religious obscurantism and bigotry.[176]

As secularism presupposes tolerance,[177] it becomes vital to see what sort of tolerance this secularism stands for. The RSS harps on the point that the Hindu State cannot but be secular as tolerance is his inherent character. It even argues that the word 'tolerance' does not correctly represent the Hindu way of life. 'The word is very inadequate. You can hate a man but still tolerate him. But here there is no hatred. You recognize the right of every person to have his own belief. He is recognized and respected—religion is no barrier for mutual love and understanding. This is the Hindu attitude.'[178] On the other hand, there are innumerable examples to show that the RSS preaches hatred. Therefore, its assurance of respect or accommodation for other religions could hardly be trusted. Moreover, by claiming the superiority of Hinduism with regard to religious tolerance, the RSS further justifies that other religions are not worthy of respect.

The positive secularism of the RSS also swears by *sarva dharma sama bhava*. However, this interpretation is quite unlike the interpretation provided by Indian secularism. For the RSS, equal respect for all religions implies that all religions must be treated equally, that is, treated the same in law. Accordingly, any law or policies that provide special treatment for minorities are opposed, as being 'pseudo-secular' and appeasing the minorities. Article 30 of the Constitution, which allows minorities to run their own educational institutions, and Article 370 which grants special status to Jammu & Kashmir, are thus opposed as these provisions are nothing but minority appeasement rather than secularism. In consonance with its interpretation of equal treatment it demands a Uniform Civil Code which would treat all religious communities in the same manner. Therefore, it criticizes the notion of secularism practiced in India as it grants special treatment to the minorities. Deoras declared that 'if secularism means treating all religions on an equal footing, proselytization and secularism can't go together'.[179] Behind the emphasis of the RSS on equal treatment one notices a thinly veiled attack on the legitimacy of minority rights. Their norm is a Hindu norm—indeed it is a Hindu religious norm. In their vision, the role of the State in religion is not one of neutrality at all, but of fostering the Hindu nation.[180]

It would be proper to ask whether the RSS brand of secularism could qualify to be named as 'true' or 'genuine' or 'positive'? The 'positive' aspect of its secularism is very much suspect as it emphasizes denial rather than the granting of rights to minorities. Hence, this secularism is quite negative from the point of view of the minorities. But the concern of the RSS is not the minorities, but the Hindus. Therefore, the RSS claim of 'positive secularism' seems to be justified in the sense that Hindus would enjoy preponderance over the minorities under the pretext of equal treatment.

Reasserting Hindu Rashtra *and* Hindutva

The present ideological writings of the RSS, besides denouncing the Nehruvian concept of a nation, also attempt to convince about the positive features of the *Hindu Rashtra* and *Hindutva*. 'We Hindus are a nation'—this is the present thrust of all ideological writings of the RSS.[181] These writings passionately plead that the Hindus are just not a religious community, but a nation; *Hindu Rashtra* is not a political concept. Nation (*Rashtra*) and State (*Rajya*) are two different concepts and should not be mixed up. State is purely a political concept. Nation (*Rashtra*) is eternal while the State is transitory. If the State is the body, the nation is its soul (*atma*). In Hindu philosophy the *atma* is eternal and only the bodies and their forms are changed. By equating the *rashtra* with the Hindu concept of *atma*, the ideologues of the RSS plead that the Hindu Nation has been existing since time immemorial and it shall continue to exist forever.

Thus, the RSS strongly denies that the concept of *Hindu Rashtra* is not religious as it does not aim to establish a theocratic or a religious Hindu State. To substantiate this point, the RSS leaders speak of Hindu catholicity by quoting from '*Asya Vamasya*' hymn of the *Rig Veda* quite frequently: *Ekam sad viprah bahudha vadanti* (Truth is one, the wise call it by many names) and *Vasudhaiva Kutumbakam* (The Cosmos is one family). On the basis of this they claim Hinduism as a universalistic and tolerant religious philosophy. However, these words have drifted free of their textual moorings; the particular contexts of these phrases are rarely mentioned.[182]

For the RSS, *Hindu Rashtra* is a cultural and emotional concept, eternally asserting itself. It makes clear that national sentiment is supreme, and all other sentiments, whether religious or sectional, should remain subservient to it. The RSS emphasizes that Hindu culture is the national culture, Hindu society is national society, Hindu art is national art, Hindu literature is national literature and Hindu history is national history. People belonging to various religions in this country are all Hindus by culture and are nationals of this *Hindu Rashtra*. As there are Shaivas, Vaishnavas, Jains, Buddhists and Sikhs amongst Hindus, there can be Christians and Muslims also, argue RSS ideologues.[183] In other words, the nationals of this nation may have different religious faiths, but they all have to subscribe to *Hindutva* or Hinduness, which is the cultural ethos of the nation.[184] Therefore, in today's parlance, the RSS adopts a broader conception of 'Hindu', which means: 'any person born in this country, irrespective of his or her religion', with the *proviso* that he or she loves it or respects its cultural tradition.[185] Logically, the national heroes of *Hindu Rashtra* like Ram and Krishna should be revered by all the nationals irrespective of their religious faiths.

Thus, the RSS has been attempting to construct a *Hindu Rashtra* by providing an alternate discourse on community, history and the nation. For the RSS, all the Hindus share a common historical and cultural experience, and therefore, constitute a monolithic Hindu identity. By projecting the Muslim other as the principal enemy of the Hindus, and recently, focusing on the Christians, it further tries to consolidate this identity. The next chapter will analyse how the RSS makes a concerted effort to homogenize Hindus.

NOTES AND REFERENCES

1. See Robert A. Nisbet, *Community and Power* (Oxford: Oxford University Press, 1968), p. 7; Sudhir Kakar, *The Inner World: A Psychoanalytic Study of Childhood and Society in India* (Delhi: Oxford University Press, 1981), Chap. VI.
2. The community is emerging in India's political culture as a political actor, which seeks to reshape not so much face-to-face intimate relations of the private sphere, but control over law and history in the predominantly public sphere of life. See Veena Das, *Critical Events: An Anthropological Perspective on Contemporary India* (Delhi: Oxford University Press, 1995).
3. Social historians offer two quite different definitions of community: localized and relational, or broad-based and inclusive. However, these two notions are not necessarily contradictory just because they represent different forms, or different historical moments and configurations. For a discussion on the 'relational' and 'ideological' definitions of community, see Sandria B. Freitag, *Collective Action and Community: Public Arenas and the Emergence of Communalism in North India* (Delhi: Oxford University Press, 1990), Introduction to Part-I and Part-II. Freitag concludes that collective action, whether ceremonial or violent, serves to define community symbolically. Ibid., p. 280.

4. A.P. Cohen, *The Symbolic Construction of Community* (London: Ellis Horwood Limited, 1985). For a discussion on the rightist conception of community, see George L. Mosse, 'Nationalism, Fascism and the Radical Right', in Eugene Kamenka, ed., *Community as a Social Ideal* (London: Edward Arnold, 1982), pp. 27-42, and for a socialist perspective of community, see Eugene Kamenka, 'Community and the Socialist Ideal', ibid., pp. 3-26.
5. See Ghanshyam Shah, 'Identity, Communal Consciousness and Politics', *Economic and Political Weekly*, XXIX (19), 7 May 1994, pp. 1133-40.
6. A detailed argument on the fuzzy character of communities can be found in Sudipta Kaviraj, 'The Imaginary Institution of India', in Partha Chatterjee and Gyanendra Pandey, eds., *Subaltern Studies VII: Writings on South Asian History and Society* (Delhi: Oxford University Press, 1993), pp. 1-39. Oberoi and Pandey also talk of 'fuzzy' identities. See Harjot Oberoi, *The Construction of Religious Boundaries: Culture, Identity and Diversity in Sikh Tradition* (Delhi: Oxford University Press, 1994); Gyanendra Pandey, *The Construction of Communalism in Colonial North India* (Delhi: Oxford University Press, 1990).
7. Dipankar Gupta, *The Context of Ethnicity: Sikh Identity in a Comparative Perspective* (Delhi: Oxford University Press, 1996), p. 141.
8. See Sudhir Kakar, *The Colours of Violence* (Delhi: Viking, 1995), p. 247.
9. Veena Das recognizes that violence plays an important role in defining the community. See Veena Das, *Critical Events*, op. cit., p. 51.
10. For an 'instrumentalist' view of identity, see Paul Brass, *Ethnicity and Nationalism* (Delhi: Sage Publications, 1991); Asghar Ali Engineer, ed., *Communal Riots in Post-Independence India* (Delhi: Sangam Books, 1985), pp. 238-71.
11. Sudhir Kakar, *The Colours of Violence*, op. cit., Chap. Six.
12. It derives from primarily geographical terms, Hindus and *al-Hind*, used in the Achaemenid inscriptions of ancient Persia and later by Arab writers. See Romila Thapar, 'Communalism and the Historical Legacy: Some Facets', in K.N. Panikkar, ed., *Communalism in India: History, Politics and Culture* (Delhi: Manohar, 1991), p. 23. Also see Heinrich von Stietencron, 'Hinduism: On the Proper Use of a Deceptive Term', in Gunther-D. Sontheimer and Hermann Kulke, eds., *Hinduism Reconsidered* (Delhi: Manohar, 1989), pp. 11-12.
13. W.C. Smith, *The Meaning and End of Religion: A New Approach to the Religious Traditions of Mankind* (New York: Macmillan, 1962).
14. Romila Thapar, 'Imagined Religious Communities? Ancient History and the Modern Search for a Hindu Identity', *Modern Asian Studies*, 23 (2), 1989, p. 223.
15. Ibid.
16. For several centuries, the people here 'did not identify themselves in terms of "Hinduism" at all. Either a given *varna* or *jati* determined their identity or (and at times in addition to it) it was determined by the area or the region they come from.' See G.P. Deshpande, 'The Plural Tradition', *Seminar*, 365, January 1990, p. 24.
17. See Robert E. Frykenberg, 'The Emergence of Modern "Hinduism" as a Concept

and as an Institution: A Reappraisal With Special Reference to South India', in Gunther-D. Sontheimer and Hermann Kulke, eds., *Hinduism Reconsidered*, op. cit., pp. 29-49.

18. Ibid., p. 29.
19. Wilhelm Halbfass, *Tradition and Reflection: Explorations in Indian Thought* (Albany: State University of New York Press, 1991), p. 15.
20. Ibid.
21. See Dharma Kumar, 'Left Secularists and Communalism', *Economic and Political Weekly*, XXIX (28), 9 July 1994, p. 1805. She brings out a critique of 'left secular' historians in this article.
22. Bhai Paramananda, *Hindu Sangathan* (Lahore: The Hindu Yuvak Sabha, 1936), p. 9.
23. V.D. Savarkar, *Who is A Hindu? Hindutva* (Poona: S.P. Gokhale, 1949). Savarkar more likely borrowed it from one of a number of writers and thinkers of nineteenth century Bengal who had used this definition in roughly the same form. See Ashis Nandy et al., *Creating a Nationality: The Ramjanmabhoomi Movement and Fear of the Self* (Delhi: Oxford University Press, 1995, p. 67).
24. M.S. Golwalkar, *Bunch of Thoughts* [1966] (Bangalore: Jagarana Prakashana, 1980), p. 80. Golwalkar avoided the use of Savarkar's definition of 'Hindu' and 'Hindutva'.
25. Ibid., p. 73.
26. Ibid.
27. Ibid. He dismisses the view that the term 'Hindu' is of recent origin: 'Others learnt to denote us by it only later on.' Ibid., p. 129.
28. Besides this Golwalkar perhaps thought that its use could favour Arya Samajists, which might create resentment among other Hindu sects, particularly the Sanatanis.
29. M.S. Golwalkar, *Bunch of Thoughts*, op. cit., p. 129.
30. Golwalkar used the term society rather than community. The RSS also frequently talks of Hindu *Samaj* (society) thereby equating community with society.
31. Baba Saheb Apte, 'A True History of India is Yet to be Written', *Organiser*, XXI (12), 29 October 1967, pp. 15-16.
32. The RSS has set up *Bharatiya Itihas Sankalan Yojana Samiti* to encourage 'new researches' and propagate an alternate history. Making an humble start, this body has managed now to get the support of a respectable number of historians.
33. The RSS endorses the views of R.C. Majumdar, who was a great protagonist of Greater India. However, Majumdar ignores the indigenous cultures of South-East Asia and highlights Hinduization.
34. Baba Saheb Apte, 'A True History of India is Yet to be Written', op. cit.
35. See Gyanendra Pandey, 'The Appeal of Hindu History', in Vasudha Dalmia and H. von Stietencron, eds., *Representing Hinduism: The Construction of Religious Traditions and National Identity* (New Delhi: Sage Publications, 1995), pp. 369-88.

36. M.S. Golwalkar, *Bunch of Thoughts*, op. cit., p. 181.
37. Many writings have come up these years by the *Hindutva* historians supporting this thesis. See, K.D. Sethna, *The Problem of Aryan Origins: From an Indian Point of View* (Delhi: Voice of India, 1992); Shrikant G. Talageri, *Aryan Invasion Theory: A Reappraisal* (Delhi: Voice of India, 1993); Navaratna S. Rajaram, *Aryan Invasion of India: The Myth and the Truth* (Delhi: Voice of India, 1993); David Frawley, *The Myth of the Aryan Invasion of India* (Delhi: Voice of India, 1995).
38. Romila Thapar, 'Communalism and the Writing of Ancient Indian History', in *Selected Writings on Communalism* (Delhi: People's Publishing House, 1994), pp. 1-18.
39. Rasheeduddin Khan, 'Prejudice, Myth and History', *Mainstream*, 31 (41), 21 August 1993, p. 12.
40. Gargi Chakravarty, 'BJP-RSS and Distortion of History: Myths and Realities of History', in *Selected Writings on Communalism*, op. cit., p. 163.
41. R.S. Sharma, *Communal History and Ram's Ayodhya* (Delhi: People's Publishing House, 1990), p. 7. Sharma points out that while Sastri and Jayaswal stresses the alien character of the Sakas, K. Gopalachari praises the Satavahanas and others for opposing Sakas as they were foreigners.
42. M.S. Golwalkar, *We or Our Nationhood Defined* (Nagpur: Bharat Publications, 1939, with a foreword by Loknayak M.S. Aney), p. 9.
43. Sitaram Yechuri, *What is Hindu Rashtra?: On Golwalkar's Fascistic Ideology and the Saffron Brigade's Practice* (Madras: Frontline Publication, 1993), p. 9.
44. For a fine discussion on philosophical aspects of Hindu tolerance, see Arvind Sharma, *Hinduism of Our Times* (Delhi: Oxford University Press, 1997), Chap. 4.
45. There is even evidence of violent confrontations between the Shaivas and the Vaishnavas in the later medieval period, mainly over matters like possession of certain religious places or of resources. At a later period the Marathas of Nagpur invaded Bengal and massacred the Hindu population, especially women, in order to snatch away their ornaments.
46. Arvind Sharma, *Hinduism of Our Times*, op. cit., p. 74.
47. R.S. Sharma describes Majumdar as 'a vocal exponent of the communalist approach to history'. Hindu historiography is greatly inspired by him. See R.S. Sharma, *Communal History and Ram's Ayodhya*, op. cit., p. 8.
48. Koenraad Elst, *Negationism in India: Concealing the Record of India* (Delhi: Voice of India, 1992), p. 136. Also see B.N. Jog, *Threat of Islam: Indian Dimensions* (Bombay: Unnati Prakashan, 1994).
49. See Romila Thapar, 'Imagined Religious Communities? . . .' , op. cit., p. 224.
50. Ibid.
51. Girilal Jain, *The Hindu Phenomenon* (Delhi: UBS Publishers' Distributors Ltd., 1994), p. 5.
52. For an exhaustive list of examples of cultural synthesis, see Rasheeduddin Khan,

Bewildered India: Identity, Pluralism, Discord (Delhi: Har Anand Publications, 1994), introduction.

53. In the *shakhas* stories are told about Aurangzeb's cruelty and of Shivaji's bravery. However, of late, Babur has occupied the centrestage in the anti-Muslim campaign.
54. For a different dimension of Aurangzeb, see M. Athar Ali, *The Mughal Nobility Under Aurangzeb* (Bombay: Asia Publishing House, 1968); B.N. Pandey, *Islam and Indian Culture* (Patna: Khuda Bakhsh Oriental Public Library, 19-21 December 1985). Even Jadunath Sarkar, one of the favourites of RSS historians, depicts Aurangzeb as more complex and human than a bigot.
55. See R.S. Sharma et al., *Ramjanmabhumi-Baburi Masjid: A Historians' Report to the Nation* (Delhi: People's Publishing House, 1991).
56. Gyanendra Pandey, 'Modes of History Writing: New Hindu History of Ayodhya', *Economic and Political Weekly*, XXIX (25), 18 June 1994, p. 1523.
57. Neeladri Bhattacharya, 'Myth, History and the Politics of Ramjanmabhumi', in S. Gopal, ed., *Anatomy of Confrontation: The Babri Masjid-Ramjanmabhumi Dispute* (Delhi: Viking, 1991), p. 122.
58. Sheldon Pollock, 'Ramayana and Political Imagination in India', *The Journal of Asian Studies*, 52 (2), May 1993, p. 264.
59. This overt political use of historiography would undermine its dignity. In parrying event against event what is forgotten is that one has already ceded in principle to the opponent's logic of historical presentation. See Dipankar Gupta, *The Context of Ethnicity*, op. cit., p. 142.
60. Dharma Kumar, 'Left Secularists and Communalism', op. cit.
61. See Richard Eaton, *The Rise of Islam and the Bengal Frontier: 1204-1760* (Berkeley: University of California Press, 1993), Chap. 5, 'Mass Conversion to Islam: Theories and Protagonists', pp. 113-36.
62. Supporting this point, Dharma Kumar observes: 'The Mughals may have given grants to temples and sadhus, but they gave much more to mosques and "pirs". And similarly, each Hindu ruler gave special support to his sect.' See Dharma Kumar, 'Left Secularists and Communalism', op. cit., p. 1806.
63. Ibid., p. 1807.
64. Ibid., p. 1806.
65. See C.A. Bayly, 'The Pre-History of "Communalism"? Religious Conflict in India, 1700-1860', *Modern Asian Studies*, 19 (2), 1985, pp. 177-203. Bayly's arguments find support from other scholars. See Rosalind O'Hanlon, 'Historical Approaches to Communalism: Perspectives from Western India', in Peter Robb, ed., *Society and Ideology* (Delhi: Oxford University Press, 1992), pp. 247-66.
66. Dipankar Gupta, *The Context of Ethnicity*, op. cit., p. 144.
67. Sheldon Pollock, 'Ramayana and Political Imagination in India', op. cit., pp. 261-97.
68. Gyanendra Pandey, *The Construction of Communalism in Colonial North India* (Delhi: Oxford University Press, 1990), p. 115.

69. Robert Eric Frykenberg, 'Hindu Fundamentalism and the Structural Stability of India', in Martin E. Marty and R. Scott Appleby, eds., *Fundamentalisms and the State: Remaking Polities, Economies and Militance*, Vol. 3 (Chicago: University of Chicago Press, 1993), pp. 233-55.
70. Ibid.
71. Kenneth W. Jones, 'Politicized Hinduism: The Ideology and Program of the Hindu Mahasabha', in Robert D. Baird, ed., *Religion in Modern India* (Delhi: Manohar, 1989), p. 240.
72. Kenneth W. Jones, 'Religious Identity and the Indian Census', in N.G. Barrier, ed., *The Census of British India: New Perspective* (Delhi: Manohar, 1981), pp. 73-101. The Census has become a handy instrument of the RSS. It issues warnings to the Hindus whenever there is a decline of their numbers and increase of non-Hindus.
73. For a detailed discussion on the topic, see David Kopf, *British Orientalism and the Bengal Renaissance* (Berkeley: University of California Press, 1969); Ronald Inden, 'Orientalist Constructions of India', *Modern Asian Studies*, 20 (3), 1986, pp. 401-46.
74. Peter van der Veer, *Religious Nationalism: Hindus and Muslims in India* (Delhi: Oxford University Press, 1996), p. 20.
75. Robert E. Frykenberg, 'Hindu Fundamentalism and the Structural Stability of India', op. cit., p. 239.
76. K. Suryanarayana Rao, *Hindu Rashtra: It is not a mere Slogan but the Vibrant Reality* (Madras: Vigil, 1990), p. 1.
77. The most comprehensive source on the Brahmo Samaj is David Kopf, *The Brahmo Samaj and the Shaping of the Modern Indian Mind* (Princeton: Princeton University Press, 1979).
78. For Dayananda's life and ideas, see J.T.F. Jordens, *Dayananda Saraswati: His Life and Ideas* (Delhi: Oxford University Press, 1981).
79. Christophe Jaffrelot, 'Hindu Nationalism: Strategic Syncretism in Ideology Building', *Economic and Political Weekly*, XXVIII (12-13), 20-7 March 1993, p. 517.
80. Romila Thapar, 'Syndicated Moksha', *Seminar*, 313, September 1985, p. 18.
81. Christophe Jaffrelot, 'Hindu Nationalism: Strategic Syncretism in Ideology Building', op. cit., p. 518.
82. For a wider discussion, see Anand A. Yang, 'Sacred Symbol and Sacred Space in Rural India: Community Mobilization in the "Anti-Cow Killing" Riots of 1893', *Comparative Studies in Society and History*, 22 (4), 1980, pp. 576-96; Sandria B. Frietag, 'Sacred Symbol as Mobilizing Ideology: The North Indian Search for a "Hindu" Community', ibid., pp. 597-625.
83. The RSS took up some of the issues, which the Arya Samaj pursued. Initially, it expanded in the north and the north-west with the support of Arya Samajists. For a comparative discussion on the ideas and organization of the RSS and the Arya Samaj, see Daniel Gold, 'Organized Hinduisms: From Vedic Truth to Hindu Nation', in Martin E. Marty and R. Scott Appleby, eds., *Fundamentalisms Observed*, Vol.1 (Chicago: University of Chicago Press, 1991), pp. 531-93.

84. Kenneth W. Jones, *Arya Dharm: Hindu Consciousness in Nineteenth Century Punjab* (Delhi: Manohar, 1976), p. 30.
85. Javed Alam, 'Composite Culture and Communal Consciousness: The Ittehadul Muslimeen in Hyderabad', in Vasudha Dalmia and H. von Stietencron, eds., *Representing Hinduism*, op. cit., p. 342.
86. The RSS fully subscribes to this concept of manliness with its stress on regular physical exercise. It also conducts sham fights to test as well as instill courage among the *swayamsevaks*. Vivekananda's celibacy is also cited as ideal to the *bal* and *kishore swayamsevaks*. An ideal *pracharak* is supposed to maintain strict celibacy. However, beef is strictly prohibited and virtues of vegetarianism are propagated.
87. See Wilhelm Halbfass, 'Practical Vedanta', in Vasudha Dalmia and H. von Stietencron, eds., *Representing Hinduism*, op. cit., p. 213.
88. To the RSS, *Bande Mataram* rather than *Jana Gana Mana* should have been adopted as the national anthem as the former is more authentic. The hymn is sung by the *Sangh Parivar* in its entirety as it symbolizes the undivided India of the pre-Partition days. The BJP government in Delhi made the song compulsory in state-run schools.
89. Tapan Raychaudhury, *Europe Reconsidered: Perceptions of the West in Nineteenth Century Bengal* (Delhi: Oxford University Press, 1988), pp. 127-8.
90. Amales Tripathi, *The Extremist Challenge: India between 1890 and 1910* (Calcutta: Orient Longman, 1967), p. 17.
91. Tanika Sarkar, 'Imagining a Hindu Nation: Hindu and Muslim in Bankimchandra's Later Writings', *Economic and Political Weekly*, XXIX (39), 24 September 1994, p. 2553.
92. Quoted by Amartya Sen, 'Secularism and Its Discontents', in Kaushik Basu and Sanjay Subrahmanyam, eds., *Unravelling the Nation: Sectarian Conflict and India's Secular Identity* (Delhi: Penguin Books, 1996), p. 33 fn.
93. For a detailed discussion on Tilak's arguments, see Stanley Wolpert, *Tilak and Gokhale: Revolution and Reform in the Making of Modern India* (Berkeley: University of California Press, 1962), pp. 64-5.
94. Quoted by Stanley Wolpert, ibid., pp. 135-6.
95. Ibid., pp. 178-9.
96. See K.P. Karunakaran, *Continuity and Change in Indian Politics* (Delhi: People's Publishing House, 1964), p. 96.
97. While Governor Harris ascribed the cause of the riot to excessive preaching by cow-preservation societies, Tilak ascribed it to the universal belief amongst Muslims that the government was afraid of them and therefore would not side with the Hindus in the matter of such riots.
98. Quoted by D.P. Karmarkar, *Bal Gangadhar Tilak: A Study* (Bombay: Popular Book Depot, 1956), p. 61. The RSS inherited this legacy of Tilak.
99. Gail Omvedt, *Cultural Revolt in a Colonial Society: The Non-Brahman Movement in Western India 1873-1930* (Bombay: Scientific Socialist Education Trust, 1976), p. 104.

100. Ibid.
101. Stanley Wolpert, *Tilak and Gokhale*, op. cit., p. 80.
102. Mark J. Harvey, 'The Secular as Sacred? The Religio-Political Rationalization of B.G. Tilak', *Modern Asian Studies*, 20 (2), 1986, p. 331.
103. V.D. Savarkar, *Hindutva*, op. cit., p. 3.
104. The imagery of *Pitrubhu*, rather than common usage of *Matrubhumi*, was adopted from European nationalism.
105. V.D. Savakar, *Hindutva*, op. cit., p. 95.
106. Savarkar's *Hindutva* is seen as a Brahminical effort of appropriation of non-Brahminical schools of thought, from Jainism down the Virashaiva movement.
107. Quoted by Tapan Basu et al., *Khaki Shorts and Saffron Flags*, op. cit., p. 9.
108. Bankim and Aurobindo showed a more nuanced understanding of the politics of culture and were sensitive to the diverse cultural traditions of India.
109. T.C.A. Raghavan, 'Origins and Development of Hindu Mahasabha Ideology: The Call of V.D. Savarkar and Bhai Parmanand', *Economic and Political Weekly*, XVIII (15), 9 April 1983, p. 597.
110. Dhananjay Keer, *Veer Savarkar* (Bombay: Popular Prakashan, 1966), p. 265.
111. Hedgewar's conceptualization of *Hindu Rashtra* has been explained in Chap. II.
112. Deendayal was born in 1916 in Mathura district of UP in an astrologer's family. Orphaned at an early age, he went through a hard life. He was a bright student. He passed his intermediate examination from Pilani in 1937 with distinctions and his B.A. from Kanpur in 1939 in the first division. He joined the RSS in 1937 and became a full-time worker in 1942. He organized the Jana Sangh in UP, soon became general secretary of the BJS and continued till 1967. In 1968, he became the President of the BJS. He remained a bachelor and led a simple life until his death in mysterious circumstances on the railway track near Mughal Sarai in 1968. His philosophy of *Integral Humanism* was adopted by the BJS. He was not just the ideologue of the BJS, but also of the RSS. His integral humanism was very much in consonance with Golwalkar's understanding of *Rashtra* though Upadhyaya added some original ideas. The RSS *swayamsevaks* put Deendayal in high esteem. For his detailed life history and philosophy, see Sudhakar Raje, ed., *Pandit Deendayal Upadhyaya: A Profile* (Delhi: Deendayal Research Institute, 1972); *Pandit Deendayal Upadhyaya: Ideology and Perception*, Vols. I-V (Delhi: Suruchi Prakashan, 1991); M.S. Golwalkar et al., *Integral Approach* (Delhi: Suruchi Prakashan, 1991); Sudhakar Raje, ed., *Destination: Nation's Tribute to Deendayal Upadhyaya* (Delhi: DRI, 1978); P. Parameswaran, ed., *Gandhi, Lohia and Deendayal* (Delhi: DRI, 1978).
113. M.S. Golwalkar, *We or Our Nationhood Defined*, op. cit., p. 18.
114. Golwalkar observes that 'socialism is modern Russia's religion. It is a Godless religion but a religion nonetheless. For the Russians, their prophet is Karl Marx and his opinions are their Testament.' Ibid., p. 37.
115. Ibid., pp. 40-1.
116. Ibid., p. 42.

117. Ibid., p. 43.
118. Ibid., p. 44.
119. Ibid., p. 6.
120. Ibid., p. 45.
121. Ibid., p. 47.
122. Ibid., pp. 47-8.
123. As Golwalkar writes: 'To keep up the purity of the Race and its culture, Germany shocked the world by her purging the country of the Semitic Races—the Jews. Race pride at its highest has been manifested here. Germany has also shown how well-nigh impossible it is for Races and cultures, having differences going to the root, to be assimilated into one united whole, a good lesson for us in Hindusthan to learn and profit by.' Ibid., p. 35.
124. See M.S. Golwalkar, *Bunch of Thoughts*, op. cit., Chap. XVI, pp. 233-68.
125. Ibid., p. 248.
126. Ibid., p. 249.
127. Ibid. To support his charges, Golwalkar cites Niyogi Committee Report: 'All the philanthropic acts of the missionaries are simply a mask for carrying on proselytising activities, sometimes by intimidating and sometimes by tempting the simple folk. At the root of the activities is their ambition to carve out a separate Christian state for themselves on the strength of their numbers. They are spending crores of rupees for that single purpose.' Ibid., pp. 251-2.
128. Ibid., p. 254.
129. Ibid.
130. Ibid., p. 255.
131. Ibid., p. 256.
132. Ibid., p. 264.
133. Ibid.
134. Ibid., p. 263.
135. Gyanendra Pandey, 'Hindus and Others: The Militant Hindu Construction', *Economic and Political Weekly*, XXVI (52), 28 December 1991, p. 3001.
136. Mlechhas are 'those who do not subscribe to the social laws dictated by Hindu Religion and Culture'. See M.S. Golwalkar, *We or Our Nationhood Defined*, op. cit., p. 62.
137. Gyanendra Pandey, 'Hindus and Others: The Militant Hindu Construction', op. cit., p. 3003.
138. M.S. Golwalkar, *We or Our Nationhood Defined*, op. cit., p. 60.
139. Ibid., p. 61.
140. Ibid., p. 62.
141. M.S. Golwalkar, *Bunch of Thoughts*, op. cit., p. 182.
142. Tapan Basu et al., *Khaki Shorts*, op. cit., p. 26.
143. Hans Kohn, an authority on the theory of nationalism, observes that there are two forms of nationalism—political, which is rational, and cultural, which is mystical. For a comparative analysis, see John Hutchinson, 'Cultural Nationalism and Moral Regeneration', in John Hutchinson and Anthony D.

Smith, eds., *Nationalism* (Oxford: Oxford University Press, 1994), pp. 122-31. Also see Marguerite Ross Barnett, *The Politics of Cultural Nationalism* (Princeton: Princeton University Press, 1976). Barnett studies Tamil nationalism.

144. M.S. Golwalkar, *Bunch of Thoughts*, op. cit., p. 45.
145. Golwalkar observes: 'It seems, in their concept of our culture, of the ideal of our womanhood, a Sita or a Savitri, a Padmini or a Nivedita has no place. In that contest, indeed we miss the real beauty of India.' Ibid., p. 54.
146. Ibid., p. 47.
147. Ibid., p. 48.
148. Sarah Joseph, 'Identity, Culture and Community', *Economic and Political Weekly*, XXVIII (17), 24 April 1993, pp. 807-9.
149. See Deendayal Upadhyaya, *Integral Humanism* (Delhi: Bharatiya Jana Sangh Central Office, 1965).
150. V.V. Nene, *Pandit Deendayal Upadhyaya: Ideology and Perception, Part-II, Integral Humanism* [trans. by M.K. Paranjape and D.R. Kulkarni] (Delhi: Suruchi Prakashan, 1991), p. 11.
151. M.S. Golwalkar et al., *Integral Approach* (Delhi: Suruchi Prakashan, 1991), p. 26.
152. The task of the RSS is to build the 'integral man' through the *shakhas*.
153. M.S. Golwalkar et al., *Integral Approach*, op. cit., p. 31.
154. Sudhakar Raje, ed., *Pandit Deendayal Upadhyaya: A Profile* (Delhi: DRI, 1972), p. 172.
155. The concept of *swadeshi* that the RSS has been championing at present is not really new. More discussion on the topic will be taken up in Chap. VII.
156. Abhas Chatterjee, *The Concept of Hindu Nation* (Delhi: Voice of India, 1995), pp. 10-14.
157. For a critique of existing arguments on secularism, see Amartya Sen, 'Secularism and Its Discontents', in Kaushik Basu and Sanjay Subrahmanyam, eds., *Unravelling the Nation: Sectarian Conflict and India's Secular Identity*, op. cit., pp. 11-43.
158. See T.N. Madan, 'Secularism in its Place', *The Journal of Asian Studies*, 46 (4), November 1987, pp. 747-58. Madan argues that while the second definition is broad, the former implies a relatively narrow formulation of negative or defensive policy of religious neutrality on the part of the state.
159. Most of the discourses in social science, mainly Marxist historiography, subscribed to this position. However, this group has shed its old rigidities and even made the beginnings of an unacknowledged self-criticism as religion gains a new academic respectability as a component of subaltern consciousness.
160. These secular seekers are driven not by the imperatives of any ideology, but by a certain ambivalence which compels them to view matters of the state, social injustice, and the struggle against all kinds of intolerance in a constant dynamic with affinities to other, perhaps non-rational, mythic, fictional states of being. See Rustom Bharucha, 'In the Name of the Secular: Cultural Interactions

and Interventions', *Economic and Political Weekly*, XXIX (45-6), 5 and 12 November 1994.

161. Ibid.

162. Sumit Sarkar counters this objection by arguing that far from being an importation from the modern West, secularism in its broadest sense of tolerance and respect for faiths other than one's own may even have had a longer ancestry in India than in Europe. This followed not from any unique and superior virtue of Hindus (evidence does exist of Buddhists and Jain shrines being occasionally destroyed), but because a centralized priesthood claiming to be indispensable for salvation was much less powerful in Hindu or even Islamic traditions than in medieval Europe. See Sumit Sarkar, 'Roots of Secularism', *The Times of India*, 26 March 1993.

163. Many scholars criticise the role of the State on this point, though their understanding differs from that of the RSS. Ashis Nandy in several articles criticises 'statist secularism'. See his 'Culture, State, and the Recovery of Religious Tolerance', *Economic and Political Weekly*, XIV (49), 8 December 1984, pp. 2079-83; 'An Anti-Secularist Manifesto', *Seminar*, 314, October 1985, pp. 14-24; 'The Politics of Secularism and the Recovery of Religious Tolerance', *Alternatives*, XIII (2), April 1988, pp. 177-94. Also see Subrata Kumar Mitra, 'Desecularising the State: Religion and Politics in India after Independence', *Comparative Studies in Society and History*, 33 (4), October 1991, pp. 755-77.

164. The counter version is given in Prakash Chandra Upadhyaya, 'The Politics of Indian Secularism', *Modern Asian Studies*, 26 (4), 1992, pp. 815-53.

165. See Rajeev Bhargava, 'Giving Secularism its Due', *Economic and Political Weekly*, XXIX (28), 9 July 1994, pp. 1784-91.

166. However, the RSS resents the fact that the word 'secular' was introduced in the Preamble of the Indian Constitution only in 1976 during the authoritarian days of the Emergency. The RSS certainly does not relish this word but finds it useful to give it a new meaning rather than discarding it.

167. These charges are reminiscent of the British nationalists as a 'microscopic minority'. See Sumit Sarkar, 'Roots of Secularism', op. cit.

168. The 'pseudo-secular' is the Hindu who defends the right of the Muslim citizen. Similarly, the Hindu immigrant from Bangladesh is by definition a 'refugee' while the Muslim is an 'infiltrator'. See Partha Chatterjee, 'Secularism and Toleration', *Economic and Political Weekly*, XXIX (28), 9 July 1994, pp. 1768-77.

169. Employment of Muslims in government services presents a dismal picture: engineers 2 per cent; doctors 2.5 per cent; IAS officers 2.86 per cent; IPS officers 2 per cent; Class I officers 3.3 per cent; bank employees 2.18 per cent and other categories 3.10 per cent. Likewise with an income considerably lower than the national average, Muslims are among poorest in the society. Surveys conducted by the National Council of Applied Economic Research (NCAER) put the average Muslim household income at Rs 22,807. Compare this with Rs 29,786 for the Hindus; indeed the Muslim household income is

even lower than the 1993-4 national average for rural India, which is Rs 25,653. No wonder then that more than 43 per cent of the Muslims have turned landless compared to 20 per cent amongst the Hindus. The National Sample Survey provides other revealing statistics: 10.9 per cent of Muslims compared to 6.4 per cent of Hindus have a per capita monthly income of Rs 90 or less; 41.4 per cent of Muslims compared to 28.43 per cent of Hindus fall in the income group of Rs 96-158.31, while only 3.87 per cent Muslims compared to 9.3 per cent of Hindus belong to Rs 475 per month income group. See Zafar Jung, 'Prejudices that Defy Constitutional Rights', *The Times of India*, 11 June 1999.

170. The *Sangh Parivar* has coined some catchy phrases like *Ham Panch, Hamare Pachees* to highlight the rapid growth rate of the Muslims.
171. See Madhu Kishwar, 'Religion at the Service of Nationalism: An Analysis of Sangh Parivar Politics', *Manushi*, 76, May-June 1993, pp. 2-20; Sitaram Yechury, *Pseudo Hinduism Exposed: Saffron Brigade's Myth and Reality* [Delhi: A CPI(M) Publication, 1993].
172. Quoted by Sudhir Kakar, *The Colours of Violence*, op. cit., p. 213.
173. Ibid., p. 163.
174. See Partha Chatterjee, 'Secularism and Toleration', op. cit. But it can not be overlooked that the *Sant-Samiti* of the VHP, at its meeting of 13-14 October 1992, had set up a committee to rework the 'anti-Hindu' Constitution. The committee headed by Swami Muktananda had prepared a draft report. For details, see Yoginder Sikand, 'Manusmriti versus Constitution of India', *Mainstream*, 31(23), 17 April 1993, pp. 15-18. The *Sangh Parivar* had been demanding a review of the Constitution for quite some time. The present BJP government has finally initiated the process, thereby indicating that the present Constitution may be overhauled.
175. See Partha Chatterjee, 'Secularism and Toleration', op. cit.
176. Ibid.
177. For a critical analysis of Indian secularism's tolerant credentials, see Bidyut Chakrabarty, 'India's Secularism: Tolerance and Coercion', in Bidyut Chakrabarty, ed., *Secularism and Indian Polity* (Delhi: Segment Book Distributors, 1990), pp. 93-106.
178. K. Suryanarayana Rao, *Hindu Rashtra: It is not a mere Slogan but the Vibrant Reality*, op. cit.
179. *Balasaheb Deoras Answers Questions* (Bangalore: Sahitya Sindhu, 1984), p. 53.
180. Ratna Kapoor, Brenda Crossman, 'Communalising Gender/Engendering Community: Women, Legal Discourse and Saffron Agenda', *Economic and Political Weekly*, XXVIII (17), 24 April 1993, p. WS-37.
181. In a similar manner M.A. Jinnah expressed five words to describe the concept of Pakistan: 'We Muslims are a nation'. For recent ideological writings on *Hindu Rashtra*, see H.V. Seshadri et al., *Why Hindu Rashtra?* (Delhi: Suruchi Prakashan, 1990); K. Suryanarayana Rao, *Hindu Rashtra: It is not a mere Slogan but the Vibrant Reality*, op. cit.

182. For a brilliant discussion on the contextual position of *vasudhaiva kutumbakam*, see Brian A. Hatcher, '"The cosmos is one family" (*vasudhaiva kutumbakam*): Problematic mantra of Hindu humanism', *Contributions to Indian Sociology*, 28 (1), 1994, pp. 149-62.
183. K. Suryanarayana Rao, *Hindu Rashtra*, op. cit.
184. During the last decade RSS leaders have been swearing on *Hindutva* more frequently than the Golwalkar era. As the Hindu Mahasabha has become a spent force, the RSS has no constraint to adopt Savarkar's *Hindutva* as the watchword. Moreover, the RSS having successfully appropriated the legacies of various Hindu sects and thinkers, now claims to be the sole representative of the Hindus. This enviable position gives it the prerogative to incorporate any ideological concept of the previous Hindu leadership.
185. S.H. Deshpande, 'RSS and the Muslims: No Escape from Secularism', in *The Times of India*, 25 May 1994.

CHAPTER V

Homogenizing Hindus: Caste, Tribe, Woman and Progeny

RSS discourse on community, history and nation leaves no doubt that *Hindu Rashtra* stands for Hindu hegemony. But Hindus are not a homogeneous entity—there exists a multiplicity of identities among them. Golwalkar recognized this reality, though never admitted so. As *Hindu Rashtra* aimed at a monolithic Hindu identity, he understandably underplayed these diverse identities under the pretext of one culture, one language and one nation (*Hindu, Hindi, Hindustan*). Though Golwalkar did not favour any dilution of ideology, he, at the same time, created an array of affiliates to work among various sections of the society with the objective of assimilation and homogenization of these identities into an all-embracing and omnipotent 'Hindu' identity.

In the post-Golwalkar phase, Deoras and other RSS leaders recognized that some of these identities were getting restive and it would be wise to address them with more courage, rather than simply ignoring their existence. They further understood that the RSS would not succeed in its quest for political power without integrating these identities into the framework of *Hindutva*. An attempt has been made in this chapter to examine how the RSS has made certain strategic shifts in its ideology in order to homogenize different identities like castes, tribes and women into the monolithic framework of *Hindu Rashtra*. It is also shown how it has modified its strategies in a slow and subtle manner without reversing its original ideological position; new ideas have been incorporated, but not at the cost of the traditional ones.

INTEGRATING CASTES

As community politics intensified in early twentieth century, the integration of the depressed classes and tribals into the Hindu fold became a major concern of the then Hindu leaders. Lajpat Rai claimed that 'the depressed classes are Hindus' as 'they worship Hindu Gods, observe Hindu customs, and follow Hindu laws'.[1] Regarding the 'Santals, Kolis, Bhils, Panchamas, Namashudras and other such [depressed] tribes and classes', V.D. Savarkar argued, 'this Sindhusthan is as emphatically, the land of their forefathers as of those of the so-called Aryans; they inherit the Hindu blood and the Hindu culture; and even those of them who have not as yet come fully under the influence of any orthodox Hindu sect, do still worship deities and saints and follow a religion however primitive, are still purely attached to this land, which therefore to them is not only a Fatherland, but a Holyland'.[2] Swami Shraddhanand strongly advocated for the abolition of untouchability. The RSS developed its understanding of caste and tribes upon this legacy; it strongly argued that the untouchables and the tribals are very much part and parcel of Hindu society.

RSS' Understanding of Caste

Hedgewar made it clear that in the *shakha* the identity of the *swayamsevak* was *only* Hindu, and nothing else; he should not be conscious of any other identity, especially the caste identity. The *shakha* was designed to discipline the *swayamsevak,* reinforce his Hindu identity and impart Hindu *sanskar.* As most of Hedgewar's recruits belonged to the upper castes, mainly the Brahmins, the *swayamsevaks* got naturally inclined to imbibe and imitate the values and norms of upper caste Hindus. Despite a significant change in the composition of membership over the years, even today, the imprint of an upper-caste behavioural pattern and value system is unmistakably visible on the *swayamsevaks.* An upper caste legacy still continues in the organization.

Golwalkar, the ideologue of the RSS, attempts to provide a theoretical formulation of caste and tries to integrate it into the framework of the *Hindu Rashtra.* He makes a distinction between *varna* and caste[3] and explains that while *varnas* are four,[4] castes are countless. As he proceeds, while the basis of caste is occupation, *varna* is based on the ancient form of the modern theory of heredity enunciated by Mendels. *Varna* refers to quality, not to the colour of the skin, argues Golwalkar; therefore, a Brahmin may be dark and a Shudra may be fair. *Varna* is determined by *guna* and *karma,* including that of previous birth, observes Golwalkar. He further contends that when the Brahmin gave up his *dharma* and started competing for jobs, he knocked out the basis of *varna.*

Golwalkar rejects the view that caste was an evil institution and was imposed on society by some section which had a vested interest. He does not find any reason to believe that Brahmins exploited other castes and got the benefits.[5] Present RSS writings, in a similar vein, strongly refute that the upper castes are responsible for perpetuating caste oppression for centuries.[6] In Golwalkar's opinion, caste was a great institution, which served society and held it together when everything else seemed to collapse all around. He particularly highlights the contribution of caste as a bulwark against Islam: 'It was because caste was weak in West Punjab and East Bengal that these two areas, of all other, succumbed to Islam.'[7] Despite the 'positive' contributions of the caste system, Golwalkar however feels that this 'ancient armour' is no longer relevant. That is why the RSS does not recognize any caste; it underscores only one identity, i.e. Hindu identity.

Thus, Golwalkar glorifies the rationale of the ancient Hindu caste system, underplays its exploitative nature, exonerates the upper castes from perpetrating caste exploitation and applauds the positive role of a strong Hindu caste system in thwarting the march of Islam. Then why and how does the caste become irrelevant? Golwalkar does not offer any convincing answer; he merely states that caste has no more role to play.

Though caste has lost its relevance, Golwalkar regrets that the caste system still prevails. Then how is it to be abolished? Golwalkar offers a 'natural approach' in contrast to the 'most un-natural approach' of the 'national integration-wallas', who focus on the division of Hindus into various castes, tribes, backward classes, etc. He does not believe in 'cheap attacks on caste' and prefers 'to abolish it sweetly . . . not by making noises'.[8] Obviously, Golwalkar's construction of a unified Hindu identity gets jeopardized if too much stress is laid on the divisive dimensions of Hindu caste system.

Abolishing Untouchability

The major bane of the Hindu caste system is untouchability and Golwalkar pleads for its abolition; 'the Harijan can, and must, enter the temple as a Hindu. Nobody is going to stop him.'[9] However, here again, he argues that creating scenes and throwing challenges might create news, but it will not solve the problem. The right approach is to treat the Harijans as equal members of Hindu society and make efforts for their upliftment 'with the same solicitude with which one works for the recovery of a sick member of the family'.[10] The legal ban is not enough; Golwalkar appeals to religious leaders of various sects to give a religious sanction to the legal ban to make it really effective.[11]

The VHP, which was entrusted by Golwalkar to strive for the abolition of untouchability, has also made a strident demand in favour of a religious sanction by Shankaracharyas against untouchability: 'For whatever may be said about the correctness of the position of the so-called "Untouchables" in different epochs, the age we live in demands a revision of the obligations and rights on the basis of equality and brotherhood.'[12] The VHP emphasizes the abolition of untouchability to save Hindu society from divisions and puts special responsibility on the Shankaracharyas 'to relegate the inessentials to a back place', so that all the folds and layers, castes, communities and *sampradayas* could be integrated to turn this society into one huge organism. For this supreme objective of Hindu unity, the VHP does not hesitate to dump the injunctions of the Shastras and modify them as per the need of the present time: 'A healthy and free society need not follow the prescriptions enjoined during adverse times.'[13]

The solution provided by the RSS to eradicate untouchability and caste discrimination appears to be quite simplistic and superficial—the declaration of Shankaracharyas will have very little impact. Its suggestion that a 'beginning can be made to do away with these evils through community festivals, social gatherings and temple worships',[14] hardly makes any headway in getting rid of such an age-old practice. The RSS is yet to address the fundamental questions of untouchability especially those involving larger social, economic and political issues. Nevertheless, it is true to a substantial extent that the *swayamsevaks* do not prefer to be introduced according to their respective castes. They claim that their primary identity is Hindu, not their belongingness to any particular caste.[15] True, once an untouchable becomes part of the RSS brotherhood, he is not treated differently by fellow caste-Hindu *swayamsevaks.* But it is doubtful whether the *swayamsevaks* have the same attitude to those untouchables and dalits who are not part of their brotherhood. A discussion on the issue of reservation for the Scheduled Castes (SCs) and Scheduled Tribes (STs) would clarify the RSS position further.

Reservation on Reservations

The reservations for SCs and STs in public employment has become a major issue since independence, particularly since the early 1970s. How does the RSS look at affirmative action which the Indian State has adopted for the upliftment of neglected sections? A resolution of the Akhil Bharatiya Pratinidhi Sabha the RSS will better illustrate. As it reads:

the RSS 'considers it necessary that reservations be continued for the present with a view to bringing all these brethrens of ours who have remained backward in educational, social and economic fields over the centuries, at par with the rest of society'.[16] At the same time it emphasizes that the reservations cannot be a permanent arrangement and that these crutches have to be done away with as soon as possible. It strongly pleads that merit and efficiency should not be allowed to be adversely affected because of reservations. The RSS has also shown concern for the economically backward section of the upper castes who are deprived of the benefits of the reservation policy.

The ABPS of the RSS deplores that the reservation issue has become a tool of power politics and election tactics, thereby generating mutual ill-will and conflict. The RSS believes that a harmonious and egalitarian society cannot be achieved on the strength of constitutional and political measures alone, but through the combined efforts of social and governmental agencies. RSS claims to its credit that as a main social organization it has been striving to create social harmony and goodwill. As the RSS believes 'in the indivisible unity of the entire Hindu Society including Harijans and tribals', it has 'consistently been endeavouring to arouse this inherent spirit of oneness'.[17]

The *Organiser* came up with similar arguments that the 'crutch' of reservation should be dispensed with at the earliest. It gave a call to the politicians to do enough for these sections so that there would be no need to extend its time period further. It opposed reservations for the children of the beneficiaries. It also came down heavily on extending the reservation to other backward sections and pleaded that the whole country is backward.[18] It feared that the enlargement of reservation would not only compromise the quality of services and professions, it would also dilute the development of Harijans and tribals.

The question of extension of reservation to other backward castes became a hot issue with the implementation of the Mandal Commission Report by the V.P. Singh government. The RSS described it as a 'retrograde step'. Besides 'casteising' society further, this led to a gathering storm of appeasement of communities, the RSS argued.[19] The RSS started emphasizing the primacy of an economic criterion in giving the benefits of reservation. It criticized that affluent sections like Yadavs and Kshatriyas had also been included in the backward caste grouping. It was also critical of the then vice-president of India who had sought benefits of reservation for his progeny, thus making a mockery of the issue. Though the RSS favoured providing everybody the right to education, it opposed reservation in institutions of higher learning and in employment avenues. It cited the example of Europe and even the socialist countries to strengthen its anti-reservation arguments.[20]

Rajendra Singh, the successor of Deoras, did not favour caste-based reservation. Championing the cause of merit, Singh argued, the reservations should not exceed 50 per cent of the jobs as 'it is also necessary that integrity, ability and meritorious qualities find the highest place in administration'.[21] He deplored that the politics of reservation 'has been creating bitterness and hatred between various sections of the society' and argued that this can only be removed with the help of service projects 'inspired by compassion, fellow-feeling and social harmony'.[22] In this light the RSS launched a drive called *samarasya sangam* (confluence of harmony); the *swayamsevaks* were asked to adopt a village in their respective locality in order to promote 'social harmony between various sections of the society and social assimilation'.[23]

Is the Dalit a Hindu?

Now a days a Scheduled Caste person is increasingly being referred to as Dalit (Downtrodden). 'Dalit', a term of popular usage in Maharashtra, means 'suppressed or exploited people'. From the early 1970s, spearheaded by the militant Dalit Panthers of Maharashtra, new social movements emerged on the Indian political arena challenging the system of exploitation as well as the Hindu-dominant symbolism of Indian identity.[24] Since then the new militant term 'Dalit' has replaced the Gandhian term 'Harijan' and the colourless governmental 'Scheduled Castes'.[25]

Is the Dalit a Hindu? As a leading Dalit intellectual answers: 'Dalits were never Hindus, are not Hindus and can never be Hindus.' They are 'a separate people themselves—the descendants of the great Adi-Dravida or Dravida indigenous race of India (Mool Bharatis)'.[26] Another Dalit intellectual claims that the Dalit-bahujans and the Hindus belong to two different cultural worlds opposed to each other.[27] Therefore, the Dalits assert a separate identity other than Hindu, which is contrary to the position of the RSS. They do not want to be treated as sick members of the Hindu family as they claim that they do not belong to this family at all. They also categorically reject the solution of the RSS which emphasizes a gradual change of heart without making much noise. As the Dalit Panther manifesto emphasizes: 'We do not want a little place in Brahman Alley. We want the rule of the whole land. We are not looking at the persons but the system. Change of heart, liberal education, etc., will not end our state of exploitation. When we gather a revolutionary mass, rouse the people, out of the struggle of this giant mass will come the tidal wave of revolution.'[28] Thus the Dalits want a fundamental change in the system in which they would be the rulers. They want a complete reversal of the system. This approach certainly does not go along with the ideology of the RSS.

Hindutva *Represents Caste Hierarchy*

Dalit intellectuals equate *Hindutva* with Brahminism. They define Brahminism as 'a process of fixing finality of relations or human interactions on the basis of the axiom that, by birth the Brahmins are superior to all other beings' and as a natural corollary, the Shudras are inferior to them. This is 'a natural and unalterable arrangement'.[29] They blame Brahminism for perpetuating caste hierarchy, and therefore, equate *Hindutva* with casteism. They further argue that the stratified Hindu caste based society denies social mobility by brainwashing the members of each of the caste groups to remain confined within the socio-economic jurisdiction of their respective caste. Brahminism does not grant any right to others to choose their vocation according to their merits, aptitude or active tendencies of character. Merit was made a monopoly of the Brahmins; whatever belonged to the Brahmins was declared to be meritorious. Therefore, Dalit intellectuals argue that 'Hindu society lost potency of both vertical and horizontal mobility'.[30]

The Dalit view-point challenges the very definition of Hinduism as the majority religion and the core of Indian tradition. It insists that it was rather a Brahmanic Hinduism that represented the hegemony of an elite and that this hegemony has to be overthrown.

Attempting to Co-opt Dalits and Ambedkar

The RSS quickly grasped the potential of the Dalit movement. Golwalkar created the VHP to work for the eradication of untouchability from Hindu society. The VHP asserts that ancient Hindu society was free from untouchability. If a section of Hindus, the *chandalas* were treated as untouchables, it was only because they were criminals. VHP leader Ashok Singhal observes that present-day Dalits were a glorified community at the time of the Muslim invasion. He argues that the Dalit community 'was a creation of Islam because they refused to join the ranks of their religion'.[31] He further contends, the Muslim rulers wanted the Dalits to adopt Islam, but on their refusal the Muslim rulers 'snatched away the properties of these communities and threw them out of the villages and thus was born the dalit community'.[32]

The Dalits not only reject this thesis, on the contrary, they advocate for a strong 'Dalit-Muslim unity' to fight Brahmanical oppression. Some Dalit theoreticians argue that a vast majority of the Muslims of India are descendants of Dalits, backward castes, tribals or *shudras* who embraced Islam to seek liberation from Brahminical tyranny. Therefore, Dalits and Muslims are really blood brothers and sisters. Both are beef-eaters, both are the victims of Hindu rule and oppression, and both have a culture that stresses justice, brotherhood and freedom. Both live with each other in the same slums and segregated localities. Both are social slaves. Both have common economic, social and political interests.[33]

The *Sangh Parivar*, on the other hand, attempts to create an anti-Muslim consciousness among the Dalits by systematically breaking the syncretic religious practices prevalent among the Dalits and the Muslims. For instance, in Madras slums, it organizes and finances the Vinayaka Chaturthi celebrations. Idols 'representing' each slum are carried in public procession for immersion under the supervision of the *Sangh Parivar*. Sometimes, anti-Muslim riots take place due to rumour-mongering and communal propaganda. These riots heighten communal consciousness amongst the Dalits. Therefore, while on the one hand, the Dalits feel an integral part of a pan-Hindu identity, on the other hand, they develop an anti-Muslim consciousness.[34]

As Ambedkar has emerged as a rallying factor of Dalit identity, the RSS tries to relate some of his ideas with the philosophy of *Hindutva*. In RSS's analysis, though Ambedkar was critical of the practice of casteism in Hindu society, he was much opposed to the predominance of fundamentalist forces in the Muslim community. As the RSS interprets, Ambedkar 'viewed the former as a cause of the weakening of social harmony in Hindu society, and the latter as a threat to the survival not only to the pacifist Hindu society, but also of nationalism, secularism and democracy—cherished ideals of our civilization and polity'.[35] Therefore, in the perception of the RSS, Ambedkar was much more concerned about the Muslim threat to Hindu society than the caste discrimination among the Hindus.

The RSS takes pain to explain that for all his bitterness against Hindu society, Ambedkar's verdict on Muslim society is even harder. As the RSS argues, for Ambedkar, Islamic society is not more egalitarian or better than Hindu society; Koran permits slavery; Islam has its own caste system; the Muslims are opposed to reforms and Islam imposes a uniformity of thought.[36] The RSS regrets that the present Ambedkarite movement is not at all in consonance with Ambedkar's view of Islam.

Pointing out Ambedkar's conversion to Buddhism, the RSS tries to score a point. Ambedkar, the RSS observes, rejected the offers of Muslim and Christian missionaries for the following reasons: first, he wanted a rational and humanist religion, for which the bizarre beliefs of Christianity and Islam did not qualify; and second, Buddhism was an indigenous religion which would not bring with it extra-territorial loyalties.[37] The RSS sources claim that Ambedkar preferred Buddhism to any other religion as it was 'a part and parcel of Bharatiya culture' and his conversion would not harm 'the tradition of the culture and history of this land'.[38] This interpretation ignores the substantive and rational dimensions of Buddhism that really attracted Ambedkar. Thus, the RSS fails to contextualize the Dalit movement and the socio-political thought of Ambedkar.[39]

Dalits are aware that *Hindutva* has failed to provide a sound critique of the caste system, which is mainly responsible for their degraded existence. Many Dalit thinkers view the *Hindutva* agenda as an upper caste game plan against the poor cutting across the religious boundaries. They also understand that the RSS appropriation of Ambedkar is not genuine.[40] However, the Dalit community is not a monolith and is pulled by diverse contradictions. Different regions have different objective situations and political compulsions. Dalit leadership is also fragmented; except the BSP, other Dalit organizations have barely crossed their local frontiers. All these factors favour the RSS to carry out its agenda of assimilation of the Dalits into a pan-Hindu identity. Its affiliates like Seva Bharti carries out certain projects in Dalit localities, such as literacy drives, health and hygiene, etc.[41] The RSS organizes *shakhas*, *bhajan* sessions and conducts night schools to attract Dalits.

The *Sangh Parivar* also periodically indulges in symbolic gestures to bring Dalits into the *Hindutva* fold—the laying of a foundation stone of a Ram temple by Kameshwar Chaupal, a Dalit, was one such powerful gesture. Dalit women were also encouraged to participate in public ceremonies such as *Shila Pujan*, etc., organized by the *Sangh Parivar*. Sometimes these gestures do create some impact; a section of Dalits feel elated and honoured when Brahmins and upper caste people come to them and ask for their support and participation in public functions. Some of them also believe that a pan-Hindu identity would make it possible for them to transcend their caste identities and give them an honourable place in Hindu society.

INTEGRATING TRIBALS

Are Tribals Hindus?

The RSS also claims that tribals are Hindus. It does not accept the term *adivasi* as the prefix *adi* implies that tribals were the original inhabitants and the Aryans came from outside. Instead the RSS has coined the term *vanavasi* (forest dwellers) to address the tribals. Golwalkar explains that tribals are very much Hindus though they have no knowledge of their religion (Hinduism). He rejects the view that the tribals cannot be called Hindus as they are animists and worship trees and serpents. He argues that the Hindus throughout the country worship *Tulsi, Bilva* and *Aswattha* and also *Nag*, the cobra.[42]

Does beef-eating keep the tribals outside the pale of the Hindu community? Here Golwalkar shows flexibility and defends them by arguing that the fault does not lie with them but with the Hindus: First, no one taught them to look at the cow as their mother. Secondly, as they do not have sufficient food to feed themselves with, they are forced to eat beef out of sheer necessity. Therefore, argues Golwalkar, the Hindus have a responsibility to teach the tribals the traditions and customs of Hindu community as they are ignorant about these.

However, the critics point out that acceptance of Varnashrama Dharma (in effect caste) and the supremacy of the Brahmin, the worship of the cow, and the burning of the dead are three features of commonality in the beliefs and practices of all Hindus. On the question of veneration for cow and the manner of disposal for the dead, Hindu protagonists would surely agree; and on that ground much of the tribal population living in and around the forests of India must be reckoned as being outside the Hindu fold even today, for many among them eat beef and bury their dead.[43] 'A similar question mark must lie over sections of the remainder of the "depressed classes" (or untouchables) who live in closer proximity to plains Hindu society.'[44]

The RSS does not agree that the Hindu social system was at the root of the neglect of the tribals. Golwalkar tries to convince that in the olden times when the Panchayat system was the basic unit of society, those forest dwellers had an honoured place in it. Golwalkar applauds the qualities of the tribals, such as courage, intelligence, industry, honesty, warmth of heart, culture and spiritual refinement. 'Probably it was only Maharana Pratap who had established close links with them and made them equal partners with the rest of society. The forest-dwellers in those regions, the Bhills, stood shoulder to shoulder with Rajputs generation after generation in the heroic defence of *Swadesha* and *Swadharma*.'[45] Thus, Golwalkar attempts to prove that these tribals fought against the Muslims for the honour of the Hindu religion and a Hindu kingdom.

To bring the tribals into the fold of Hinduism, the RSS encourages them to change their names; instead of Oraon one should write Ram as one's family name. This attempt will clearly destroy the history, language, and culture of the tribals. By encouraging the tribals to trace their ancestry to some Rajput figure, the *Sangh Parivar* in fact strikes at the very roots of the social and cultural history of the original settlers of this land.[46]

Integrating the Vanavasis: Sangh Parivar *in a Tribal District, Phulbani (Orissa)*

Though the RSS is unable to explain adequately the reasons behind the present deplorable socio-economic conditions of the tribals, it recognizes their plight and proposes to adopt such plans by which their primary physical needs could be taken care of. Accordingly, the RSS first created the VHP and then Vanavasi Kalyan Ashram (VKA) for the purpose. It would be useful to examine the method of operation of these affiliates of the RSS in the tribal district of Phulbani, Orissa.

Tribals constitute roughly one-fourth of Orissa's population.[47] The tribal areas, because of the presence of Christian missionaries, offer an ideological advantage to the RSS.[48] The missionaries are active in welfare projects as well as conversion. Therefore, here the other is clearly identified and resentment amongst Hindus against conversion could be ideally exploited. However, the ideological challenge will not be enough unless the tribals are 'Hinduized' and an alternate welfare system is provided to woo them away from the missionary welfare system. Once this is achieved, the *Sangh Parivar* will make attempt to bring back 'the lost brothers' to the Hindu fold through reconversion (*paravartan*). Keeping these objectives in mind, the RSS deputed a Hindu missionary, Laxmanananda Saraswati[49] to Phulbani, a district having a tribal majority[50] and a centre of Christian missionary activities. Raghunath Sethi,[51] a *pracharak*, was deputed to assist Laxmanananda.

Hinduizing the Tribals

As the tribals were lacking in 'Hindu religious consciousness', the VHP, during the initial years, tried to convince the tribals to observe four main duties: first, to worship Hindu gods and goddesses; secondly, to understand the themes of Hindu religious texts (Shastra and Purana); thirdly, to adopt non-violence towards birds and animals, particularly towards the cow; and finally, to protect and serve the nation, which is *Hindu Rashtra*. Accordingly, the VHP distributed photographs and images of different gods and goddesses among the tribals and asked them to worship these deities regularly. It also taught them to follow a standard religious practice, as followed in coastal Orissa. It organized *bhajans*, *kirtans*, discourses on the *Gita*, the Upanishads and other Hindu religious texts and propagated the prescriptions of Shankara, Ramanuja, Madhabacharya and other Hindu preachers. The VHP organized about 100-50 *yajnas* and set up more than 300 *kirtan mandalis* in the district to start the process of Hinduization.

Hinduization was promoted not only by introducing these alien practices, but also by adopting certain measures at the expense of traditional customs and religious practices of the tribals. For instance, as the tribals usually worship the primitive goddess, *Thakurani*, every tribal village has a *Thakurani ghara* (abode of the goddess). This is just not a conventional religious place, but also a centre of tribal socio-cultural life. Moreover, it is used as a meeting place by young tribal boys and girls where they choose their respective partners for staying together, the practice popularly known as *dhangda dhangdi*. The VHP found such practice 'un-Hindu' and 'uncivilized' and started a campaign against this.[52] The VHP leaders proudly boast of demolishing many *Thakurani gharas* in the district and replacing them with the *Bhagabata toongis*.

This mission of the VHP thus makes an assault on the distinct cultural identity of the tribals; their age-old traditions and customs are forcefully trampled upon on the pretext of civilization and Hinduization. Moreover, the *Bhagabata toongi* is the religio-cultural feature of coastal Orissa. The VHP has adopted the dominant religio-cultural practices of coastal Orissa and wants it to be the standard for the entire state. Its purpose is to impose uniformity and in the process dismantling the diverse religious practices prevalent in Orissa.

Alternate Welfare System

After some time the *Sangh Parivar* leaders realized that the initial enthusiasm of the tribals for Hinduization could not be sustained for long. Now they should follow the line of the Christian missionaries, who had been promoting Christianity through welfare activities, particularly by running hospitals and schools.[53] Therefore, the RSS should devise an alternate welfare system not only to check the growth of Christianity but also to promote Hinduization and to encourage reconversion. Accordingly, the Vanavasi Kalyan Ashram (VKA)[54] was established to consolidate the gains made by the VHP.

Chakapada Ashram of Laxmanananda Saraswati

Laxmanananda, popularly known as Swamiji, came to Chakapada and camped near the Shiva temple. He set up an ashram and a school in 1969. The Vanavasi Kalyan Ashram took over the management of this ashram from the VHP in 1979. Chakapada Ashram, which started with a donation of 3-4 acres of land and a pair of bullocks by an old man who had no heir, has now a huge tract of agricultural land with a *goshala* having fifty to sixty cows.[55]

Laxmanananda started a number of activities.[56] First, he campaigned for prohibition. He also got the backing of the administration for this endeavour. As an Ashram inmate claims, due to his militant approach there has been a drastic reduction in drinking and the sale of liquor in the area. Secondly, he organized religious congregations like *nam sankirtan* and *yajnas* once or twice a year to attract tribals and others towards Hindu religious practices. Thirdly, as the RSS activists boast, because of Swamiji's organization and mobilization of tribals, the Christian missionaries have ceased their operation within the 30 km radius of Chakapada. Finally, the Ashram has become a model agricultural farm for the villagers. Now the villagers look forward to the Ashram and not to the traditional village head (*mukhia*) as their role model in farming and veterinary science.

Ashram School

The Ashram runs a Sanskrit school, which provides *madhyama* (matric) and *upa shastri* (higher secondary) courses. Now it has included *shastri* (a degree course). The school has 260 students, 90 per cent of them are tribals (*vanavasis*). Nearly 80 per cent of the students reside in the Ashram. The government provides a stipend of Rs 150 and Rs 165 per month to each school and college student respectively. The Ashram spends about Rs 100 per month on each student, partly managing the deficit from its agricultural production. While all 13 school teachers get their salary from the government, the 3 college teachers get *mandhan* (honorarium) from the Ashram.

All the teachers and the students are *swayamsevaks*. While the school *swayamsevaks* attend the *shakha* in the morning, their college counterparts participate in the evening. However, the *shakhas* are conducted outside the Ashram premises.[57] Besides studying, these inmates periodically undertake *seva prakalpas* (service projects) in the nearby villages. These boys teach the villagers to keep their surroundings clean and maintain health and hygiene. Sometimes the boys contribute physical labour in these service projects, thus gaining the appreciation of the villagers.

The inmates of the Ashram propagate family values among the *vanavasis* as they find that family ties are not strong among them. They also campaign against the prevailing *kusanskar*, like *dhangda dhangdi*. Obviously, the objective is to impose the Hindu marriage system upon the Adivasis who do not believe in the institution of marriage. The pupils of the Ashram make constant attempts to inculcate the values of Hindu religion, culture and festivals. Thus, the Ashram actively undertakes the process of Hinduization among the tribals.

Shankaracharya Sanskruta Kanyashram, Jalaspatta

Laxmanananda once came to deliver a *boudhik* at the RSS *shakha* in Kurtamgarh. The *swayamsevaks* and sympathizers requested him to open a Chakapada-like Ashram at this place. When he found a *Shivling* inside the river at Jalaspatta and the serene environment, he agreed to the proposal. However, he had two conditions: first, a Shankaracharya temple would be constructed; and secondly, the school and the Ashram would be exclusively for girls as the Hindu family is woman-centred.[58] Subse-quently, Bhupendra Basu, the *prant sanghchalak* and Harihar Nanda, *prant karyavah* of the RSS visited the place, a *yajna* was performed and thus the ashram took off.

The Ashram was named Shankaracharya Sanskruta Kanyashrama and started functioning in 1989. The school provides Sanskrit education. It started with *prathama* (7th), then *madhyama* and *upa shastri* were added subsequently. The school has a strength of 8 teachers and 148 students. While 134 of these students are tribals, all of them except 4 reside in the Ashram. Each student gets a stipend of Rs 155 per month from the government. The Ashram generates its resources from agriculture to make up the deficiency.

Activities

All students are members of the Rashtra Sevika Samiti and lead a very disciplined life.[59] A regular *shakha* is conducted in the Ashram premises.[60] Cultural programmes are organized every Saturday evening for two hours. These include patriotic dance-dramas and tribal dances as 'the tribal cultural treasure needs to be protected'.[61] Thus, the RSS has no objection in promoting certain tribal traditions which do not contradict core Hindu values. On Sunday afternoons, the inmates visit the nearby villages in groups. They teach the alphabet to children and women, and acquaint the women with different Hindu rituals and practices. Occasionally, they distribute seeds and plants and impart environmental education. A monthly *baithak* (meeting) takes place once a month in which the important national and international problems are discussed.[62] In that meeting a review of the activities for the month is done and duties are distributed.

'Malanchal Chhatrabas', Raikia

This hostel for tribal boys started with a donation of one acre of land by the Arya Samaj leader Brahmananda Saraswati. Mahant Avaidyanath of the VHP laid the foundation stone; a paper merchant of Calcutta donated Rs 1 lakh for the construction of the hostel. The hostel is managed by the VKA and a RSS whole-timer is incharge of the hostel.

The hostel has two rooms and 38 residents. These boys attend the nearby schools, including one run by the Christian missionaries. Like the other two hostels of Chakapada and Jalaspatta, each resident pays to the hostel his scholarship amount of Rs 150 per month, and the deficiency is met by the VKA.[63] The residents sometimes receive clothes and blankets as gifts. Here again all the inmates are *swayamsevaks* and regular *shakhas* are conducted. The boys lead a disciplined life and get thoroughly trained with the ideology of the *Hindu Rashtra.*

Other Welfare Activities and Operational Problems

VKA runs dispensaries at Cutingia and Kurtamgarh. They also have a mobile dispensary.[64] VKA has opened about 15 *ratri pathashalas* (night schools) in Raikia block, out of which only 3 are functioning.[65] The RSS activists gives reasons for the non-functioning of these schools: first, the lack of activists (*karyakartas*) and secondly, the shortage of funds. Both these problems are interrelated. The RSS tries to recruit teachers from the respective villages by appealing in the name of patriotism, duty towards one's own village and neighbourhood, the religious benefit of teaching, etc. But this has only a temporary effect; when the recruits compare their income with the teachers of the government and other voluntary agencies, they feel frustrated and desert the RSS-sponsored projects.

VKA also runs Bal Sanskar Kendras either weekly or regularly. Here the boys in the age group of 3-8 are imparted Hindu *sanskar*. In Raikia block the VKA started 20 such centres which gradually came down to 3. It also proposes to start one-teacher schools, like in Bihar where about 800 such schools are reportedly functioning. The VKA also organizes various *khel-kud* (sports and games) competitions.

Religio-political Activities and Reconversion

After focussing on Hinduization during the initial years, the *Sangh Parivar* has systematically speeded up various religio-political activities. *Satsangs* are organized every Thursday or Sunday. In Orissa, various *satsangs* are organized by the devotees of godmen like Anukul Chandra, Satya Sai Baba and others. But the RSS-sponsored *satsangs* 'are different in nature as they emphasize society and nation rather than individual salvation'.[66] The VKA arranges special training camps to train the *satsang pramukhs* so that identical religio-political discourse could be imparted.

The other major programme undertaken is reconversion or 'homecoming', with the purpose to bring back the *Vanavasi* 'Hindus' who have been 'lured' away by the Christian missionaries. *Paravartan* is organized according to Hindu rituals and customs laid down by the Shastra. A *Shuddhi Sanskar* ceremony is followed by the acceptance of *panchamrita*. People from the nearby villages come and witness this ceremony. The VHP leaders, in their speeches, describe Christianity as an evil. At the end of the ceremony the reconverts declare: *Ame Mishilu* (We have come back) and the villagers announce *Ame Grahana Kalu* (We have accepted). Then the reconverts change their old clothes as well as the old earthen cooking pots (*handi badala*). This is followed by their visit to the nearest *matha* or temple for *darshan* and the ceremony comes to an end.[67]

However, the *Sangh Parivar* faces a dilemma because of *punaravartan* (re-reconversion). The *Sangh Parivar* leaders show their displeasure that many reconverts are not genuinely attracted to Hinduism. As their religious status denies them the privilege of reservation in employment, they get reconverted simply to avail a certificate which they could use it for this purpose. As soon as they avail it they go back to Christianity. Therefore, the *Sangh Parivar* has become very cautious in this regard.

Ignores Genuine Socio-economic Problems

The *Sangh Parivar* has thus posed a challenge to the Christian missionaries in the tribal district of Phulbani in Orissa by providing an alternate educational and welfare system. For instance, the opening of Saraswati Shishu Mandir at Baliguda town has forced the closure of the old Catholic school.[68] The process of Hinduization asserts a 'Hindu religion' and a 'Hindu culture' over the primitive tribal religious faith. The VHP *satsangs* are not just religious congregations, their mission is to propagate the RSS ideology. Further, through *paravartan*, it stirs up anti-Christian propaganda.

Golwalkar was clear that besides striving for the physical amelioration of these neglected tribals, 'love and pride in Hindu Dharma and the spirit of identity with the rest of Hindus have to be rekindled in their minds through the channel of devotion to God'.[69] Therefore, the emphasis is much more on the process of Hinduization and propagation of *Hindutva* rather than socio-economic amelioration. The *swayamsevaks* and other Hindus are advised to treat the *Vanavasis* in a spirit of equality: 'We should freely mix with them, eat with them, and sing and chant with them the holy songs of devotion.' Here again the focus is on the 'change of heart' and a 'human touch' like in the case of Dalits. Schools and welfare programmes disseminate these aspects of integration. No rigorous socio-economic analysis addressing the genuine problems of the tribals is visible.

It might be pointed out that the approach of the RSS ignores problems which are the heart of the Adivasi issue. These problems include their economic exploitation at the hands of moneylenders as well as ecological imbalances caused by the pursuits of the big business houses.[70] Instead of raising these issues, the RSS victimizes the people who have been struggling against this exploitation.[71] Also, the RSS ignores the political, economic and cultural practices of tribals and creates a myth of the static Adivasi society. This understanding of the RSS implies that tribal society lacks the potential for change from within and it has to be brought about from without.

Co-opting Dalits and Tribals: Success or Failure?

In its attempt to co-opt the Dalits and the Adivasis the RSS has made changes in its earlier position on the reservation issue. In the early years of the 1970s, it consolidated its *savarna* middle class constituents by its consistent anti-reservation stance. As Dalit politics started asserting itself, the *Sangh Parivar* reformulated its old strategy. It favoured co-opting the Dalits and the Adivasis to the fold of *Hindutva*. Accordingly, the VHP and the Vanavasi Kalyan Ashram got activated. Untouchability was decried and a legal ban was sought. The RSS speeded up various welfare activities among these communities, showing its 'genuine' concern for these neglected sections. The ABVP, which earlier opposed the reservation of seats for SCs and STs, started favouring reservation for them.[72]

How far has the RSS succeeded in co-opting the Dalits and the tribals to the *Hindutva* fold? In many parts of India, the better-off section among the Dalits and the tribes need proximity with the *savarnas* and therefore finds a meaning in *Hindutva*.[73] *Hindutva*, in way, has turned out to be a *Savarna Purana*.[74] Behind the *Sangh Parivar*'s change of strategy, the wider objective has been to shift the focus of hate from the Dalit to the Muslim: 'At least the Gujarat middle class—spread out over large cities . . . consisting mainly of Savarna, but also Dalit and Adivasi government servants, teachers and petty contractors—had begun to find security within the ideology of Hindutva. . . . Hindutva had become for this class a new purana to validate their pre-eminence.'[75] A section belonging to the lower strata of Dalits and tribes is also aspiring to transcend their low-caste status by Hinduization or Sanskritization. The RSS, the VHP, Kalyan Ashram and Seva Bharti have been actively propagating the possibility of an equal status and even upward mobility within Hindu society. Moreover, they assure equal treatment to the Dalits within their organizations if they embrace the saffron brotherhood. The dedicated *pracharaks*, working among the tribals and the Dalits, influence these communities through their dedication and commitment.

Despite these efforts of the *Sangh Parivar* a sizable section of Dalits and tribals still remain outside the *Hindutva* fold as it fails to offer anything concrete to ameliorate their socio-economic problems. The people who are struggling for survival do not find much solace in Sanskritization. Even if some do, it is for a temporary period. Moreover, the proponents of Dalit and tribal identity politics resist the RSS project of homogenization, ideologically as well as politically.

WOMEN

Women in Hindu Tradition

The proponents of Hindu nationalism claim that women always enjoyed an exalted position in Hindu tradition. They cite many examples to prove their theses, the most common being the prevalence of goddess worship among the Hindus.[76] They also boast that there were women seers in the Vedic period.[77] Though it is true that women had an honourable position and enjoyed certain important rights during the early Vedic period, since the later Vedic period the Dharmashastras started depriving them of social and political participation. The *Manusmriti* denied women access to the *Upanayana* or initiation which marked the beginning of access to sacred learning. Manu deprived women of their power and dignity as priestesses and worshippers. *Skand Purana* mentioned: 'Should a woman still wish to perform religious adulations herself she is to wash the feet of her husband and drink the water.'[78] The woman thus lost her equal status and became subjugated by man and her entire role became confined to homemaking.

Besides these texts, many Hindu rituals also symbolically express the control of man over his wife. The structuring of women as gendered subjects through Hindu rituals and practices is fundamentally implicated in the constitution and subordination of women.[79] The *Kanya dan* ritual of the Hindu marriage, for instance, treats the woman as property. This religious ceremony makes it clear that the two partners in marriage are in an unequal power relationship.

Critics point out that women in Hindu society are discriminated. They do not enjoy any autonomy. They are not allowed to make any rational self-choice. There exists a harsher indictment against women's sexual transgressions than those of men. Moreover, the identification of the creator as male places a high premium on the paternity of the child. By treating her as a mere 'field' for the 'seed', and thereby conferring on the father the natural guardianship of his children, Hindu society has consistently underplayed the significance of women's contribution to biological reproduction.[80] The motherhood ideology, paradoxically, entrusts the mother with the duties of child rearing, without giving her any real control over the child. It successfully entrenches women within domestic spheres by putting restraints on their sexuality.[81] In the Hindu discourse, from Shraddhanand to Golwalkar, the woman appears as Mother and Nurturer, a Preserver of tradition and property. A parallel is drawn between the position of woman and the cow as both are treated as property and as sacred symbols.[82] Yet the woman's position 'is in some respects worse: for as bearers of a powerful, necessary but dangerous sexuality, and as potentially independent actors, women are threatening in a way that cows are not'.[83]

Hedgewar's Conceptualization of Women

Hedgewar's RSS was designed to be an exclusively male organization. Lakshmibai Kelkar approached Hedgewar with an appeal to admit women as members. Though Hedgewar believed that women had a definite role to indoctrinate the young minds in 'proper' directions, he refused their entry into the RSS as the Sangh leaders have taken the vow of 'brahmacharya'.[84] However, he helped her to set up a parallel but separate organization called the Rashtra Sevika Samiti. Thus, this first affiliate of the RSS was started on the Vijayadashami day of 1936. Delivering a *boudhik* on 24 June 1938, organized by the Wardha *shakha* of the samiti, Hedgewar spoke: 'Time and again there have been suggestions to start Sangh work among women. But it was not feasible. Nor was it correct to ignore it. Therefore a decision was taken to start an independent organization for women working along the aims and objects of the Sangh and encourage it to grow.'[85] Therefore, despite making it formally independent, the RSS very much designed and controlled the course it would charter. It is also important to note a small yet significant difference in name: the members of the RSS are *rashtriya swayamsevaks* while the members of the women's wing are *rashtra sevikas*.[86] This partly explains Hedgewar's conceptualization of woman.

Golwalkar's Re-articulation of a Traditional Woman

In Golwalkar's scheme of *Hindu Rashtra* women had a special responsibility as faithful mothers[87] who would carefully guard their children from 'corrupting' Western influences and instill in them the right *sanskaras* such as 'devotion to duty, spirit of personal endeavour, love of the motherland and readiness for service to society'.[88] The mothers would also teach them about patriotic heroes and religious texts. Besides this the women could keep contacts in their neighbourhood to carry out programmes to inculcate these ideals. The other important role Golwalkar earmarked for women was the role of dutiful wives. He wrote: 'The ideal of Savitri, before whom even the Lord of death accepted defeat, is before them. May them all invoke within themselves such single-minded devotion to the ideal, such purity of character and such peerless heroism.'[89]

Thus, Golwalkar's discourse on women emphasizes the woman as Mother and Nurturer, begetter of glorious sons of the *Hindu Rashtra.* Its religious overtone is pronounced when defining women in the images of Hindu goddesses and constructs—as dutiful and sacrificing mothers and wives. The discourse also looks at woman as container or vehicle, the repository of Hindu tradition, the essence of the spirituality of Hindu civilization. Critics look at it as 'an amplification of the image of individual upper-caste ("middle class"?) Hindu women: "traditionally" dressed, "traditional" in taste, eternally serving, self-sacrificing, gentle, tolerant, passive'.[90]

The RSS seeks to reclaim a glorious past in which the women once enjoyed an honourable position. In its emphasis on returning to the past this view is totally opposed to the women's liberation movement of the West. Unlike the latter, it does not want to go for any fundamental change in values; what it aspires is only a sort of readjustment in the social and economic set up. The RSS contends that women in India always had a dignified position within the household, and society. That has only to be re-established and re-affirmed.

Perpetuating Gender Inequality?

The RSS did not approve of any overt political role for women during the Golwalkar era. It could not swallow the fact that the highest political office in India was held by a woman. The RSS mouthpiece *Organiser*[91] described Indira Gandhi's rule as disastrous and admiringly quoted Napoleon: 'A statesman has his heart in his brain; a woman's brain is generally in her heart.' It argued that whenever women were invested with power, they caused havoc to the state and the nation. That is why, the argument ran, a woman has never been entrusted with the highest office of a country in the West, except those countries where constitutional monarchy still survives. Even in the USA, where women are much more on par with men, no woman has ever been a Secretary of State. The article further mentioned that 'it would scandalise the Americans, both men and women, to have a woman as the President of the United States'.[92] The article also cited examples of France, the erstwhile USSR and other countries to strengthen its argument that nowhere did women attain the highest political office. In spite of emancipation and the acquisition of the right to vote, 'women in the Western world have preferred to be wives and mothers rather than Ministers and public celebrities'.[93] The article did not appreciate Indira Gandhi's elevation to the highest political office.

The article did not stop here. It further suggested that middle-aged women, particularly widows, should live a retired life rather than aspiring for political power. Justifying this on so-called physiological and psychological grounds, it argued: 'For instance, Freudian tests of women over fifty and of women who are widows, with a frustrated life behind them, show that the desire to take revenge or to cling to power arise because of some biological changes which take place in womanly bodies after a given time.'[94] It finally advised widowed women 'to find satisfaction in family circles', as laid down by Hindu custom.[95]

All these arguments are far beyond traditionalism; they are fundamentalist, explicitly anti-woman, blatantly male chauvinistic and very much in tune with Manu's concept of woman. This understanding of the RSS contradicts its claim that women enjoyed prestigious positions in Hindu society. When the RSS denies them the equal status even now, how can it claim that women enjoyed a higher status earlier?

Divergent Discourses in post-Golwalkar Era: Traditional and Modern

The RSS was compelled to revise its monolithic discourse on women during the post-Golwalkar era for obvious reasons. First, the increasing socio-economic independence of women had created the material conditions for them to have recognition outside the family. Secondly, women's participation in the political process had been steadily increasing. Thirdly, there emerged a possibility to use women as an important instrument to arouse communal passions during the time of communal conflict. Therefore, in this changing scenario, woman's traditional role needed to be revised. A modernist discourse had to supplement the traditional. Despite adherence to a traditional role, the woman needed to be granted more freedom and equality. The RSS could no more afford to argue that investing women with political power would spell danger to the nation. In this light, a new flexible discourse had to be designed.

The *Organiser* made a significant shift vis-a-vis its earlier position. K.R. Malkani, came out with an article titled 'Role of Religion and Politics',[96] which unlike the earlier article, did not contain any pronounced anti-woman outbursts. Malkani observed that ancient Greek civilization was male-dominated where the woman was a mere child-bearing machine. In his analysis, both Christianity and Islam demonstrated a 'strong male bias'. Buddhism expressed 'a certain distaste for the female sex'. He charged Western man with treating the woman not as a better half, but the 'worse half'. He criticized the French and Russian Revolutions as they failed to meet the aspirations of women. He lamented that Europe had no woman ruler since Catherine the Great, quite contrary to the earlier position. He did not even spare the USA since it granted voting rights to women much later, even after the Negro male.

However, he was proud that India had maintained a 'balanced' man-woman relationship.[97] Trying to find the reason, he wrote: 'May be because our rich soil made food-gathering easy and hunting not so necessary; may be also because of the prevalence of Tantrism, with its feminine emphasis on mystery—and on the superiority of instinct over intellect.' He continued that 'the woman looks beyond logic—and into life. She looks beyond intellect, into mystery of things. She is a born mystic. She knows the myth to be the higher truth.' Though subtle, like the earlier article, Malkani still questioned the intellectual capability of the woman.

Malkani claims that the Indian recognition of a woman's due role is not an act of charity, but a recognition of reality. And that reality is that she performs the great act of creating a child. Therefore, there is no retreat from Golwalkar's traditional perception. In the post-Golwalkar era, RSS sources have frequently claimed that the woman is seen in high esteem by the *Parivar* and *swayamsevaks* worship the ideal women of India in their *Ekatmatastotram*. As the stanza in this prayer reads:

Arundhatyanasuya cha Savitri
Janaki Sati
Draupadi Kannagi Gargi Meera
Durgavati tatha
Lakshmirahalya Chennamma
Rudramamba Suvikrama
Nivedita Sharda cha pranamya
matrudevata

These Hindu women (Arundhati, Anasuya, Savitri, Janaki, Sati, Draupadi, Kannagi, Gargi, Meera, Durgavati, Luxmibai, Ahalyabai Holkar, Chennamma, Rudramamba, Nivedita and Sarada), the RSS mentions, have excelled as rulers, fighters, politicians, intellectuals, saints, artists, social reformers, etc. It even praises non-Hindu women like Sister Nivedita and The Mother (disciple of Aurobindo), who adopted Hindu culture and the Hindu way of life.[98] Thus the RSS tries to project that the women have always played a vital role in India and enjoyed a place of respect. Now women can play a multifarious role, including political, unlike the Golwalkar era.

Balasaheb Deoras understood the importance of organizing the women who constituted around 50 per cent of the population. He stressed the leading role of Rashtra Sevika Samiti in this endeavour.[99] Recognizing the need to reach different sections of women, some affiliates of the *Sangh Parivar* have set up their respective women's wings. Besides the oldest affiliate of the RSS, the Rashtra Sevika Samiti, the BJP has its Mahila Morcha and the VHP controls Durga Vahini. With these developments, the discourses constituting the Hindu woman within the *Parivar* are multiple: moderate and extremist, traditional and modern. At times these discourses seem contradictory. For example, the moderates within the Rashtra Sevika Samiti and the BJP Mahila Morcha oppose *sati*, whereas the extremists favour a woman's right to choose to commit *sati*. Similarly, moderates support the legal amendments that have been made to Hindu personal law and plead for similar changes of Muslim law through a Uniform Civil Code. The BJP even speaks of ensuring women's equal access to their husbands' property. On the other side, the *sants* and *sadhus* of the VHP are strongly opposed to the reform of the Hindu Personal Law and argue for the restoration of the laws of Manu. Some even go to the extent of demanding restoration of Hindu polygamy.

However, both the moderate and extremist discourses contain, to differing extents, elements of modernity and tradition. For example, the moderate voice of the BJP Mahila Morcha contains very strong traditional overtones in their emphasis on women's role in the family as wives and mothers. Similarly, the Rashtra Sevika Samiti which brings women out of their homes and their traditional roles is careful not to challenge the family's ultimate authority over its members, particularly, its female members. Similarly, even the more extremist discourse contains elements of modernity. For example, in the debate around Roop Kanwar's *sati*,[100] some of the more extremist voices within the BJP—the same voices that publicly deplored the enslavement of Muslim women in the Muslim Women's Act—publicly defended Roop Kanwar's *sati*. Vijayraje Scindia went on record at that time to say that the tradition of *sati* is a part of 'our' cultural heritage and that it is the fundamental right of all Hindu women to commit *sati* if they want to.[101] The statement amounts to a careful intermingling of two discourses: traditional, and a modernist appeal to the liberal rights discourse.[102]

Therefore, though all these multiple discourses appear contradictory, they are not really so. Underlying these divergent discourses exists a common thread—the recognition of women as *matri shakti*, as wives and mothers, as strong Hindu women. Within these discourses, the Hindu woman is a product of both a traditional and a modern discourse. She is both the subject of the traditional discourses of religion—celebrated as *matri shakti*, as mother—and the subject of the modern discourses of liberalism and secularism—she has rights.[103]

Emergence of the Militant Communal Hindu Woman

Golwalkar's construction of woman has undergone a sea-change during the last decade. He did not approve of a demonstratively public or an active political role for women. The Ram Janmabhoomi movement foregrounded the militantly communal Hindu woman, thereby inverting her traditional invisibility. The movement brought some unprecedented changes in the process of the political self-activization of women.[104]

The earlier national and communal movements, which sought participation of women, promised to restore the honour of a feminine figure—the cow, the abducted Hindu woman, the motherland. However, the role was reversed in this movement in which women were being activated to liberate the *janmabhoomi* and restore it to Ram, a male deity. The reversal of roles equips the communal woman with a new and empowering self-image. The woman has stepped out of a purely iconic status to take up active position as a militant.[105] Thus, the woman has acquired a new militant role, which was perhaps not devised by Golwalkar.

The present discourse of the RSS favours a strong Hindu woman. The RSS provides physical training to women for this purpose. A strong Hindu woman is seen as essential for the constitution of a strong Hindu society. The new woman has also become active and much more visible in the public sphere. However, this new RSS construction of woman would never allow her to abandon her traditional role as home-maker, as faithful and dutiful mother and wife. It continues to believe that women 'have a unique responsibility of keeping the family united by their service, love and understanding'.[106] The RSS has expressed concern that the development of children would suffer as educated mothers go out to earn. It argues that 'the consideration that those women who are not doing a job, do not have a place in the society and in the family is totally wrong'.[107] Thus, the woman retains her traditional role despite the fact that she has acquired a certain new role in the changing socio-political context. This new Hindu woman, though educated and working, enjoys a strong presence within her family and her community, and is still required to retain her purity and loyalty as wife and mother.

PROGENY

The *Hindu Rashtra* not only demands an ideal wife and mother, it needs ideal progeny as well. The children of the *Hindu Rashtra* need to be imparted *sanskar* and patriotism not just by their mothers, but also by a carefully designed pedagogy.[108] The RSS set up its first Saraswati Shishu Mandir at Gorakhpur (Uttar Pradesh) in 1952 'aiming at all-round development of boys and girls on the basis of Indian culture'. Golwalkar was present on the occasion.[109] The decision to set up a school came at a moment of dejection and of virtual non-activity.[110] However, this decision was very much the product of a conscious activity rather than non-activity in many ways: first, as parents were getting hesitant to send their children to the *shakhas*, particularly after the first ban, it was thought that the children could be attracted through the schools without any suspicion; secondly, these students, properly trained in the ideology of the *Hindu Rashtra*, would supplement the core cadre, the *swayamsevaks*; thirdly, the dominant role of Christian missionaries in the educational sphere could be effectively challenged, particularly in tribal and remote areas.

Vidya Bharati: The Umbrella Organization

Since 1952, the RSS has been promoting these schools with a missionary zeal. Initially, it concentrated in UP, Bihar, Andhra Pradesh and a few other states. An all India body called Vidya Bharati was set up in 1977 to provide an organizational umbrella to these schools.[111] A huge camp of children was organized at Delhi to mark the occasion.[112] Vidya Bharati's growth has been phenomenal. In 1977, it managed only 500 schools and just over 20,000 students; by the end of 1990, the number of these schools reached 4,000 having 35,000 teachers.[113] Vidya Bharati claimed that by the end of 1991, their educational network covered the whole of India except a few states of the north-east and it consisted of about

4,000 schools, 36,000 teachers and over 10 lakh (one million) students. Its target was to reach 10,000 schools in the next five years.[114] It kept its target; by 1998 it has come to be regarded as the largest NGO in education, running 13,000 institutions which employ 74,000 teachers and educate 17 lakh students. It has 8,145 primary schools, 40 colleges, 15 teacher training colleges and 7 technical institutions.[115] All except the single-teacher schools and about half the primary schools are recognized by the respective state education boards. By 1999, the organization has expanded further; it now runs 14,000 schools having 18 lakh pupils. These schools have presence in every state except Mizoram, and they employ 80,000 teachers.[116] These schools are popularly known as Saraswati Shishu Mandir; besides this name, they are also run in the names of Bharatiya Vidya Niketan, Gita Vidyalaya and Saraswati Bal Vidyalaya.

Content of Education

The RSS is opposed to the 'colonial educational heritage' left behind by Lord Macaulay and aims to replace it with a system based exclusively on Hindu lines. It is to be noted that the school is called *mandir* and the teachers are called *acharyas.* Thus the RSS gives a Hindu touch to the nomenclatures. All schools have a prayer hall with idols of Hindu deities. These schools observe Teachers' Day not on 5 September, the birth anniversary of Dr. S. Radhakrishnan, but on the birth anniversary of the sage Vyasa. Similarly, they observe Children's Day not on 14 November, Nehru's birth anniversary, but on Krishna Jayanti. The aim of these schools is 'character-building'. The theme of education is represented in the daily prayer: *Jag-sir Mor Banaye Bharat* (Let India be the pride of the world). An organizer of the Vidya Bharati set-up explains their philosophy by saying: 'dedicated to the motherland with a deep Bharatiya spirit inculcates in the child the will to change his character, adjust his nature and programme so as to fulfill the nation's will and necessity.'[117] In consonance with this objective, the ideas of prominent Hindu thinkers like Vivekananda, Tilak, Aurobindo are propagated and their 'strength of character' is idealized among the students.

Initially, Vidya Bharati developed curricula for four subjects: Physical Exercises, including *yoga, asanas,* etc.; Music; Sanskrit; and Cultural Knowledge. But the RSS always eyed one subject—Indian history. In its view, the textbooks on history give the 'communist' rather than the 'Hindu' viewpoint. Therefore, they need to be rewritten and reinterpreted afresh.[118] The opportunity came with the rule of the Janata Party at the centre. Morarji Desai, under the RSS influence, made an attempt to withdraw those textbooks whose 'controversial and biased material' would lead their readers to acquire 'a prejudiced view of history'. Attempts were also made to control the ICHR, ICSSR, NCERT, NBT and the UGC, the bastions of 'communist' historians and social scientists.[119] Though the short Janata experiment aborted the RSS plan, it never gave it up. During early 1990s, with the patronage of the BJP governments of UP, Rajasthan, Himachal Pradesh and Madhya Pradesh the Vidya Bharati not only expanded in terms of numbers, it was also granted autonomy to frame the syllabi for lower classes and conduct examinations as well.

Thus, the saffron syllabus was introduced in these states. History textbooks were rewritten and Akbar painted black. In UP, moral classes were introduced in schools, headed by RSS *pracharaks*. Students were to respond to the roll call saying '*Vande Mataram*' instead of *upasthit* or 'yes sir'. Singing of *Saraswati Vandana* was made compulsory. In 1991 the BJP introduced *Vedic* Mathematics in the state of UP. Vidya Bharati's projection of the map of India includes in it Nepal, Pakistan, Bangladesh and parts of Myanmar—the RSS dream of Akhand Bharat. The Indian Ocean is introduced as Hindu Mahasagar and the Arabian Sea as Sindhu Mahasagar. The writings of Deendayal Upadhyaya and contributions by RSS stalwarts—Rajendra Singh and Sudarshan discussing science and environment respectively—have entered school textbooks.[120]

With BJP's assuming power at the Centre in 1998, the RSS made certain that the key portfolio of education (HRD) remained with a hardcore loyalist. M.M. Joshi was assigned this ministry and Uma Bharti became his deputy. Joshi's job was to complete the unfinished RSS agenda that was initiated in 1977. In the top-level central research institutes, Joshi replaced left-leaning academics with those close to the *Sangh Parivar*. The Indian Council for Historial Research became the first target, followed by the Indian Council of Social Science Research and the Indian Institute of Advanced Studies. In some BJP ruled states, the RSS standpoints were unobtrusively introduced. In Rajasthan, RSS supporters were nominated to the education boards.[121]

Joshi's enthusiasm got a set back when he tried to push through the RSS agenda in a meeting of state education ministers. The controversial annexure to the agenda of the meeting, which was withdrawn later due to protest by a number of state education ministers, made the following suggestions on curricular reform:

- The curriculum from the primary to the highest classes should be Indianized, nationalized and spiritualized. At all levels of education and in all courses, even vocational courses, essentials of Indian culture should be introduced covering 10 per cent to 25 per cent of every course.
- No differentiation should be made in the curriculum for boys and girls at the primary stage. At later stages, the curriculum for girls may include training in home keeping.
- A comprehensive programme for the use of one's mother tongue as a medium of instruction at all stages of education should be launched.
- Considering the contribution of Sanskrit to the development of Indian languages and its unique contribution to the cultural unity of the nation and ancient wisdom, it should be made a compulsory subject from Classes III to X.
- Moral and spiritual education should be introduced at all stages in all the schools and the universities for the inculcation of a good character and desirable social and national values.
- Value Education Centres with facilities for the comparative study of all religions should be established.
- Access to higher education should not be virtually unrestricted as at present. Changing the mass character of higher education will not only raise academic standards but also lead to substantial savings. Savings thus effected should be utilized for greater vocationalization of higher education.
- Sanskrit universities should be established in the four zones of the country. Research on outstanding Sanskrit works should be encouraged.
- A course on Indian philosophy in all higher education courses/programmes, especially vocational courses should be provided.
- Article 30 of the Indian Constitution be amended to read as follows: 'Right of citizens to establish and administer educational institutions of choice.' Every section of citizens, whether based on religion or language, shall have the right to establish and administer educational institutions of their choice.

Methodology

The RSS has been consistently disseminating '*sanskar* and *sanskriti*' through the teachers of these schools. Most of these *acharyas* are *swayamsevaks*, properly trained in the ideology of the *Hindu Rashtra*. The classroom is an ideal place to teach the RSS viewpoint on culture and history. A periodic examination called Sanskriti Gyan Pariksha is conducted among the students belonging to Classes IV to XII to assess their knowledge on Indian history and culture.

Besides classroom teaching, where culture and history are accordingly taught, the ideology is also conveyed through co-curricular activities and publications, including children's magazines.[122] The children sing the prayers and songs steeped in devotion to the *Hindu Rashtra*. Assemblies and stage performances organized on Hindu festivals are another example of ideologically relevant activities. Occasionally an activist of the *Sangh Parivar* addresses them, further cementing their ideological belief. The virtual absence of non-Hindu children in these schools adds to the collective sense of a distinct self-identity, which these activities evoke in a RSS school. Arousing a sense of collective Hindu identity may be seen as the underpinning philosophy of education in these schools.[123]

These children, indoctrinated with the ideology of the *Hindu Rashtra*, are supposed to spread their knowledge to the children of nearby slums and villages through the Sanskar Kendras.[124] However, at present, these *kendras* have been operating primarily in the remote and tribal areas where few schools exist. Also, about 500 such *kendras* are functioning in the urban slum areas. These extension centres have been set up with two aims: first, education is to be imparted to those children who are unable to attend the school; secondly, these children will be implanted with 'noble virtues' by exposing them to the Hindu culture and tradition through songs, stories and ceremonies.

Thus, the RSS meticulously shapes the future citizens of the Hindu nation. The popularity of this education system is soaring among the middle and lower middle classes for various reasons. While government schools have almost become defunct and private English-medium schools have become prohibitively expensive, the RSS-run schools charge a reasonable fee. Also, as the RSS schools impart cultural values like respect to the elders and learning of Hindu traditions, middle-class parents feel that their children are getting a well-rounded education at a nominal price.

The RSS, since the time of Hedgewar, has been attempting to construct a Hindu identity and homogenize the Hindus. Despite his ideological rigidity, Golwalkar gave a decisive push to the agenda of homogenization when he created the *Sangh Parivar* to attract and assimilate different identities into the framework of *Hindu Rashtra*. But the actual credit goes to Balasaheb Deoras for giving a dynamic orientation to the RSS project of homogenization. Deoras was shrewd enough to sense that the Dalits, the tribals, and the women were getting conscious of their socio-political rights and looking for self-expression. He also had the foresight to see the immense political potential of the future citizens. Therefore, all these sections needed to be carefully integrated, assimilated and homogenized for the success of the RSS mission. As he favoured direct political intervention, he did not hesitate to make a few strategic changes within the broad framework of the *Hindu Rashtra* to entice these identities and solicit their support in his endeavour. He activated the affiliates to work rigorously among these sections and they made significant inroads. The RSS experiment of homogenization may not have had a resounding success, but its ceaseless efforts and flexible strategies certainly fostered its tryst with politics.

NOTES AND REFERENCES

1. Lajpat Rai, *A History of the Arya Samaj* [1915] (Delhi: Orient Longman, 1967), pp. 123-4.
2. V.D. Savarkar, *Hindutva* (Poona: S.P. Gokhale, 1949), pp. 120-1.
3. See Golwalkar's interview published in *Organiser*, XXII (29), 8 March 1969.
4. These four *varnas* emerged from the *Virat Purusha* (Primeval Man) as mentioned in the *Rig Veda*: his mouth became the Brahmins, his arms the Kshatriyas, his thighs the Vaishyas, and his feet the Shudras. For more discussion on *varna* and the concept of race, see Christophe Jaffrelot, 'The Idea of Hindu Race in the Writings of Hindu Nationalist Ideologues in the 1920s and 1930s: A Concept Between Two Cultures', in Peter Robb, ed., *The Concept of Race in South Asia* (Delhi: Oxford University Press, 1995), pp. 327-54.
5. Defending the Brahmins he observes that they 'are as poor as anybody else in this poor country. Ninety per cent of them do not get two square meals a day'. See *Organiser*, XXII (29), 8 March 1969.
6. M.V. Kamath, 'The Demonization of Upper Castes', *Organiser*, Deepavali Special, 30 October 1994, pp. 23-4.
7. *Organiser*, XXII (29), 8 March 1969.
8. Ibid.
9. Ibid.
10. *Organiser*, XXII (28), 28 February 1969.
11. Ibid.
12. *Organiser*, XXII (45), 21 June 1969.
13. Ibid.
14. H.V. Seshadri, *The Way* (Delhi: Suruchi Prakashan, 1991), p. 29. This brings to

mind the suggestion of Swami Shraddhanand. For him inter-dining alone could solve the problem of untouchability and exclusiveness among the Hindus.

15. BJP's electoral debacle in UP in the 1999 Lok Sabha elections suggested otherwise; there appeared to be a vertical division along the caste lines within the *Sangh Parivar.*
16. Resolution of the ABPS of the RSS adopted at Nagpur on 27-9 March 1981. See *Organiser,* XXXII (47), 12 April 1981.
17. Ibid.
18. *Organiser,* XXXII (39), 15 February 1981.
19. *Organiser,* XLVII (3), 20 August 1995.
20. *Organiser,* XLVI (40), 7 May 1995.
21. *Organiser,* XLVIII (15), 10 November 1996, p. 10.
22. *Organiser,* 27 March 1994, p. 17.
23. *Organiser,* XLVII (24), 14 January 1996, p. 7.
24. See Gail Omvedt, *Dalit Visions: The Anti-Caste Movement and the Construction of an Indian Identity* (Delhi: Orient Longman, 1995). Though the Panthers rose and fell like a flash, the Dalit movement has spread across the country. Kanshi Ram's Bahujan Samaj Party (BSP) has emerged as a strong political force in north and north-west India.
25. The manifesto of Dalit Panthers defines Dalit as members of scheduled castes and tribes, neo-Buddhists, the working people, the landless and poor peasants, women and all those who are being exploited politically, economically and in the name of religion. Thus the term has broad connotations. See Dalit Panther Manifesto in Barbara Joshi, *Untouchable! Voices of Dalit Liberation* (London: Zed Books, 1984), pp. 141-6.
26. See V.T. Rajsekhar's Foreword in Ram Nath, *Dalit-Muslim Unity: Why and How?* (Bangalore: Dalit Sahitya Academy, 1995), p. 7.
27. See Kancha Ilaiah, *Why I am not a Hindu: A Sudra Critique of Hindutva Philosophy, Culture and Political Economy* (Calcutta: Samya, 1996).
28. V.T. Rajsekhar's foreword in Ram Nath, *Dalit-Muslim Unity,* op. cit., p. 7.
29. S.K. Biswas, *Hindu Raj: Today-Yesterday-Tomorrow* (Bangalore: Orion Books, 1996), p. 3.
30. Ibid., p. 5.
31. *Organiser,* XXLVII (3), 20 August 1995.
32. Ibid.
33. V.T. Rajsekhar's Foreword in Ram Nath, *Dalit-Muslim Unity,* op. cit., p. 6.
34. See S. Anandhi, *Contending Identities: Dalits and Secular Politics in Madras Slums* (Delhi: Indian Social Science Institute, 1995), pp. 30-43.
35. S.K. Aggarwal, *Dr. Ambedkar on Muslim Fundamentalism* (Delhi: Suruchi Prakashan, 1993), p. 53.
36. Koenraad Elst, *Dr. Ambedkar: A True Aryan* (Delhi: Voice of India, 1993), pp. 3-14.
37. Ibid.
38. Ibid.

39. For a detailed discussion on Ambedkar's socio-political thought see M.S. Gore, *The Social Context of an Ideology: Ambedkar's Political and Social Thought* (Delhi: Sage Publications, 1993); Gail Omvedt, *Dalits and the Democratic Revolution: Dr. Ambedkar and the Dalit Movement in Colonial India* (Delhi: Sage Publications, 1994).
40. Dalit intellectuals strongly object to Arun Shourie's criticism of Ambedkar in his book *Worshipping the False Gods*. Despite the clarification of the RSS that it has nothing to do with this work, the Dalits are not convinced as they know Shourie's RSS connection. For a critique of Shourie's book, see Gopal Guru, 'Understanding Ambedkar's Construction of National Movement', in *Economic and Political Weekly*, XXXIII (4), 24-30 January 1998.
41. Seva Bharti of Delhi has over 200 projects, with Balwadis, Bal Sanskar Kendra, Tailoring Classes, Coaching Classes, Medicare Centres, Night Schools, Reading Rooms, etc., covering about 75 slum areas.
42. M.S. Golwalkar, *Bunch of Thoughts* [1966] (Bangalore: Jagarana Prakashana, 1980), p. 471.
43. Veer Bharat Talwar, *Jharkhand ke Adivasi aur RSS* [in Hindi] (Chhaibasa: St. Martin's Printer, n.d.), pp. 142-3.
44. Gyanendra Pandey, 'Hindus and Others: The Militant Hindu Construction', in *Economic and Political Weekly*, XXVI (52), 28 December 1991, p. 3003.
45. See M.S. Golwalkar, *Bunch of Thoughts*, op. cit., pp. 474-5.
46. Nirmal Minz, 'Identity of Tribals in India', in Walter Fernandes, ed., *The Indigenous Question: Search for an Identity* (Delhi: Indian Social Institute, 1993), pp. 23-32.
47. As per the 1991 Census, the Scheduled Tribes constitute 22.2 per cent of the population of Orissa. The population of the Scheduled Castes is 16.2 per cent.
48. For an account of the activities of the Christian missionaries in nineteenth century Orissa, see Dasarathi Swaro, *The Christian Missionaries in Orissa: Their Impact on Nineteenth Century Society* (Calcutta: Punthi Pustak, 1990). Also see Rev. Amos Sutton, *Orissa and Its Evangelization* (Derby, England, 1850).
49. The early life of Laxmanananda is obscure. He spent some years at one Kailash Ashram in the foothills of the Himalayas. In 1966 he participated in the *Goraksha Andolan*, then joined the VHP and came to Orissa. After consulting Bhupendra Kumar Basu, the Orissa RSS chief, he started his mission at Phulbani.
50. Phulbani has now been bifurcated into two districts: Boudh and Kondhmal. The new district of Phulbani (Kondhmal) has the following population ratio: Scheduled Tribes 54.23 per cent, Scheduled Castes 18.20 per cent and General Category 27.57 per cent. See *Panchayati Raj Department Publication* (Bhubaneswar: Government of Orissa, 1994).
51. Raghunath Sethi was invited to a meeting in which Bhupendra Kumar Basu was also the speaker. He got attracted towards RSS ideology and became a *pracharak*. He was appointed as the state secretary of the VHP, then came to Phulbani as zilla *pracharak* in 1967-8. Sethi comes from a Scheduled Caste background.
52. VHP leaders never approve the idea of staying together; they insist on institutionalized marriage.

53. RSS activists argue that the missionaries have spread Christianity by cheating the innocent tribals. For example, they cured malaria with cheap anti-malaria drugs (quinine tablets), but made prior condition that the patient would embrace Christianity soon after the cure. As malaria is the most common disease in the tribal areas, maximum conversion took place due to this.
54. Though the VKA was set up in 1952, it started its activities in Orissa only in 1979. Earlier the VHP was active in the tribal areas of Orissa. In its report (1994-5) the Kalyan Ashram claimed to be running the following programmes in Orissa: Hostels–4 (boys and girls–2 each); Schools–2; One Teacher Schools–72; Non-formal Education Centres–204; Bal Sanskar Kendras–89; Dispensaries–9; Khel Kud Kendras–129; Satsang Kendras–641; Sewing Centres–4. It also mentioned that there were 86 wholetime workers (78 males and 8 females) working for ABVKA in Orissa. See *Report of Akhil Bharatiya Vanavasi Kalyan Ashram*, Orissa, Sundergarh: 28 February 1995.
55. The *goshala* also has a curious beginning. One day an old man reportedly came to the Shiva temple to offer a cow. As no one was there to receive, he donated the cow to the Ashram. Thus started a *goshala*. Interview with Raghunath Sethi.
56. Interview with Laxminarayan Acharya, a teacher of the Ashram school and RSS activist.
57. Perhaps Laxmanananda wants to ensure that the payment of salaries to teachers and scholarships to students should not be affected because of the open RSS affiliation.
58. Interview with Mukund Deo, secretary of the ashram. Deo is also a BJP activist.
59. Daily Routine: 4 a.m.–Collective recital of *Ekatmata Stotra*; 4-30 a.m.-5-30 a.m.–Study; 5-30 a.m.-6 a.m.–cleaning of the Ashram; 6 a.m.-6-30 a.m.–*nityakarma*, go the river for bath; 6-30 a.m.-7-30 a.m.–*Surya namaskar*, *yoga* and mass prayer; 7-30 a.m.-8 a.m.–breakfast; 8 a.m.-9-45 a.m.–study; 9-45 a.m.-10 a.m.–break; 10 a.m.-1 p.m.–school; 1 p.m.-2 p.m.–lunch; 2 p.m.-4 p.m.–school; 4 p.m.-5 p.m.–agriculture; 5 p.m.-5-30 p.m.–*nityakarma*; 5-30 p.m.-6-15 p.m.–*shakha*; 6-15 p.m.-6-30 p.m.–break; 6-30 p.m.–prayer; 7 p.m.-9 p.m.–study; 9 p.m.–dinner; 10 p.m.–bedtime.
60. The whistle blew exactly at 5-30 p.m. The *Rashtra sevikas* assembled at the Ashram ground and made 6 rows. First, there was *dhwja pranam*, then *gana sankhya* (counting of numbers) followed by prayers such as *Swarnamayi Lanka, Janani Janmabhoomischa* and then slogan of *Akhand Bharat ki Jai*. After this the girls played *luchakali* and *kabaddi*. I was told that they also practise *danda* (push ups). That day there was no *boudhik* as they had just participated in the monthly *baithak*.
61. Interview with Mukund Deo, secretary of the Ashram. It is strange that the tribal custom of *dhangda dhandi* is not considered as a cultural treasure, but a *Kusanskar*.
62. My visit coincided with the day of the monthly *baithak*. The topics for discussion were *Swadeshi* and Somalia. Deo was explaining these issues in detail to the inmates as well as to the teachers.

63. The boys face a lot of hardship if the scholarship money is disbursed late. The young RSS whole-timer faces difficulty in arranging the ration. In comparison to the other two Ashram schools, this hostel faces more financial crisis as it does not have its own agricultural land.
64. On my visit to Cutingia dispensary I found that it was a very small one and not well-equipped. It was without a doctor for quite sometime and a paramedical person was managing it. However, the regular *shakha* was taking place in the compound of the dispensary.
65. Though 400 such *pathashalas* were opened, only 100 have been functioning. However, the VKA report claims that operational number is still 400.
66. Interview with Chandrakanta Nath. The number of these *satsangs*, which picked up during the *Ram Janmabhoomi* agitation, is declining steadily. For example, 53 such congregations were held regularly in Raikia block, the number came down to 28 later. Similarly in Udayagiri tahshil the number has come down from 300 to 100.
67. Under the supervision of Laxmanananda *paravartan* ceremonies had taken place at the district. While one activist claims that about 6,000 people have been brought back to the Hindu fold in the district, ABVKA pamphlet puts the number at 1,700. Even this number seems to be much exaggerated.
68. Saraswati Shishu Mandir at Baliguda, which only provides primary education, has a student strength of 350. People prefer this school because it imparts quality education and puts emphasis on Indian culture, argues one local RSS leader. This school primarily trains the future missionaries of *Hindu Rashtra*. In the next 25 years the Christian missionaries will stop functioning and these trained students of the RSS schools will 'dominate each sphere of social life', predicts one RSS activist.
69. See M.S. Golwalkar, *Bunch of Thoughts*, op. cit., p. 473.
70. It is argued that as the RSS is closely linked with the capitalists, its silence on these vital issues are not surprising. See Walter Fernandes and Arundhati Roy Choudhury, 'Search for a Tribal Identity: The Dominant and the Subaltern', in Walter Fernandes, ed., *The Indigenous Question*, op. cit., pp. 9-22.
71. For instance, B.D. Sharma, an activist bureaucrat, who worked dedicatedly for the upliftment of the Adivasis, was stripped and paraded on the roads of Jagdalpur, Madhya Pradesh by the *Sangh Parivar* members.
72. The same strategy was followed in the case of the Mandal Commission Report. The RSS opposed it tooth and nail, but when backward caste politics asserted itself, it projected Kalyan Singh, who belonged to the backward caste, as the BJP chief minister of UP.
73. However, a radical section consisting of students, intellectuals and professionals has emerged among the Dalits which strongly advocates a separate Dalit identity and opposes its integration into the Hindu fold.
74. This term is borrowed from Ashis Nandy et al., *Creating a Nationality: The Ramjanmabhoomi Movement and Fear of the Self* (Delhi: Oxford University Press, 1995).

75. Ibid., p. 104.
76. However, the notion of Goddess worship within 'patriarchal religions' can be seen as attempts to devise normative patterns of female behaviour as wife and mother. See Uma Chakravarti and Kumkum Roy, 'In Search of Our Past: A Review of the Limitations and Possibilities of Historiography of Women in Early India', in *Economic and Political Weekly*, XXXIII (18), 1988, pp. WS 2-10.
77. This claim becomes weak when one analyses the *Rig Veda*, which consists of over a thousand hymns—of which, those attributed partly or wholly to women seers do not number more than twelve or fifteen, that is approximately one per cent. See Kumkum Roy, '"Where Women are Worshipped, there the Gods Rejoice": The Mirage of Ancestress of the Hindu Women', in Tanika Sarkar and Urvashi Butalia, eds., *Women and the Hindu Right: A Collection of Essays* (Delhi: Kali for Women, 1995), p. 14.
78. Frieda Hauswirth, *Purdah: The Status of Indian Women* (London: Kegan Paul, 1932), p. 28. Quoted by Kiran Saxena, 'Legitimising Subjugation of Women', in Hem Lata Swarup and Sarojini Bisaria, eds., *Women, Politics and Religion* (Etawah: A.C. Brothers, 1991), pp. 75-89.
79. Leela Dube and Saurabh Dube, 'Women in India, Religion, and the Category of Politics', in Hem Lata Swarup and Sarojini Bisaria, eds., *Women Politics and Religion*, op. cit., pp. 59-65. Analysing the rituals associated with Hindu girls during the pre-pubertal and post-pubertal stages they suggest that these rituals set certain limits for the women within the family.
80. Leela Dube, 'Seed and Earth: The Symbolism of Biological Reproduction and Sexual Relations of Production', in Leela Dube et al., eds., *Visibility and Power: Essays on Women in Society and Development* (Delhi: Oxford University Press, 1986), pp. 22-53.
81. Veena Poonacha, 'Hindutva's Hidden Agenda: Why Women Fear Religious Fundamentalism', in *Economic and Political Weekly*, XXVIII (11), 13 March 1993, p. 438.
82. Gyanendra Pandey, 'Hindus and Others: The Militant Hindu Construction', in *Economic and Political Weekly*, op. cit., p. 3004.
83. Elaborating this point Pandey writes that though the woman is 'pure' as a symbol of the nation, she is considered sexually 'impure' in the Hindu discourse. On the contrary, cow is never impure. In this discourse the woman is not only to be 'protected but also disciplined and controlled'. Ibid.
84. J.A. Curran, Jr., *Militant Hinduism in Indian Politics: A Study of the RSS* (New York: Institute of Pacific Relations, 1951), p. 81.
85. *Organiser*, XLVI (40), 7 May 1995.
86. Tanika Sarkar, 'The Woman as Communal Subject: Rashtrasevika Samiti and Ram Janmabhoomi Movement', in *Economic and Political Weekly*, XXVI (35), 31 August 1991, p. 2058.
87. Summing up the concept of mother, Golwalkar writes: 'As the human life evolves, the concept of mother also takes a wider and more sublime form. When man looks around with his discerning intellect, he sees so many other

things which he owes a debt of gratitude. He begins to look upon them also as mother. He sees the rivers which give him food and water. He calls them mother. Once he outgrows the use of mother's milk, he sees the cow which feeds him with her milk throughout his life. He calls it mother-cow. And then he reaches a state of understanding that it is the mother soil which nourishes him in her bosom even after he breathes its last. He becomes conscious that she is his great mother. Thus to look upon one's land of birth is a sign of high state of human evolution.' M.S. Golwalkar, *Bunch of Thoughts*, op. cit., pp. 120-1.

88. Ibid., p. 485.
89. Ibid., p. 493.
90. Gyanendra Pandey, 'Hindus and Others: The Militant Hindu Construction', *Economic and Political Weekly*, op. cit., p. 3004.
91. *Organiser*, XXII (50), 26 July 1969. Also see the editorial of *Organiser*, XXIV (25), 30 January 1971, which describes Indira Gandhi as a 'bad woman' and a blot on Indian womanhood.
92. *Organiser*, XXII (50), 26 July 1969.
93. Ibid.
94. Ibid.
95. The *Sangh Parivar* vehemently opposed Rajiv Gandhi's widow Sonia Gandhi's entry into politics. During the 1999 election campaign, besides attacking her foreign origin, it also questioned her ability as a woman.
96. *Organiser*, XXIX (12), 15 August 1977.
97. Tracing the history of such a relationship Malkani argues that Mohenjo-Daro treated women equally though the Vedic civilization was male-dominated. During the later Puranic period, goddesses were given equal status with the gods; even their names preceded their divine counter-parts, e.g. Lakshmi-Narayan, Sita-Ram, etc.
98. *Organiser*, XLVI (40), 7 May 1995. However, Sonia Gandhi is not acceptable despite her adoption of Hindu culture; the RSS primarily objects to her political role.
99. *Organiser*, XXIX (37), 5 February 1978.
100. For a discussion on the politics of *sati*, see Lourens P. Van Den Bosch, 'Burning Question: Sati and Sati Temples as the Focus of Political Interest', *Numen*, 37 (2), December 1990, pp. 174-94.
101. See John S. Hawley, 'Hinduism: Sati and Its Defenders', in John Stratton Hawley, ed., *Fundamentalism and Gender* (New York: Oxford University Press, 1994), pp. 79-110.
102. Ratna Kapoor, Brenda Crossman, 'Communalising Gender/Engendering Community: Women, Legal Discourse and Saffron Agenda', *Economic and Political Weekly*, XXVIII (17), 24 April 1993, pp. WS–35-44.
103. Ibid.
104. Tanika Sarkar, 'The Woman as Communal Subject: Rashtrasevika Samiti and Ram Janmabhoomi Movement', *Economic and Political Weekly*, op. cit.
105. Ibid.

106. *Organiser*, XLVI (40), 7 May 1995.
107. Ibid.
108. For a critical discussion of the educational activities of the RSS, see Krishna Kumar, 'Hindu Revivalism and Education in North-Central India', in K.N. Panikkar, ed., *Communalism in India: History, Politics and Culture* (Delhi: Manohar, 1991), pp. 173-95; Also see Tanika Sarkar, 'Educating the Children of the Hindu Rashtra: Notes on the RSS Schools', *South Asia Bulletin*, XIV (2), 1994, pp. 10-15.
109. The other important personalities who graced the occasion were veteran Congress leader Purushottam Das Tandon and Hanuman Prasad Poddar, editor of *Kalyan*, a widely circulated religious monthly in north-India. See *Organiser*, XXX (25), 12 November 1978.
110. Tanika Sarkar, 'Educating the Children of the Hindu Rashtra', op. cit., p. 10.
111. *Organiser*, XXX (25), 12 November 1978.
112. The camp was attended by 15,000 children of the 9-11 age group. The then President of India, Neelam Sanjeeva Reddy inaugurated the camp. Other prominent persons who addressed the camp were, Balasaheb Deoras, Jagjivan Ram, P.C. Chunder, Union Minister of Education and noted educationist D.S. Kothari. For details on the camp, see *Organiser*, XXX (26), 19 November 1978.
113. See *Organiser*, XLII (11), 21 October 1990.
114. Tanika Sarkar, 'Educating the Children of the Hindu Rashtra', op. cit., p. 11.
115. *The Week*, 15 November 1998.
116. See Nalini Taneja, *BJP's Assault on Education and Educational Institutions* [Delhi: CPI(M) Publication, 1999], p. 29.
117. S.P. Gulati, 'Shishu Mandirs and the Concept of Developed Child', *Organiser*, XXX (25), 12 November 1978.
118. The RSS faces the dilemma because the existing textbooks on history and other social science subjects are recommended by the NCERT to its students in middle and secondary levels. Though their contents contradict the RSS version, they have to be taught as they are not only compulsory, but also qualitatively superior.
119. Lloyd I. Rudolph, Susanne Hoeber Rudolph, 'Rethinking Secularism: Genesis and Implications of the Textbook Controversy, 1977-79', *Pacific Affairs*, 56 (1), Spring 1983, pp. 15-37.
120. For details on the saffronization of syllabi and school textbooks, see Nalini Taneja, *BJP's Assault on Education and Educational Institutions*, op. cit.; *The Week*, op. cit.; 'Saffron Generation', *The Hindustan Times*, 19 December 1999.
121. See Nalini Taneja, *BJP's Assault on Education and Educational Institutions*, op. cit.
122. Vidya Bharati brings out a quarterly journal, named *Vidya Bharati Pradipika*.
123. See Krishna Kumar, 'Hindu Revivalism and Education in North-Central India', op. cit.
124. The objective is to have one such centre for each school. See *Organiser*, XLII (11), 21 October 1990.

CHAPTER VI

Quest for Political Power: Balasaheb Deoras

The evolution of the RSS, its organizational structure and functions, the ideology of the *Hindu Rashtra* and its homogenizing agenda unveil its political mission despite its insistence that it is merely a cultural organization. This chapter seeks to contest this 'cultural' claim further by explaining the emergence of the RSS as an important political actor on the Indian political scene, particularly under the leadership of Balasaheb Deoras. Responding to the changing dynamics of Indian politics the RSS has changed the course of its political journey—from moderate, pragmatic, and accommodative to militant, rigid, and intolerant. It also examines how the RSS promoted its political mobilization during the *Ram Janmabhoomi* agitation through an innovative use of Hindu cultural and religious symbols, thereby wrapping its political agenda in a cultural cover.

Deoras: A Child of the Organization

Three sealed letters of Golwalkar addressing 'To All Swayamsevak Brothers' were opened soon after his death in 1973. As per his wish expressed in the first letter, Balasaheb Deoras became the next *sarsanghachalak.*[1] Golwalkar thus followed the same tradition set by Hedgewar. Unlike Golwalkar, who was a late entrant to the RSS, Balasaheb[2] came under the influence of Hedgewar at the age of twelve and soon became one of his favourite *swayamsevaks.* Having thus entered the RSS that had been formed only two years earlier, Balasaheb grew with it and in it. He was adventurous and displayed leadership qualities since childhood.[3] In 1939, Balasaheb became a full time RSS *pracharak* in Nagpur. Then he was sent on an assignment to Calcutta for a year. After his return, he became the city secretary of Nagpur. This was a strategic position as Nagpur was the key to organizational control. In 1942, Balasaheb trained a big batch of RSS workers of Nagpur as *pracharaks* and dispatched them to different provinces. When Bhayaji Dani was *sarkaryavah*, Balasaheb acted as *sah-sarkaryavah* for many years. In 1965, Balasaheb was appointed *sarkaryavah* and continued in that office till 1973. Deoras was thus rightly described as a true child of the organization. He was more of a 'machine operator' who had been controlling the RSS ever since the days of Hedgewar.

Practical and Pragmatic

Balasaheb himself admitted that though he was a student of philosophy, he lacked interest in pursuing the systems of thought. Like Hedgewar, he was known for his pragmatism, prompting Golwalkar to announce before a group of *swayamsevaks* as early as 1944: 'If you want to know Dr. Hedgewar, look at this young man!'[4] He has been described as a person 'without inhibitions', 'practical and pragmatic', and 'without any taboos regarding rites and rituals, or the practice of religiosity'.[5] Besides his pragmatism, he had 'a sharp critical understanding and ability to analyse situations and suggest solutions'.[6] Thus the RSS clarified that his pragmatism did not shun ideology, and *Hindutva* was no less important to Deoras.

Organizational Reorientation: Evolving an Innovative Mechanism

As a man of organization and pragmatic orientation, Deoras brought about changes in the organizational set-up to make it capable of political action.[7] First, the old hierarchical structure was brought in line with the electoral constituency divisions. Each RSS district would now cover one or two parliamentary constituencies; below that came the assembly and municipal constituency divisions. The purpose was to build up a well-oiled election machinery. The *shakhas* were assigned a much wider role; they became the basic centres not only for elections to legislatures but also for managing elections of various trade unions, student unions and other socio-cultural organizations of the *Sangh Parivar* working within their respective areas.[8] Secondly, the areas of work between the RSS and its affiliates were properly divided; while the latter would concentrate on propaganda, the ground organization would be controlled and manned by the former. Thirdly, married men were encouraged to take up full-time work. And to tackle the financial burden, an elaborate plan was prepared to secure control over educational and other institutions where the full-time workers could be given employment without any cost to the RSS as such. Finally, changes were brought in the system of fund collection. In the past the collection through *Guru Dakshina* was kept secret. This was replaced by a new system whereby the head of a *shakha* would come to know what contribution has been made by whom. As a result it was found out that the amount of collection was more in the Jana Sangh-ruled areas.[9]

Soon after his takeover, Deoras reiterated his commitment to Golwalkar's *Hindu Rashtra.* For him, too, the problem of Hindustan is not the Muslim or the Christian, but the disunity among the Hindus. Therefore, the aim of Hindu *Sangathan* should never be undermined: 'We are convinced that when the Hindu becomes strong and united, the whole country will become strong and united.'[10] Despite this confirmation of ideological continuity, Deoras made a break with the Golwalkar's hesitation towards politics. Unlike Golwalkar, he had 'no inclination towards the spiritual'.[11] In contrast to Golwalkar's idealism and quietism, Deoras displayed a flair for pragmatism and activism. But it was not just his personal flair for politics that impelled him to carve out an active political role for the RSS. Rather certain objective conditions in the country facilitated the direct political intervention of the RSS.

Seeking an Alternative National Ideology and Politics

The Indian political scene was quite volatile when Deoras took over the RSS. The Congress system[12] seemed to have exhausted its potential and was losing its political hegemony by the early 1970s. Many senior and well-known leaders (the syndicate) had deserted the Congress party, but were neither able to challenge Indira Gandhi effectively nor provide an alternative socio-economic model of development. On the other hand, Indira Gandhi's *Garibi Hatao* campaign was turning out to be more populist than substantive. Meanwhile, in 1964, there occurred a split in the Communist Party of India; both the Communist Parties, the CPI and the CPI(M), were mainly confined to their regional bases. The Naxalite movement, which emerged subsequently by challenging the CPI(M), had also splintered into a dozen of groups.

Further, post-independent India had passed through some unique experiences. A sovereign polity had already emerged on the foundation of universal franchise. Centralized rule had consolidated the national market. The communications network had expanded with the use of radio and television. There was also a substantial increase in literacy rates.

These developments had brought the Indian masses from diverse regions and social backgrounds into direct contact and inter-dependence. All these factors had created an objective situation for the re-casting of an all-encompassing, pan-Indian identity. India required a powerful ideological cement in the form of a national ideology.[13] In the absence of any anti-imperialist struggle, anti-colonialism had lost all attraction as a binding force. An alternative national definition was needed in such a changed socio-economic-political scenario. But neither the Congress nor the Left were capable of providing such a definition.

Deoras was quick to grasp this fluidity and uncertainty in the national political scene and thought it ideal for the RSS to enter the political fray with its alternative national agenda. He thus announced that 'the extreme opinion that the Swayamsevak of the Sangh should have nothing to do with the world around him is patently wrong'[14] and gave a call to *swayamsevaks* 'to participate in every field of national life for reformation according to RSS thinking'.[15] It was a daring venture of Deoras to bring the RSS into open politics, a strategic shift from the cautious approach undertaken by Golwalkar.

A New Political Strategy: Rejuvenating the Affiliates

This decision of Deoras to enter the political arena was also partly attributed to the growing strength of the RSS over the last 33 years of Golwalkar's long reign; it had undergone a phenomenal expansion having *shakhas* in almost every part of the country. Besides the parent organization, the other family members were shaping up quite well, particularly the BJS, the ABVP and the BMS. The political front, the BJS, had travelled a long way since its first session at Kanpur in 1952. The 1973 Kanpur session of the party showed the strength the party had acquired in the last two decades.[16] Its labour affiliate, the BMS, had emerged as one of the strongest labour organizations in the country. Its student affiliate, the ABVP, had set up 600 branches having 1,65,000 members and 24 full-time workers.[17]

Therefore, Deoras was confident that the RSS, with its wider family network, could take up a new challenging role. Accordingly, he adopted a new strategy that reflected his political astuteness. Deoras rightly understood that despite the expansion of the BJS, its performance in the parliamentary election of 1971 and subsequent assembly elections of 1972 was quite dismal. Hence, instead of relying totally on this affiliate, the RSS should look forward to other affiliates. Thus Deoras concentrated on the two most promising affiliates, the ABVP and the BMS, working among students and labour respectively. He foresaw that both these affiliates along with the BJS would play a leading role in political struggle in the future.

Gujarat provided the first opportunity to Deoras to test the viability of his new strategy. The Congress party had begun to lose its political base there. After the 1969 split in the party, Indira Gandhi adopted a personalized and populist style to establish her party in the province. The state government announced reservations for lower castes, which was opposed by massive agitations. Thus Gujarat became the site for competitive populism[18] resulting in riotous street politics.

The RSS galvanized the ABVP to spearhead the struggle, under the banner of Nav Nirman Samiti, against the allegedly corrupt government of Chimanbhai Patel. The movement succeeded by overthrowing the government. The ABVP proved its political potential. The RSS gained confidence at this success and thought of carrying out such struggles 'against the corrupt and inefficient' Congress governments in other states.[19] Thus using mass street mobilizations to topple governments became a standard practice. The next stage was set in Bihar.[20]

Aligning with Jayaprakash Narayan against Indira Gandhi

Meanwhile Indira Gandhi's authoritarian style of functioning was getting pronounced day by day.[21] The RSS was quick to understand the nature of her functioning and started opposing it. For example, the RSS took strong objection to the question of supercession of senior judges of the Supreme Court in the appointment of the Chief Justice. An editorial of the *Organiser* warned that 'the politically conscious elements of the Indian society will have to exert themselves to keep the press free, the judiciary independent and the legislatures responsive—if India is not to drift into the nightmare of a corrupt dictatorship'.[22] Referring to the appeal of the Congress leader Shashi Bhushan for 'limited dictatorship', L.K. Advani cautioned: 'it seems the Congress-I is seriously toying with the idea of scuttling democracy, and supplanting it with a totalitarian or a quasi-totalitarian set-up.'[23] Thus, the RSS had started taking a strong position against the authoritarian tendency of Indira Gandhi.

Jayaprakash Narayan launched a protest movement against the corrupt Congress government of Bihar. The ABVP became a part of the Chhatra Sangharsh Samiti (CSS)[24] and joined the JP movement. In late 1974, the movement changed its character by moving beyond Bihar and targeting Indira Gandhi. JP's concept of 'total revolution' was endorsed by the RSS. The ABPS of the RSS took the unusual step of supporting Narayan's 'total revolution', though it maintained its tradition of keeping aloof from political activities. In a rally at Delhi, Balasaheb Deoras called JP a 'saint' who had 'come to rescue society in dark and critical times'.[25]

Jayaprakash reciprocated the compliment by publicly praising the *Sangh Parivar.* He attended the 20th All-India session of the Jana Sangh and declared, 'If Jana Sangh is fascist, then I, too, am a fascist'. He further complimented the RSS for its efforts to reduce economic inequality and corruption.[26] Both JP and the RSS needed each other. While JP had the leadership, the RSS had a committed cadre. Any struggle against Indira Gandhi demanded a close cooperation between the two. JP's approbation certainly enhanced the public stature of the RSS. The old stigma of 'Mahatma Gandhi's murderer' was considerably blunted with the certificate from a former close associate of Mahatma Gandhi.

RSS and anti-Emergency Struggle

On 5 June 1975, the Allahabad High Court declared Indira Gandhi's election to the parliament invalid due to violations of election law. The opposition parties demanded her resignation. They formed the Lok Sangharsh Samiti (LSS) to coordinate the activities of the JP movement. Nana Deshmukh, a former RSS *pracharak* and the organizing secretary of the BJS, became its general secretary. On 25 June 1975 JP gave a call to the defence forces not to carry out the 'illegal order'. The next morning a state of Emergency was declared and the political opponents of Indira Gandhi including Balasaheb Deoras were arrested. The RSS was banned on 4 July 1975 under Defence of India Rules, 1971, and a large number of RSS members were arrested.

The initial response of the RSS was cautious. Madhavrao Mulay, the general secretary, declared that the organization had been dissolved. However, the RSS kept alive an effective skeleton organization, although its *shakhas*, training camps, parades and other activities were stopped. Soon some leading *pracharaks*, after consulting imprisoned Balasaheb Deoras, met at Bombay in late July to chart out the action plan for their banned organization. They decided that the RSS would work closely with the LSS, thus breaking the RSS tradition of keeping the organization aloof from political movements.[27] The coordinating work of the RSS with the LSS would be carried out by the four zonal *pracharaks*: Yadavrao

Joshi (south), Rajendra Singh (north), Moropant Pingale (west), and Bhaorao Deoras (east). In addition, while Rambahu Godbole was entrusted with the task of contacting the opposition party leaders, Eknath Ranade was to liaison with the government. Incidentally, Ranade was assigned the same job during the previous ban of 1948-9. This meeting also charted the following course of action for the banned organization: (a) to keep up the morale of the *swayamsevaks* by arranging some form of congregations;[28] (b) to establish an underground press; (c) prepare for a nationwide *satyagraha*,[29] establishing contact with significant non-political figures and with prominent representatives of the minority communities; and (d) solicit overseas Indian support[30] for the RSS in the underground activities of the LSS. However, many critics believe that the RSS was keen on a compromise rather than fight Indira Gandhi.[31]

Despite these versions, other evidence suggests that the RSS played a key role in the struggle against Emergency. Its cadre was the backbone of the LSS, which spearheaded the JP movement. After the arrest of JP, Nana Deshmukh assumed the responsibility of leading the LSS. When Deshmukh was arrested, D.B. Thengadi, the general secretary of the BMS, took charge.[32] Thus, the RSS contributed its cadres and leaders to the LSS, the instrument of anti-Emergency struggle. Thousands of its members were arrested while offering *satyagraha* against authoritarian regime of Indira Gandhi.

However, it is not to argue that it was only the RSS and its affiliates that participated in the struggle. All the opposition parties like the Samyukta Socialist Party (SSP), the Bharatiya Lok Dal (BLD), the Congress (Organization), the CPI (Marxist), and Naxalites opposed the Emergency. Even many students, teachers, lawyers, doctors, actors, writers, peasants, workers and other professionals, who did not have any party-affiliation, sacrificed their career to join the struggle against dictatorship and authoritarianism. Thus, it was a concerted effort of all individuals, groups and political parties who wanted the restoration of democracy in India. Therefore, the credit goes to the Indian people who participated and sympathized with this struggle.

Post-Emergency Era: Politics of Accommodation and Ideological Flexibility

The Emergency experience greatly exposed the cadres and the leaders of the RSS to the political environment of the country and made them ambitious. They felt proud of having participated in the 'second freedom struggle'. This baptization was badly needed for any political claim in the future as the RSS avoided the fight against colonialism during the freedom struggle. This participation gave them a unique opportunity to feel the political pulse of the people. It also widened their limited political outlook of the Jana Sangh experiment. Their interaction with different political parties, groups and individuals proved to be immensely beneficial.[33]

All these new experiences compelled the RSS leaders to ponder whether they should continue to stick to the old ideological framework of the *Hindu Rashtra* or should they redefine it in the light of the changed political dynamics.[34] Deoras rightly realized that to remain in the mainstream of national politics, the RSS should opt for a politics of accommodation. Therefore, as the realpolitik demanded, there should be no hesitation to redefine its exclusivist ideological moorings and seek a politics of pragmatism and accommodation. This changing attitude of the RSS leadership helped the formation of the Janata alliance of the opposition parties when general elections were announced. The RSS cadre campaigned vigorously against Indira Gandhi. The Janata alliance won the elections. After the victory the ban on the RSS was lifted on 4 July 1977.

RSS during Janata Period

The Janata alliance became Janata Party[35] on 1 May 1977. The RSS approved the merger of the BJS in this new party which formed the first non-Congress government at New Delhi. Three of its *swayamsevaks* from the Jana Sangh group, A.B. Vajpayee, L.K. Advani and Brij Lal Verma, got cabinet berths in the Morarji government. After the June assembly elections, the Jana Sangh members became the chief ministers in three States, Himachal Pradesh, Madhya Pradesh and Rajasthan and in the Union Territory of Delhi; and shared power in UP, Bihar, Haryana and Orissa. Again most of them were RSS *swayamsevaks.*

The other constituents of the Janata Party, particularly the erstwhile socialists, were quick to grasp the growing influence of the RSS. They feared, on the basis of its large disciplined cadres and its influence over the erstwhile Jana Sangh members, that the RSS would soon become too powerful and eclipse other constituents of the Janata Party. Therefore they devised a strategy to keep the RSS under control. It was suggested that the RSS should merge with the youth wing of the Janata Party to form a united volunteer organization. This was rejected by the RSS.[36]

Deoras did not accept the proposal, which he thought, would certainly adversely affect the long-term objective of his organization. This would not only invite intense political attack from its detractors, but would also bring decadent political culture to the RSS. Therefore, the RSS, as an organization, should never become a part of the government. Even the BMS and the ABVP were not allowed to merge their identities with respective labour and student counterparts of the Janata Party. Besides, being strongly entrenched in the Janata government and with its political affiliate taking care of the RSS interest, Deoras did not feel any real need for such a merger.

Thus Deoras cleverly avoided the politics of competition and bickering. He rather preferred to concentrate and spend his energy on other areas where there was hardly any competition and the RSS could expand its support base more quietly and effectively. Accordingly, the RSS sought mutual cooperation with the Janata government in the areas of adult education, social welfare, youth affairs, etc. Government patronage, the RSS reasoned, would ensure the flow of resources for these welfare activities.

There was another dimension: the RSS and its affiliates had been growing at a fast pace[37] and the financial burden was becoming heavier for the maintenance of its growing number of whole-timers and other *karyakartas.* The involvement in the welfare projects would provide them engagement as well as financial assistance. With this strategy, the RSS expanded its sphere of influence in the government as well as non-government sectors and grew rapidly during the Janata regime.

Controversy on 'Dual Membership' and Admitting non-Hindus

This rapid growth of the RSS alarmed other Janata constituents. They became apprehensive that the erstwhile BJS, backed by the strong and disciplined RSS cadre, would soon control the organizational apparatus of the party. Therefore, they raised the question of 'dual membership' and demanded that the members of the old BJS should sever their links with the RSS as the party constitution denied membership to anybody belonging to another political party, communal or other, which has a separate membership, constitution and programme. They pleaded that any association of the members of the Janata Party with the RSS, a 'Hindu communal organization', would undermine the secular credentials of the party. The Jana Sangh faction countered that the RSS was a cultural organization and there was no restriction to be associated with it.

Surprisingly, the RSS phenomenon did not come up either during the Parliament elections or at the time of the merger of the Jana Sangh with the Janata Party. They were raised only when the struggle for power became intense among the constituents of the party. This issue of 'dual membership' was used both to gain leverage against the Jana Sangh group and to damage their capacity to mobilize additional support within the Janata Party.[38]

To tackle the issue of dual membership, the RSS announced the opening of its doors to non-Hindus. As discussed earlier, the Emergency experience had softened its attitudes towards non-Hindus. Jayaprakash Narayan, the new political mentor of the RSS, had been emphasizing this issue for quite sometime. Moreover, the Jana Sangh constituent of the Janata Party wanted its parent body to adopt an inclusive policy of admission, which would save its leaders from constant criticism and embarrassment in the Party forum. While adopting the open-door policy, the RSS did not compromise on its traditional goal of uniting the Hindu community. Its leadership was clearly reluctant to take any action which might undermine the brotherhood's commitment to each other and to the RSS.[39]

Demise of the Janata Party and Disillusionment of the RSS

Even this gesture of the RSS could not stop the division of the party. Raj Narayan was the first to leave the party to form the Janata (Secular) party, thereby claiming that the Janata Party was 'unsecular'. The next exit was of the Charan Singh group, which also took a strong anti-RSS stance. Morarji Desai lost his majority and resigned on 15 June 1979. The Jana Sangh faction threw its weight with Jagjivan Ram, a Harijan leader, thus attempting to shed its upper-caste image. However, the President invited Charan Singh to form the government. The caretaker government, being unable to muster support, resigned and general elections were held in January 1980. The election gave a massive mandate to Indira Gandhi and proved to be a disaster for the Janata Party.[40]

The leaders of the Janata Party analysed the causes of the electoral defeat. On the one hand, Jagjivan Ram attributed the defeat to the 'hostile activities of the RSS', and also charged that a 'secret' understanding existed between the RSS and Indira Gandhi.[41] On the other hand, some other leaders argued that the presence of RSS members in the party gave it a communal image, thereby resulting in the loss of support of the minorities and lower castes and leading to the poll debacle. The Janata Party had to sort out the RSS issue once and for all.

Some leaders of the Janata Party again raised the question of 'dual membership' and wanted the Jana Sangh group to sever its ties with the RSS. This time the Jana Sangh constituent left it on the wisdom of the RSS leadership, which preferred to keep deliberate silence. In the light of the new political configuration, it was perhaps a wise option. The RSS was thoroughly disillusioned with the internal bickering of the Janata Party. It saw its writing on the wall and thought it would be futile to attempt its resurrection. The RSS leadership realized that it was high time for the Jana Sangh constituent to come out of the party and form an alternative of its own.

RSS Dilemma: Power Politics or Ideological Purity?

The political experience, though exciting, was not all that pleasant for the RSS leaders. It was exciting because it gave them an opportunity to acquire an all India status. They felt elated when each major decision of the national government required their approval, or at least their considered opinion. The RSS got a lot of publicity, its organization and affiliates became known throughout the country and its leadership acquired a national stature and respect. Perhaps, except the Congress party, no other organization had achieved this status.

However, many traditionalists within the RSS got disillusioned with the evil effects of power politics. They thought that the ideology of the *Hindu Rashtra* was compromised when the RSS opened its doors to non-Hindus despite the fact that there was hardly any entry. Many RSS leaders did not appreciate the way the RSS was dragged into each and every controversy and advocated to go back to Golwalkar's policy of quiet expansion. Moreover, factional politics was alien to their culture. Though they managed to suppress the revolt of Balraj Madhok with no difficulty, Subramaniam Swamy's public criticism of Vajpayee caused a lot of embarrassment to the RSS leaders.[42]

All these mixed experiences called for an introspection. What should be its ideological parameters? Should it go back to the old and rigid ideological roots of the *Hindu Rashtra* of Golwalkar era or stick to the softer version that it had been experimenting with during the post-Golwalkar phase? The positive gains of power politics far outweighed the negative experiences. It could not overlook the fact that its newly acquired power and status were primarily the fruits of power politics and a politics of accommodation. At the same time the RSS also could not ignore that there always remained a threat of slipping into 'pure' power politics and losing its ideological goal. Therefore, it was gripped by a dilemma; in its search for an alternative political structure, the RSS could neither ignore the strength of its ideology nor the benefits of power politics.

Attempting a Synthesis: Birth of the Bharatiya Janata Party (BJP)

In the midst of this dilemma, the Jana Sangh group of the Janata Party organized a convention on 5 April 1980, and announced the birth of the Bharatiya Janata Party. The new party, reflecting the RSS mind, tried for a synthesis of ideology and realpolitik. Accordingly, the new party was not a mere resurrection of the old Jana Sangh. As it aspired to extend its geographical, demographic and ideological reach, the BJP required retaining and continuing certain traditions of the Janata Party. It retained the name of Janata, adopted the lotus as a party symbol rather than the lamp of the Jana Sangh. Its new flag was half saffron and half green, the latter symbolizing secularism. Though the party appointed RSS men in key positions, it co-opted a few leaders from a non-RSS and non-Jana Sangh background. Its organizational structure was designed on the basis of participatory democracy rather than the democratic centralism of the RSS. However, in terms of the leadership structure and recruitment patterns, the BJP continued with its Jana Sangh and RSS heritage.[43]

In terms of ideology, the party retained the Integral Humanism of Deendayal Upadhyaya, while adopting Gandhian Socialism as the party's statement of first principles. Its ideological modification of the militant Hindu nationalism of the Jana Sangh could be further noticed in its commitment to five principles (*pancha-nishtha*), such as nationalism, national integration, democracy, positive secularism, and value-based politics.[44]

All these attempts of synthesis reflected the ground political reality within the *Sangh Parivar.* The leading affiliates of the RSS, after a national political exposure and power sharing, were in no mood to return to the traditional 'cultural' line. More importantly, the BJP leaders hoped to convert their party to a national alternative to the Congress. Therefore, it felt the necessity of moving beyond its old confines of high-caste, urban middle class, Hindi-speaking north India. The RSS fully endorsed this understanding of its political affiliate and tried to offer an ideological rationale through a mix of *Hindu Rashtra* and Gandhian Socialism. But certain hardliners in the party ranks were opposed to this hybrid ideology. These protests were perhaps supported by a section of RSS leadership, which did not appreciate this new ideological line.

To some of the observers of Indian politics, this new ideological line of the BJP, particularly the adoption of Gandhian Socialism, indicated its ideological independence from the RSS. But it needs to be remembered that it was Deoras, who a year before the formation of the BJP proudly claimed that 'we are real followers of Gandhiji's principle of tolerance and non-violence'.[45] Then the RSS had argued that on most issues nobody was closer to Gandhi than itself and claimed that his *Hind Swaraj* could very well be a RSS text.[46] Further, since the days of the Bihar agitation, the RSS had closely identified itself with Jayaprakash Narayan, a practitioner of Gandhian politics.[47] Under his influence, the RSS had been consciously integrating Gandhian ideals in its various programmes to enhance its popularity and acceptability. Rajendra Singh, successor of Deoras, claims that the *Sangh Parivar* has been following the legacy of Gandhi by striving 'to fulfil his cherished dream of Ramrajya and Swadeshi': cow protection by VHP, swadeshi by SJM, upliftment of the tribals by VKA, Gandhiji's *gram-swaraj* by DRI, and restoration of Bharatiya languages by Vidya Bharati. Moreover, the *swayamsevak's* life is the best example of Gandhiji's precept of simple living.[48]

Therefore, BJP's adoption of Gandhian Socialism was not at all contradictory to the RSS position. It rather reflected the ideological dilemma and confusion of the RSS, which was pondering whether to go back to its ideological roots of *Hindu Rashtra* or to adhere to Gandhi for political expediency.[49] Further, A.B. Vajpayee and other moderates might have influenced the RSS leadership to permit them to experiment with this new line. But there was no evidence to suggest that they were pursuing a line at the expense of the RSS. They could hardly afford to do so.

New Religio-political Strategy: Revival of the VHP

During these years of introspection, an incident occurred at Meenakshipuram in Tamil Nadu. Here, in 1981, some fifteen hundred Harijans were converted to Islam. The RSS expressed its deep concern over the mass conversion and calls upon the government to impose a legal ban on conversions.[50] It also called upon 'the entire Hindu Society to bury deep the internal caste dissensions and pernicious practice of untouchability and stand up as one single homogeneous family'.[51] In the prevailing circumstances, the incident provided an opportunity to the RSS to re-orient its strategy.

As discussed earlier, Deoras, after taking over the leadership, adopted a strategy of activating and assigning the affiliates like the ABVP and the BMS a frontal role in the turbulent political years. These affiliates carried out their tasks quite successfully during and after the Emergency and also in the Janata days. In the context of new emerging possibilities on the issue of Meenakshipuram a new strategy had to be adopted. Which affiliate could be entrusted to carry out the new assignment? The RSS found none of the tried affiliates suitable for the purpose. The VHP seemed to be ideal. Though set up way back in 1964, it was lying low till then. The VHP was primarily active among the tribals and untouchables by setting up schools, clinics and temples. Its main purpose was to block the influences of Christianity and Islam.

The Meenakshipuram incident brought a metamorphosis in the VHP.[52] In the RSS strategy for the coming years, it was going to be the torchbearer. The VHP took the assignment and raised the alarm of 'Hinduism in Danger!' It warned that, unless the conversions were immediately banned and reversed, Hindus would become minorities in India. The RSS sought to introduce the VHP to the various sects of Hindu religions and seek legitimacy for its future role as the vanguard of Hindu interests. Therefore, it organized a Hindu Unity conference at Delhi in September 1981 on the issue of Meenakshipuram, in which representatives from different Hindu organizations including the VHP participated. Karan Singh chaired the conference and it was decided to float a society called 'Virat Hindu Samaj'. The following office-bearers were nominated to manage Virat Hindu Samaj: Karan Singh, president; Lala Hans Raj Gupta, working president; P.C. Gupta, secretary and Ashok Singhal, organizing secretary. All of them were trusted RSS men except Karan Singh whose presence was primarily symbolic. As an able statesman and man of letters he was widely known among the educated. Moreover, as an erstwhile scion of the Hindu royal family of Jammu, his symbolic leadership would ensure the support of various Hindu sects to the imminent VHP-led movement. The Samaj decided to hold a 'Virat Hindu Sammelan' in Delhi on October 1981.[53]

The *Sangh Parivar* organized the Virat Hindu Sammelan, a massive rally of the Hindus 'for national identity and national integrity'.[54] The slogans raised in this rally are significant enough to be mentioned.

'Hindu sare ek, ped ek hai shakha anek' (All Hindus are one; it is one tree, even though it has innumerable branches); *'Dhokha, lalach petrodollar, nahin chalega, nahin chalega'* (Fraud, temptation and petrodollars shall not prevail); *'Ek hi patni, ek vidhan, Hindu ho ya Musalman'* (Let there be one law and monogamy—for Hindus and Muslims). These slogans remind one of the ideological thrust of the Golwalkar era by proposing a Hindu unity on the foundation of an anti-Muslim tirade. Another slogan which needs a special mention was, *'Hindu Hindu sab mil jao, chhooa chhoot ka bhoot bhagao'* (Let all Hindus unite, and exorcise the monster of untouchability). Golwalkar never gave priority to the abolition of untouchability. The Meenakshi-puram conversion compelled the RSS to adopt a clear line on the issue. Deoras also understood that to become a national political force, the RSS had to co-opt the untouchables in a much bigger scale. Therefore, the Virat Hindu Sammelan adopted the abolition of untouchability as one of its five objectives.

Strategic Shift of the Congress: Indira Gandhi's 'Hindu' Card

This religio-political strategy of the RSS got a further boost by Indira Gandhi's new political approach. In fact the post-Emergency Indira government was a different one from her pre-Emergency regime. The radical slogan of *Garibi Hatao* was no more heard. Terms like 'secular' and 'socialist' fell out of favour. Rather, she preferred to remain under the spiritual guidance of Swami Dhirendra Brahmachari, made pilgrimages to sacred rivers, shrines and temples across the country and spoke of 'Hindu hegemony' in the Hindi heartland. Karan Singh was a prominent Congressman and his participation in a RSS-sponsored meeting must have been in her knowledge.[55]

All these may be tactical as the Congress base among the minorities was shrinking and the conflict in Punjab and Kashmir had acquired a religio-political dimension. But Indira Gandhi's new approach certainly generated enthusiasm among the leaders and cadres of the RSS. They felt happy that she was facilitating the growth of Hindu consciousness in the Hindi heartland, which the RSS had been aspiring all along. Some people in the RSS raised the question: how far was it correct for the BJP to pursue a diluted *Hindutva*, when ironically the Congress was taking a pro-Hindu posture.

Indira Gandhi's thrust on Hindu rhetoric and rituals paid rich dividends to the Congress in the elections of Jammu & Kashmir and

Delhi held in early 1983. Surprisingly, the BJP was completely wiped out from the Jammu area, which had been a traditional stronghold of the Jana Sangh. More surprisingly for the party, in the Delhi elections, the Congress scored a convincing victory in the metropolitan council and corporation.[56] Some speculated that the RSS cadres maintained a neutral stance in the elections as there was an understanding between the RSS and the Congress. However, no authentic information is available to substantiate this allegation.[57] Many *swayamsevaks*, of course, voted for the Congress, as the RSS showed no enthusiasm for the BJP.

Though it is difficult to ascertain whether Indira Gandhi had a secret pact with the RSS, but her electoral victory certainly taught the RSS a few lessons: first, a distinct Hindu constituency still existed in the Hindi heartland, and if properly aroused, could give definite electoral dividends; and, secondly, the loyalty of this constituency was not fixed and could be manipulated by any political party which had the ability to arouse it more passionately. These lessons had some implications for the RSS: first, its religio-political strategy, with the VHP at the centre, needed to be further accentuated for mass mobilization of Hindus; secondly, the future ideological-political line of the BJP ought to be redefined.

Mass Mobilization by VHP: Politics of Yatras

In the context of Indira Gandhi's wooing of the Hindus, the VHP was perceived as an ideal instrument for the rival mobilization of the Hindus, particularly in north-India. The RSS carefully planned out the strategy. The traditional Hindu rituals of pilgrimage (*tirth-yatras*) had to be revived to reinforce a community consciousness among the Hindus.[58] Accordingly, the VHP organized three major 'pilgrimages' under the slogan of 'Pilgrimage for Unity' (*Ekatmata Yatra*) between mid-November and mid-December 1983, for the whole of India: from Haridwar in the foothills of Himalayas to Rameshwaram in Tamil Nadu; from Pashupatinath in Nepal to Kanyakumari; and from Gangasagar in West Bengal to Somnath in Gujarat.[59] Incidentally, all these three *yatras* intersected at Nagpur, the headquarters of the RSS.

The aim of these pilgrimages was to gloss over caste, sect and denominational differences and invoke the spirit of unity among Hindus. The message was clear: 'Hinduism was in danger, and no danger was more sinister than the possibility of a concerted movement of Muslim and untouchable communities working together.'[60] The signatories of the appeal to join the *yatras* included not only the members of the *Sangh*

Parivar, but also the Arya Samaj, the Rotary Club, the Lions Club and also, more notably, the Jain Sampradaya, Vaishnav Parivar, Sikh Sampradaya, Bauddha Sampradaya and Bharatiya Dalit Varga Sangh. Therefore, an attempt was made to associate virtually all non-Hindu communities with the *yatras* and to isolate the Muslims.[61]

According to the VHP this month-long campaign mobilized sixty million people and covered 85,000 km. The routes of the *yatras* were so planned that they touched maximum numbers of Hindu shrines and religious places. The chariots (*rathas*) of the VHP carried a huge portrait of Mother India (*Bharat Mata*) and urns (*kalasha*) containing Ganga water throughout the journey. During the campaign, religious books, portraits of *Bharat Mata*, badges and stickers depicting 'Om', yogasan charts and pictures of great men were sold through stalls set up on the route. Thus the VHP used a lot of Hindu religious ritual paraphernalia and sacred symbols to create a community consciousness among the Hindus.

Invoking Politics of Ram: Deploying the Most Popular Hindu Symbol

The favourable response of the Hindus to these *yatras* encouraged the RSS to search for a powerful and popular Hindu symbol that would further boost the mobilization. Ram, the most popular Hindu god of north India, fitted ideally into their scheme. In April 1984, the VHP, for the first time, announced its intention of liberating the *Ram Janmabhoomi*, the 'birthplace of Ram' at Ayodhya, which was allegedly destroyed by Babur to construct a mosque in the early sixteenth century.[62] Few popular symbols like this could have mobilized the Hindus on such a gigantic scale.

The mobilization strategy was carefully worked out. The VHP *Dharma Sansad* gave a clarion call to free Lord Ram who was still 'behind bars' and the *Ram Janmabhoomi Mukti Yajna* was launched. A huge chariot-cavalcade—actually a motorcade of trucks carrying images of 'Lord Ram behind bars', accompanied by thousands of *kar sevaks* armed with swords and tridents—marched from Bihar towards Ayodhya. However, this march was interrupted due to Indira Gandhi's assassination. 1985 witnessed the *Ram-Janaki Rath Yatra*. The stated aims were: first, to create a Hindu awakening and Hindu unity by emphasizing the need to transcend caste and sect differences in the worship of Lord Ram; secondly, to popularize the concept of *Ram Rajya*, the ideal state.[63]

Thus the most popular Hindu religious symbol of Ram was deployed to facilitate the politics of the *Sangh Parivar.*

The RSS announced that places like Somnath, Rameshwaram and Ayodhya were not merely religious places—but also points of national faith and unity. 'Desecration of such points of national faith is an open aggression on our national life. And all such desecrated spots are verily blots on our national freedom. And eradication of all such stigmas is nothing less than vindication of our national ethos and honour.'[64] It viewed the *Ram Janmabhoomi* agitation as 'a battle for national self-assertion'.[65] In a surprising judgement in 1986, the Faizabad district judge ordered opening of the locks on the shrine allowing unhindered access to Hindu devotees. The VHP threatened to start a *satyagraha* if the locks were not opened. The government complied with the court order and the temple was opened to the devotees amidst much fanfare on 1 February 1986.

Meanwhile, the issue of the Muslim Personal Law became a centre of controversy with the judgement of the Supreme Court in the Shah Bano case. The Rajiv Gandhi government did not accept the Supreme Court ruling and introduced the Muslim Women's Bill under severe communal pressure. Why did the government yield to communal pressure? The Congress felt the need to stem the anger of the Muslims over the Shah Bano verdict which was reflected in the results of various by-elections in Assam, Kishanganj (Bihar), Baroda (Gujarat) and other places. These defeats compelled the Congress to bring the Muslim Women's Bill to regain its Muslim constituency.[66] The Shah Bano controversy provided the *Sangh Parivar* a convenient handle to intensify their anti-Muslim campaign under the pretext of 'appeasement of minorities'. In the assessment of the *Parivar* leaders, this event marked a watershed in the mobilization of Hindus.[67]

Consolidating the Organization for Militant Offensive

During the decade 1979-89, the number of *swayamsevaks* of the RSS had swelled from 10 lakh to 18 lakh. The number of *shakhas* increased to 25,000 spreading over 18,880 cities and villages. It had 38 front organizations and 50 lakh people were connected with their activities. More importantly, the RSS showed spectacular growth in south India. For example, 3,000 daily *shakhas* and 900 weekly gatherings were organized in 12 out of 14 districts in Kerala.[68] Therefore, the RSS was confident of its strength before it decided to go in for the offensive.

The centenary celebration year (1988-9) of K.B. Hedgewar provided the opportunity to the RSS to galvanize the cadre and propagate its ideology. Deoras spelt out three objectives during the year: first, to acquaint people with Hedgewar's pre-RSS life;[69] secondly, to propagate its ideology of *Hindu Rashtra*; and thirdly, to acquaint the people with its service projects.[70] While centenaries of other patriots were '*sarkari* centenaries' being sponsored by the government, this would be 'the people's centenary' being solely sponsored by the RSS. On the government's refusal to release a centenary stamp, the RSS, in protest, printed 1 crore cards having the picture of Hedgewar on the front and the map of Akhand Bharat with the saffron flag at the back.[71] It planned that its *swayamsevaks* would reach more than 2 lakh villages during the year. Thus this year was spent in preparation before the onslaught. Incidentally, the year 1989 was also celebrated as the silver jubilee of the VHP and various programmes were undertaken to revitalize it.

A meeting of the top leaders of the *Sangh Parivar* took place at Ahmedabad on 24 March 1989. Besides Deoras, other important leaders of the *Parivar* who attended it were H.V. Seshadri, Rajendra Singh, Yadav Rao Joshi of the RSS, Ashok Singhal of VHP, L.K. Advani, A.B. Vajpayee and S.S. Bhandari of BJP, D.B. Thengadi of BMS and Madan Das Devi of ABVP.[72] A close coordination among the leading members of the RSS family was obviously required before going for the offensive.

Militant Offensive: Ramshila Pujan

Soon after the VHP's decision to construct a temple in Ayodhya, the ABKM of the RSS appealed to all Hindus to extend their generous help for the purpose.[73] The Allahabad High Court issued an interim directive to maintain status quo of the disputed property. The RSS announced that the *Ram Janmabhoomi* was beyond the purview of the court. The VHP now argued that if the government could overrule a judgement in the Shah Bano case through legislative action, it should also override the judgement on Ayodhya.

The event that became the eye of the storm, was *Ramshila Pujan*. The VHP launched a campaign to carry consecrated bricks, called *Ramshilas*, from every village with a population of 2,000 or above for the construction of the Ram temple. This programme was meticulously planned out.[74] The bricks were taken to Ayodhya through *panchayat* centres, district headquarters and state capitals. A minimum contribution of Rs 1.25 per head was collected. The VHP organized *kirtans*, prayers, discourses, musical concerts and symposia in the villages. The aim was to carry the ideology of *Hindutva* to each village and town and mobilize the Hindus through the medium of Ram. RSS leaders attended all the important *Shila Pujan* functions.[75] The brick programme was simult-aneously traditional in its vestments while highly innovative in form. Hindus of all regions and persuasions would engage in a common act of devotion to a single deity—Ram. No sponsor of a temple had ever before involved the general public in temple building on such a large scale.[76]

The beatific smile of Ram in VHP posters had been replaced by a war-like image—Ram with his trident and bow at ready.[77] This new imagery of Ram came from television epics—Ramanand Sagar's *Ramayana* and B.R. Chopra's *Mahabharata*. The latter especially glorified a militaristic and virile Hinduism. The telecasting of these epics on *Doordarshan* resulted from the decision of an insecure Congress party. Though Ram existed all along, popular perceptions were vague and varied. The telecasting of *Ramayana*, which was primarily based on the *Ramcharitmanas* of Tulsidas, ignored the traditions of 'many *Ramayanas*' projecting a uniform version.[78] The serial certainly concretized certain perceptions of Ram. For instance, when people were asked about Ayodhya before the telecast, though they identified Ayodhya as the birthplace of Ram, their idea about the place was still vague. After the telecast they defined it as a town in UP.[79] Thus the broadcasting of *Ramayana* and *Mahabharata* helped to create a national Hindu identity, a form of consciousness that had not hitherto existed.[80]

It became easy for the VHP to project a militant Ram, a symbol of strength and power. Passionate slogans rent the air: '*Saugandh Ram ki khate hain hum mandir vaheen banayege*' (We swear by Ram we will build the temple at the same site), '*Bachcha-bachcha Ram ka, Janmabhoomi ke kaam ka*' (Every child belongs to Ram and for *Ram Janmabhoomi*) and '*Jis Hindu ka khoon na khaule, khoon nahin vo pani hai; Janmabhoomi ke kaam na aye, vo bekaar jawanee hai*' (That Hindu whose blood does not boil has water in his veins, youth that does not serve *Ram Janmabhoomi* is youth lived in vain). Therefore, the *Ramshila* campaign was not only mobilizational, it was confrontational as well. It became aggressively anti-Muslim and provoked communal violence.[81] The government again yielded to the pressure of the RSS and the VHP and permitted *Shilanyas*.

BJP's Metamorphosis: From Communal Harmony to Ultra-Hinduism

Since the Meenakshipuram incident the VHP had taken a frontal role in religio-political mobilization. Being pushed back to the background, the BJP had been undergoing a transformation in tune with the new RSS strategy. The ideological dilemma that prevailed during its birth had gradually disappeared. In the beginning, in its attempt towards a synthesis, it demonstrated its commitment towards communal harmony. BJP's 'positive secularism' promised 'full protection of the life and property of the minorities'.[82] In his address to National Council of the party in 1982, Atal Behari Vajpayee advised the opposition parties to 'resist the temptation of compromising with religious and communal fanaticism . . . simply to get power'. The National Executive of the party passed a resolution on 'Communal Harmony and Social Cohesion' in 1983, which stated: 'No religion encourages or condones hatred or violence against one's fellow beings . . . A Hindu, Moslem, Christian or whosoever maimed or killed is an Indian disabled or lost. Life and property lost is not just Hindu loss or Muslim loss but a national loss.'[83]

The BJP began reverting to its ultra-Hindu posture after its 1984 electoral rout. It realized that the dilution of its earlier position as a champion of the Hindus had cost it dearly.[84] Rajiv Gandhi's landslide victory was attributed partly to his ability to win over most of the upper-caste support that previously went to the BJP. Therefore, a return-to-the-roots was to be adopted as the BJP's main strategy. Deendayal's 'Integral Humanism' replaced 'Gandhian Socialism' as the basic philosophy of the party in October 1985. L.K. Advani was installed as the new president of the party in May 1986.

The BJP hardened its anti-Muslim position on the Shah Bano judgement and the subsequent Muslim Women's Bill. While the party welcomed the judgement of the Supreme Court as 'pre-eminently just and sensible', it strongly rejected the Muslim League view that this judgement was an interference in the religious affairs of Muslims. Rajiv Gandhi's move to amend the law was described as 'retrograde, anti-woman and a surrender to obscurantism and bigotry'. Advani observed that the Muslim Women Bill ran counter to the Directive Principles of the Constitution (Article 44) enjoining the state to frame a Uniform Civil Code. He reiterated that the concept of *sarva dharma sama bhava* should never make any distinction between one citizen and another on the ground of religion. The BJP intensified its anti-Muslim campaign by accusing the government of promoting 'minorityism'. L.K. Advani summed up 'minorityism' as the promotion of a minority complex among the minorities, which serves neither national interest nor even minority interest. He branded the secularism of the government as 'pseudo-secularism'.

Besides the Shah Bano case, certain other factors facilitated the BJP's anti-Muslim propaganda. A massive Hindu backlash was building up because of the situation in Punjab and Kashmir. The poll analysis of the Assam assembly elections confirmed the understanding of the RSS that if a party could get a block of Hindu votes, it had a fair chance of coming to power. The Asom Gana Parishad (AGP), despite the Muslim opposition, could get the majority on the basis of block Hindu votes.[85] Henceforth the BJP decided to aim at the consolidation of Hindu votes in its favour. For garnering the Hindu votes, it became a practical necessity to harden its stance on controversial issues like Art. 370, UCC, Minorities Commission and Ayodhya. The BJP found particular potential in the Ayodhya dispute, which could not only refurbish its Hindu identity, but also create a solid Hindu vote bank.

Babri Masjid to Ram Janmabhoomi

It is interesting to note that the early party documents recognized the existence of the Babri Masjid at Ayodhya without any reservations. In the national executive meeting of the party held between December 1986 and January 1987, L.K. Advani condemned a Muslim organization's boycott call of Republic Day celebrations 'in protest against the Babri Masjid issue'. Hence the BJP did not mention *Ram Janmabhoomi* or Ram Temple till then. It is only on June 1989 that the national executive of the BJP adopted its first detailed resolution on Ayodhya at Palampur (Himachal Pradesh). The resolution categorically blamed Babur for destroying the temple situated at *Ram Janmasthan* at Ayodhya and constructing a mosque in its place. It made clear that the court 'cannot adjudicate' this dispute. As the resolution of the party demanded: 'The sentiments of the people must be respected, and *Ram Janmasthan* handed over to the Hindus—if possible through a negotiated settlement, or else, by legislation. Litigation certainly is no answer.'

Thus, with the Palampur resolution, the Babri Masjid was changed to Ram temple; and the BJP publicly committed to a militant Hindu line. The Palampur resolution signalled that the time had come for the BJP to take the leading role in the *Ram Janmabhoomi* agitation, which was so far under the control of the VHP. This new role further demanded that the party had to intensify its fanatically anti-Muslim and aggressively pro-Hindu campaigns. In this atmosphere Lok Sabha elections took place at the end of 1989.

Giant Electoral Leap: Courtesy Hindutva

The BJP election manifesto criticized the Congress on the Shah Bano case, its attempt to recognize Urdu as the second language in UP and above all, for not allowing the rebuilding of the Ram temple at Ayodhya. After the 1989 elections, no party won an absolute majority in parliament. However, the BJP increased its strength to a hefty 86 compared to a meagre 2 in the previous parliament.[86] In the Uttar Pradesh assembly elections, it increased its tally from 16 to 57.[87] During the subsequent elections for the 8 state assemblies held in early 1990, the BJP increased its tally to 496 from 162 in the previous assemblies.[88] This electoral performance further convinced the *Sangh Parivar* that militant *Hindutva* could pay further electoral dividend.[89]

The Janata Dal led National Front formed a minority government with the support of the BJP as well as the left parties. BJP's support to the National Front government, spelt out in Advani's letter of 29 November 1989, referred to specific 'reservations'—Article 370, Uniform Civil Code, Human Rights Commission and *Ram Janmabhoomi*.[90] However, the BJP, as a major supporter of the government, acquired a decisive say in the affairs of governance. Though it did not participate in the government, it had its pound of flesh; its leaders were appointed as governors in a few states. Through the appointment of Jagmohan as the Governor of Jammu & Kashmir it tried to monitor the Kashmir policy. As the nature of this new government was fragile, major political parties soon competed to expand their own support bases anticipating a mid-term poll. While the BJP continued to consolidate its Hindu constituency through the *Hindutva* movement of the RSS, V.P. Singh announced various concessions to the Muslims in order to strengthen his hold among the Muslims.

RSS objects to V.P. Singh's Muslim 'Appeasement'

The *Sangh Parivar* objected to the following gestures of V.P. Singh's government towards the Muslims.[91] First, the Prime Minister met the Shahi Imam of Jama Masjid to express his 'indebtedness'. Secondly, he appointed a Muslim as the Home Minister of India for the first time. Thirdly, he ordered to throw open all protected mosques under the supervision of the Archeological Survey of India for prayers during the *Ramzan* period. The RSS reminded the Prime Minister that Indira Gandhi had resisted this pressure and allowed prayers at Safdarjang Mosque only for a day in 1984. Moreover, V.P. Singh granted Rs 50 lakh for renovation of the Jama Masjid, which did not fall under the protected category of monuments. The RSS argued that the masjid did not require any renovation and the grant would only benefit the Imam.

V.P. Singh's announcement from the Red Fort that Prophet Muhammad's birthday would be observed as a public holiday received further hostile opposition from the *Sangh Parivar*. L.K. Advani pleaded that no public holiday was observed in Arab countries including Saudi Arabia on the Prophet's birthday. Moreover, important Hindu festivals like Ram Navmi were not national holidays. He criticized the government's 'dual standards' and accused it of following a discriminatory policy against the Hindus in this regard. Advani demanded that Ram Navmi, Janmashtami and Shivratri should be declared as national holidays.[92] Though all these gestures of V.P. Singh did not benefit the Muslims in any concrete terms, these were exploited by the *Sangh Parivar* to its fullest advantage in its anti-Muslim campaign.

Mandal Report and the RSS Dilemma

Besides Muslims, V.P. Singh also tried to woo the backward castes. With his acceptance of the Mandal Commission Report which made an additional reservation of 27 per cent of jobs for the backward castes, Indian politics took a decisive turn. Various explanations are offered suggesting the motive of the implementation of this report which was in cold storage for about a decade. First, it was a counter-move to assert his leadership by containing the proposed rally of Devi Lal. Secondly, the Janata Dal was in need of creating a support base among these caste-groups in north India to counter the Congress. Finally, its objective was to blunt the edge of the pan-Hindu identity, which was so assiduously being shaped up by the RSS.

This action of V.P. Singh immediately identified the Janata Dal with the interests of the numerically preponderant backward castes. But Singh and the Janata Dal incurred maximum hatred and condemnation from the upper castes and the urban middle class, specially the professionals. Mandal decision also greatly antagonized the media and the intelligentsia, dominated by the upper castes and fearful of losing their earlier access to power due their educational advantage.[93]

But above all, the acceptance of the Mandal reports threatened to split the political base of the BJP. The *Sangh Parivar* had been working meticulously to expand its upper-caste support by utilizing the ideology of Hindu nationalism. Its targets were primarily the numerically strong and politically assertive backward castes. Singh's strategy now seemed to strike at the roots of Hindu electoral consolidation so important to the BJP. The RSS criticized V.P. Singh's 'antique politics' and described him as 'a broker of the few affluent backward castes' who would be the real beneficiaries of Mandalization of India.[94]

Both Advani and Vajpayee threatened to withdraw support if the government did not review its stand. The BJP ruled Himachal Pradesh rejected the report. However, the party was caught in a trap: if it supported the issue, it would alienate its followers of the urban areas, particularly among the educated middle class; and if it opposed the Mandal report, it would lose the support of backward class Hindus of the rural areas. Moreover, many of its backward caste members in parliament prevailed upon it not to oppose the issue directly.

The RSS was trapped. The best option to overcome this Mandal dilemma was to shift the focus to the *Mandir* and the Muslims.[95] Deoras focused on the *Ram Janmabhoomi* issue in his annual Vijaya Dashmi speech and announced: 'We are no longer slaves and hence tolerate any symbols of slavery' and rejected any approach which implied that *sarva dharma sama bhava* was 'a one-way track for Hindus while the others should continue to be intolerant'.[96] He was firm on the abrogation of Article 30 and 370 of the constitution and adoption of a Uniform Civil Code. Accordingly, on 12 September Advani announced that he would commence his *Rath Yatra* from Somnath in Gujarat to Ayodhya in Uttar Pradesh, a distance of 10,000 km.[97]

Rath Yatra: *A Concerted Effort of the* Sangh Parivar

Advani's *Rath Yatra* was not the decision of the BJP. It was a carefully designed strategy of the RSS. The *yatra* was a concerted effort of all the leading members of the RSS family. Bhaorao Deoras, brother of Balasaheb and a master political strategist of the RSS, reportedly spent two weeks in Delhi coordinating Advani's *Rath Yatra* plans.[98] The motive of this *yatra* was clearly political rather than religious. The Toyota *rath*, carrying the party symbol prominently, made their political intentions very clear.

Advani was ideally suited to the purpose. He was the chosen hero. Despite his insistence that it was the VHP who was leading the movement, it was Advani, who became identified as the leader of the movement. He was presented a *dharma dhwaja* by the priest of Somnath temple before he started his *dharma yuddha* (holy war).[99] However, Advani very shrewdly interpreted that the issue was not Hindu *vs.* Muslim or the construction of the temple but 'a crusade for strengthening national unity and promoting nationalism in the country'.[100] He was out to restore 'national pride'. The *Rath Yatra* would be 'a great act of national integration'. During the entire journey he severely criticized the 'pseudo-secularism' and 'minorityism' of the Congress, Communists and the Janata Dal. He also made scathing references to the havoc caused by the Mandal report.[101]

For the people, the decorated *rath* was a temple. They greeted it with folded hands, touched the tyres and took the sand below it placing it on their forehead. Women danced and performed *aarti.* At every place the most common offering was traditional weaponry: arrows, dices, maces, swords, *trishuls* and *kripans.*[102] At Jetpur in Gujarat 101 Kshyatriya youths offered him a bowl containing their blood.[103] The slogans raised were highly inflammatory: *'Jab jab Hindu jaga hai, Desh me molla bhaga hai'* (When the Hindus have arisen, the *mullahs* have fled the country); *'Mussalmano ko dono sthan, Pakistan aur kabarsthan'* (Muslims have two places—Pakistan or the graveyard).

Advani was arrested at the fag end of his journey at Samastipur, Bihar. The BJP predictably withdrew support to V.P. Singh resulting in the downfall of his government. Though he failed to reach Ayodhya, he had already achieved his mission. The journey was a spectacular success in western and north India from the point of view of the *Sangh Parivar.* Advani had 'succeeded in momentarily uniting a deeply fragmented Hindu society in a symbolic show of strength'.[104] Advani might have succeeded in uniting the Hindus, but he certainly divided the nation by igniting anti-Muslim hysteria among the Hindus. The entire country witnessed unprecedented communal violence.[105] The Mulayam Singh government resorted to police firing on the *kar sevaks* to protect the mosque on 30 October and 2 November killing 50 odd *kar sevaks.*[106]

The killing of the *kar sevaks* provided the opportunity to the leaders of the *Sangh Parivar* to fuel the agitation. The RSS described this action as 're-enactment of Jallianwala' and V.P. Singh and Mulayam Singh Yadav were compared with Babur and Mir Baqi respectively.[107] The killed *kar sevaks* were declared martyrs and their ashes were to be carried in urns—called *asthi kalash*—in a procession all over the country. The objective was not just to highlight the atrocities of the state, but also to make the Muslims responsible for being the indirect cause of these killings. As a symbol, the mortal remains of the martyrs were 'more powerful than the frigid bricks which were used first for the "shilanyas ceremony"'.[108]

The popular Hindu support to the *Rath Yatra* was described by Advani as the 'greatest Mass Movement' in independent India. The response was certainly spectacular in bringing various sections of Hindus towards the ideology of *Hindutva.* The assertion of Hindu identity further widened the gulf between Hindus and Muslims. The response of the State, like on previous occasions, was ambivalent. It allowed Advani to complete major part of his journey. The communal virus had already spread before his arrest. The firing on *kar sevaks* complicated the situation further and provided a convenient handle to the RSS.

The *Ram Janmabhoomi* movement and the *Rath Yatra* enabled the *Sangh Parivar* to penetrate the domain of Indian politics that had eluded it so far. No longer did it remain confined to its traditional geographical boundary—the pockets of urban north India; now it extended its presence all over the country, both urban as well as rural, more than ever before. Further, the RSS made a conscious attempt to widen its narrow upper caste support base. Though it is true that angry anti-Mandal upper-caste youths lent their overwhelming support to the *Ram Janmabhoomi* agitation,[109] the movement undoubtedly generated a lot of enthusiasm among the youths belonging to the backwards,[110] Dalits, tribals and created a pan-Hindu identity.

1991 Elections: Focus on Ayodhya

Soon after the *Rath Yatra* the RSS galvanized the BJP and other affiliates for the elections. The BJP changed its president in February 1991; Murli Manohar Joshi, another hardcore RSS man, replaced Advani. An aggressive electoral campaign was launched by the *Sangh Parivar* to reap an electoral harvest from the Ayodhya affair. The VHP announced plans for a *gherao* of parliament house on 4 April and went ahead with the plan despite the dissolution of the Lok Sabha. This huge rally in which more than a million people participated, was addressed by a host of *Sangh Parivar* leaders: Sudarshan, Singhal, Dalmia, Advani, Vajpayee, Joshi, Uma Bharti, Rithambara, Mahant Avaidyanath.[111] An appeal was made to the electorate to fill the parliament with *Rambhakts*—the devotees of Ram. Thus the 1991 election campaign was launched on a VHP platform on a strident note.

BJP's election manifesto, entitled *Towards Ram Rajya,* promised '*Ram,*

Roti and *Insaf*'. It underlined its 'high integrity, consistent ideology, internal discipline and stability, mature leadership, and a dedicated cadre to do them all'.[112] During the campaign video-vans toured different parts of the country and one of the video tapes that was shown frequently was that of the *kar seva* at Ayodhya. It aroused great passion among the Hindus. Emotive slogans such as '*Jo Hindu hit ki bat karega, wahi desh par raj karega*' (Only those who can take care of the interests of the Hindus will rule the country) and '*BJP ko lana hai, Ram rajya banana hai*' (Bring the BJP to power to bring Ram's rule) were raised. Firebrand speakers like Rithambara and Uma Bharti toured the country propagating *Hindutva* through their inflammatory anti-Muslim speeches and appealed to the people to vote for the construction of the Ram temple at Ayodhya.

BJP's Emergence as National Alternative

The BJP contested a record number of 477 seats. In comparison to the 1989 elections, when it won 86 Lok Sabha seats and got only 11.5 per cent of votes, this time it increased its strength to 120 by polling 20 per cent of votes. In as many as 167 constituencies the BJP polled more than 16.33 per cent of votes.[113] The party achieved a landslide victory in Gujarat by pocketing over 50 per cent of votes and winning 20 out of 25 Lok Sabha seats. In UP the BJP polled 32.8 per cent of votes and won 51 of the 85 seats.[114] In Delhi it polled over 40 per cent of votes and captured 5 out of 7 seats. Though it suffered some losses in Rajasthan and Madhya Pradesh in terms of seats, it gained in votes. Only in Maharashtra and Himachal Pradesh did it lose seats as well as votes. The party also showed a presence in the southern states of Karnataka (9 seats) and Andhra Pradesh (1 seat), polling over 28 per cent and 9 per cent of votes respectively. It also improved its performance in the eastern states. In Assam it won 2 out of 14 seats. Though it could not open its account in West Bengal and Orissa, it got 11.7 and about 10 per cent votes respectively. This widespread support base of the BJP made it a potential national alternative.

Thus the BJP emerged on the Indian political scene with reinvigorated self-confidence; it became the largest Opposition party in the tenth Lok Sabha and L.K. Advani became the leader of the Opposition. Unlike the 1977 and 1989 Lok Sabha elections, this time its electoral victory was because of its own strength rather than an outcome of alliances with non-Congress opposition parties. The BJP projected itself as an independent political force and succeeded in attracting the electorate despite the attempt of the opposition parties to isolate it. Though the growth of the BJP could be attributed largely to the 'temple politics', it was also benefited by a steady decline of the Congress in the north Indian states. Moreover, the BJP, since the Janata experiment in 1977, had been making an inroad into the rural areas through its alliance partners. Besides its focus on the *Mandir* issue, its anti-Mandal stance and withdrawal of support to V.P. Singh's government enhanced its credibility among the upper castes. They rallied behind the BJP firmly, particularly in UP, to counter Mulayam Singh Yadav's attempt to forge the unity of Muslims, backward castes and Dalits.

Another landmark for the *Sangh Parivar* was the electoral victory of the BJP in UP; the capture of power in the state would give an impetus to its Ayodhya campaign. Kalyan Singh, who belonged to a backward caste, was chosen to become the chief minister bypassing the claims of old RSS loyalists and BJP heavyweights like Kalraj Mishra and Lalji Tandon. Obviously, the strategy was to enlist the support of the backward castes to counter the influence of Mulayam Singh Yadav, the *bete noire* of the *Sangh Parivar.*

Sustaining anti-Muslim Propaganda

The *Sangh Parivar* continued its politics of *yatras*; Murli Manohar Joshi, Advani's successor, undertook the *Ekta Yatra* from Kanyakumari to Kashmir focussing on national unity. During the campaign he attacked Art. 370 and asked the people to reflect seriously on the dangers faced by the Indian nation. He unfurled the national flag at Lal Chowk in Srinagar on 26 January 1992. Despite being a low-key affair in comparison to Advani's *Rath Yatra*, it undoubtedly served a purpose by keeping anti-Muslim propaganda alive. In November 1992, L.K. Advani and M.M. Joshi led two pilgrimages, which on this occasion set off from Ayodhya towards Kashmir. The plan was to draw attention to the situation of the martyred Hindus in the state. These marches built up the pressure that would lead to the destruction of the Ayodhya mosque.[115]

Salman Rushdie's powerful and complex novel *Satanic Verses* created a furore among the Muslim community. The book was banned as it was allegedly an assault on their beliefs. The Muslim community stood up in defence of the divine nature of the truth as revealed via the Prophet. This very argument was turned against the Muslims in the Ayodhya controversy. Hindu fundamentalists insisted that the actual historical record was irrelevant. Religion is a matter of faith and belief, and since the Hindus believed that a temple to Ram once stood on the site, this belief gave an extra-constitutional sanction to their programme. The continuing existence of the mosque on a site so sacred to Hindus, they argued, was a continuing personal assault on every Hindu.[116]

The teleserial 'Chanakya' was telecast in 1991-2 by Doordarshan, the state-run TV channel. Though its theme appeared to be different from the epic serials 'Ramayana' and 'Mahabharata', in reality it was a mere continuation. Its recurrent motifs were 'the twin concerns proclaimed by the proponents of today's Hindu "rashtravadis": the need for an "akhand" Bharat to combat the fragmentation which lays "us" open to the external enemy; and the need to combat through the creation of a new Hindu male, the hydra-headed corruption spawned by the wielders of state power, which represents the eating away of the vitals of the nation by the "internal enemy"'.[117] The RSS was getting ready for its next assault in this milieu.

Operation Demolition

On 6 December 1992, 3,00,000 *kar sevaks* assembled at Ayodhya and thronged the domes of the Babri Masjid. Within five hours the mosque was razed to the ground and a new make-shift Ram temple was constructed amid the rubble of the disputed structure. It was a smooth operation. The *Sangh Parivar* celebrated the event as a historic victory. H.V. Seshadri observed that the demolition was 'undoubtedly a morale-boosting for the Hindu psyche. On 30 October 1990, hoisting of the Bhagwa was symbolic assertion of the nation's Hindu identity. But now, that standing monument to a foreign invader's insult to the nation's honour and independence has itself been erased.'[118] O.P. Kohli, the president of the Delhi unit of the BJP and a trusted RSS worker, expressed that it was good that the mosque was destroyed because it had been a blot on 'the face of India' and, therefore, on our national honour.[119] Even Vajpayee spoke in the same vein: Babri Masjid 'was a symbol of shame and has been erased',[120] and put the blame on the Allahabad High Court for delaying the judgement which provoked 'a group' to demolish the disputed structure.[121] Girilal Jain, who had been vociferously championing *Hindutva* in his columns, wrote that the Muslims must learn a 'lesson' from the destruction of the mosque, and that they should remember that there was no going back to the pre-6 December situation since political mobilization of Hindus as Hindus had never occurred before.[122]

The Ayodhya demolition was carefully planned by the *Sangh Parivar* and was facilitated by the UP government headed by Kalyan Singh. According to the 'Citizen's Tribunal on Ayodhya'[123] the demolition was pre-planned and finalized at a meeting held on 5 December 1992 and attended by H.V. Seshadri, K.S. Sudarshan, L.K. Advani, M.M. Joshi, Vijaya Raje Scindia, Ashok Singhal, Vinay Katiyar, Uma Bharti, Sadhvi Rithambara, Acharya Dharmendra, Pramod Mahajan, B.L. Sharma, and Champat Roy, apart from Moreshwar Save of the Shiv Sena. However, the RSS does not admit so. Seshadri[124] argued that the demolition was not a part of the plan on that day and they could not gauge the intensity of the feelings of the *kar sevaks.* Unexpectedly they broke the human chain of *swayamsevaks* guarding the place.[125] Deoras attributed the demolition to outside elements. *BJP's White Paper on Ayodhya* claims that the demolition 'was an uncontrolled and, in fact uncontrollable upsurge of spontaneous nature'.[126]

The Fall Out: Communal Riots

The demolition intensified Muslim anger and despair resulting in riots at many places. Celebrations and victory processions of the Hindus led to riots at some places. As the Srikrishna Commission[127] observes: 'The irresponsible act of the *hindutva* parties in celebrating and gloating over the demolition of Babri Masjid was like twisting a knife in the wound and heightened the anguished ire of the Muslims. The celebration rally organized by Shiv Sena in Dharavi is an example.'[128] In Bombay, a large number of Muslims assembled near Minara Masjid in Pydhoni at about 23.20 hours on 6 December to protest against the demolition. Despite the fact that the protestors were not armed, the police mishandled the situation and by their aggressive posture turned the peaceful protests into violent. The riots continued till 12 December.[129] The targets were mainly policemen and Hindu temples.[130] The riots later turned to be less a case of Hindu-Muslim conflict than Muslims against the police and vice-versa. During these riots the police forces went completely berserk, showing again the process of communalization of police forces, which had been going on for years.[131] Srikrishna Commission observed that 'the response of police to appeals from desperate victims, particularly Muslims, was cynical and utterly indifferent. On occasions, the response was that they were unable to leave the appointed post; on others, the attitude was that one Muslim killed, was one Muslim less.'[132]

Another spate of rioting started on 6 January 1993, which was markedly different from the previous riots.[133] This time, the Hindus started it under the provocation and guidance of the Shiv Sena, which had been inciting them by anti-Muslim propaganda through the writings in its newspapers like *Saamna* and *Navakal*. Bal Thackeray, the Shiv Sena supremo, advocated the doctrine of 'retaliation'[134] and the Shiv Sainiks, the cadre consisting of lumpen elements, unleashed organized violence. The Sena went on offensive by selecting the issue of *namaz*, the congregation of Muslims at mosques for Friday prayer.[135] To confront this, it organized *maha aartis* (great pujas) at various temples in the city; between 26 December 1992 and 5 February 1993, the Shiv Sena organized 498 *maha aartis*, of which 172 were attended by 1,500 persons or more.[136] These congregations provided physical gathering points and emotional rallying spaces from which gangs moved out to attack Muslim targets.[137] During the eight days of severe, and ten further days of less severe rioting in January 1993 at least 550 people were killed and Rs 4,000 crore of property destroyed.[138] BJP local leaders or members of other affiliates of the RSS were also involved in the rioting.[139] But it was the Shiv Sena which was instrumental in organizing the riots in Bombay. Communal violence also broke out in other parts of India. 200 people were killed at Surat[140] and 139 at Bhopal.[141] The *Sangh Parivar's Hindutva* politics thus plunged India into the worst communal violence since Partition, with 1,700 dead and 5,500 injured.

Third RSS Ban: Narasimha Rao's Ambivalence

On the evening of 6 December 1992 President's rule was imposed in UP shortly after Kalyan Singh resigned. Three days later, L.K. Advani, M.M. Joshi, Uma Bharti, Sadhavi Rithambara, Ashok Singhal and Vinay Katiyar were arrested on charges of inciting communal violence. The following day the RSS, the VHP, the Bajrang Dal, the Jamaat-e-Islami and the Islamic Sevak Sangh were banned. Their offices were sealed and all activities including the holding of RSS *shakhas* were prohibited. The two common grounds for the banning of the RSS, the VHP and the Bajrang Dal were the participation of their members in the demolition of Babri Masjid and their incitement of communal antagonism. The notification issued against the RSS added that it was intent on asserting 'that members of certain religious communities have alien religions and cannot, therefore, be considered nationals of India'.[142] Subsequently the BJP governments in MP, Rajasthan and HP were dismissed on 15 December and President's rule imposed. Deoras protested the sacking of the BJP governments and described it as 'unconstitutional, illegal and immoral'.[143]

Unlike the previous bans of the RSS in 1948 and 1975, this time the government adopted a conciliatory rather than a firm attitude toward the RSS. Only a relatively small number of people were taken into custody under the Unlawful Activities (Prevention) Act.[144] Key cadres had gone into hiding. Even this crackdown was soon relaxed and the seven leaders were freed on 10 January 1993. The government's policy was further constrained by certain judicial decisions. The Madhya Pradesh High Court ordered in the end of December that the RSS offices in Jabalpur and Indore be opened. On 2 April 1993, it overturned the imposition of President's Rule in the state and ordered the restoration of the legislative assembly in Madhya Pradesh. The central government appealed before the Supreme Court.

The ban was covered by the Unlawful Activities (Prevention) Act, 1967, which required that notification should be confirmed by a Tribunal headed by a High Court judge. Justice P.K. Bahri of the Delhi High Court was appointed in this capacity, and on 4 June 1993 he upheld the ban on the VHP for a statutory period of two years because of the inflammatory nature of some of its members' speeches but cancelled those against the RSS and the Bajrang Dal.[145] It was a major victory for the RSS.

The Narsimha Rao government's attitude was ambivalent in the entire Ayodhya episode. It decided to pursue a 'legal' rather than a 'political strategy'. The government literally believed Kalyan Singh's assurance to the Supreme Court that his government would prevent the *kar sevaks* from damaging the mosque if they were allowed a symbolic *kar seva* nearby. Further, Rao was not in favour of dismissing Kalyan Singh's government as he found Art. 356 'too restrictive'. Thus he allowed a huge congregation of *kar sevaks* and failed to protect the mosque from their onslought; the police forces were asked to intervene only after the construction of a make-shift temple. The district administration allowed the *sadhus* to have *darshan*, thereby according legitimate sanctity to the temple; then this order was withdrawn. Later the Allahabad High Court permitted *darshan*. On 13 December, the CBI was entrusted with the task of investigating the demolition of the Babri Masjid.[146] On 27 December, the central government issued an ordinance for the acquisition of all the disputed areas in Ayodhya and later passed a Bill. The centre thereby acquired 67.7 acres of the land for two trusts which would construct a Ram temple and a mosque respectively. The government also requested the President to seek the opinion of the Supreme Court under Article 143(1) whether a Hindu temple or any Hindu religious structure existed prior to the construction of the *Ram Janmabhoomi*-Babri Masjid in the area on which the structure stood.[147]

Narasimha Rao was clearly outsmarted by the *Sangh Parivar* in the Ayodhya episode. His hesitation, vacillation, indecision and inaction were perhaps guided by the organizational strength of the RSS, its capacity of militant mobilization and the enormous Hindu support it enjoyed at that juncture. He obviously wanted to avoid confrontation with the RSS which could have brought down his government and Rao was not ready for such a sacrifice.

RSS Mobilization to Counter the Ban

RSS did not sit quiet during the ban period. It had a fair assessment of the government's weaknesses and its own strength. Its confidence to face this ban was quite different from 1948 and 1975; it rightly coined slogans like '*Pachattar nahin yeh banwe hai/Ek nahin hum lakhon hai*' (This is not 1975 but 1992, We are not one but lakhs).[148] Though it suspended its routine activities, it resolved to 'fight through all constitutional avenues this unjust, undemocratic and politically motivated action of the Central Government'.[149] It devised an 'Action Plan'[150] to mobilize support, which included: (i) to collect at least five crore signatures on a memorandum to the President demanding that the Ram temple be rebuilt at the *garbha-griha*; (ii) to organize a massive demonstration at Delhi during the coming session of parliament to demand lifting of the ban on RSS, VHP and Bajrang Dal and to protest against the dismissal of BJP governments in 4 states and; (iii) 'Direct Action' to force the government to seek a fresh mandate from the people for Lok Sabha and hold elections in UP, MP, Rajasthan and Himachal Pradesh.

The RSS was sure that the demolition was 'bound to prove decisive in the next round of battle in the ballot'[151] and galvanized the BJP to launch a political offensive through a *Jan-Jagaran* Programme from 1 January 1993 for the mid-term poll for the Lok Sabha.

VHP and Bajrang Dal Emerged Stronger

The *Ram Janmabhoomi* agitation and the demolition of the mosque enhanced the popularity of the VHP and Bajrang Dal.[152] VHP's *Dharma Sansad* appeared to have more sanctity and authority than the parliament of India. The popularity of the VHP leaders like Ashok Singhal, Acharya Dharmendra, Giriraj Kishore and Vinay Katiyar gave them a sense of superiority vis-a-vis their BJP counterparts. Their statements at times created embarrassment for the BJP. While the VHP stated that Kashi and Mathura would be their next targets, the BJP dissociated itself from such demands. The VHP also demanded its pound of flesh in the forthcoming elections, thus attempting to enter into the political arena which the BJP had monopolized so far.

The Bajrang Dal, a VHP subsidiary, was a loose structure till Ayodhya demolition; its members were recognized by their saffron headband bearing the word 'Ram'. Their role in demolition elevated their status in the *Sangh Parivar*. Though the RSS applauded its role, it wanted to keep this potentially violent organization under discipline and ideological control. Thus, in 1993, the Bajrang Dal became an all-India body with a more rigid organizational structure that resembled that of the RSS in several respects. Uniforms were introduced (blue shorts, white shirts and saffron scarf), trained RSS cadres were deputed to control the organization and some 350 training camps were held during 1993.

Setback to Sangh Parivar

The *Sangh Parivar* got a severe jolt when the BJP suffered major electoral reverses in the 1993 assembly elections in UP, MP, and Himachal Pradesh. These elections were widely regarded as a referendum on the demolition. The demolition and the subsequent riots scared the traditional supporters of the BJP—the middle classes and small traders. Despite the middle class support for Ram temple, they did not feel happy about the demolition. The business interests of the trading community were often affected by riots. The aggressive campaign of the VHP and the Bajrang Dal further added to their anxiety and insecurity. Naturally these supporters of the BJP had a suspicion whether the party would be able to handle the law and order situation effectively. Therefore, the 'religious Hindus' started deserting soon after the demolition; the 'political Hindu' appeared to be vacillating; sections of the middle class, and the petty trading and entrepreneurial class found benefits in the new economic reforms of Narasimha Rao government; the Backward Classes and Dalits were not prepared to overlook the upper caste bias of the *Hindutva* forces.[153]

Thus, the RSS made a decisive political journey under the leadership of Balasaheb Deoras. His daring decision to go for direct political intervention reached a climax with the demolition of the Babri Masjid in 1992. The RSS participation in the anti-Emergency struggle and subsequently in the Janata experiment helped it to master the art of realpolitik. It showed willingness to accommodate and did not mind introducing some strategic changes in the notion of *Hindu Rashtra* for the sake of political power. Even after the disillusionment with the Janata Party and the formation of the BJP, it continued with its politics of accommodation. Subsequently, however, the fear of losing its Hindu agenda and constituency to Indira Gandhi and Rajiv Gandhi and the political marginalization of its political affiliate, the BJP, compelled it to adopt the strategy of militant Hinduism. Thus, *Ram Janmabhoomi* movement was launched and politics was contextualized in terms of 'Hindus' and 'Others'. Political mobilization was expressed in a new nomenclature—*Kar Seva*; Hindu religious and cultural symbols were carefully selected for political mobilization. The *Rath Yatra* turned out to be a mammoth political congregation to assert a 'Hindu' identity. The *Ram Janmabhoomi* movement and the *Rath Yatra* reversed the political future of the BJP, from a marginal political party to the national alternative. The RSS, its ideological mentor and organizational master, no longer remained peripheral; it had now come to occupy the centrestage of Indian politics as an indispensable player.

NOTES AND REFERENCES

1. The first letter informed that after discussing with various 'veteran, experienced and dedicated workers' and provincial *sanghachalaks*, Golwalkar had decided to nominate Balasaheb Deoras as his successor. This suggests that various factors determine the selection to this top post, not just the predecessor's fancy. While the second letter instructed not to build his memorial, in the third letter he asked for forgiveness for his shortcomings. See 'Shri Guruji's Three Last letters', *Organiser*, XXVI (45), 16 June 1973.
2. Balasaheb was born on 1915. His ancestors were from Andhra Pradesh like that of Hedgewar. The family name was Deoraju, which turned into Deoras after decades of living in Maharashtra. Balasaheb used to visit a *vyayamshala* (gymnasium) in the childhood and was a champion *kho-kho* player. He passed out from New English School in 1931. He joined Morris college and became a graduate in 1935 with Philosophy and Sanskrit as his optional subjects. Also passed the Bachelor of Law examination in 1937, but never practiced. He joined Anath Vidyarthi Griha School as a teacher with the objective of bringing the young boys to the RSS. However, he soon left the job to become a full-time *pracharak* and decided to remain a bachelor.

3. In the early days of the Sangh there was a small troop of *swayamsevaks* called *kusha-pathak*. This group of *swayamsevaks*—brave, adventurous, intelligent and imbibed with revolutionary inclinations—was the most favourite of Hedgewar. Balasaheb was the leader of this batch which got engaged in preparing bombs. Hedgewar took ten sittings of this batch and impressed upon them the ineffectiveness of such a course and weaned them to the organizational way. See *Organiser*, XXVI (46), 23 June 1973. This suggests that the RSS accords primacy to collective organizational action vis-a-vis adventurous individual/group action.
4. Ibid.
5. At the same time, he was 'an ardent believer in the fundamental principles of life conceived and contained in the one word "Hindutva"'. Ibid.
6. Ibid.
7. For details on these organizational changes, see D.R. Goyal, *Rashtriya Swayamsevak Sangh* (Delhi: Radha Krishna Prakashan, 1979), pp. 114-16.
8. The first experiment of the new line took place when the RSS *shakha pramukhs* actively participated in the elections to the Delhi University Students' Union and Delhi University Teachers' Association in 1973 to secure votes for the RSS nominees. Ibid., p. 115.
9. Ibid., p. 116.
10. 'Hindus are Problems of Hindusthan: Sarsanghchalak's Penetrating Analysis of Current Situation', *Organiser*, XXVII (15), 17 November 1973.
11. See *Organiser*, XXVI (46), 23 June 1973.
12. See Rajni Kothari, 'The Congress System in India', *Asian Survey*, 4 (12), December 1964, pp. 1161-73.
13. See Aijaz Ahmed, 'Culture, Community, Nation: On the Ruins of Ayodhya', *Social Scientist*, 21 (7-8), July-August 1993, pp. 17-48.
14. 'Sangh Cannot Remain Aloof From World Around: Interview with the New Sanghchalak', *Organiser*, XXVI (46), 23 June 1973.
15. See 'Balasaheb Asks Swayamsevaks to Enter Every Field of National Life', *Organiser*, XXVII (10), 13 October 1973.
16. J.P. Mathur, a leader of the BJS, wrote about the growth and transformation of the party. See his 'Kanpur To Kanpur: Jana Sangh's Journey of Growth', *Organiser*, XXVI (36), 14 April 1973. In this session, the BJS resolved to adopt a more pragmatic approach. This was facilitated with the expulsion of Balraj Madhok from the party. The RSS leadership supported the pragmatic Vajpayee line over the conservative line of Madhok.
17. *Organiser*, XXVII (31), 9 March 1974.
18. Atul Kohli, *Democracy and Discontent: India's Growing Crisis of Governability* (Cambridge: Cambridge University Press, 1991), pp. 37-60.
19. 'Vidyarthi Parishad gives all-out support to Gujarat Revolution', *Organiser*, XXVII (32), 16 March 1974.
20. The protest movements in Gujarat and Bihar are discussed in Ghanshyam Shah, *Protest Movements in Two Indian States: A Study of the Gujarat and Bihar Movements* (Delhi: Ajanta Publications, 1977).

21. For an analysis of Indira Gandhi's distinctive style of leadership, see Nayantara Sahgal, 'The Making of Mrs. Gandhi', *South Asian Review*, 8 (3), 8 April 1975, pp. 189-210. An excellent psychological interpretation of Indira Gandhi's authoritarianism can be found in Ashis Nandy, *At the Edge of Psychology: Essays in Politics and Culture* (Delhi: Oxford University Press, 1993 rep.), pp. 112-30.
22. *Organiser*, XXVI (40), 12 May 1973.
23. L.K. Advani, 'An Open Threat of Dictatorship', *Organiser*, XXVII (1), 11 August 1973.
24. One-third of the 24 member-governing body of the CSS belonged to the ABVP. At some places RSS activists became the office-bearers of the CSS. See Ghanshyam Shah, *Protest Movements in Two Indian States*, op. cit., pp. 97 and 131.
25. *Organiser*, XXVIII (17), 7 December 1974.
26. *Organiser*, XXVIII (41), 24 May 1975.
27. Walter K. Andersen and Shridhar D. Damle, *The Brotherhood in Saffron: The Rashtriya Swayamsevak Sangh and Hindu Revivalism* (Delhi: Vistaar Publications, 1987), p. 212. The authors describe the political activities of the RSS during the ban period primarily on the basis of an interview with Rajendra Singh. For the RSS account of its role during the Emergency, see *Organiser*, XXIX (1) and (2), 28 May and 4 June 1977.
28. Most of these get-togethers were secretly organized in temples, clubhouses and in the houses of prominent personalities where the police would not usually enter.
29. The adoption of the non-violent Gandhian method as an effective means of protest demonstrates the tactical shrewdness of the RSS. The RSS claims that over 1,00,000 of its members participated in the *satyagraha*. From the *Parivar*, ABVP and BMS contributed 12,000 and 10,000 volunteers respectively. See *Organiser*, XXIX (1), 28 May 1977.
30. In November 1976, the Friends of India Society, International was formed in England for the same purpose.
31. Madhu Limaye points out that the first priority of the RSS leadership was to secure the removal of the ban. Deoras greeted Indira Gandhi on her 'victory' in the election appeal before the Supreme Court. He even distanced himself from the JP movement and appealed to Indira Gandhi to lift the ban. Vinoba's intervention was also sought. See Madhu Limaye, *Janata Party Experiment: An Insider's Account of Opposition Politics 1975-1977*, Vol. I (Delhi: B.R. Publishing Corporation, 1994), p. 134. Similar version can be found in D.R. Goyal, *The Rashtriya Swayamsevak Sangh*, op. cit., Appendix VI (Deoras Letters).
32. *Organiser*, XXIX (1), 28 May 1977.
33. The RSS worked closely with the communists, socialists, Naxalites, Jamatis and other groups, who were ideologically poles apart.
34. Madhu Limaye, *Janata Party Experiment*, op. cit., p. 138. Limaye produces Dattopant Thengadi's letter to Madhavrao Mulay in which he underlined the need to redefine the concept of the *Hindu Rashtra* in the light of changed circumstances.

35. For a comprehensive study of the Janata Party, see C.P. Bhambri, *The Janata Party: A Profile* (Delhi: National Publishing House, 1980).
36. Reacting to Madhu Limaye's suggestion, the RSS leader Madhav Rao Mulay said: 'The suggestion is amazing and objectionable. RSS is a voluntary organisation, but that does not make it a volunteer organisation. The swayamsevaks of the Sangh are not volunteers who will spread the *durries* and fix the mikes for some leaders to come and make speeches. It should be clearly understood that we are nobody's Boy Scouts.' *Organiser*, XXIX (14), 19 August 1977.
37. The number of *shakhas* increased from 8,500 in 1975 to 11,000 in 1977. See *Organiser*, XXIX (41), 5 March 1978. One year later, the RSS boasted of having added another 2,000 new *shakhas*. The labour affiliate, BMS, also grew from 1.2 million members in 1977 to 1.8 million in 1980. For a discussion on the growth and activities of the BMS, see Kiran Saxena, 'The Hindu Trade Union Movement in India: The Bharatiya Mazdoor Sangh', *Asian Survey*, XXXIII (7), July 1993, pp. 685-96. The ABVP also increased its membership from 1,70,000 in 1977 to 2,50,000 in 1982.
38. Andersen and Damle, *The Brotherhood in Saffron*, op. cit., p. 217.
39. Ibid., p. 223.
40. The Janata party won only 31 seats out of which the Jana Sangh group won 16, compared to its tally of 93 in 1977.
41. It is hard to prove the allegation. However, after the election, the RSS hoped that the ruling party would replace the politics of hate with the politics of cooperation. *Organiser*, XXXII (2), 6 July 1980, p. 3.
42. For an account of Swamy's accusation, see Janardan Thakur, *All the Janata Men* (Delhi: Vikas Publishing House, 1978), Ch. VIII.
43. Y.K. Malik and V.B. Singh, *Hindu Nationalists in India: The Rise of the Bharatiya Janata Party* (Delhi: Vistaar Publications, 1995), p. 38.
44. Bharatiya Janata Party, *Our Five Commitments* (Delhi: Asiatic Printers, n.d.), pp. 1-20.
45. 'RSS is Gandhian, says Balasaheb', *Organiser*, XXX (34), 14 January 1979.
46. Ibid.
47. JP movement witnessed a strange conjunction of Gandhian socialism with Hindu nationalism. See Richard G. Fox, 'Gandhian Socialism and Hindu Nationalism: Cultural Domination in the World System', *Journal of Common-wealth and Comparative Politics*, 25 (3), November 1987, pp. 233-47.
48. *Organiser*, XLIX (28), 8 February 1998.
49. Gandhi continues to baffle *Sangh Parivar*. Shiv Sena Chief Bal Thackeray made certain derogatory remarks on Mahatma Gandhi. However, realizing that it could antagonise the powerful Gujarati business community of Bombay, he soon withdrew his remarks. The BJP General Secretary Pramod Mahajan, defending Thackeray, said that Gandhi could at best be regarded as India's '*suputra*' (a great son) but not '*rashtra pita*' (father of the nation): 'a country which is over 5,000 years old doesn't need a father'. See *The Times of India*, 4 January 1997. Incidentally, Mahajan only reiterates the dominant view on Gandhi within

the RSS. Baburao Deshpande, the oldest RSS *pracharak* in Orissa, expressed the same in an interview in 1994. Interview with Baburao Deshpande.

50. For RSS viewpoint on conversion, see Devendra Swarup, ed., *Politics of Conversion* (Delhi: Deendayal Research Institute, 1986).
51. *Organiser*, XXXIII (9), 19 July 1981.
52. A comprehensive account of VHP's emergence as a powerful member within the *Sangh Parivar* as well as its role in the RSS scheme of religio-political mobilization can be found in Peter van der Veer, 'Hindu Nationalism and the Discourse of Modernity: The Vishwa Hindu Parishad', in Martin E. Marty and R. Scott Appleby, eds., *Accounting for Fundamentalisms: The Dynamic Character of Movements*, Vol. 4 (Chicago: University of Chicago Press, 1994), pp. 653-68; Also see his *Religious Nationalism: Hindus and Muslims in India* (Delhi: Oxford University Press, 1996).
53. The Virat Hindu Sammelan set five objectives: unite Hindus, abolish untouchability, ban conversions, ban foreign money for conversions and bring people back to their ancestral faith. *Organiser*, XXXIII (22), 18 October 1981.
54. *Organiser*, XXXIII (23), 25 October 1981.
55. *Organiser* reported that the ruling party was not opposed to the *Sammelan*. Even a senior leader of the All India Harijan League of the ruling party, Krishna Swarup, endorsed the *Sammelan*. *Organiser*, XXXIII (22), 18 October 1981.
56. The BJP won only 19 of 56 seats in the Metropolitan Council and 37 out of 100 seats in the Corporation.
57. Andersen and Damle, *The Brotherhood in Saffron*, op. cit., pp. 231-2.
58. For an account of the different *yatras* undertaken by the *Sangh Parivar*, see Jackie Assayag, 'Ritual Action or Political Reaction? The Invention of Hindu Nationalist Processions in India during the 1980s', *South Asia Research*, 18 (2), 1998, pp. 125-45.
59. All these places were carefully selected for their religious importance and geographical location, covering the length and breadth of India. The inclusion of Pashupatinath in Nepal confirmed the high esteem the RSS offered to this only Hindu kingdom of the world. For the details of these *yatras*, see Peter van der Veer, *Religious Nationalism: Hindus and Muslims in India*, op. cit., pp. 119-28.
60. Robert Eric Frykenberg, 'Hindu Fundamentalism and the Structural Stability of India', in Martin E. Marty and R. Scott Appleby, eds., *Fundamentalisms and the State: Remaking Polities, Economies and Militance*, Vol. 3 (Chicago: University of Chicago Press, 1993), p. 246.
61. Ashis Nandy et al., *Creating a Nationality: The Ramjanmabhoomi Movement and Fear of the Self* (Delhi: Oxford University Press, 1995), p. 107.
62. Some historians of the Centre for Historical Studies of the JNU issued a statement opposing the RSS-VHP account of history of the Babri Masjid-Ram Janmabhoomi. See 'The Political Abuse of History: Babri Masjid–Ram Janmabhumi Dispute', *India Alert—Special Bulletin*, 2 (3), December 1983; R.S. Sharma et al., *Ramjanmabhumi-Baburi Masjid: A Historians' Report to the Nation* (Delhi: People's Publishing House, 1991). Also see Sushil Srivastava,

The Disputed Mosque: A Historical Inquiry (Delhi: Vistaar Publications, 1991). For RSS–VHP viewpoint, see Koenraad Elst, *Ramjanmabhoomi vs. Babri Masjid: A Case Study in Hindu-Muslim Conflict* (Delhi: Voice of India, 1990). Also see Arun Shourie and Jay Dubashi, *Hindu Temples: What Happened to Them—A Preliminary Survey* (Delhi: Voice of India, 1990).

63. *Organiser*, XXXVIII (8), 6 July 1986.
64. H.V. Seshadri, 'Wiping Out the Blot of Foreign Slavery', *Organiser*, XXXVII (34), 5 January 1986.
65. Ibid. This assertion prompts Engineer to comment that the *Mandir-Masjid* controversy is above all a political controversy and also involves much deeper questions of identity and power. See Asghar Ali Engineer, ed., *Politics of Confrontation: The Babri Masjid-Ramjanmabhoomi Controversy Runs Riot* (Delhi: Ajanta, 1992). Introduction. For an incisive analysis on different aspects of the conflict, see S. Gopal, ed., *Anatomy of Confrontation: The Babri Masjid-Ramjanmabhumi Dispute* (Delhi: Viking, 1991).
66. While the temple doors were opened to cajole the Hindu vote-bank, the Muslim Women Bill was introduced not to antagonize the Muslim vote-bank. In both the cases the State yielded to communal pressure. See Zoya Hasan, 'Changing Orientation of the State and the Emergence of Majoritarianism in the 1980s', in K.N. Panikkar, ed., *Communalism in India: History, Politics and Culture* (Delhi: Manohar, 1991), pp. 142-52. Ramesh Thakur also argues that the retreat of the Congress was for crass political reasons: 'an effort to shore up crumbling Muslim bloc support for a party that was clearly in deep electoral trouble'. See Ramesh Thakur, 'Ayodhya and the Politics of India's Secularism: A Double-Standards Discourse', *Asian Survey*, 33 (7), July 1993, p. 650.
67. L.K. Advani, *The Times of India*, 14 October 1990.
68. *India Today*, 30 June 1989.
69. As the RSS never participated in the anti-colonial struggle, it always shows its keenness to project Hedgewar's pre-RSS life. It emphasizes that he had close links with the Bengal revolutionaries and that he participated in the freedom struggle and got imprisoned.
70. *Organiser*, XL (36), 5 March 1989.
71. This wish of the RSS to have a commemorative stamp of its founder was fulfilled by the Vajpayee government.
72. 'Top Level meeting of RSS-BJP Leaders', *Organiser*, XL (41), 16 April 1989.
73. *Organiser*, XLI (4), 30 July 1989.
74. *Organiser*, XL (47), 28 May 1989.
75. For instance, D.B. Thengadi was present in the first *Ramshila Pujan* held at Badrinath and H.V. Seshadri attended the final function at Ayodhya on 10 November.
76. Richard H. Davis, 'The Iconography of Rama's Chariot', in David Ludden, ed., *Making India Hindu: Religion, Community and the Politics of Democracy in India* (Delhi: Oxford University Press, 1996), p. 41.
77. See Anuradha Kapur, 'Deity to Crusader: The Changing Iconography of Ram',

in Gyanendra Pandey, ed., *Hindus and Others: The Question of Identity in India Today* (Delhi: Viking, 1993), pp. 74-109.

78. See Paula Richman, ed., *Many Ramayanas: The Diversity of Narrative Tradition in South Asia* (Delhi: Oxford University Press, 1992).
79. See Victoria L. Farmer, 'Mass Media: Images, Mobilization, and Communalism', in David Ludden, ed., *Making India Hindu*, op. cit., pp. 102-3. For more on the impact of mass media on the Ram Janmabhoomi movement, see Romila Thapar, 'The Ramayana Syndrome', in *Seminar*, 353, January 1989, pp. 71-5; Sheldon Pollock, 'Ramayana and Political Imagination in India', *Journal of Asian Studies*, 52 (2), May 1993, pp. 261-97.
80. Lloyd I. Rudolph, 'The Media and Cultural Politics', in Subrata K. Mitra and James Chiriyankandath, eds., *Electoral Politics in India: A Changing Landscape* (Delhi: Segment Books, 1992), p. 92.
81. After *Ramshila Yatras* started in mid-1989, the communal graph raced upwards. In 1987, communal violence took toll of 383 lives, in 1988 the number receded to 223. While the number of people killed during the first half of 1989 were 94, in the later half of the year the toll spurted to 708 as the *Ramshila* campaign gathered momentum. See *India Today*, 15 October 1990.
82. *Our Five Commitments*, op. cit., p. 4.
83. Quoted by Kameshwar Choudhary, 'BJP's Changing View of Hindu-Muslim Relations', *Economic and Political Weekly*, XXVI (23), 17 August 1991, p. 1901.
84. The BJP distributed a questionnaire among the party members to study the causes of the defeat. Most of the respondents felt that the main reason of the defeat was the loss of the party's previous Hindu identity and therefore, the party should come closer to the RSS organizationally to refurbish its image. See Manini Chatterjee, 'The BJP: Political Mobilization for Hindutva', *South Asia Bulletin*, XIV (1), 1994, pp. 14-23.
85. *Organiser*, XXXVII (36), 9 January 1986.
86. BJP's performance could be attributed to two factors: opposition unity against the Congress and the Ram Janmabhoomi campaign. For details, see James Chiriyankandath, 'Tricolour and Saffron: Congress and the neo-Hindu Challenge', in Subrata K. Mitra and James Chiriyankandath, eds., *Electoral Politics in India: A Changing Landscape*, Delhi: Segment Books, 1992), pp. 55-80.
87. However, Mitrasen Yadav of Communist Party of India won in Faizabad (the parliamentary constituency of Ayodhya).
88. It increased its strength from 58 to 220 in Madhya Pradesh, from 38 to 86 in Rajasthan, from 8 to 44 in Himachal Pradesh, from 16 to 42 in Maharashtra, from 11 to 66 in Gujarat, from 13 to 39 in Bihar and 0 to 2 in Orissa. *Organiser*, XLI (34), 18 March 1990.
89. The RSS believed that the *Shilanyas* issue and the BJP's stand on *Ram Janmabhoomi* 'played a big role in these elections'. *Organiser*, XLI (20), 3 December 1989. H.V. Seshadri admitted that the major factor in the electoral victory of the BJP was 'the rising Hindu awareness' and observed that the future of the party would depend on 'how consistently and commitedly' it would

continue to attune its policies with the 'Hindu content'. *Organiser*, XLI (36), 1 April 1990.

90. A.G. Noorani, 'History of the BJP (1980-1990)', *Mainstream*, 29 (23), 30 March 1991, p. 11.
91. *Organiser*, XLI (40), 6 May 1990.
92. *Organiser*, XLII (6), 16 September 1990.
93. For a critical discussion on the role of media during the agitation, see S. Shivanandan, 'Mandal, Mandir and Masjid: Dubious Role of Media', in *Mainstream*, 28 (52), 20 October 1990.
94. *Organiser*, XLII (6), 16 September 1990.
95. For a discussion on the complex Mandal and Mandir controversy, see Sukumar Muralidharan, 'Mandal, Mandir aur Masjid: "Hindu" Communalism and the Crisis of the State', in K.N. Panikkar, ed., *Communalism in India: History, Politics and Culture*, op. cit., pp. 196-218.
96. For the address of Balasaheb Deoras at the Vijaya Dashmi function at Nagpur held on 29 September 1990, see *Organiser*, XLII (10), 14 October 1990.
97. The *Yatra* was to start on 25 September and culminate on 30 October covering eight states such as Gujarat, Maharashtra, Andhra Pradesh, Madhya Pradesh, Rajasthan, Haryana, Bihar and Uttar Pradesh.
98. Reported in *India Today*, 15 October 1990.
99. *Organiser*, XLII (10), 14 October 1990.
100. *Organiser*, XLII (9), 7 October 1990.
101. It has been argued that the *Rath Yatra* had 'taken away the cynicism' of the middle class students that had been fostered by the Mandal Commission. See Swapan Dasgupta, 'Invoking Ram to Fight Mandal', *The Times of India*, 30 October 1991.
102. *Organiser*, XLII (10), 14 October 1990.
103. Advani reportedly did not approve of this gesture and advised them to donate blood in the nearby hospital. But these gestures certainly signalled that violence would be inevitable. Surprisingly, Advani kept on insisting that his journey would be peaceful.
104. Swapan Dasgupta is cited in *Organiser*, XLII (11), 21 October 1990.
105. For an incisive analysis of the communal violence in Gujarat and Rajasthan, see Ashis Nandy et al., *Creating A Nationality: The Ramjanmabhoomi Movement and the Fear of the Self*, op. cit., Chap. IV, pp. 99-155. For a case study of 1990 communal riots in Agra city, see Jayati Chaturvedi and Gyaneshwar Chaturvedi, 'Dharma Yudh: Communal Violence, Riots and Public Space in Ayodhya and Agra City, 1990 and 1992', in Paul Brass, ed., *Riots and Pogroms* (Houndmills: Macmillan Press, 1996), pp. 177-200.
106. For a comprehensive discussion, see Nilanjan Mukhopadhya, *The Demolition: India at the Crossroads* (Delhi: Indus, 1994).
107. *Organiser*, XLII (14), 11 November 1990.
108. Sumanta Banerjee, '"Hindutva": Ideology and Social Psychology', *Economic and Political Weekly*, XXVI (3), 19 January 1991, p. 100.

109. Most of the 21 'martyrs' of the 1990 *Kar Seva* at Ayodhya belonged to Brahmin and Bania castes.
110. Though a substantial section of the OBC leaders agreed that a temple should be built in Ayodhya, they did not approve demolition of a holy shrine. See G.K. Lieten, 'On Casteism and Communalism in Uttar Pradesh', *Economic and Political Weekly*, XXIX (14), 1994, p. 781.
111. The RSS-VHP combine, while campaigning against cow slaughter, also attempted to seize the Parliament in 1966. While on that occasion they tried to pressurize the members of Parliament to adopt a pro-Hindu legislation, this time they were speaking as if they wanted to push through a vote of no-confidence against the government, 'thereby suggesting that the judgement of the crowds in the street was preferable to that of the electorate'. See Christophe Jaffrelot, *The Hindu Nationalist Movement and Indian Politics 1925 to the 1990s: Strategies of Identity-Building, Implantation and Mobilisation [with special reference to central India]* (Delhi: Viking Penguin India, 1996), p. 437.
112. BJP advertisement published in *The Times of India*, 4 May 1991.
113. Yogendra K. Malik and V.B. Singh, *Hindu Nationalists in India*, op. cit., p. 200.
114. Mahinder Singh Tikait, the BKU supremo, who had considerable support among the Jats of western UP, instructed his cadre 'to take the name of Ram and with *Om* on your lips, vote according to your conscience'. This was clearly a signal in favour of the BJP. See Dipankar Gupta, *Rivalry & Brotherhood: Politics in the Life of Farmers in Northern India* (Delhi: Oxford University Press, 1997), p. 81.
115. Jackie Assayag, 'Ritual Action or Political Reaction? The Invention of Hindu Nationalist Processions in India During the 1980s', *South Asia Research*, op. cit., p. 138.
116. Ramesh Thakur, 'Ayodhya and the Politics of Secularism', op. cit., pp. 651-2.
117. See Uma Chakravarti, 'Saffronising the Past: Of Myths, Histories and Right-Wing Agendas', *Economic and Political Weekly*, XXXIII (5), 31 January 1998, p. 229. Although Chanakya's appeal was limited to an upper caste elite, it was part of a larger process in which a brahmanic view of history and culture was consolidated alongwith a rightward shift in politics. Ibid., p. 232.
118. *Organiser*, XLIV (20), 20 December 1992.
119. *The Times of India*, 16 December 1992.
120. *Sunday*, 27 December 1992–2 January 1993.
121. 'Speech of Shri Atal Behari Vajpayee in Lok Sabha on 17-12-92', in *Hindus Betrayed* (Delhi: Suruchi Prakashan, 1993).
122. *The Times of India*, 14 December 1992.
123. O. Chinappa Reddy et al., *Citizens' Tribunal on Ayodhya*, p. 68.
124. *Organiser*, XLIV (20), 20 December 1992.
125. Ibid.
126. *BJP's White Paper on Ayodhya*, op. cit., p. 131.
127. Srikrishna Commission was appointed on January to investigate the post-

Babri demolition Mumbai riots of December 1992 and January 1993. The Commission laboured hard for five years, and heard and examined more than 500 witnesses, and surfed through 2,135 affidavits. It covered 72 police station areas which were affected by riots. The witnesses included the then chief ministers of Maharashtra, Sudhakarrao Naik and Sharad Pawar. Bal Thackeray, though summoned, did not appear before the Commission. The Shiv Sena–BJP government disbanded the Commission on 23 January 1996 but revived it again on the intervention of Atal Behari Vajpayee. The findings of the Commission have established that it was the Shiv Sena led by Bal Thackeray which was mainly responsible for organizing the riots. See Asghar Ali Engineer, 'Srikrishna Commission Report: Painstaking Documentation', *Economic and Political Weekly*, XXXIII (33 and 34), 15-21 and 22-8 August 1998, pp. 2215-16.

128. Quoted by Asghar Ali Engineer, 'Srikrishna Commission Report', op. cit., p. 2215.
129. For an account of the December riots in Bombay see P. Sainath, 'Bombay Riots of December 1992: A Report', in Mehdi Arlsan and Janaki Rajan, eds., *Communalism in India: Challenge and Response* (Delhi: Manohar, 1994), pp. 191-9. Also see Justice S.M. Daud and Justice H. Suresh, *The People's Verdict: An Inquiry into the Dec' 92 and Jan' 93 Riots in Bombay* (Bombay: Indian People's Human Rights Commission, 1993), and pp. 48, 65 and 66; D. Padgaonkar, ed., *When Bombay Burned* (New Delhi: UBSPD, 1993).
130. A.A. Engineer, 'Bombay Shames India', in *Bombay's Shame: A Report on Bombay Riots* (Bombay: Ekta Samiti, 1993), pp. 6 and 15.
131. P. Sainath, 'Bombay Riots of December 1992: A Report', op. cit., p. 192.
132. Asghar Ali Engineer, 'Srikrishna Commission report', op. cit., p. 2215.
133. For an incisive analysis of 1993 January riots, see J. Masselos, 'The Bombay Riots of January 1993: The Politics of Urban Conflagration', in John Maguire, Peter Reeves and Howard Brasted, eds., *Politics of Violence: From Ayodhya to Behrampada* (Delhi: Sage Publications, 1996), pp. 111-26.
134. In an interview with Anita Pratap as reported in *Time* (Australia), 25 January 1993, p. 37, Thackeray said: 'Muslims started the riots, and my boys are retaliating. Do you expect Hindus to turn the other cheek? I want to teach Muslims a lesson. Our fortitude has gone.'
135. As the mosques did not have enough capacity to accommodate the Muslims, they often occupied the streets, thus causing inconvenience to the people. The Sena cleverly channelled hostility to *namaz* into a Hindu-derived ritual. The *maha aartis*, the evening prayers of the Hindus in the temples, ironically, blocked the streets in much the same way as the Friday *namaz* did. See J. Masselos, 'The Bombay Riots of January 1993', op. cit., p. 116.
136. A.A. Engineer, *Bombay's Shame*, op. cit.
137. See J. Masselos, 'The Bombay Riots of January 1993', op. cit., p. 116.
138. Ibid., p. 112.
139. S.M. Daud and H. Suresh, *The People's Verdict*, op. cit., p. 43.

140. J. Breman, 'Anti-Muslim Pogrom in Surat', *Economic and Political Weekly*, XXVIII (16), 17 April 1993, pp. 737-41; Sudhir Chandra, 'Of Communal Consciousness and Communal Violence: Impressions from Post-riot Surat', *Economic and Political Weekly*, XXVIII (36), 4 September 1993, pp. 1883-7; P. Sheth, 'Degeneration of a City', *Economic and Political Weekly*, 30 January 1993, pp. 151-2.
141. *Bhopal Riot: A Report* (Bhopal and Delhi: Sanskritik Morcha and PUDR, 1993).
142. See the notification in *White Paper on Ayodhya*, op. cit., p. 115.
143. *Organiser*, XLIV (21), 27 December 1992, p. 3.
144. The number of persons arrested was 1,500 in UP and 1,000 in MP. Not more than 3,500-4,000 activists of the *Sangh Parivar* went to jail. *The Pioneer*, 15 December 1992.
145. A.G. Noorani, 'A Touch of Gloss—Bahri Report: Bizzare Conclusions', *Frontline*, 10 September 1993, p. 111.
146. The CBI filed a charge sheet against forty activists belonging to *Sangh Parivar* and Shiv Sena (including Advani, Kalyan Singh and Thackeray) on 5 October 1993.
147. *White Paper on Ayodhya*, op. cit., pp. 97-106.
148. *Organiser*, XLIV (21), 27 December 1992.
149. *Organiser*, XLIV (20), 20 December 1992.
150. *Organiser*, XLIV (26), 31 January 1993, p. 11. Rajju Bhaiya launched a signature campaign on 15 January 1993.
151. *Organiser*, XLIV (21), 27 December 1992, p. 5.
152. Ashis Nandy, 'Three Propositions', *Seminar*, 402, February 1993, p. 15.
153. Manini Chatterjee, 'The BJP: Political Mobilization for Hindutva', in Praful Bidwai et al., eds., *Religion, Religiosity and Communalism* (Delhi: Manohar, 1996), pp. 105-6.

CHAPTER VII

Consolidating Political Power: Rajendra Singh and Sudarshan

On 11 March 1994, after handing over the mantle to Rajendra Singh[1] alongwith the symbolic *shreephal* (coconut), Balasaheb Deoras announced before the Akhil Bharatiya Pratinidhi Sabha of the RSS: 'I am no longer the Sarsanghchalak. Mananeeya Rajendra Singhji is the Sarsanghchalak now.'[2] Deoras cited his physical disability as the reason for his retirement and also disclosed that he had nominated Rajendra Singh three years ago after consulting with his senior colleagues in the KKM.[3] This was an unprecedented announcement. Deoras deviated from the past practice of his predecessors by passing the baton during his lifetime.

Why did Deoras choose Rajendra Singh? There were other veterans for this coveted post—Dattopant Thengadi, Moropant Pingle, H.V. Seshadri and K.S. Sudarshan. Singh's educational qualifications, organizational skills, tested leadership during the anti-Emergency agitation, mastery of the Indian political topography, international contacts, and above all, his proximity to Deoras, helped him score over other contenders. Moreover, his non-Brahmin and non-Maratha background were his additional assets as it was necessary to take the RSS out of the Maharashtrian–Brahmin circuit in the context of its national agenda and the resurgence of caste politics. The battle for hegemony of the Hindi heartland had reached a crucial stage and it would be ideal if a north Indian Hindi speaker headed the RSS. Deoras perhaps understood the mindset of the north Indian elite and masses. Another important reason that perhaps went in favour of Rajendra Singh was his political pragmatism, which Deoras considered crucial for managing the burgeoning affiliates, particularly the BJP. Further, when the BJP was inching towards political power at the centre, the RSS needed somebody who could effectively guide and control the political affiliate. To his advantage, Rajendra Singh's political acumen was much better than his competitors. All these factors influenced Deoras to nominate Rajendra Singh as his successor, despite the fact that he had abdicated the post of *sarkaryavah* sometime back due to his ill health.

Apart from being a 'man of firm resolve and conviction with a sharp mind and clear understanding', Rajendra Singh is 'very simple and unassuming'.[4] He is addressed by the ordinary *swayamsevak* as Rajju Bhaiya, in contrast to the images of previous *sarsanghchalaks.* As Seshadri explained: 'Mananeeya Raju Bhaiyya's style of functioning deserves to be emulated. He has a unique way of leading people with his informal talk carried on in a lighter vein.'[5] In the post-Ayodhya period this would be extremely useful, as the *Sangh Parivar* had undergone the process of massification, which demanded an informal and intimate relationship between the supreme leader and the common *swayamsevak.* And the *sarsanghchalak* had to perform this new role of elder brother to each *swayamsevak* along with the role of a guide and philosopher.

The present chapter will discuss how the RSS, under the leadership of Rajendra Singh, the successor of Deoras, continued its tryst with politics and succeeded in installing its political affiliate at the seat of power in Delhi. As the BJP does not monopolize, but shares political power with its alliance partners, it will examine what new strategies the RSS has adopted in view of the political compulsions. Does the RSS dilute its *Hindutva* agenda or re-orient it? It will also discuss how political power has strained not only the RSS-BJP relationship, it has also started threatening the saffron brotherhood. Finally, it will analyse the developments after K.S. Sudarshan succeeds Rajendra Singh.

HINDUTVA: HARD OR SOFT?

Soon after his take over, Rajendra Singh, paid his customary obeisance to *Hindutva* by announcing that Ayodhya issue would remain alive until the construction of a Ram temple at the same site.[6] He endorsed the stand of the VHP on Kashi and Mathura and warned that demands for restoring Hindu places of worship were bound to crop up as long as the 'three most sacred places of Hindus' are not 'returned' to them. He also gave his approval to VHP *Dharma Sansad's* decision to organize *yatras* and forcibly occupy the disputed site in November 1994. Advani also made it clear that the Ayodhya issue would remain the 'ideological mascot' of the BJP, and that *Hindutva* was a 'shortcut' to cultural nationalism and the most distinctive feature of the party's identity and approach.[7] The BJP think tank put their heads together at Sariska in Rajasthan, to define *Ram Rajya* and *Hindutva* in terms of the nation-state.[8] Thus *Hindutva* remained in focus.

Mandalization and Dalitization of the Sangh Parivar

The Mandalization of Indian polity and the rising consciousness of Dalits put the RSS in a dilemma. The *Sangh Parivar* could no more afford to continue with the image of an upper caste formation; it had to accommodate these castes if it wanted to succeed in mainstream politics. The conservatives, at the same time, were not prepared to allow any such move as it would dilute *Hindutva* and result in upper caste alienation. However, the *Sangh Parivar* was compelled to make some tactical changes. First, *Hindutva* needed to tone down its stridency in public; and secondly, and more importantly, it had to give due credence to the inescapable Mandalization and Dalitization as the electoral loss of the BJP in UP and MP was partly because of the OBC and Dalit voters. K.N. Govindacharya, a RSS *pracharak* and BJP leader, advocated social engineering and the BJP inducted a large number of backward class activists in the key positions within the party. For instance, Uma Bharti became the chief of the party's youth wing.

Besides tackling the Backward Classes, the *Sangh Parivar* thought of extending its support base among the Dalits. The BSP had already emerged as the political expression of the Dalit voice, particularly in UP. The *Parivar* felt the need to strike a deal with the BSP to have an easy access to the Dalit base. But the BSP was sharing power with Mulayam Singh Yadav, *Sangh Parivar's bete noire*. A strategy was carefully worked out and the BJP supported the BSP leader Mayawati against Mulayam, thereby breaking the Backward-Dalit alliance and making her the first Dalit Chief Minister of UP. Mayawati was also looking for the opportunity; with the given electoral arithmetic, she could not have become the Chief Minister without the support of the BJP. The honeymoon was short-lived, however; the BJP brought down the Mayawati government in October 1995.

1996 Lok Sabha Election: Reflecting the Dilemma

In October 1995, the VHP launched the *Ekatmata Yatra* (March of Unity), intended as a kick off to the 1996 Lok Sabha campaign. The grand plan of local level processions joining up with major processions from all parts of India uniting finally at Nagpur, was met with public indifference.[9] The VHP's attempts to rally support behind Kashi and Mathura were also met with a lacklustre response and the VHP and the BJP were at odds with each other and with their own stated policies.[10]

The preamble of the 1996 BJP manifesto asserted: 'Hindutva or cultural nationalism, . . . will guide from *swarajya* [self rule] to *surajya* [good governance].'[11] It further emphasized: 'Hindutva is a unifying principle which alone can preserve the unity and integrity of our nation. It is a collective endeavour to protect and re-energise the soul of India, to take us into the new millennium as a strong and prosperous nation.'[12] The BJP assured, after assuming power, it 'will facilitate the construction of a magnificent Shri Rama Mandir at Janmasthan in Ayodhya which will be a tribute to *Bharat Mata*. This dream moves millions of people in our land; the concept of Rama lies at the core of their consciousness.'[13]

The BJP further promised to promulgate a Uniform Civil Code (UCC), disband the Minorities' Commission in favour of a National Human Rights Commission (NHRC), make 'fraudulent conversions' a punishable offence and introduce a system of registering all conversions. It denounced 'illegal immigration' as a 'demographic invasion' and proposed measures to prevent infiltration from Bangladesh. On Kashmir, it reiterated its demand to abrogate Article 370 but talked of 'regional development councils' in J & K.

Alongwith its commitment to a strong nation-state, it promised to strengthen federalism and criticized the frequent resort to President's rule. It also gave an assurance to divide big states such as UP, MP, Bihar and Maharashtra in order to carve out Uttaranchal, Chhatisgarh, Vananchal and Vidarbha. The BJP further advocated decentralization at the grassroots by proposing to make 'the panchayats financially self-sufficient'.[14]

The Campaign: Hindutva *Diluted*

While the manifesto resonated with *Hindutva* and highlighted 'minority appeasement', the campaign, however, exhibited the party's realization of the declining appeal of its *Hindutva* plank. The party thus emphasized economic reform and a smaller and cleaner government at the centre. The BJP campaign also faced the almost insurmountable difficulty of reconciling the conflicting aspirations of the core groups of the party with the party's compulsion to dilute *Hindutva* to widen its base.

BJP's most important symbol to underline its moderate image was its leader A.B. Vajpayee. The party projected him both as the future Prime Minister in the event of its victory. Vajpayee avoided any reference to Ayodhya in his campaign speeches. Unlike Advani, he seldom referred to the party's slogan of *Hindutva* and cultural nationalism. He also tried to establish a rapport with Muslims that they had nothing to fear by voting for the BJP.[15]

The three major planks of the BJP—*suchita* (cleanliness in public life), *suraksha* (security), and *swadeshi* (economic nationalism)—grew weaker as the campaign moved closer to the election. The party's plan to wage a campaign against corruption lost some of its appeal when leaders like Advani, Madan Lal Khurana were implicated by the CBI in the *hawala* scandal. The Rao government's decision not to sign the Comprehensive Test Ban Treaty (CTBT) and to continue the Prithvi Missile Programme took the heat out of its allegation that the Congress was compromising on national security. However, the BJP harped on about Kashmir and the Purulia arms dropping as security threats. The *swadeshi* plank was also eroded by the revival of the Enron deal.

Unlike previous elections, religious specialists did not tour and campaign for the BJP candidates and kept a low profile. Sadhvi Rithambara, whose fiery speeches and cassettes shot up the temperature in the 1989 and the 1991 Lok Sabha elections and the 1993 assembly elections, was not visible anywhere. Though part of this was a genuine fear of the Election Commission's regulations, 'Seshan phobia', part of it was also because of the popular indifference to the *Hindutva* programmes. Moreover, being unsure of public support, religious leaders were compelled to focus on their own districts and did not have time to campaign elsewhere.[16] At the same time, the BJP continued to attack the policy of 'minority appeasement' during its campaign, concentrating mainly on the Uniform Civil Code (UCC), Article 30, the influx of Bangladeshi Muslims, ISI networks, etc. The party even hoped that its campaign for the UCC would generate another Hindu wave.[17]

The Supreme Court's judgement on *Hindutva* further emboldened the campaign of the *Sangh Parivar*. Manohar Joshi, the Chief Minister of Maharashtra, promised the electorate that if the Shiv Sena were voted back to power, Maharashtra would become the first 'Hindu state'. Exonerating Joshi, the Court interpreted this statement as only an expression of 'a hope' and that 'no precise meaning can be ascribed to the terms "Hindu", "Hindutva" and "Hinduism", and no meaning in the abstract can confine it to the narrow limits of the religion alone, excluding the content of Indian culture and heritage'.[18] Moreover, it vindicated the *Sangh Parivar's* attempt to equate nationalism with Hinduism.[19] Though the BJP refrained from highlighting the Ayodhya issue in its campaign, the VHP launched a vigorous campaign for the protection of cows to galvanize Hindu votes.

Another important aspect of the campaign was the issue of formal appeal by the *sarsanghchalak* Rajendra Singh to the voters to defeat 'anti-Hindutva elements'. Singh stated: 'Contribute your time and mite to the fullest in this popular awakening, which actually is God's work, so that our politics—eclipsed by anti-Hindutva thinking—can come out and shine forth.'[20] Thus the RSS was extremely anxious to get hold of political power at New Delhi.

BJP's Electoral Performance

The BJP polled 21.34 per cent of national votes compared to 20 per cent in 1991. Congress (I) was ahead of the BJP with 28 per cent of the national vote. The BJP won 52 seats in UP, thus adding one seat to its 1991 score of 51. In Bihar it won 18 out of 32 seats it contested compared to its tally of only 5 seats in 1991. In Gujarat it could manage to pocket 16 out of 26 seats in comparison to its 1991 strength of 20 seats. In Madhya Pradesh, it got an impressive victory by winning 27 seats in comparison to only 12 in 1991. It maintained its score of 12 seats in Rajasthan like the 1991 position. In Haryana, it showed a gain of 4 seats compared to none in 1991. In Karnataka, it improved its performance, from 4 in 1991 to 6 in 1996.

The party's improvement with regard to its share in votes was also impressive. In Assam and Orissa it polled 16 and 13 per cent respectively over its 1991 share of 9 and 10 per cent. In Arunachal Pradesh the party polled 17 per cent over only 6 per cent in 1991. Two factors were mainly responsible for the BJP's seat gains.[21] First, was the ability of the party to forge election alliances with Samata Party in Bihar, Haryana Vikas Party in Haryana and Shiv Sena in Maharashtra. Secondly, the party also succeeded in consolidating its support among the upper castes while fracturing the votes of the OBCs. Though the BJP could not gain much beyond the Hindi belt, its voters were found to be both committed and certain compared to the hopelessly split opposition voters.[22]

BJP's 13-day Government

The President invited the BJP leader Atal Behari Vajpayee to form the government as the BJP and its allies were the largest political combine though they did not have absolute majority. Vajpayee was sworn in as the Prime Minister on 16 May 1996. It was a memorable occasion for the RSS—its long cherished dream of occupying Delhi came true. But the elation was short-lived. Vajpayee had to prove his majority within a fortnight and the support was nowhere in sight. To woo the opposition, the Vajpayee government's presidential address did not include the *Hindutva* agenda, viz., Ram temple, Article 370 and the UCC. Despite this gesture, the opposition parties made a scathing attack on the RSS and talked of its 'hidden agenda'. On 28 May, the Vajpayee government resigned, as it could not muster support, paving way for the Deve Gowda-led United Front government.

Being unable to keep itself in power at the centre, the BJP made a concerted effort to retain its supremacy in UP. But in the assembly elections, the BJP's share of seats came down to 174, in comparison to 177 seats in 1993. BJP was forced to have an alliance with the BSP. A BJP-BSP coalition government was formed with Mayawati as the Chief Minister. As per the understanding, Kalyan Singh would take over after the expiry of six months.[23]

Back to Hindutva?

The electoral performance of the BJP belied the expectation of the *Sangh Parivar* and demanded an introspection. Was it desirable to dilute the *Hindutva* agenda? This raised some serious differences between the BJP leadership on the one hand and the RSS-VHP combine on the other. The latter argued that in the 1996 Lok Sabha polls as well as in the Uttar Pradesh assembly elections the BJP experimented with the policy of downplaying *Hindutva* with disastrous results. M.G. Vaidya, the then *prachar pramukh* of the RSS, remarked that 'the BJP should make Hindu nationhood its main plank. It should not bother about the charges of communalism. It will not lose a single vote by using the word "Hindu".'[24] Even Rajendra Singh questioned both the policies and the direction of the BJP.[25] In his Dussehra rally, he admonished the BJP for straying from the path of *Hindutva*. The VHP too joined in the attack and declared its intention to revive the issue of Mathura and Kashi.

The BJP's executive meeting at Jaipur in November 1996 also

reflected this mood. M.M. Joshi, Kalraj Mishra and Lalji Tandon vehemently opposed Govindacharya's theory of social engineering, which had the backing of Kalyan Singh. The critics attributed BJP's poor performance to social engineering which aimed at bringing Dalits and the most backward castes closer to the party by giving them tickets. There was a strong move to push Mandalization backward and reassert *Hindutva*.

1998 General Elections

The United Front government refused to accede to the Congress demand to severe ties with the DMK as the Jain Commission mentioned its support to the LTTE, the organization behind the assassination of Rajiv Gandhi. Therefore, the Congress withdrew support to the Gujaral government, thereby forcing the twelfth general elections. The Congress, first forcing the UF to replace Deve Gowda by Gujral and subsequently withdrawing support to the UF precipitated instability.

BJP was quick to make stability its main poll plank. The title of the BJP manifesto[26] was 'A Stable Government and An Able Prime Minister'. But the party manifesto did not give up its *Hindutva* agenda. It remained committed to 'One nation, One people and One Culture' though it acknowledged the unique cultural and social diversity in India. It observed that people had rejected the efforts to characterize *Hindutva* as a sectarian or exclusive idea. The BJP was convinced that *Hindutva* offered immense potentiality to re-energize this nation and strengthen and discipline it to undertake the arduous task of nation-building. The party promised to facilitate the construction of the Ram temple in Ayodhya and explore all consensual, legal and constitutional means for the purpose. It also promised to abrogate Article 370 and entrust the Law Commission to formulate a Uniform Civil Code (UCC), based on the progressive practices from all traditions to gender equality and equal rights for women. It also proposed to review the Constitution of India in the light of the experience of the past 50 years and make suitable recommendations.

But the manifesto also focused on other major issues. On the question of federalism, the BJP promised to take necessary steps to prevent misuse of Article 356 of the Constitution and implement Sarkaria Commission recommendations. It would carve out Uttaranchal, Vananchal, Vidarbha and Chhattisgarh as separate states. On the economic front, it ensured 8 to 9 per cent of growth of GDP and promised to protect the small-scale sector, which constituted the backbone of the Indian economy, from unequal competition, both from large houses and from the transnational corporations. The manifesto promised to increase state spending on education progressively to six per cent and more of the GNP within five years. It was committed to provide free education to women up to graduation and passage of the bill reserving 33 per cent seats for women in all elected bodies.

The Campaign: Hindutva *on Backburner*

The focus of the BJP's 1998 election campaign was 'stable government and able Prime Minister'. The party put *Hindutva* on the backburner as it realized that to have a nationwide electoral presence it needed support from the alliance partners. Besides its alliance with the Shiv Sena in Maharashtra and the Samata Party in Bihar, its other prominent alliance partners were: Shiromani Akali Dal in Punjab, Haryana Vikas Party in Haryana, Biju Janata Dal in Orissa, Lok Shakti in Karnataka, and AIADMK in Tamil Nadu. The BJP also made conscious efforts to woo the minorities and Dalits. In a rally of the minorities organized at Delhi, Vajpayee and Advani sought to dispel minority apprehension and assured them to look after their interest if their party was voted to power.[27] The party established contacts with the community leaders, offered more tickets to Muslim candidates and promised to resolve their problems.[28]

The RSS agreed with the BJP that the key issue would be stability and competent government; Ayodhya, though important, would not be the core issue in the campaign.[29] At the same time, it clarified that the BJP was committed to the reconstruction of the temple at Ayodhya.[30] Rajendra Singh also asked the Muslims to forego their claim on Ayodhya, Kashi and Mathura. The *Sangh Parivar* organized various activities to keep the *Hindutva* issue alive among its core constituency. The RSS celebrated the golden jubilee year of India's independence as a year of *Bharat Mata Pujan* (Mother India's Worship) from 5 to15 January 1998 organizing programmes at about 70,000 places in which more than 57 lakh people reportedly participated.[31] The VHP appealed to the Hindus to elect a *Rambhakt* Government at the centre; only a *Rambhakt* government could clear the reconstruction of the temple at Ayodhya. The VHP had prepared a 5-point Hindu agenda for the 1998 elections: '1) enacting a law banning the slaughter of cow and her progeny besides declaring it a cognizable offence so as to close down all the mechanized slaughterhouses in the country; 2) removing all the hurdles in reconstruction of temples at Ayodhya, Mathura and Kashi, and the handover of all these places to Hindus respectfully; 3) ban on religious conversion by enacting a law; 4) stopping interference of several state governments in management of Hindu *maths*, temples and *akharas*, and; 5) ensuring the free flow of Ganga as well as making it pollution-free.'[32] To create awareness among the voters, some Hindu saints and the VHP decided to perform *Ram Mahayajna* at 7,000 places.

During the campaign, the *Sangh Parivar* got apprehensive over Sonia Gandhi's entry into the Congress campaign and her potential to revive and revitalize it as a strong contender for power. The RSS interpreted that Sonia's entry was primarily because of personal compulsions, as she feared that the BJP would carry the Bofors probe to its logical end. It commented that the Indian National Congress had become the Italian National Congress as Sonia's 'roots are firmly in foreign soil—whether financial, cultural, ethical or emotional—capturing the country's premier party solely on the strength of her money power and foreign connection'.[33] Thus took off the *Swadeshi-Videshi* campaign.

BJP's Victory: RSS Claims Credit

The BJP won 180 seats in the twelfth Lok Sabha and together with its allies 250 seats. In terms of vote share, the BJP was also able to break the 25 per cent barrier in its own right. With the help of the alliance partners, the BJP was able to penetrate new areas, particularly in the east (Orissa, West Bengal) and the south (Karnataka, Tamil Nadu, Andhra Pradesh). On 19 March 1998, Vajpayee was sworn in as the Prime Minister. The majority was ensured when Telugu Desam decided to extend its support to Vajpayee.

The RSS claimed its due credit for the victory of the BJP. Before the elections, Rajendra Singh had identified three main factors responsible for the BJP's ascendancy: 'A clear-cut ideology, leaders of proven merit and a large number of devoted and committed workers are the main reason for the growth of the BJP.'[34] Celebrating the victory after the elections, the RSS reiterated that the victory was the result of the ideology of *Hindutva*, the disciplined and dedicated RSS cadre and the leadership of the BJP.[35] Paying tribute to the RSS workers, Rajendra Singh stated that 'this happy change in the political arena is chiefly the fruit of the silent, self-sacrificing and relentless efforts put in the various spheres of national regeneration by Hindutva-dedicated workers and organizations over the past several decades'.[36] He called upon the *swayamsevaks* to expand their organizational work in this 'pro-Hindutva atmosphere', especially in the areas where it had not taken deep roots and hoped that the *Parivar* would expand at a much faster rate.[37]

RSS AGENDA: *SURAKSHA* AND *SWADESHI*

The Vajpayee led government soon released the 'National Agenda for Governance' (NAG), a document which accommodated the viewpoints of the alliance partners. It did not contain the controversial *Hindutva* agenda of the RSS, as there was no reference to Ayodhya, Article 370, and UCC. The RSS obviously agreed to it because of political compulsions. But some of its favourite issues like national security (*suraksha*) and *swadeshi*, figured prominently in the NAG.

On the question of *suraksha*, NAG mentioned: 'To ensure the security, territorial integrity and unity of India we will take all necessary steps and exercise all available options. Towards that end we will re-evaluate the nuclear policy and exercise the option to induct nuclear weapons.' Besides *suraksha*, the RSS wanted to push through its agenda of *swadeshi*. As the document noted: 'We will continue with the reform process, give it a strong swadeshi thrust to ensure that the national economy grows on the principle that "India shall be built by Indians"; . . .'[38] The RSS was sure that despite its approval to drop the *Hindutva* agenda, it would gain substantial political mileage from these two issues.

SURAKSHA

Militarizing Hindutva

As Golwalkar observed: 'It is significant that every Hindu God is armed',[39] thereby suggesting that the *Hindu Rashtra* should be a strong military power. On 26 February 1966, just before the his death, Savarkar had called on the Indian government to 'immediately equip India with nuclear weapons and missiles'.[40] The RSS rejects the Gandhi-Nehru legacy in military and security matters. It denounces Mahatma Gandhi for preaching and practicing 'the doctrine of non-violence in the most perverted form' and attempting to establish superiority of his non-violent methodology over physical resistance.[41] It accuses Nehru of being completely oblivious to the country's defence requirements and advocating that India had no enemy.[42] However, Sardar Patel is commended for recognizing the security threat from India's neighbour and warning Nehru and the people about it.[43]

The RSS feels that the Nehru-Gandhi legacy fostered 'defeatism', 'pseudo-secularism' and internal division and it needs to be completely discarded in favour of an aggressive policy about the nation's security. For a long time, the RSS has been advocating the adoption of the nuclear weapon option. It also demands a hard line vis-a-vis Pakistan, labelling it as a 'terrorist state' for abetting terrorism in Kashmir and suggests tough measures such as bombing the terrorist camps in the Pakistan territory and pursuing Pakistan-sponsored insurgents back into Pakistan. The ambitious plan of the RSS also includes building up a 'blue water navy' capable of exercising power in the Indian Ocean 'from Singapore to Aden' and of protecting the interests of overseas Indians in the Indian Ocean. The BJS espoused a hard agenda on security and military matters. It argued in favour of universal military training and observed a *Rashtra Suraksha Saptah* (National Security Week) in December 1953 to highlight the question of national security. After the Chinese aggression in 1962, it stepped up the demand for the allocation of more resources for defence. It sensed danger after the acquisition of nuclear weapons by China and asked the government to shed its 'pseudo-pacifist inhibitions'.[44] The BJP has been advocating both these 'hard' options alongwith the 'soft' ones.[45]

After the BJP's installation at the centre, the RSS shifted its focus to the issue of national security. It sharply reacted to Pakistan's testfiring of the Ghouri missile and observed that it would disturb peace in Asia and cause concern for India, especially in the context of Pakistan's promotion of terrorism and insurgency. It further added: 'By naming the missile after the 12th century invader who plundered half of India and destroyed the culture here, Pakistan has added a new dimension to her missile programme.'[46] Pakistan's aggressive stance, the RSS observed, was rooted in a 'conquest fixation'.

Nuclear India

Possession of nuclear weapons has always remained dear to the *Sangh Parivar*. In 1951, the Jan Sangh manifesto had proclaimed the need for India to go nuclear. It rejected the argument on economic non-viability of nuclear weapons and argued that no price could be considered too high where the country's defence was involved. Soon after China tested nuclear bomb in 1964, its propaganda for nuclear agenda got momentum. Vajpayee spoke thus in the Rajya Sabha: 'The answer to an atom bomb is an atom bomb, nothing else.' The party had greatly welcomed the 1974 Pokhran nuclear test. It urged the government not to sign the Nuclear non-Proliferation Treaty (NPT). This aggressive stance of the BJS was considerably diluted when the party merged its identity with the Janata Party and Vajpayee became the Foreign Minister in the Janata government (1977-9). However, Subramanyam Swamy, the then blue-eyed boy of the RSS, repeatedly advocated making India nuclear. The BJP, the new *avatar* of the BJS, in all its manifestoes, has always given priority to the nuclear agenda.

With the BJP's coming to power the RSS precipitated its campaign for the nuclear option. It asked for a re-evaluation of India's nuclear status, which had been overdue since in the last quarter of the century the global strategic balance had tilted towards a unipolar power system. The RSS argued that India's security concerns demanded an in-depth evaluation of its defence requirements and, if after such an exercise, it were felt that Pokhran had to be repeated, the country should go ahead with it.[47] While going nuclear, the RSS warned, India would face international opposition, similar to the one Indira Gandhi had to face after the first explosion at Pokhran on 18 May 1974. But, then, the RSS argued, the nation's security and the morale of our fighting forces should get precedence.

Pokhran II

On 11 May 1998, on the auspicious Buddha Purnima day, the Buddha smiled again. India exploded nuclear bombs at Pokhran and Vajpayee proudly claimed that India had achieved the status of the sixth nuclear weapon State. While the international community was aghast and replied by imposing sanctions, an overwhelming number of people in the country approved of the testing of the nuclear bombs, celebrated the blasts and applauded the Vajpayee government.[48]

The *Sangh Parivar* was very happy, as the 'Hindu Bomb' would give a boost to Hindu Nationalism. The VHP announced its plan to construct a temple to commemorate the nuclear tests at Pokhran. The temple, proposed to be constructed about 50 km from the test site, would be dedicated to Shakti—the goddess of strength.[49] To justify the sanctity of the site, the VHP came up with the argument that Baba Ramdev had come to Pokhran to preach social reforms and a better status for women. Even Govindacharya, the BJP Secretary, stated: 'Like the feeling attached to Ayodhya, the nuclear tests are an emotional nationalist assertion.'[50]

An even more fundamental way in which Pokhran is geared to

overall *Sangh Parivar* objectives 'is through vastly accelerating processes of militarisation of culture and education. The "national"-cum-"Hindu" chauvinism very obviously stimulated by the bomb fosters unthinking, jingoistic, aggressively-male mind-sets, for which the RSS has been systematically working for decades, and which are quite evident, to some extent autonomously, among a significant section of privileged, high-caste, upwardly mobile Indians.'[51] The RSS has always remained critical of the 'effeminate' Hindu and the possession of nuclear weapons symbolically asserted Hindu masculinity and virility.

SWADESHI

Any concept of the nation must include the economic path it would pursue. For a long time, the RSS did not have a viable economic programme.[52] Though D.B. Thengadi makes a detailed list[53] on Golwalkar's economic thinking, Golwalkar in fact only talked of some elementary economics and never made any detailed economic analysis. Thengdi's exhaustive list attributed to Golwalkar actually includes certain viewpoints of Deendayal Upadhyaya. While Golwalkar deserves the credit to be the propounder of a sound political ideology of *Hindu Rashtra*, he paid little attention to its economic philosophy. However, he spelt out that the material economic objective must be controlled by higher and more spiritual goals of life. The desire and lust for unrestrained economic gain, which characterized the 'materialism of the west', should be abhorred. Consumption has to be regulated. Every man should act as a trustee. All these features should ensure that every citizen conforms to the culture of the Hindu nation and completely identifies with it. Summing up Golwalkar's economic thinking, Vajpayee wrote:

> In his eyes all wealth belonged to God and man was just a trustee. He held that possessing more wealth than was necessary for the worship of the almighty was usurping wealth belonging to God and was hence to be condemned. At the same time he was strongly opposed to the present statist tendency. He was an advocate of a selfless polity and decentralized economy.[54]

Deendayal's Economic Thinking

The political affiliate, the BJS, subscribed broadly to Golwalkar's nascent economic philosophy. During 1950s and 1960s, the party was vehemently opposed to the planning regime of the Nehru government and pleaded for the cause of the petty traders and small industrialists of north India, who constituted its political base and financial strength. In 1965, Deendayal Upadhyaya came out with some innovative economic ideas in his ideological treatise 'Integral Humanism', which was adopted by the BJS. He sketched the economic philosophy of the Hindu nation and outlined a new economic blueprint that he argued would suit our 'national genius'.

He rejects both Marxism and capitalism because while the former denies individual freedom, the latter encourages profit motives and aggrandizement. He observes that the centralization of power, economic and political, is implied in both. Both, therefore, result in dehumanization of man. Instead of capitalism or socialism, Upadhyaya aims at progress and happiness of man—the 'Integral' man. And his philosophy of integral humanism keeps human beings at the centre. Upadhyaya also categorically rejects the Nehruvian model of economic development, as it does not conform to our cultural and spiritual heritage. He was of the firm view that *swadeshi*[55] and decentralization would constitute the essence of an alternate economic system. In this respect, Upadhyaya identifies more with Gandhian economic philosophy, at least thematically. Foreign capital and technology should be accepted as long as they are under firm national control. There should be no blind imitation of the Western pattern of industrialization; the stress should be on labour-intensive rather than capital-intensive industries. The changes in the traditional techniques of production should be reasonably adaptable so that there would be no increase in unemployment. This would, in turn, reduce urbanization and all the evils of modernity flowing from big cities, Upadhyaya argued.[56] Though having different political views from Gandhi, a convergence between Gandhi and Upadhyaya is apparent in their anti-utilitarian inclinations.[57]

However, after Upadhyaya's death in 1967, the economic philosophy of the RSS was more or less eclipsed ideologically by Indira Gandhi's rhetorical socialism and aggressive economic nationalism with an emphasis on import substitution and industrialization. The Janata experience compelled the RSS to find some relevance with Gandhian socialism, but hardly anything substantial could be achieved during the period. The *Sangh Parivar* gave least priority to an economic agenda and concentrated more on the construction of a militant Hinduism.

The RSS could not ignore for long the economic developments at the national as well as at the global level. The expansion of its support base and the emergence of its political affiliate as the national alternative compelled it to rethink a viable economic strategy. Further, globalization has accelerated and intensified global capital movements and transnational corporations have emerged as key players in the world economy. This has had an adverse impact on national economies across the world.

In 1991, the Congress government adopted the new economic policy, which favoured liberalization, deregulation and privatization of the public sector. K.S. Sudarshan, the present RSS chief and an ardent champion of *swadeshi*, argues that the post-1991 reforms are as bad as the pre-1991 socialist policies. He criticizes trade liberalization because it 'destroys our national self-confidence', ridicules the 'urban orientation' of economic policy-makers and lambasts the import of 'job-killing' technologies which is 'pushing our youngsters into terrorism and crimes'.[58]

The RSS, therefore, embarked upon a campaign for a *swadeshi* approach to economic development. It published a pamphlet listing the brand names of 326 consumer products manufactured by multinationals and mentioned an Indian product alternative to each product. The pamphlet called for a popular movement against multinationals, and called upon its members and supporters to divert their consumption pattern away from the products of 'exploitative multinational companies' and towards goods produced in India. The consumerism induced by foreign companies erodes and undermines the cultural ethos of India and it weakens the economic foundations of the Indian economy. Deoras compared multinationals to the East India Company and claimed that *swadeshi* was but the natural continuation of the nationalist pre-independence struggle and called upon 'patriots to shun everything foreign and prize everything swadeshi'.[59]

Rewriting Swadeshi

Swadeshi became a battle cry during the campaign against the partition of Bengal in 1905; the protestors adopted a strategy of an economic boycott of British goods. Mahatma Gandhi expanded the idea of *swadeshi*, emphasizing production by Indians so as to exclude foreign goods from the Indian market. The basic premise of *swadeshi* was to develop indigenous capabilities so that domestic resources could be processed with domestic labour and technology. Basically, it aimed at ending economic exploitation by the British. The RSS version of *swadeshi* does not really follow the conventional Gandhian outline, but vaguely subscribes to the broader nationalist content of the Japanese model. Japan has become a powerful nation on its inner strengths, both cultural and economic, and that should be the ideal of this economic philosophy.[60]

What is the RSS notion of *swadeshi*?[61] 'Swadeshi principle of economic development [means that] each country has its natural resource and manpower. It has its genius. It can discover its own course of economic development. . . . Swadeshi however does not teach hatred for any country. It wants to learn from all countries in the world. This is the guidance of Vedas in India.'[62] What would be the nature of this economic nationalism? The economists of this school argue that it neither means autarky nor self-sufficiency. No nation can shut all its doors and refuse to deal with the world outside. They argue that the Hindus have never done that before. What economic nationalism means is the 'the refusal to be dominated by foreigners'. Foreign investment is welcome as long as it serves the national interest.[63] As the BJP argues, *swadeshi*, however, is not defined in isolation from the world economy but an approach that relies for economic growth primarily on internal capital and human resources.[64] Without severing links with the world economy, the BJP argues that 'integration into a global economy should not mean obliteration of national identity' and subordination to external forces. On the contrary, through *swadeshi* it should be possible for a country to exercise its 'judgement', to define its needs and 'chart its own course'.[65]

The major arguments espoused by the *swadeshi* exponents of the RSS are as follows: that multinational companies are taking over the entire economy; that their monopolization would lead to an upward movement of prices and a continual drain of wealth. Their demand for a free exchange rate and relaxation of government controls would lead to a submission to 'the manipulations of western imperialist economies'. All patents, copyrights and trademarks also represent monopolies and are nothing but further means of exploitation. *Swadeshi* exponents treat India as an undifferentiated entity in which all castes and classes have an equal interest in opposing this 'western imperialist' takeover.[66]

Swadeshi is not against liberalization as such. Rather, it advocates 'internal liberalization' and rejects 'external liberalization'. It favours freedom from government controls for industry within the country, but opposes removal of trade barriers and exposing the *swadeshi* industries to foreign competition. Its main thrust is to fight multinational imperialism by making Indian goods competitive through low prices. How could an internally competitive market economy be achieved? If this could be achieved by curtailing the cost of production, the producers may be the losers. Who would decide the administered prices? Though the *swadeshi* exponents argue that state agencies along with social interest groups would do the job, it sounds unrealistic. Various groups would try to achieve maximum interest. The other method to be adopted is to counter the 'consumerist culture' of the West by raising consciousness among the people to keep their needs to a minimum. All these measures may lead to further intensification of the statist model rather than weakening it.[67]

How is this economic nationalism of the *Hindutva* variety different from the nineteenth century economic nationalism? The RSS keeps an essential link between *Hindutva* and economic nationalism; that the latter is only an offshoot of the former. *Hindutva* is the spirit behind Hindu economics. It understands that the success of Hindu economics depends on the adherence to *Hindutva*; for example, to resist the temptation of consumerism would be an uphill task unless it develops an ideological commitment to *Hindutva*. On the other hand, the economic nationalism advocated by the nineteenth century economic nationalists was secular in nature. There is another fundamental difference between the two. The RSS has never kept poverty as the central issue of its economic philosophy. In this respect the RSS differs not only from the socialists but also in a major way from the nineteenth century economic nationalists. However, of late, the RSS leaders have realized that no economic programme could be acceptable to the broad masses of the people unless it tackles the question of poverty and unemployment. Therefore, *swadeshi* criticizes private foreign investment for not producing adequate employment for the people.

Swadeshi Jagaran Manch

To propagate *swadeshi*, a new affiliate named Swadeshi Jagaran Manch (SJM) was set up by the RSS.[68] The battle against Enron[69] brought it to the national focus. Besides taking on multinationals, the national agenda of the SJM was to counter the religious divide of Ayodhya and, at the same time, to attract Sarvodaya activists, socialists and even some environmentalists into the folds of the SJM.[70] It took up several issues to emphasize its agenda. One was the problem of depletion of local native resources with the entry of multinationals in the area of deep-sea fishing. The target was to enlist support from the 75 lakh fisherman community of the nine coastal states. Another campaign focused on Al-Kabir, the mechanized abattoir in Medak district of Andhra Pradesh. SJM's economic flavour to the issue supplemented the religious flavour of the VHP.

The SJM became a strong critic of certain economic policies adopted by the Vajpayee government. In protest, the SJM organized a three-week long *Chetna Yatra* in 1998 carrying the anti-globalization message and demanding the following: (1) Roll back most of the 380 items that the former Commerce Minister R.K. Hegde transferred in his exim policy from the 'restricted' list to the OGL; (2) Cancel the blanket invitation of 100 per cent Foreign Direct Investment (FDI) in liquor and tobacco sectors; (3) Re-open some public sector contracts already awarded, notably the one for extension of the Neyveli Lignite Project given to the Italian conglomerate Anslado; (4) Review the agreement between the Union Government and Suzuki Motor Company on Maruti Udyog Limited which dilutes the government's authority; and (5) Remove from advisory posts a few personalities identified by the SJM as 'anti-swadeshi'.[71] The SJM has also been harping on the need to seek amendments to the WTO agreement and to thwart all moves towards a full convertibility of the rupee. Both these policies suit the strategic interests of the large domestic corporations, which are seeking a reprieve from foreign competition, and a stable rupee to make imports affordable.

ACCELERATING MILITANT *HINDUTVA*: TARGETING CHRISTIANS

Changing Context

Though the government's steps on national security, particularly the nuclear explosion, pleased the RSS, it was not at all happy the way the *swadeshi* issue was treated. The bomb euphoria dissipated gradually. The situation in Kashmir remained grim. The quality of governance was being increasingly questioned. The alliance partners were constantly threatening, thereby eroding the credibility of the government everyday.

After the climax of the Ayodhya demolition, the anti-Muslim tirade of the RSS was fast losing its resonance. Repetition of the same old charges was looking a little shopworn. It was much easier for the RSS to target the governments run by 'Muslim appeasers' and 'pseudo-secularists' for every lapse, from the terrorist killings in Kashmir to ISI activities; it became a big dilemma when all this continued under the regime of its own political affiliate. Therefore, excessive anti-Muslim propaganda offered no more political advantages, rather it threatened to act adversely by forcing the Muslims back to the Congress, which they had deserted after the demolition. A shift was needed, a new target had to be invented.

Sonia Gandhi's entry onto the political scene provided an opportunity to the RSS. It launched an offensive propaganda against her foreign origins whilst simultaneously targeting her religion—Christianity. The electoral reverses of the BJP in four states in November 1998 at the hands of a rejuvenated Congress under Sonia Gandhi further compelled the RSS to precipitate the campaign. In order to counter Sonia Gandhi's political ascendancy, the RSS thought it would be tactically right to attack her faith. Hence, the new focus on Christians.

Besides the Sonia factor, the other important reason for inventing the Christians as the latest enemy, was the *Sangh Parivar's* dilemma over *swadeshi*. Despite its campaign against the multinationals and globalization, the BJP government was zealously pursuing the liberalization agenda. This was creating embarrassment for the RSS. It was wondering how to reconfirm its nationalist credentials without seriously disturbing the liberalization agenda of the BJP. 'What could be more convenient for the *Sangh Parivar* than giving to residual anti-imperialist sentiments a purely religious-cum-culturalist twist, targetting Christians, not—at least with any real seriousness—multinationals?'[72]

History of anti-Christianity

Christians have always remained one of the enemies of the *Hindu Rashtra*. Despite their obsession with Muslims, Hindu nationalists, since 1920s, have not failed to focus on the 'threat' from Christians. While Muslims have been perceived as the 'Enemy Number One', the Christians have occupied the status of 'Enemy Number Two'. For Hindu nationalists, including Hedgewar, Muslims rather than Christians posed a bigger threat because of their numerical strength and militant mobilization; the Christians, constituting a minuscule minority, were much less vociferous.[73] Secondly, as the colonial rulers believed in Christianity, any anti-Christian activity would have incurred their wrath. Thirdly, the Hindu elite and the middle class—the main supporters of the RSS—were apparently less hostile to the Christians as they benefited to a great extent by the education and health-care system maintained by Christian missionaries. Hedgewar and other Hindu nationalist leaders were themselves beneficiaries of the British/missionary education system.

During the colonial period, the RSS focused on the Muslims. After independence and partition, Golwalkar turned his attention towards the Christians and considered them as an 'internal threat' to the Hindu nation. He charged the Christian missionaries for proselytizing the Hindus, encouraging secessionism in the north-eastern states, and acting as the agents of a global conspiracy to evangelize India. He created the VHP and deputed *pracharaks* to tribal areas to counter the activities of the Christian missionaries.

Deoras carried on the legacy of Golwalkar. He activated the Vanavasi Kalyan Ashram in tribal areas to take on Christian missionaries. Along-with the VHP it continued with the process of 'Hinduization' of tribals and set up an alternate welfare system of schools and hospitals to attract tribals towards the *Sangh Parivar*. Deoras, for a long period, adopted a policy of accommodation and pushed militant Hinduism to the background. However, the RSS revived militant Hinduism by launching the *Ram Janmabhoomi* agitation. Though the thrust of the Ayodhya campaign was anti-Muslim, at selected places, where Christians had a sizeable presence in comparison to Muslims, the *Sangh Parivar* projected them, and not the Muslims as the main enemy. The VHP carried on a well-orchestrated propaganda against Christians and organized 're-conversion' (*paravartan*) of the Christians back to the Hindu fold. Thus, the Ayodhya movement that had no connection with the Christians was conveniently diverted against them, particularly in some tribal areas.

Reiterating Golwalkar's anti-Christian Arguments

'Christianity has two pillars: a narrow piety and word-juggling theology. . . . Above all, like Islam, it is inwoven with bigotry and fanaticism and lacks charity, understanding and the deeper vision of the spirit', writes Ram Swarup, a *Hindutva* ideologue.[74] Another RSS ideologue com-ments: 'Jesus is junk. It is high time for Hindus to learn that Jesus Christ symbolizes no spiritual power, no moral uprightness. He is no more than an artifice for legitimizing wanton imperialist aggression. The aggressors have found him to be highly profitable so far. By the same token, Hindus should know that Jesus means nothing but mischief for their country and culture.'[75]

Rajendra Singh expressed grave concern over the massive conversion of tribals by Muslim and Christian missionaries by exploiting poverty, illiteracy, ignorance and a sense of alienation among these sections of society. These religious conversions were a serious threat to the country's unity and integrity, warned Rajendra Singh.[76] The RSS charged that international Christian agencies were pumping in millions of dollars and sending trained workers to India to exterminate Hinduism. These missionaries were also accused of dishonouring Hinduism, its gods and goddesses and converting vulnerable tribals by treacherous means.[77] H.V. Seshadri[78] thus warned that conversion of the *Vanvasi*, backward and other poorer sections of Hindu society by the Church through various types of allurements and make-believe disease-curing miracles, was bound to provoke a severe reaction among the Hindus.

The Kendriya Karyakari Mandal (Central Working Committee) of the RSS reiterated old Golwalkarian arguments[79] by harping on the alleged fear of a 'deeply-laid global conspiracy' of massive conversion of Hindus to Christianity. It cited the objective of the global project 'Evangelisation 2000 and Beyond' to provide 'a Church for every village and a Bible for every individual', particularly in India, by the year 2000 AD. The RSS argued that this target could only be met by a mass conversion of Hindus.[80] It showed its concern that an incredibly large array of missionaries, equipped with the most modern and sophisticated devices had already started their operation in this direction; even the Pope himself has shown his keenness on the cultural evangelization of Bharat. The Karyakari Mandal reminded the missionaries that Mahatma Gandhi had described the mass conversion of Hindus to Christianity as an immoral act and asked them to stop it. The RSS called upon Hindu society to be alert to the threat faced by vulnerable sections of the Hindu society in particular and Hindus in general by these foreign subversive forces.

Conversion: A Contentious Issue

Conversion has remained a contentious issue ever since the missionaries started this operation. Swami Shraddhananda, in his *Hindu Sangathan: Saviour of the Dying Race* (1926), blamed conversion as the main cause of Hindu decline. He showed concern at the conversion to Islam as well as Christianity by 'force' and 'means other than force' and cited intra-Christian polemic to prove his point about Christian coercion and trickery.[81] The Constituent Assembly debated the propriety of unregulated conversions and there were charges of missionaries enticing tribals through allurements. Though many Congressmen objected to the freedom of religion extending the right to propagate, finally they 'agreed to keep the word "propagate" out of regard for our Christian friends'.[82] In early 1950s, propaganda against the Christian missionaries remained in the agenda of the BJS, the political affiliate of the RSS. The party organized an anti-foreign missionary week in November 1954. In reaction to the Jana Sangh agitation, the Madhya Pradesh government set up a committee under Justice B.S. Niyogi to study Christian missionary activity. The Niyogi report was harsh in its indictment of missionaries. It accused them of promoting separatism and even creating 'a state within a state'. The Niyogi report has since then remained a hot favourite of the *Sangh Parivar* and has been frequently quoted to prove its allegations against the Christian missionaries. During 1967-8, the Madhya Pradesh government, in which the BJS was a major partner, tried to implement some of the recommendations of the Niyogi Committee Report, and imposed a strict test for providing voluntary choice on Christian converts. In 1968, Orissa, Madhya Pradesh and Arunachal Pradesh enacted legislations to discourage conversions. In 1979, O.P. Tyagi, a member of parliament of the Janata Party belonging to the erstwhile Jana Sangh faction, introduced a bill which favoured extension of this legislation nationwide. Although this failed, it was around this time that the RSS decided to work systematically among the tribals and fight the Christian missionaries. By the mid 1980s, the *Sangh Parivar* started the reconversion or 'homecoming' of tribals and this took an aggressive turn during the 1990s.

The *Sangh Parivar* has used conversion as a convenient weapon against Christian missionaries. The ideologues of *Hindutva* associate the conversion activities with the use of force, allurement or fraudulent means. They also charge that conversion makes the convert anti-national, even a traitor. Echoing Golwalkar, VHP's Giriraj Kishore observes: 'Conversions not only change the religion of the converted, but also their nationality.'[83]

The Christian missionaries, on the other hand, maintain that the right to practice, preach and propagate one's religion is enshrined in the Indian Constitution and that this opportunity is available to every religious group. They strongly deny the use of any kind of force, allurement or fraudulent means to convert people to Christianity. They plead that love and service always remains an integral part of their faith; it is their humanitarian work, like that of Mother Teresa, which attracts some people to embrace Christianity. There are about 16,000 Christian schools in India and nearly half of them are more than a hundred years old. Crores of children either study there now or have passed out. If the *Sangh Parivar's* allegation were true, they argue, then the Christian population would have multiplied by a number of times during this period.[84] Moreover, if converting the poor by allurement were as simple, as it has been made out to be, the number of Christians would have overtaken that of the Muslims in India as roughly one-third of Indian population lives below the poverty line. Further, there are more than 6,000 other Christian institutions in India, which include hospitals, dispensaries, social-welfare centres, orphanages, etc. The number of beneficiaries from these again runs into millions. If the only aim of Christian missionaries was conversion to their religion, then by now nearly three-fourth of the Indian population would have been Christians. But the fact is that Christians constitute only 2.32 per cent of India's population.

Dangs' example would perhaps illustrate the complex process of conversion. In Dangs (Gujarat), the Catholic Church has nurtured welfare programmes, including three boarding schools, dispensaries and some income-generation schemes. Ironically, it is the Protestant Friend Missionary Prayer Band (FMPB) and the Indian Evangelical Mission that have drawn the greatest number of converts. Faith healing, of course, has played an important role in drawing tribal Bhils to these congregations. 'The poor tribal', admits a Dutch priest who has been working in tribal areas for three decades, 'doesn't accept Christianity purely out of love for the God. The motives are mixed. It can be the hope of a better life, a job or even food security.'[85] Yet, he observes, 'forced conversions' occur rarely.

Conversion does not necessarily imply passivity on the part of the converted; the convert is not a mere 'object', as the RSS interprets. There are more than a million Christians in the West who have converted themselves to Hinduism, Sikhism, Islam and Buddhism. Since 1960s hundreds of Hindu religious sects have flourished there, including the Harekrishna movement. How does one explain these conversions? Would it be fair to treat these conversions as those by force, allurement or fraudulent means?

Another of the *Sangh Parivar's* charges directed at the missionaries is that they have eroded Indian culture and imposed their own instead. Verrier Elwin was a fine example, who, instead of converting a single Indian to Christianity, got himself converted into a tribal.[86] Belgian Camil Bulke's Hindi-English dictionary still remains the most authentic till today. The contribution of the Spaniard Carlos Valles to the Gujarati language and of Beski to the Tamil are few examples of those missionaries who preserved and promoted Indian culture whole-heartedly. Indian Christianity has also consciously blended itself with local cultures; in the seminaries, a greater understanding of Hinduism is very much a part of theological studies. The Catholic Church has been particularly sensitive to non-Christian traditions, some churches have even adopted Hindu symbols like the *Om*. Trainee Catholic priests extensively study the Upanishads, the Vedas, the *Ramayana* and the *Mahabbharat.*

There is another side of the story too. There are evangelists who utilize generous foreign funding for offensive proselytization.[87] The Texas-based Gospel for Asia Order describes Hindus in Gujarat as 'still living in the bondage of Satan' and the *Global Prayer Digest* charges Bhils with 'appeasing false gods'. Dubious faith healers like the California-based Roger Houtsma openly invite minimum donations of $ 25 for 'church plants' in India: 'The harvest is ripe now, and now is the time to put in the sickle and reap. . . .'[88] It is these fundamentalist groups who provide ammunition to the *Sangh Parivar's* anti-Christian campaign.

The real worry of *Hindutva* forces is not conversion and evangelization, but the perceived threat from Liberation Theology, argue the critics. Some of the Christian missions preach that Liberation Theology could empower and liberate the Dalits, tribes and other oppressed sections. This is seen as a danger as it 'would certainly disturb Hindu society'.[89] Missionary presence, the RSS fears, might not lead to significant conversions, but it would act as a catalyst in the empowerment of the lower-castes as it did in the case of the Namashudras of Bengal.[90] That would perhaps challenge the *Hindutva's* upper-caste hegemony.

Counter Challenge: Reconversion and Hindu Missionaries

Though the RSS opposes conversion, it promotes re-conversion. The *Sangh Parivar* has been actively organizing reconversion of converted tribals and Dalits to Hinduism. It is an irony that though it blames the Christian missionaries for converting the poor on the strength of their money, the RSS is reportedly receiving huge funds from overseas Indians for the cause of Hindu revival in India. It imitates the strategy of the Christian missions. The Vanavasi Kalyan Ashrams have been emulating the welfare activities of the church. Moreover, a new breed of Hindu missionaries has been deputed by the RSS in strategic tribal areas. It has been discussed how Swami Laxmanananda has been actively countering Christian missionaries and organizing reconversions in Phulbani (Kandhamal) district of Orissa. In the Dangs district of Gujarat, Swami Ashimanand, a Bengali with a Master's degree in physics, travels from village to village distributing the *Hanuman Chalisa* and promoting reconversion.[91] Dilip Singh Judeo of the Jashpur royal family has taken a pioneering role in reconversion of tribals in Madhya Pradesh. Judeo welcomes the reconverts by personally washing their feet. His Vanvasi Kalyan Ashram claims to have brought some 1.5 lakh tibals back to the Hindu fold. In Ranchi, Govind Oraon plays the role of a *Pahan* (tribal priest) to reconvert Adivasis before idols of *Shiva* and *Parvati.*

VHP's Aggressive anti-Christian Campaign

It is significant that the VHP, which had gone into hibernation for quite sometime and maintained a low profile during the first few months of the Vajpayee government, took up the anti-Christian agenda with a missionary zeal. Ashok Singhal and Giriraj Kishore, the working president and the general secretary of the VHP respectively, issued certain provocative statements: 'Mother Teresa's motive was not service (to humanity) but conversion'; 'There is a Western design behind Amartya Sen getting the Nobel Prize. His area of specialization—poverty and development—will give missionaries a chance to convert the poor'; 'Sonia symbolizes Christian power in this country. In the coming months we will further raise the pitch of our attack against her.'[92] The Christians think that with the rise of Sonia Gandhi 'they will have the best of times and get away with anything', observed VHP International President Vishnu Hari Dalmia.[93] VHP's *Dharma Sansad* even decided to conduct its own 'census' of Muslims and Christians.[94]

Ashok Singhal alleged that Mother Teresa had got Hindus converted to Christianity under the garb of serving humanity. He further charged, she had only helped Christians or those who promised her that they would embrace Christianity. Singhal blamed the media of building an aura around her under which she flourished and eventually received the Nobel Prize. He did not spare Nobel laureate Amartya Sen and linked Sen's concern for literacy to the spread of Christianity in India. [95]

VHP leader B.L. Sharma, popularly known as 'Prem', who had earlier rationalized the rape of a nun at Jhabua in Madhya Pradesh, accused the converts for their loyalties to 'London and Vatican'. He further charged Indian Christians as having on their hands 'the blood of thousands of Gomantak Brahmins who were murdered by the Portuguese in Goa'. This reminds one of Golwalkar's doctrine as well as the thrust of the Ayodhya campaign, which linked Indian Muslims with Babur, the invader.

VHP's anti-Christian campaign, in some ways, was reminiscent of the early days of the Ayodhya movement.[96] It projected Indian Christians as the inheritors of the legacy of the colonial invaders; like the Muslim invaders, they also conquered India and ruled over the Hindus. Like the Muslims, the loyalty of the Christians to the nation is also under suspicion as their *janmabhoomi* and *punyabhoomi* are not identical. The strategy in this campaign was to arouse Hindu anger by reminding them of the injustices committed by the colonialists and their continued attack on Hindus through conversion, in the garb of missionaries, being carried on by the descendants of foreign invaders and imperialists.

GUJARAT

Gujarat became the epicentre of the *Sangh Parivar's* anti-Christian pogrom. A report of the Gujarat government, Socio-Economic Review,[97] became quite handy. As the report revealed, between the 1981 and the 1991 census, while the Hindu population in Dangs district rose from 1,10,522 to 1,33,828, that of the Christians increased from 1,514 to 7,824. While the overall growth of population in the district was 27 per cent, that of the Hindus was 21 per cent, the growth rate of the Christians was a phenomenal 416 per cent. The share of the Hindu population declined from 97.24 per cent in 1981 to 92.88 per cent in the last census while that of the Christians rose from 1.33 per cent to that of 5.43 per cent. Even in respect of the overall growth rate of population in the state during the decade, the growth of the Christian population, particularly in the tribal-dominated districts, was significant. Against the overall growth rate of 21 per cent of the population, the Muslim population increased by 24 per cent and of the Christians by 37 per cent. The growth of the Christian population in other tribal-dominated districts in south Gujarat was 120 per cent in Surat, 66 per cent in Bahruch, 53 per cent in Bulsar and 46 per cent in Baroda, all much above the state's average. The *Sangh Parivar* suspected that such a quantum jump in the Christian population was the result of large-scale conversions. 'A Christian conspiracy' thesis gained ground. Dilip Singh Judeo, the MP, and a pioneer of the *Sangh Parivar's* reconversion movement, claimed that 4.5 lakh Hindus were being converted to Christianity each year. Veteran Sarvodaya workers Chunibhai Vaidya and Ghelubhai Nayak of Dangs cautioned that there was a clamour to bring proselytization to the national agenda. Vaidya demanded that the government should immediately enact an anti-conversion law; 'When even Gandhiji and Vinoba Bhave were against conversions, where is the hitch?'[98]

The attack on the Christian community gathered momentum. The body of Samuel Christian was exhumed from Kapadwanj cemetry in Nadiad district and thrown outside the Methodist Church. In Rajkot, a Christian missionary girls school was attacked amidst slogans of 'Jai Shri Ram' and copies of the New Testament burnt by the VHP-BD activists who charged that the school was encouraging conversion of Hindu girls to Christianity. The incident in Zankhavav stemmed from a personal dispute over land gifted by a Hindu, Shantilal Shah, to a missionary school for tribals. Chandulal Shah, who had VHP links, claimed to be a tenant of the disputed land. The VHP activists led an attack on the school. The VHP memorandum submitted to the Collector speaks of forcible conversions of tribals, propagating anti-national activities and misuse of religious places.[99]

Even Muslims became the targets in places such as Bardoli and Radhikapur. At Radhikapur in Dohad district, two 'Ghanchi' Muslim boys from a backward community fell in love with two Hindu girls and reportedly eloped. The VHP and Bajrang Dal issued a 48-hour ultimatum asking the Muslims to trace the two girls or quit the village. Fifty-nine terrified Muslim families had to flee to another town. The VHP put up a signboard in the village: 'VHP welcomes you to Hindu rashtra's village.'[100]

The Director General of the Gujarat police had categorically stated that the charges being made on forced conversions and inter-religious marriages were baseless and squarely blamed the VHP and the Bajrang Dal for the violent incidents in parts of the state: 'The VHP and the Bajrang Dal have taken law into their hands and this is not a good trend.'[101] Even Keshubhai Patel, the saffron Chief Minister, was forced to issue a statement warning the VHP and BD: 'If they are found involved in the incidents, they will be strongly dealt with.'[102]

Dangs

Hindu Jagaran Manch (HJM), a *Sangh Parivar* outfit, decided to organize a rally on Christmas Day, 25 December, in Ahwa. Its provocative leaflet condemned Christ and the Bible. It declared that Ishu (Christ) had come on earth to divide family and people. He was an apostle of war. The Bible asked its followers to destroy the God of those who lived in the hills and to finish those people who worshipped these gods and goddesses.[103] On 24 December the procession started at 12 noon. The main slogans of the rally were: 'Christians are "chor"' (thieves), '*Hindu jago, Christians bhago*' (Hindus awake, Christians run away), '*Gali gali me shor hai, Padri sab chor hai*' (everybody in the street is shouting that Christian priests are thieves). Then a public meeting was held, in which the *Sangh Parivar* leaders gave provocative speeches against missionaries and conversions. People were asked to protect 'our tradition and Hindu religion and teach a lesson to the Christians so that they do not convert people'.[104] The Christians standing outside the ground protested; police resorted to *lathi* charge to disperse the meeting. After the dispersal fifty to sixty persons went to the market and looted the shops of Muslims and Christians. And the attack on Christians conti-nued. Between 25 December and 3 January, 24 churches, 3 schools, and 6 houses or shops were burnt, destroyed or damaged, and 9 Christian tribals suffered serious injuries. The *Sangh Parivar*, on the other hand, blamed the missionaries for first attacking the Hanuman temple which provoked the HJM to take out the rally.

Despite all this noise about conversion, Christians constitute less than 1 per cent of the state's population. Conversion to Christianity, though insignificant in numbers, occurs not by force but basically for faith healing, dignity and empowerment. Most of the converts belong to the lower socio-economic strata. The objective of the attack by *Hindutva* forces is to create a fear psychosis among these vulnerable sections so that they do not seek any alternate mode of empowerment. The RSS message is quite clear—the downtrodden should only look forward to the patronage of *Hindutva* for their upliftment.

ORISSA

Orissa, a relatively peaceful state, surprisingly became another centre for an anti-Christian hate campaign. The state has a Christian population of 2.9 per cent as per 1991 census, an increase from 1.98 per cent in 1981. This Christian population is primarily confined to the tribal areas. The tribals constitute about 22 per cent of the state population suggesting that a large number of them are non-Christians. The Christian missionaries are primarily working in the tribal areas. There are about 8,000 churches in Orissa; Phulbani district alone has 2,000 churches. It is estimated that 5,000 people get converted to Christianity every year.[105] RSS *pracharaks* are also active in these areas, contesting and competing with the missionaries. The VHP leader Ashok Singhal's announcement to recruit 20,000 cadres to work in Orissa's tribal areas created further tension between the *Sangh Parivar* and the missionaries.

R. Udaygiri

At R. Udaygiri in Gajapati district, about 2,000 tribals broke into the jail on 8 December 1998, dragged out Jai Singh, a *Pana* Christian (a scheduled caste convert), and his associate and burnt them alive. Then this crowd moved to the nearby *Pana* locality and set their houses on fire. Jai Singh was a known anti-social element and was engaged in robberies and extortion of money, mainly from the Adivasis. On 1 December, he and his accomplice reportedly looted money from the passengers of a bus, mostly Adivasis. The tribals approached the local police officer, a *Pana* Christian, to press Jai Singh to return their money. No action was taken for a few days, thereby infuriating the tribals. The police finally arrested Jai Singh and his associate, allegedly to save them from tribal anger. The tribals took out a procession and demanded that both Singh and his associate be handed over to them. When this was not met, the tribals committed this horrible crime. It was alleged that Balram Ranhati, a local BJP leader (earlier in Congress), was leading and instigating the tribals against Christians.

For quite some time, the VHP and the VKA have been mobilizing the Saura tribals of this area against the *Panas*, the Scheduled Castes, who were converted to Christianity. The *Sangh Parivar's* hostility towards the *Panas* is not simply because of their religion. The *Panas* are educated, politically conscious, vocal, well-placed in bureaucracy, and resourceful and do not look for RSS patronage for their empowerment. With their strong presence in this district as well as the neighbouring district of Phulbani, the RSS finds it difficult to challenge the Christian community in this territory.[106]

Ranalai

Tension had been building up in the area ever since the Christians found that not only was a cross painted on the Khamari hill partially disfigured but a trident (*trishul*) had also been painted. For the past few months Hindus, led by Kanucharan Paik, a BJP activist, were objecting to the sign of the cross painted on the hillock. A peace committee was formed, which agreed to restore the cross. But it was again disfigured. On 16 March, a mob consisting of men from Ranalai as well as a neighbouring village went to the Khamari hill, erased the cross symbol and set fire to the spot, and descended on the village, shouting that the power of *trishul* had prevailed over the cross. The Christians feared the worst and gathered outside on the road. A confusion led to the clash; the mob set Christian houses on fire.[107] The police allegedly sided with the Hindus. In retaliation, an angry Christian mob attacked the police jeep, in which Police Inspector Asit Mohanty was travelling. When some women, mostly Hindus tried to save him, they were pushed back by the mob.[108]

Gajapati district had witnessed Hindu-Christian conflict on a few occasions. A few years ago, tribals attacked a faith healing camp in the district believing it was aimed at converting people. Police had to escort American Pentecostal missionaries out of the state. The *Sangh Parivar* has been very active in the district as well as in the neighbouring district of Phulbani. It distributed a booklet *Orissare Dharmantrikaran* (Conversion in Orissa), written by Subhas Chauhan, Convener of the Hindu Jagaran Manch, and Mohini Mohan Mishra, a university teacher. This 70-page booklet carries details of Christian activities in Orissa. It quoted 1991 census report to support the contention that the Christian population in the state was increasing and this was possible 'only by conversion'.

Manoharpur (Keonjhar District)

Australian missionary Graham Stewart Staines and his two sons were burnt alive when they were sleeping in their jeep at Manoharpur in Keonjhar district on the night of 22 January 1999. The man who organized this gruesome murder was Rabindra Kumar Pal alias Dara Singh, a migrant from Etawah (Uttar Pradesh). In seven First Information Reports (FIRs), Dara was linked to the BD and in four to the BJP. It states that he worked for the BJP in 1998, that he was active in the Goraksha Samiti and attacked Muslim cattle traders. It has been testified that the murderous crowd shouted 'Jai Bajrang Bali' and dispersed when a whistle was blown. A witness, Debendra Pradhan, who claimed to be a RSS member himself, said that he had seen Dara Singh at the RSS camp for the first time.[109] However, the Wadhwa Commission, which was set up to probe the Staines killings, though established Dara Singh's involvement in this 'gruesome killings', it ruled out the involvement of any organization, thereby giving a clean chit to the *Sangh Parivar*.

In a less than 30-km radius of the site of Staines killing, Dara's next victim was a 30-year old Muslim trader Sheikh Rehman. On 26 August, Dara alongwith 10 tribals ransacked his garment shop at Padiabeda market and hacked his forearms. Rehman succumbed to the injuries. Previously, during 1998, Dara had engineered many attacks on Muslim cattle traders and earned popularity among the local Mahanta community, who reveres the cow. Within a week of Rehman's killing, on 1 September, a group of men came with bows and arrows and killed Rev. Arul Doss, a Tamil Roman priest, and set fire to the church in the jungle hamlet of Jamuboni in the Mayurbhanj district.

Anti-Christian Strategy of the RSS

As discussed in Chapter V, the *Sangh Parivar* entered into the tribal areas of Orissa through the VHP during the late 1960s and early 1970s to counter missionary proselytization. During the late 1970s and 1980s, Vanavasi Kalyan Ashrams were set up and an alternate welfare network of schools, hospitals and sports centres were built to woo tribals away from the missionary influence. During the *Ram Janmabhoomi* agitation, the *Sangh Parivar* carried out a systematic anti-Christian campaign in the tribal areas of Orissa, though its nationwide thrust was anti-Muslim.

The *Sangh Parivar* has been actively pursuing a multifold strategy. First, it has been 'Hinduizing' the tribals and pressurizing them to renounce their 'uncivilized' tribal way of life and adopt the 'Hindu' culture and customs. It not only preaches hatred against Christians, it also instigates the reconverts against the converts.

Secondly, it has made cow-protection a major issue in certain tribal areas of Keonjhar and Mayurbhanj where the dominant local community reveres the cow. The VHP and the BD activists have been snatching cows from the Christian and Muslim cattle traders to win over the support of this community. The rise of the Dara phenomenon could be attributed to these activities. In fact, the cow-protection activities of the VHP and BD receive support from all over the state as Oriyas are emotionally attached to the cow.

Thirdly, the *Sangh Parivar* has been mobilizing the tribals against the *Panas*—a community of Dalits who have been converted to Christianity—particularly in the districts of Gajapati and Kandhamal (Phulbani) of southern Orissa. It has been instigating the Hindu tribals against the Christian *Panas*, who are economically better off, and politically assertive.

Finally, the *Sangh Parivar* exploits the community sentiment of the tribal Hindus against the converts, for their defiance of age-old tribal customs and traditions. For instance, at Manoharpur, during the Raja festival, when the earth is said to be menstruating, the converts violated local customs by continuing to till the land, thereby provoking the tribal Santhals. At Jambuboni, before his murder, Father Doss was reportedly celebrating *Nuakhai*, a harvest festival, ahead of the tribal calendar.[110] Though these tribes strongly feel the need to protect their cultural traditions from an 'Christian onslaught', they perhaps fail to assess the assault of 'Hinduization' on their community identity.

National Debate on Conversion: Five-Point RSS Agenda

During the midst of the attacks on Christians, the Prime Minister made a suggestion to have a national debate over the issue of conversion, thus implying that the violence was an outcome of the proselytizing activities of the churches. The RSS was quick to grab the opportunity. The RSS, of late, has been demanding national debates over contentious issues, which could be exploited to arouse passion and emotion in favour of *Hindutva*. Therefore, it welcomed the Prime Minister's suggestion and enumerated a five-point agenda for such a debate.[111]

First, in contrast to the position upto 1941 census, the tribals have been put in the category of 'Hindus' in all the censuses thereafter. The church needs to explain whether it accepts this fundamental change in the religious categorization of tribals. Secondly, the Church defends its proselytizing activities under the right to propagate granted in Article 25 of the Constitution. But the right to propagate implies respect for other faiths. 'Will not the unrestricted freedom granted to those religions whose underlying principle is that theirs is the only true religion and other religions are false and debasing, result in making human beings intolerant of other faiths and hence fanatic?', questions the RSS. Should the secular state allow its citizens to become intolerant and fanatic? Or should it restrict this freedom only to those who accept the existence and therefore validity of other faiths? Thirdly, though conversion by force is illegal, force has many forms. If anybody's poverty, or ignorance or disease is exploited for his conversion, should it be deemed voluntary conversion or conversion brought about by fraud? Fourthly, Article 30 is discriminatory. Why should the majority community—the Hindus—be deprived of the privileges that Article 30 confers on the minorities? Fifthly, the term 'minority institution' needs a precise definition. Any institution should not be declared a minority institution just because the management of that institution is in the hands of people subscribing to a minority religion. All these conditions, the RSS argues, have serious implications for the fabric of Indian secularism.

'Oust Christians' Campaign

With BJP's installation in Delhi for the third time, the spate of anti-Christian violence that began in Gujarat and Orissa earlier, erupted again in random acts across the country—UP, MP, Punjab, Andhra Pradesh, Karnataka, and Goa. Between January and June 2000, 36 anti-Christian attacks have been reported, though some of them are disputed by Hindu organizations.[112] There were a series of attacks on Christian institutions particularly in UP. This was perhaps a desperate attempt to overcome the declining popularity of the BJP, internal squabbles within the *Sangh Parivar*, miserable performance in the 1999 Lok Sabha elections, Kalyan Singh's exit and above all, the failure to implement the Ram temple agenda. While the Christian leaders accuse the *Sangh Parivar* of using Christian-bashing to consolidate the Hindu vote-bank, the *Parivar* leaders look at it as an ISI plot, the handiwork of Pakistan, to foment hatred between Christians and Hindus and undermine the credibility of the Vajpayee government.

Despite the *Sangh Parivar's* denial of its involvement and its subsequent exoneration by the Minority Commission, it is true that the VHP and the Bajrang Dal have stepped up their anti-Christian campaign. Bajrang Dal, instead of being defensive about its alleged role in the incidents, rather proudly boasts of its extremist and violent character; it believes that violence enhances its respectability and glorifies its image: 'Hindus will respect us more and Christians will fear us.'[113] Clearly stating Bajrang Dal's intention to drive the Christians away from the state, one of its leaders observes: 'The Christians want to take over the country. What is the point of us targeting one or two? Our aim is to drive them all away.'[114] He further adds: *Jis samay hum bhagana shuru karenge, yeh nahin bach payenge* (The day we start chasing them away, they won't be able to save themselves).

VHP's Giriraj Kishore attempts to prove that the Christians are more dangerous than the Muslims. Elaborating on the relative evils of the two enemy communities of the *Hindu Rashtra*, the Muslims and the Christians, he observes that the latter is worse than the former in the matter of conversion. Though the Muslims 'breed too much, the Christians go around desecrating Hindu Gods and asking tribals to accept Jesus'.[115] He further argues: 'Muslims are upfront in their hostility. Christians are a sugar-coated people. They pretend to be harmless when they are actively against Hinduism. For us, Akbar is more dangerous than Aurangzeb. One's a known evil, the other more dangerous as he is hidden.'[116] Kishore points out another difference: 'Muslims claim to be present in larger numbers than they are, Christians claim they are a declining populace when actually they are growing.'[117] Kishore thus elevates the enemy status of the Christians from number two to number one—at least for a temporary period.

Dara Singh,[118] the prime accused in the Staines murder case, after his arrest, is being projected as a saviour of the Hindus and some organizations are leading a save-Dara Singh mission. Copies of *Moon Dara Singh Kahuchhi* (This is Dara Singh speaking), full of acrimonious anti-minorities propaganda, have been circulated in thousands. There has been a spurt of anti-Christian literature in the form of pamphlets, handbills, and posters. The RSS may absolve itself from the charges of being directly involved in the anti-Christian attacks, but it certainly cannot be exonerated from the responsibility of leading a systematic hate-campaign against the Christians.

Thus, the RSS has shown that besides Ayodhya and the building of the Ram temple, it has other ideological and mobilizational arsenals in its armour. It has the potential to manoeuvre and manipulate even trivial issues because of its control over a mammoth organization. Every affiliate remains subservient to it and the political affiliate is no exception just because it controls political power. The *Hindu Rashtra's* end is not mere political power but Hindu hegemony. Hence, the immediate task before the RSS is to guide its political affiliate to move in the right direction so that this mission can be accomplished.

SANGH AND SARKAR

Saffron Intervention

Right from the very beginning of the formation of the Vajpayee government in 1998, the RSS has been trying to act as the big boss. K.S. Sudarshan, the then *sah-sarkaryavah* of the RSS, reportedly stormed into Vajpayee's residence late at night at the time of ministry-making in March 1998 to prevent Jaswant Singh from being inducted into the Union Cabinet as the Finance Minister. Vajpayee had no option but to acquiesce. Vajpayee's decision to invite Ananth Kumar, a staunch RSS loyalist from Karnataka, first to take oath as a Cabinet Minister, despite being quite junior, sent a signal to the RSS cadres that it was their own government. The RSS also reserved certain key portfolios for its trusted loyalists—for instance, Murli Manohar Joshi got Human Resources Development with Uma Bharti as his deputy to implement the saffron agenda in education. Jhandewalan, the RSS office at Delhi, replaced Nagpur, as the RSS headquarters; the political directives to the BJP and the government were issued from Delhi, not from Nagpur. The top RSS leadership, including Rajendra Singh, Thengadi, Seshadri and Sudarshan started camping here frequently to monitor the activities of the Vajpayee government.

After the initial euphoria, the RSS did not feel satisfied by the way the BJP government was being run. It acted tough; even hardcore RSS men like L.K. Advani were not spared. After the killing of 26 Hindus at Doda in Jammu & Kashmir, Acharya Giriraj Kishore of the VHP said, if the government had the will the situation in the state could be brought under control in a month's time, but he would give six months more to Advani as the problem was complex. He did not accept Advani as the 'hero' of the Ayodhya agitation and said: 'It was not Advani who built the movement . . . that naturally when politicians choose to jump in at the last minute they get the credit.'[119] It was the VHP and not Advani, who did the hard work, but Advani ran away with the credit, grumbled Kishore. He also rejected Advani's comparison as the second Sardar Patel, saying that he had to demonstrate through action. *Panchjanya*, the RSS mouthpiece, pulled up Vajpayee for forgetting to include Janmashtami (birthday of Lord Krishna) greetings in his Independence Day speech and for overlooking Deendayal Upadhyaya's name in the list of past national leaders.[120]

RSS and the State Governments

The RSS also tried to have its control in the states where the BJP was in power, either on its own or in coalition. In Uttar Pradesh, it ran a virtual 'super-cabinet' to oversee the performance of the ministers, including Kalyan Singh. Rajendra Singh, the *sarsanghchalak*, even addressed over 60 top IAS and IPS officers, including the Chief Secretary and the Director-General of police, on the state's declining law-and-order situation.[121] In Delhi, the RSS was able to appoint its favourite as the Lieutenant-Governor. In Rajasthan, the RSS pressurized Bhairon Singh Shekhawat, a non-conformist saffronite, for induction of more RSS members into the cabinet and other important positions. In Madhya Pradesh, where the party was out of power, the Sangh strategy operated through the Governor Bhai Mahavir, a trusted RSS worker. In Bihar, Sunder Singh Bhandari, a RSS *pracharak* and seasoned politician was appointed to mastermind the saffron strategy to counter Laloo Yadav.

Unlike in the north, the RSS, however, avoided a confrontationist role in Maharashtra. Here, the RSS did not insist on a superior status vis-a-vis the BJP. For instance, it backed Suresh Kalmadi in the 1998 Lok Sabha polls despite the fact that Avinash Dharmadhikari, a former IAS officer with close RSS links was contesting against him. The RSS perhaps could not afford to antagonize the Shiv Sena. Moreover, Sena supremo Bal Thackeray and BJP's Pramod Mahajan shared a perfect understanding. Similarly, the RSS and the Keshubhai Patel government in Gujarat have been sharing a cordial relationship. Most of the ministers holding important portfolios—Finance Minister Vajubhai Vala, Minister of State for Power Kaushik Patel and Minister of State for Home Haren Pandya—are trusted RSS men. The Keshubhai ministry does not take important decisions without prior consultations with the *Sangh Parivar*.

SJM's Aggressive Campaign

The saffron intervention, however, took a new turn under the leadership of the Swadeshi Jagran Manch (SJM). The Vajpayee government was embarrassed when the SJM took its protest to the street criticizing its economic policies. On 30 and 31 August 1998, a meeting of the SJM's steering committee was held, which was attended by representatives of sister organizations VHP, ABVP and, most importantly, K.S. Sudarshan—the then Joint-Secretary of the RSS. The SJM had criticized the BJP government for allowing 100 per cent foreign investment in the liquor and tobacco industries, and for retaining and promoting certain key bureaucrats in economic and trade councils, who were 'hostile to swadeshi'.[122] The RSS sources felt that the Prime Minister's Office was directly involved in these decisions and described a 'powerful member' of the PM's kitchen cabinet as an 'operator'.[123] The RSS clearly wanted a bureaucracy which would be amenable to its *swadeshi* agenda. Under its pressure, Montek Singh Ahluwalia, the Finance Secretary, was transferred. But the government did not oblige it by replacing him with the RSS favourite Y. Venugopal Reddy, but by Vijay Kelkar, thereby annoying the saffron highcommand.

The SJM's agitation was charted out almost as a revolt against the government. Accordingly, the SJM started a 24-day *Chetna Yatra* on 17 September and carried on its anti-globalization programme on 25 *raths* through public rallies and musical compositions based on 'economic patriotism'. The purpose was two-fold: first, to spread the message of *swadeshi* and anti-globalization; secondly, to embarrass the government on its economic policies. The convener of this *yatra* was BJP MP Mahesh Sharma, a RSS *pracharak* and former Secretary of the ABVP. The SJM questioned the government's rationale to 'sacrifice' the interest of Maruti 'to promote Suzuki'. It also objected to an Andhra Pradesh government tender for a Japanese grant-in-aid irrigation project which excluded the use of Indian goods and commented that such exclusion 'hurts sovereignty'. The proposed ban on non-iodized salt, the SJM argued, would favour the Cargill Corporation, one of the largest food companies in the world and warned that this 'open invitation' to Cargill would be a disaster.

RSS-BJP Relationship after Electoral Debacle

Soon after the electoral debacle of the BJP in Rajasthan, Delhi and Madhya Pradesh, there was a Bharatiya Mazdoor Sangh (BMS) rally in Delhi on 30 November 1998 to protest the BJP government's decision to allow foreign participation in the insurance sector. Leading the rally was Thengadi: '[Prime Minister] Vajpayee should learn from Nehru and [former American President] Woodrow Wilson, who lost their credibility because of selfish advisors.'[124] The message behind Thengadi's public admonishment of Vajpayee was clear—pursue the RSS line or face the wrath. Three days later, Swadeshi Jagran Manch took to the streets on the insurance issue.

The attack continued. K.R. Malkani accused that Vajpayee had succumbed to US pressure for throwing open the insurance sector. Thengadi even accused Vajpayee of becoming 'a captive of a coterie which doesn't allow him to think rationally'. Harendra Kumar, ABVP Organizing Secretary, compared Vajpayee to Bhisma Pitamah who had joined the Kauravas and, therefore, had to be fought to uphold the good.[125] Even BJP President Kushabhau Thakre went to the Press, claiming the party had not been consulted on the insurance issue. Party Secretary Narendra Modi did not find it amusing 'to read about decisions from newspapers'.[126] Some even went to the extent of speculating that Advani would replace Vajpayee as the Prime Minister. Vajpayee was pushed into a corner. Even his ministerial colleagues like Uma Bharti showed tantrums in public. The ABVP convention in Mumbai dubbed him *nikamma* (most inept) Prime Minister. Vajpayee received enough flak for the election results, price rise and all the failures of the government.

There was a growing demand in the *Sangh Parivar* that the RSS should keep the party under its firm control. RSS should have more control over the BJP, demanded Vishnu Hari Dalmia, the VHP leader. He firmly stated, the compulsions of governance should not be used as excuses not to implement some of the least controversial *Hindutva* demands like the ban on cow slaughter.

Chintan Baithak

The RSS held a *chintan baithak* (brain-storming session), a rare introspective session held in the past only at extraordinary times like the aftermath of Gandhi's assassination and the Emergency and following the BJP's 1984-5 electoral rout. The four-day meeting was attended by the leaders of important affiliates: BJP's President Kushabhau Thakre, General Secretaries Venkiah Naidu and Govindacharya, VHP's Giriraj Kishore, Bajrang Dal Chief Jiban Singh Powayya and SJM's S. Gurumurthy. Sudarshan said the RSS would not like to be treated as an 'appendage' of the BJP.[127] The BJP's recalcitrant behaviour was discussed threadbare. Some of the saffron affiliates allegedly charged the RSS leadership for being lenient towards the BJP, and asked for a clarification—who was the master—the BJP or the RSS? Angry delegates even talked of teaching the BJP leaders a lesson for straying from the path. They asked the RSS not allow the BJP to dilute its *Hindutva* ideology.

At the *chintan baithak*, the RSS decided on asserting itself and strengthening its control over the BJP. Their affiliates wanted the BJP to stop playing to what they call the 'pseudo-secular gallery'. They charged that the government first compromised on core *Hindutva* issues—Article 370, Ram temple and the Uniform Civil Code—because of the compulsions of coalition politics, as well as dumping the *swadeshi* agenda. Dalmia warned that the government's repeated condemnation of the VHP might prove costly. There was also a demand that the RSS should replace the discredited BJP. Some hardcore workers threatened that the RSS could 'finish off' the BJP in the next election and reminded it of the 1984 electoral debacle.

'National interest is supreme' declared *Panchjanya* (27 December 1998) on its cover. 'Should the government act against the national interest, we will be compelled to speak out', announced K.S. Sudarshan, and warned the Vajpayee government for going back 'on its own declared policies'.[128] Then came the ultimate threat of switching support to another party: 'Every government is ours regardless of which party heads it'. This is reminiscent of alleged RSS support to the Congress government during the early 1980s.

Vajpayee Retaliates

Clearly, the target was Vajpayee. It was enough. Instead of being defensive, he inducted Jaswant Singh and Pramod Mahajan into the Cabinet, contrary to the wishes of the RSS. He reportedly pulled up Govindacharya for endorsing the 'spirit of the statement' at the ABVP convention in Mumbai which dubbed him *nikamma* Prime Minister. The same Govindacharya, in the past, described Vajpayee as a *mukhota* (mask). Vajpayee also showed his displeasure over the attack on his government at the *chintan baithak*, where BJP chief Kushabhau Thakre was present. Vajpayee's message was clear: his government will not play second fiddle to the BJP, or even the RSS.

BJP National Executive in Bangalore, 1999

In the National Executive meet of the BJP at Bangalore, Party President Kushabhau Thakre spoke openly of the uneasy relationship between the BJP and the government.[129] His remarks reflected the views of a powerful section in the party backed by RSS hardliners, who opposed dilution of the *Hindutva* plank, resented the reference to the demolition of the Babri Masjid as 'unfortunate', and the government's betrayal of *swadeshi*. These hardliners also had a different perception of the attacks on Christians in Gujarat and on the recent electoral debacle.

But Vajpayee prevailed. Addressing the National Executive, he said: 'While widest consultations are both desirable and necessary, decisions of the Government are final.'[130] This was a complete turn around from what he said on May 1998 at the party's National Executive meeting in Gandhinagar: 'The Government will not run the party. It is the party which will run the Government.' Thus Vajpayee made it clear that he would not like to be bullied by the tactics of the *Sangh Parivar*.

Vajpayee was able to remove critical references to the functioning of his government in all the resolutions. K.R. Malkani's *swadeshi*-tinted draft economic resolution was discarded and replaced with one prepared by Finance Minister Yashwant Sinha, which asserted: 'The Government is the best judge of the country's economic situation and is best placed to take appropriate steps . . .', thereby giving a green signal to the contentious Patents and Insurance Regulatory Authority (IRA) Bills and a red card to *swadeshi*.

The amended resolution firmly stated: 'The outcome of the elections is not a reflection on the performance of the BJP-led Government.' The final resolution also deleted a pointed reference to 'aggressive proselytisaton by some sections of the Church' and was categorical in condemning the destruction of churches in Gujarat. Implicit in the condemnation was the conscious decision to dissociate the BJP from the actions of some members of the *Sangh Parivar*.

Thus, Vajpayee clearly established the supremacy of the government over both the BJP and RSS. Vajpayee's retaliation was surprisingly supplemented by Advani's proposal of a 'Kamraj Plan' to revamp the party and the government. By indicating that he was ready to opt out of government, Advani signalled that he would not be a party to the destabilizing game underway. As a shrewd strategist he understood that Vajpayee still remains the best political mascot of the RSS.

Could the RSS really afford to destabilize Vajpayee? Could Vajpayee afford to break with the RSS and run a conservative government without the RSS? Nothing of this happened as both parties understood each other's strengths and weaknesses. Khurana, a Vajpayee follower, resigned from the cabinet protesting that some elements in the RSS wanted 'to remote-control the Government and tarnish its image.'[131] Yet, Vajpayee did not play it up and coolly accepted his resignation, obviously not to alienate the RSS. He also inaugurated a *Swadeshi Mela* of the Swadeshi Jagran Manch, the most vocal critic of his government. Interestingly, despite the attack of several *Sangh Parivar* leaders, Rajendra Singh, the then *sarsanghchalak*, never criticized Vajpayee in particular; he reportedly had an excellent relationship with Vajpayee all through.

The RSS and Vajpayee, at times, share an uneasy relationship. Despite his total commitment to the Sangh, he is not a run-of-the-mill *swayamsevak*. His liberal identity, ideological flexibility and aversion to militant Hinduism have become an asset as well as embarrassment to the RSS. But it is true that only Vajpayee has made it possible for the RSS to control Delhi, a decisive step for the mission of *Hindu Rashtra*. No other member, including Advani, could do it. Vajpayee is the most acceptable leader to the alliance partners in the era of coalition politics. On the other hand, Vajpayee is the product of the RSS; without its ideological and organizational support he would have been a nobody. Thus, both the RSS and Vajpayee need each other and supplement each other. Therefore, though the relationship soured, it could hardly reach a point of no return. The RSS had no other option but to make truce with him.

Resurrection of Vajpayee Government

With Jayalalitha's withdrawal of support, Vajpayee's 13-month government lost the motion of confidence on 17 April 1999 by a solitary vote. Sonia Gandhi's inability to muster support for an alternate government led to the thirteenth Lok Sabha elections. Vajpayee continued as the caretaker Prime Minister till the completion of elections in October. While the BJP was wondering about its election strategy, there was a sudden turnaround. Pakistani insurgents were found to be occupying Indian territory at Kargil. Indian soldiers fought bravely to drive out these insurgents. There was war hysteria all over the country.

The RSS got another opportunity to display its aggressive nationalism and *Hindutva* got a new boost. It exposed Pakistan's 'evil design' on India. It asked the international community to declare Pakistan as a terrorist State. It demanded crossing of the Line of Control (LOC) and to take back Pakistan Occupied Kashmir (POK). It organized meetings in memory of the Kargil martyrs, felicitated war-widows, thereby invoking anti-Pakistan emotions and galvanizing nationalist sentiment. Its affiliates went from door to door collecting funds for the war effort.

The Vajpayee government, which was earlier criticized for its poor governance, was resurrected overnight. Its caretaker status proved to be a blessing rather than an obstacle, as it exercised its full authority to handle this crisis. The media gave round the clock coverage of 'Operation Vijay', in which Vajpayee prominently figured. Finally, the Indian defence forces triumphed. Vajpayee, of course, shared the credit, for leading India into victory. Vajpayee also got credit for scoring a diplomatic victory by isolating Pakistan among the international community; even China refused to extend any support to Pakistan. Thus, Kargil resurrected the BJP.

This was an ideal situation for a party going in for national elections. The alliance partners also realized that Kargil would be one of the major electoral planks and therefore, it would be beneficial to consolidate the alliance under Vajpayee's leadership. The RSS also realized that despite Kargil the BJP would not be able to come back to power on its own, and therefore, the alliance should continue and be strengthened. Thus a grand National Democratic Alliance (NDA) was formed.

Besides Kargil, Sonia Gandhi's origins—*swadeshi* vs. *videshi*—became a major issue in the elections. The resignations of Sharad Pawar and P.A. Sangma from the Congress opposing Sonia's bid for Prime Ministership on the basis of her foreign origin further intensified the *swadeshi-videshi* campaign. Vajpayee was centrestage again. The BJP highlighted the injustice of a Congress conspiracy pulling down his government, Vajpayee's successful leadership during the Kargil war, and Sonia's Italian origins and her political inexperience. Again, what was missing was any talk of even an outline of a socio-economic programme. The BJP did not even come out with its own manifesto; a joint-manifesto of the NDA was released. The RSS also did not mind as it decided to go by realpolitik—power at Delhi was to be regained through Vajpayee's leadership.

Vajpayee charisma worked and the alliance politics clicked; the mandate of the 13th Lok Sabha went in favour of the NDA led by Vajpayee. The BJP and its allies won 296 seats leaving the Congress led alliance far behind at 134. The NDA bagged all the parliamentary seats in Delhi, Haryana, Himachal Pradesh, Goa, and did well in Orissa (19 out of 21), Andhra Pradesh (32 out of 42), Gujarat (20 out of 26), Rajasthan (16 out of 25), Madhya Pradesh (29 out of 40), Tamil Nadu (22 out of 39), and more importantly, in Bihar (40 out of 54). It also made significant inroads into the left bastion of West Bengal with the help of Mamata Banerjee's TMC, the alliance claiming 10 of the 42 seats. The performance of the NDA in Punjab was dismal and in Karnataka, much lower than was expected. The alliance could do well in Maharashtra (28 out of 48 seats) as Sharad Pawar's newly formed Nationalist Congress Party played the spoilsport for the Congress. However, the Shiv Sena–BJP alliance could not get a majority in the assembly elections. But the shocking setback to the BJP came from Uttar Pradesh, the fortress of *Hindutva.* The BJP could get only 29 seats in comparison to its 1998 tally of 57. It, however, compensated its loss by its gain in states like Bihar and Rajasthan. The party also registered an impressive presence in Assam. Though the BJP just added 1 seat to its 1998 tally of 181, and Vajpayee's margin shrunk at Lucknow, the party comfortably regained power with the support of its alliance partners, who widely represented the country, from Jammu & Kashmir to Tamil Nadu and from Maharashtra to Orissa. Vajpayee became the Prime Minister for the third time. With a clear mandate to his leadership and a perfect understanding with the alliance partners, he was confident of running a stable government. The RSS had also realized the hard reality; it could not monopolize power at Delhi, it had to share. But it can still play big brother and have strategic control over State power.

Rajju Bhaiya did his job well. Under his stewardship the RSS's tryst with politics had reached a decisive stage with its political affiliate controlling political power in Delhi. This time, with a comfortable majority, it seems like a long innings for Vajpayee. More importantly, the Indian polity has taken a rightward turn and opposition to *Hindutva* looks feeble and fragmented. Rajendra Singh also made sure that the RSS percolated down to the *taluka* and the block level in the country; 'We now propose to ensure that it reaches every *mandal*.'[132] The *Sangh Parivar* had also extended its reach to every possible sphere and had decisively broken through caste, class and regional barriers. These gains must be consolidated further.

Sudarshan Takes Over: Asserting Hindutva

In Deoras style, Rajju Bhaiya relinquished his office on 10 March 2000 in view of his ill health. H.V. Seshadri, the Sangh veteran and the *sarkaryavah*, who was speculated to be the next chief, declined the offer on health grounds. Thus, the choice fell on *sahsarkaryavah*, Kupphalli Sitaramayya Sudarshan,[133] who was relatively young among the top leaders and possessed enough maturity and vast experience to lead the RSS. Justifying his selection to this highest office, Rajendra Singh described Sudarshan as: 'A powerful orator, articulate in several languages, with a deep study of many subjects he has ably handled many a responsibility in the Sangh—*sharirik* as well as *baudhik*. An engineer by training and with his experience as *sah-sarkaryavah* there is hardly any subject with which he is not conversant.'[134]

Besides this, the timing of the elevation of a south Indian to the top post is also important. The RSS has already reached saturation point in north India and its popularity has started petering out steadily, especially in UP which used to be its core support base. So, it is perhaps the right time for the RSS to expand in south India more effectively. The *Sangh Parivar*, despite all odds, has been trying since long to integrate south India into the *Hindutva* fold through its cohesive organizational network and dedicated *pracharaks*. This effort has certainly paid some dividends. But more importantly, the traditional south Indian hostility to north Indian *Hindutva* now seems to have been blunted, particularly because of the compulsions of coalition politics; a south Indian chief, at this juncture, could ideally exploit this favourable atmosphere and help the RSS to expand in the region quite rapidly.

Unlike Rajendra Singh, who had mastered the art of realpolitik and had the bearing of a controlled statesman, Sudarshan is open and irrepressible, thus inviting controversies. Soon after his installation Sudarshan warned of another 'epic war' between Hindus and 'anti-Hindus' after which every opposition to *Hindutva* will change. Asserting that 'even otherwise confused people have now come to believe in Hindutva', he observed: 'But it is going to change. This is yet another epic war between Hindus and anti-Hindus, a veritable Mahabharat in which sometime Abhimanyu will fall, sometime Ghatotkacha or it may be Jayadratha's turn yet another day.'[135] Sudarshan also advocated the need to scrap the Constitution, which was a 'remake of the British model of 1935' and suggested its replacement with one based on the 'aspirations of the people'.[136]

While expounding on the 'India *vs.* Bharat' theme in a function organized in honour of 'nationalist' journalists, Sudarshan observed that whereas 'Bharat' was a civilizational concept, India was a gift from the departing British. 'Bharat' was one united nation; India was many nations in one. 'Bharat' was held together by a single strong culture; India argued for multi-culturalism.[137] Sudarshan also wondered how any self-respecting country could allow English to co-exist with its own national language.

Sudarshan invited the wrath of the Sikh community when he claimed Sikhs to be Hindus while addressing a meeting organized by the Rashtriya Sikh Sangat, an affiliate of the RSS. The thrust of RSS participation in tercentenary celebrations of the Khalsa has been to popularize the thesis that Sikhism is an offshoot of Hinduism, and even today remains its sword arm. The Sikhs consider this an assault on their identity and are even prepared to eat beef to demonstrate that they are not Hindus.[138]

It is perhaps apt to understand that Sudarshan likes to play both philosopher and field marshal.[139] Both these traits of his personality perhaps blossomed when he controlled the ideological (*boudhik*) as well as the physical (*sharirik*) wings of the RSS for a number of years. He believes that politics should always aim at ideological supremacy. For him, *Hindutva* is a holistic concept with definite views on everything from politics to economics: 'Let there be an endeavour to bring forth a Hindu way of development. . . .We will soon present a complete and final blueprint of an alternative concept of development.'[140] From being a way of life or, at best, a code of conduct (*dharma*), Sudarshan wants to turn Hinduism into an ideology—complete with sub-branches of Hindu economics and Hindu science.[141]

Sudarshan's stress on ideology will serve another important purpose. He has admitted that the appeal of the *shakhas* has been depleting. The RSS fears its core values will not be transmitted to the next generation. It has found that modern influences like television and competitive careers have resulted in the dwindling appeal of the *shakhas* and adversely affected its puritanical, reclusive character. Moreover, over the last decade, frequent elections have kept the *swayamsevaks* preoccupied more with political activities rather than organization-building. Sudarshan has to reorient the *shakhas*—ensuring attendance, fortifying ideology warding off 'cultural pollution'.

Sudarshan and Vajpayee Government

Rajju Bhaiya and Vajpayee were contemporaries, had worked together on various occasions and shared excellent personal relations. Rajendra Singh, during his tenure, took all the care not to embarrass Vajpayee despite occasional RSS outbursts and threats. Just before relinquishing office, he rescued the Vajpayee government on the issue of Gujarat government's controversial circular, which permitted government employees to participate in the activities of the RSS. Rajju Bhaiya made oblique hints to the Gujarat government that the RSS would not be perturbed by a withdrawal of the order, since 'it was not dependent on official patronage for its growth'.[142] This certainly paved the way for the withdrawal of the circular.

On the contrary, Sudarshan and Vajpayee reportedly do not share the best of relationships; Vajpayee's seniority and stature are perhaps the irritants. Sudarshan's hawkish posture, intrusive style and differences with the Vajpayee government are already well known.[143] He strongly advocates *swadeshi* and is extremely critical of the government's economic policy and has called for a 'second war of independence'. He complains that the move towards globalization is detrimental to *swadeshi* interests and favours only a handful of transnational corporations. Under his patronage, the SJM and the BMS, *Sangh Parivar's* two vociferous champions of *swadeshi*, never miss any opportunity to criticize the government's economic policy. The SJM has given an ultimatum that the order making iodization of salt mandatory should be withdrawn by 9 August 2000, failing which it would re-enact Dandi March from 2 October, Mahatma

Gandhi's birth anniversary. The SJM also opposes the government decision to allow 100 per cent Foreign Direct Investment (FDI) in infrastructure areas like refineries and e-commerce; it describes the government decision in the area of business to business e-commerce as 'a virtual sell-out of a high value national potential to the prejudice of emerging Indian corporates in e-commerce'.[144] It has been equally critical of the decision to remove the cap of Rs 1,500 crore for 100 per cent automatic FDI in power projects. The RSS also questions the rationale of the government's disinvestment policy.

Besides economic issues, there are differences in other vital issues as well. The RSS took a tough stand on autonomy resolution passed by the J&K assembly and made it clear that it was totally unacceptable. It also cautioned the Vajpayee government against soft-pedalling the issue.[145] Vajpayee seemed to agree and got it rejected by the cabinet. However, Sudarshan has got the pretext to revive the demand for the abrogation of Article 370.

The issue that really haunts the RSS is the construction of the Ram temple, which has been kept on hold due to political compulsions. Despite periodic assurances of the *Parivar* outfits that the carving of stone pillars is in progress and the construction will commence at an appropriate time, the RSS is yet to make up its mind about the timing. It is caught in a dilemma. It is an irony that it was the Ram temple issue that catapulted the RSS into political power in Delhi, and now it seems that will lose Delhi the moment it takes up the same Ram temple agenda. This is a tricky problem particularly for Sudarshan, who favours the ideological assertion of *Hindutva*. However, the threat of losing Uttar Pradesh may force the RSS to revive this agenda early.

What will be the RSS-Vajpayee equation during Sudarshan's tenure? Will there be more RSS intervention and control? Will an assertive RSS be acceptable to the NDA? How long will it allow the BJP to continue with this alliance experiment? While raising these questions it should not be forgotten that the disagreements between the RSS and the BJP are not fundamental, and it can never be. The dynamics of power-politics may have resulted in strategic and tactical variations, personality clashes and perceptional differences; but it will never lead to any breakdown. They very well know their limits and always act under a well-planned strategy.

In the past, the RSS has demonstrated strategic flexibility responding to the diktats of realpolitik. At the same time, it has also taken refuge under militant ideological rigidity during times when it has been in political wilderness and isolation. The RSS, therefore, will retain and consolidate its pivotal place in Indian politics rather than renouncing power so easily. After all, this is a hard-earned effort of millions of dedicated and devoted *swayamsevaks* for the last 75 years—from Hedgewar to Sudarshan. The RSS will continue its tryst with politics to establish a Hindu hegemony and convert India into a *Hindu Rashtra.*

NOTES AND REFERENCES

1. Rajendra Singh was born on 29 January 1922 in Bulandshahr in UP. His father, Balbir Singh, was one of the first Indian Chief Engineers, who earned a reputation for his honesty, integrity and ideal life. Rajendra Singh had his early education in the prestigious Modern School, Delhi and then went to a public school in Nainital. He completed his Masters Degree in Physics at the age of 21 from Allahabad University. His examiner, Nobel Laureate C.V. Raman, reportedly commended his performance. Soon after, he joined the same university to teach nuclear physics. He joined the RSS in 1942-3. He resigned from the job in 1966 to become a full-time RSS worker. Became zonal organizer for the north-east zone in 1967. During the Emergency period (1975-7) he directed underground activities. Was appointed *sah sarkaryavah* in 1977 and in 1978, became *sarkaryavah* of the RSS. Played an important role in the formation of the Janata Party. He has widely travelled in India as well as abroad. See *Organiser*, XLV (33), 20 March 1994.
2. Ibid.
3. Ibid.
4. Ibid.
5. Ibid.
6. *Organiser*, XLV (34), 27 March 1994. Also see *Organiser*, XLV (35), 3 April 1994.
7. *The Pioneer*, 14 April 1994.
8. *The Pioneer*, 12 April 1994.
9. See Virginia Van Dyke, 'General Elections, 1996: Political Sadhus and Limits to Religious Mobilisation in North India', *Economic and Political Weekly*, XXXII (49), 6 December 1997, pp. 3149-58.
10. While the VHP wanted to push ahead with an agitation at Mathura, the BJP was not keen at that point to strain its relations with Mayawati government.
11. Bharatiya Janata Party, *For a Strong and Prosperous India—Election Manifesto 1996* (Delhi), p. 6.
12. Ibid., p. 7.
13. Ibid., p. 15.
14. Ibid., p. 14.
15. V. Venkatesan, 'Losing Momentum', *Frontline*, 17 May 1996, p. 13.

16. Virginia Van Dyke, 'General Elections, 1996 . . .', op. cit., pp. 3152-3.
17. *India Today,* 15 August 1995, pp. 28-9.
18. A.G. Noorani, 'Hindutva Judicially Licensed', *Frontline,* 26 January 1996.
19. N.K. Singh, 'Hindutva, Back on the Agenda', *India Today,* 15 January 1996, p. 22.
20. *India Today,* 30 April 1996, p. 43.
21. Pramod K. Kantha, 'General Elections, 1996, BJP Politics: Looking Beyond the Impasse', *Economic and Political Weekly,* XXXII (48), 29 November 1997, pp. 3090-3100.
22. *The Economic Times,* 6 May 1996.
23. The differences started soon after. Kalyan Singh took over after six months, but the BSP withdrew support. He retained his position only by engineering split in the BSP and the Congress.
24. *India Today,* 15 December 1996, p. 29.
25. N.K. Singh, 'Sangh Brotherhood: Hindu Divided Family', *India Today,* 15 December 1996, p. 28.
26. *Organiser,* XLIX (29), 15 February 1998.
27. *The Hindustan Times,* 17 December 1997.
28. See Partha S. Ghosh, *BJP and the Evolution of Hindu Nationalism: From Periphery to Centre* (Delhi: Manohar, 1999), pp. 136-9.
29. *Organiser,* XLIX (23), 4 January 1998.
30. Ibid.
31. *Organiser,* XLIX (36), 5 April 1998.
32. *Organiser,* XLIX (23), 4 January 1998.
33. *Organiser,* XLIX (34), 22 March 1998.
34. *Organiser,* XLIX (30), 22 February 1998.
35. *Organiser,* XLIX (35), 29 March 1998.
36. Ibid.
37. *Organiser,* XLIX (36), 5 April 1998.
38. *National Agenda for Governance.* See Partha Ghosh, *BJP and the Evolution of Hindu Nationalism,* op. cit, p. 410.
39. Quoted by K.R. Malkani, *The RSS Story* (Delhi: Impex India, 1980), p. 42.
40. Quoted by Sumit Sarkar, 'The BJP and Aspects of Nationalism', *Economic and Political Weekly,* XXXIII (27), 4-10 July 1998, p. 1726.
41. *Organiser,* L (19), 6 December 1998.
42. Ibid.
43. Ibid.
44. For a comprehensive discussion on the foreign policy of the BJS and the BJP, see Partha Ghosh, *BJP and the Evolution of Hindu Nationalism,* op. cit., Chap. VII.
45. See Sandy Gordon, 'Indian Security Policy and the Rise of the Hindu Right', in John McGuire, Peter Reeves and Howard Brasted, eds., *Politics of Violence: From Ayodhya to Behrampada,* op. cit., pp. 253-71.
46. *Organiser,* XLIX (38), 19 April 1998.
47. *Organiser,* XLIX (42), 17 May 1998.

48. A Survey showed that 87 per cent people approved of this action. See *India Today*, 25 May 1998, p. 25.
49. *The Economic Times*, 21 May 1998.
50. *India Today*, 1 June 1998, p. 37.
51. Sumit Sarkar, 'The BJP and Aspects of Nationalism', *Economic and Political Weekly*, op. cit., p. 1726.
52. However, the RSS argues that its mission of *param vaibhav* always included economic progress of the nation as one of its main objectives. One finds only stray economic thoughts but not a specific economic model as such till the early 1990s.
53. D.B. Thengadi, the present economic ideologue of the RSS, identifies Golwalkar's economic thinking as follows: (i) The basic needs of life must be available to every citizen; (ii) Material wealth is to be acquired, with the object of serving society which is but a manifestation of God, in the best possible ethical manner, and out of all that wealth, only a bare minimum should be used for our own purposes; (iii) Thus we are only the trustee of the society; (iv) Ceiling on individual accumulation, no person has a right to exploit someone else's labour for personal profit; (v) Vulgar, ostentatious and wasteful expenditure is a sin when millions are starving. There must be reasonable restriction on all consumption. 'Consumerism' is not compatible with the spirit of Hindu culture; (vi) Maximum production and equitable distribution should be our motto, national self-reliance, our immediate goal; (vii) The problem of unemployment and underemployment must be tackled on a war-footing; (viii) While industrialization is a must, it need not be a blind imitation of the West; (ix) Greater stress should be laid on labour-intensive rather than capital-intensive industries; (x) Our technologists should be required to introduce, for the benefit of the artisans, reasonably adaptable changes in the traditional techniques of production, without incurring the risk of increase in unemployment; (xi) It is necessary to reconcile efficiency with employment expansion; (xii) Labour is also one form of capital in every industry. The labour of every worker should be evaluated in terms of share, and workers raised to the status of shareholders contributing labour as their share; (xiii) Consumer's interest is the nearest economic equivalent of national interest. Society is the third, and more important party to all industrial relations; (xiv) The surplus value of labour belongs to the nation; (xv) There need not be any rigidity about the patterns of industrial ownership. For each industry the pattern of ownership should be determined in the light of its peculiar characteristics; (xvi) We are free to evolve any variety of socio-economic order, provided it is in keeping with the tenets of *dharma*; (xvii) But changes in the superstructure of society will be of no use if the mind of every individual citizen is not moulded properly; (xviii) Our view of the relation between individual and society has always been, not one of conflict, but of harmony and cooperation, both out of consciousness of a single reality running through all the individuals. The individual is a living limb of the corporate social personality; (xix) The *sanskaras* of identification with the entire nation constitute the real social-

infrastructure of any socio-economic order. See D.B. Thengadi's Foreword to M.G. Bokare, *Hindu Economics [Eternal Economic Order]* (New Delhi: Janaki Prakashan, 1993).

54. See A.B. Vajpayee, 'A Glimpse of Greatness', *Organiser*, XXVI (45), 16 June 1973.
55. The RSS therefore claims that its *swadeshi* is not really new.
56. Thomas Blom Hansen, 'The Ethics of Hindutva and the Spirit of Capitalism', in Thomas Blom Hansen and Christophe Jaffrelot, eds., *The BJP and the Compulsions, of Politics in India*, op. cit., p. 295.
57. Salim Lakha, 'The Bharatiya Janata Party and Globalisation of the Indian Economy', in John McGuire, Peter Reeves and Howard Brasted, eds., *Politic of Violence: From Ayodhya to Behrampada*, op. cit., p. 277.
58. *India Today*, 28 September 1998, p. 20.
59. *Organiser*, 26 January 1992.
60. *Organiser*, XLVII (4), 27 August 1995.
61. The philosophy of *swadeshi* can be traced to Deendayal's theory of integral humanism, which is perceived as the 'third way', ideologically different from socialism and capitalism. M.M. Joshi, a radical proponent of *swadeshi* claims that the RSS has been practicing *swadeshi* and self-reliance since the days of Hedgewar. See M.M. Joshi, 'RSS—The Man-Making Machine', *Organiser*, XLVI (40), 7 May 1995, pp. 67-9.
62. M.G. Bokare, *Swadeshi Economy for War of Economic Imperialism* (Mumbai: Swadeshi Jagaran Manch, 1993), p. 7.
63. *Organiser*, XLVII (4), 27 August 1995.
64. Bharatiya Janata Party, *Humanistic Approach to Economic Development (A Swadeshi Alternative)*, Economic Policy Statement, 1992, Gandhinagar, May 1992, p. 2.
65. Ibid.
66. Gail Omvedt, 'Of Brahmins, Sacred and Socialist', *Economic and Political Weekly*, XXVIII (44), 30 October 1993, p. 2402.
67. Ibid.
68. The SJM is a radical wing within the *Sangh Parivar* with members drawn largely from the BMS, BKS, ABVP, the leadership is almost wholly in the hands of the *pracharaks* of the RSS. Within a short period the SJM has made inroads into rural and far-flung areas.
69. The *Sangh Parivar* described the Enron issue as 'another Ayodhya'. It took pride in demolishing both Babur as well as Enron. It declared, the destiny of India does not depend on multinationals. 'Our destiny, the destiny of a nation called Bharat, depends on the Bharatis, living here, working here, not on some pot-bellied Yankee in Wall Street. We can stand up to the most powerful multinational and ask it to get lost.' See *Organiser*, XXLVII (3), 20 August 1995. But ironically, its political front resurrected the Enron project, thus confirming the cleavage between rhetoric and pragmatism. However, the SJM, who spearheaded the struggle, apparently expresses its reservations against the decision.

70. Ajit Kumar Jha, 'Hindutva Swadeshi Waves of Economic Nationalism', *The Times of India*, 6 September 1995.
71. *India Today*, 28 September 1998, pp. 22-3.
72. Sumit Sarkar, 'Hindutva and the Question of Conversions', in K.N. Panikkar, ed., *The Concerned Indian's Guide to Communalism* (Delhi: Viking, 1999), p. 99.
73. The Census reports on religion indicate that the growth rate of the Christian community is the lowest among all the religious communities in India. In fact the share of Christian community in the total population of India has fallen from 2.35 per cent in 1951 census to 2.3 per cent in 1991 census. Though the Christians form the majority in three states (Nagaland, Mizoram and Meghalaya), it needs to be emphasized that the total population of these three states constitutes only 0.45 per cent of India's total population.
74. Ram Swarup, *Hinduism vis-a-vis Christianity and Islam* (Delhi: Voice of India, 1992), p. 63.
75. Sita Ram Goel, *Jesus Christ: An Artifice of Aggression* (Delhi: Voice of India, 1994), p. 85.
76. *Organiser*, XLIX (42), 17 May 1998, p. 20.
77. *Organiser*, L (29), 14 February 1999.
78. *Organiser*, L (25), 17 January 1999.
79. Golwalkar's anti-Christian arguments have been discussed in Chap. IV.
80. *Mission Mandate*, based on the six-day 'Mission India 2000 Conference' held in Chennai from 13-18 January 1992, mentions: 'The goal of our mission is to make disciples with the end of developing a church in every village and colony of every town and city of India—about 9,00,000 churches. Therefore, when we make Christ known to the people and they respond we should establish a worship group so they will be discipled and incorporated into a community of believers.' Quoted by *Organiser*, L (9), 27 September 1998, p. 9.
81. Sumit Sarkar does not find the argument convincing as all the instances are confined to sixteenth-century Goa. Sumit Sarkar, 'Hindutva and the Question of Conversions', op. cit., p. 93.
82. Purushottamdas Tandan's statement quoted by Sumit Sarkar, ibid., p. 95.
83. *The Pioneer*, 14 November 1998.
84. Ibid.
85. Ibid.
86. For Elwin's life and work, see Ramachandra Guha, *Savaging the Civilised: Verrier Elwin, His Tribals, and India* (Delhi: Oxford University Press, 1999).
87. See *India Today*, 1 February 1999, p. 21.
88. Ibid.
89. Arun Shourie, *Missionaries in India* (Delhi: Voice of India, 1994), p. 235.
90. Sumit Sarkar, 'Hindutva and the Question of Conversions', op. cit., p. 94.
91. For more information on Ashimanand's activities, see Satyakam Joshi, 'Tribals, Missionaries and Sadhus: Understanding Violence in the Dangs', *Economic and Political Weekly*, XXXIV (37), 11 September 1999.
92. *The Hindustan Times*, 3 January 1999.

93. *India Today*, 11 January 1999, p. 23.
94. *The Hindustan Times*, 2 April 1999.
95. *The Times of India*, 30 December 1998.
96. Vir Sanghvi, 'Echoes of Ayodhya', *The Hindustan Times*, 8 January 1999.
97. *The Hindu*, 17 January 1999.
98. *India Today*, 25 January 1999, p. 28.
99. *The Pioneer*, 15 August 1998.
100. *The Hindustan Times*, 3 August 1998.
101. *The Pioneer*, 7 August 1998.
102. Ibid.
103. For details, see Ghanshyam Shah, 'Conversion, Reconversion and the State: Recent Events in the Dangs', *Economic and Political Weekly*, XXXIV (6), 6 February 1999, pp. 312-18; Satyakam Joshi, 'Tribals, Missionaries and Sadhus: Understanding Violence in the Dangs', op. cit.
104. Ghanshyam Shah, 'Conversion, Reconversion and the State', op. cit., p. 317.
105. *The Hindustan Times*, 14 February 1999.
106. Lokpal Sethi, 'Sangh Parivar Plays Tribal-Christian Card to Arouse Communal Passion', *The Hindustan Times*, 22 December 1998.
107. *The Hindustan Times*, 21 March 1999.
108. *The Hindustan Times*, 23 March 1999.
109. *The Hindu*, 8 May 1999.
110. *The Hindustan Times*, 19 September 1999.
111. *Organiser*, L (28), 7 February 1999.
112. For details, see 'Hawk Flock', *Outlook*, 26 June 2000, pp. 26-8.
113. *The Times of India*, 23 June 2000.
114. Ibid.
115. *Outlook*, 26 June 2000, p. 27.
116. Ibid.
117. Ibid.
118. Dara Singh denies having any link with the *Sangh Parivar*. He rather blames the RSS for not being militant enough to protect the cows: 'They don't practice what they preach.' See *India Today*, 22 May 2000, pp. 40-1.
119. *The Hindu*, 8 August 1998.
120. *India Today*, 28 September 1998, p. 22.
121. Ibid., p. 21.
122. *The Hindustan Times*, 6 September 1998.
123. *The Times of India*, 8 October 1998.
124. *The Hindustan Times*, 13 December 1998.
125. *India Today*, 18 January 1999, p. 26.
126. *India Today*, 14 December 1998, p. 29.
127. *The Pioneer*, 15 December 1998. Sudarshan also scotched speculations that RSS chief Rajendra Singh was being forced out of the office by the southern lobby. He also said that the electoral rout of the BJP was not discussed at all.
128. *The Times of India*, 12 January 1999.

129. *The Times of India*, 6 January 1999.
130. *India Today*, 18 January 1999, p. 24.
131. *India Today*, 15 February 1999, p. 21.
132. *The Pioneer*, 9 January 2000.
133. Sudarshan, a Kannada Brahmin, was born and brought up in Madhya Pradesh where his father was a railway employee. He was born in Raipur on 1931. He joined the RSS at the age of nine. He did his schooling at Bilaspur and then completed B.E. (Hons.) in Telecommunication from Jabalpur Engineering College, Sagar University. He became a *pracharak* in 1954 and was promoted to Madhya Bharat *Prant Pracharak* in 1964. In 1969, he took the responsibility of the Akhil Bharatiya *Sharirik Pramukh*. He was appointed as Kshetra *pracharak*, Poorvanchal in 1977 and became Akhil Bharatiya *Boudhik Pramukh* in 1979. He was *sahsarkaryavah* since 1990. Sudarshan has also written a book on the Punjab problem. Besides his mother tongue, Kannada, he is conversant in Hindi, Marathi, Bengali, Assamese, Oriya, Gujarati and English. See *Organiser*, LI (34), 19 March 2000; also see *Frontline*, 17 (6), 18-31 March 2000.
134. Rajendra Singh's Address to the Akhil Bharatiya Pratinidhi Sabha of the RSS in Nagpur on 10 March 2000. See *Organiser*, LI (34), 19 March 2000.
135. Ibid.
136. *The Hindustan Times*, 13 March 2000.
137. 'Nagpur Calling', *The Times of India*, 13 March 2000.
138. See *The Hindustan Times*, 7 May 2000.
139. Swapan Dasgupta and Farzand Ahmed, 'Hawkish Postures', *India Today*, 27 March 2000, pp. 24-6.
140. *Organiser*, LI (34), 19 March 2000.
141. *India Today*, 27 March 2000, pp. 24-6.
142. Quoted by V. Venkatesan, 'A Saffron Move Stopped', *Frontline*, 17 (6), 18-31 March 2000.
143. Vajpayee hosted a tea-party at his residence on 30 March to felicitate K.S. Sudarshan, the new RSS chief, in which Rajju Bhaiya and other leaders of the *Sangh Parivar* were present. Besides economic issues, security matters, especially the situation in Jammu & Kashmir were also discussed. See *The Hindustan Times*, 31 March 2000.
144. *The Hindu*, 10 June 2000.
145. See *Organiser*, LI (52), 16 July 2000.

CHAPTER VIII

Conclusion

The circumstances leading to the foundation of the RSS spelt out the contours of its ideology and politics. Hindu-Muslim riots, disenchantment with Congress politics and assertion of non-Brahmin identity were crucial determinants of its worldview. But the incipient organization neither had enough strength to take on Gandhian mass-politics nor to stem the tide of the non-Brahmin challenge. Therefore, in the beginning, the RSS concentrated only on organizing and training selected Hindu boys to confront the Muslims during communal riots.

Hedgewar claimed India as a *Hindu Rashtra* (Hindu Nation). Golwalkar concretized this ideology. For the RSS, the *Hindu Rashtra* has been existing since time immemorial; rather than making India Hindu, it is only discovering, recognizing and asserting this identity. However, in reality, the RSS is constructing a Hindu identity quite meticulously and methodically by reinterpreting community, history and nation.

RSS understands that culture is much dearer to an individual than politics. A cultural pledge is more enduring than political commitment. Therefore, if a political commitment were ensured through a cultural medium, it would be long-standing. Accordingly, the RSS has been imparting political training to its cadre through a cultural discourse and the innovative use of Hindu cultural symbols and rituals. Thus, ideally, the political ideology of *Hindu Rashtra* does not appear political as it is expressed in the language of culture.

This training is facilitated by a cohesive, well-knit, hierarchical organization reflecting its politico-cultural framework. It is true to a great extent that individuals get attracted to the RSS not for its politics and ideology, but primarily for its outward cultural features. The regular *shakha* activities—the assembly of disciplined cadre in uniform, unfurling of *bhagwa dhwaj*, mass prayer, sports and games, the stories of brave Hindus narrated by *ascetic pracharaks*—entice the young and impressionable to the RSS. After their entry and initiation (*diksha*), their bond with the organization is further strengthened by the practice of a unique brotherhood. A *bal swayamsevak* is addressed by a *proudha swayamsevak* as *bhaiya* (brother), thereby enhancing the self-respect of the former. The brotherhood always stands by the individual *swayamsevak* despite the fact that the RSS is increasingly being unable to solve the substantive problems of its cadre.

The organization has many other cultural traits too. The *sarsanghchalak* and the *pracharaks* remain bachelors, thus demonstrating the Hindu emphasis on *tyag, tapasya* and *brahmacharya*. Their gospel, though poor in Hindu philosophy, is replenished with repetitive phrases and stanzas from Hindu scriptures. Golwalkar's personality further added to its cultural aura; Swami Akhandananda, a disciple of Ramakrishna Paramahansa, reportedly advised him to grow a beard as it would magnify his personality! Golwalkar's flowing beard and long hair gave him the look of a *rishi* (sage) and attracted many to the RSS fold during his long tenure. This also partly contributed to his absolute authority within the organization. Sangh *karyalayas* usually don a photograph of Golwalkar performing *yagna* (holy sacrifice) with the caption below, *Rashtraya Swaha* (Sacrifice to the Nation). In *yajnas* the names of gods and goddesses are invoked and sacrifice offered. Golwalkar added *Rashtra* (Nation) to the pantheon of Hindu gods. He could do so with ease because of his saintly image. Golwalkar's 'cultural nationalism', though political to the core, incessantly emphasized the cultural characteristics of a nation.

Despite these demonstrative Hindu cultural practices and rituals, the ideology and practice of the RSS undoubtedly negates the real spirit of Hindu traditions. Traditional Hinduism was more of a faith or multitude of faiths, rather than a restricted ideology. Philosophically, its sphere was *Brahmanda* (cosmos), not a defined physical space—the nation-state. In comparison, *Hindu Rashtra* appears to be precariously narrow. Traditional Hinduism is transcendental; but the ideology of *Hindu Rashtra* which preaches hatred against the enemy other cannot really transcend time and space. While Hindu traditions offer a wide range of paths to its followers, the 'character-building' (*charitra nirman*) process of the RSS *shakha* hardly offers any choice to its *swayamsevaks*. Though the RSS certainly deserves credit for attracting millions of promising youngsters to its fold, its unimaginative standardization and regimentation, and its cramped pedagogy fail to harness their true potential. However, the objective of the RSS is to train its members not for their individual salvation, but for the service of the *Hindu Rashtra*.

The ideology of *Hindu Rashtra* shows scant regard for the pluralist cultural traditions of Hinduism. The RSS stands for a mono-cultural Hinduism. The *Sangh Parivar* demolished *Thakurani ghara* (abode of tribal goddess) and forcibly stopped the practice of *dhangda dhangdi*—an 'uncivilized' tribal practice of choosing life partners—and set up *Bhagabata toongi* in the tribal district of Phulbani. Thus, the RSS opposes multiple cultural traditions for the sake of a standardized cultural uniformity. The attack on the Sahmat exibition makes it clear that *Hindu Rashtra* recognizes only one *Ramayana*, not many *Ramayanas*. The burning down of M.F. Hussain's paintings suggests that the iconography of Hinduism is too sacrosanct to be creatively interpreted, especially by a non-Hindu. The assault on Deepa Mehta's films *Fire* and *Water* warns that every cultural expression must conform to the tenets of *Hindutva*.

The RSS may not be fascist or fundamentalist as such, though it has demonstrated such potential on some occasions, particularly during the course of *Ram Janmabhoomi* agitation. The vicious anti-Muslim propaganda and violent mobilizations ultimately led to the demolition of the Babri Masjid—a fascist event beyond any doubt. Even in tribal areas like Phulbani, where the Christians outnumbered the Muslims, the *Sangh Parivar* conveniently shifted its focus on the Christians leading to the burning down of the churches, even though the Christians had nothing to do with Babri Masjid. Initially, the RSS pleaded for the supremacy of 'We'—the Hindus—against the Muslim 'other'. Muslims were the primary enemy of the *Hindu Rashtra*. Later, Golwalkar extended the boundary of the other by including Christians and Communists. Recently, the *Sangh Parivar* has been focusing on the Christians as the new other thereby instigating its militant cadre to unleash violence against this 'enemy'. Earlier, during the Sino-Indian war, it conveniently projected the Communists as the other—who was anti-national, and therefore, anti-Hindu. During the *Ram Janmabhoomi* agitation, the RSS further extended the boundary of the other to include 'pseudo-secularists'. Besides the emotional issue of Ram temple, the strong middle-class opposition to the reservation policy was cleverly used by the RSS. The present *sarsanghchalak* K.S. Sudarshan, has already hinted at an 'epic war' between the Hindus and 'anti-Hindus', thereby clarifying that it is not the minorities alone, even those Hindus who are opposed to the *Hindu Rashtra*, are regarded as the other. Thus, the RSS has the potential to become fundamentalist as its thrust on we versus the other could turn into 'we' versus the 'rest'. However, the biggest hurdle preventing the RSS to unleash fundamentalism is the absence of a monolithic 'we' and its failure to homogenize the Hindus.

Cultural politics has its own limitations. On the one hand, culture promotes politics; on the other, politics makes culture impure. As a result, the cultural politics of the *Sangh Parivar* is trapped in its own logic. The RSS was able to suppress a powerful Balraj Madhok in early 1970s when its ideological and organizational control was total over its political affiliate. Further, it was only at the fringe of political power. But the situation became different when it had become a major political player. The Shankersinh Vaghela phenomenon, which initially seemed to be an aberration, has grown rapidly with the ascendancy of the RSS in power politics. Who could ever imagine the *Sangh Parivar* dumping Kalyan Singh—once its Man Friday and the nucleus of the Ayodhya agitation? Kalyan Singh is not Madhok and his sphere of influence is UP, the Hindi heartland. Kalyans' tacit support to Sakshi Maharaj did prove costly for the BJP in UP in the 1999 general elections. He again contributed to the BJP's humiliating defeat in the panchayat elections held in 2000. Now he is determined to throw the BJP out of Lucknow in the forthcoming UP assembly elections. If this happens, the RSS will get a severe blow and its hold on Delhi may eventually weaken.

The problem is not limited to the BJP alone. It has been spreading to other affiliates as well. Friction is also emerging between one affiliate and the other; for instance, between the BJP and the VHP, the BJP and the SJM. As other affiliates grow in strength, they challenge the political affiliate and ask for their due share in political power which the BJP has been monopolizing so far. The VHP leadership claims to be more sacrosanct than the BJP because of its commitment to undiluted *Hindutva*. The SJM demonstrates its diehard economic nationalism and blames the BJP for compromising the sovereignty of the nation. Earlier the RSS had no problem in accommodating the rising stars of each affiliate. With rising expectations of even ordinary members to have shares in the power structure, it has become impossible for the RSS to satisfy everybody.

There is also an inherent tension between the *Sangh Parivar* and its newfound allies. The Shiv Sena, despite its commitment to *Hindutva*, has its own political compulsions. Not long ago, Balasaheb Thackeray mocked the RSS. He would neither allow the RSS to grow at his expense nor toe its political line. The Shiv Sena brought back Enron though the RSS promised to dump it in the Arabian Sea. It felicitated Michael Jackson despite the avowed opposition of the RSS to 'cultural imperialism'. It is also an irony that erstwhile socialists like George Fernandes, Sharad Yadav and Ram Vilas Paswan—the habitual Sangh baiters—have become the *Sangh Parivar's* trusted allies. It is further amusing to see that the RSS once courted Jayalalitha and now shares a cozy relationship with her arch rival—the DMK, which once championed 'Tamil nationalism' and fought against 'northern imperialism'. However, this changing relationship need not be dismissed as pure political expediency; it also indicates the shift of the Indian polity towards the Right.

The RSS has been facing other ideological dilemmas as well. All along it has underplayed the reality of caste identities for the sake of a seamless Hindu identity. It talked of integrating Dalits and tribals into the mainstream of Hinduism through a 'natural' way. However, in the context of increasing assertion of caste-based identities, particularly after the acceptance of the Mandal Commission Report and the emergence of the BSP, the RSS cannot afford to ignore the politics of caste. Thus, it has added to its lexicon phrases like 'social engineering' (*samajik samrastha*). This has posed a great dilemma. Its old class-caste base, which distinctly belonged to the upper and middle segment, gets threatened by the emergence of a new backward-lower caste leadership within the *Sangh Parivar.* Kalraj Mishra, a veteran BJS/BJP leader of Uttar Pradesh, had to bow to Kalyan Singh. More interestingly, the RSS had also found a strange bedfellow in Kanshi Ram's Bahujan Samaj Party, which consistently attacked the *Manuvadi* ideology of the RSS. Despite the failed experiment, the RSS is preparing the ground to counter the Kalyan phenomenon in UP. Even if these experiments are symbolic and strategic, they have definitely eroded its traditional upper caste support base.

Strategic changes are also evident in the RSS attitude towards regional politics. Golwalkar was a champion of a unitary State and never favoured the division of bigger states. Subsequently, the *Sangh Parivar* supported Uttaranchal in Uttar Pradesh, Jharkhand in Bihar and Chhattisgarh in Madhya Pradesh. Also, in areas like western Orissa, in many states they are demanding the creation of autonomous councils. As the RSS sees political potential in such demands, it has given support to these movements in order to channelize the popular sentiment towards its own politics and ideology. The RSS seems to be prepared to dilute its old stand on the unitary State for political gain. As the BJP came to power in Delhi only because of an alliance with regional parties, the RSS will obviously look at federalism afresh. At the same time, the outright rejection of the Autonomy Resolution of the Jammu & Kashmir legislative assembly by the cabinet clearly suggests that the RSS will never like to see a weak centre.

These strategic changes adopted by the RSS to facilitate its rise in the political arena do not suggest of any ideological revision of the notion of *Hindu Rashtra.* The RSS has a remarkable capacity to take a complete reverse turn and yet ideologically justify its position. Its various fronts take up several projects simultaneously thereby giving the impression of representing different voices, though all of them actually have the same voice. The Swadeshi Jagaran Manch could still remain anti-Enron though the BJP supported its revival. The VHP could still speak of 'liberation' of Kashi and Mathura though the BJP publicly denies that they do not figure in its agenda. The Bajrang Dal could still vigorously pursue its anti-Christian pogroms while Vajpayee assures the Pope of their safety and protection. True, power politics has exacerbated conflicts and contradictions in the *Sangh Parivar.* But by and large these are more apparent than real and the RSS has managed them remarkably well.

Converting India into a *Hindu Rashtra* may remain a distant dream. But there is no doubt that the politics and ideology of the RSS is spreading at a faster pace incorporating new social groups and regions. At many places Hindu traditions are giving way to *Hindutva*—tolerance to violence and community consciousness to communal consciousness. The RSS tryst with politics has reached a crucial stage with its control over the State apparatus. Now it will consolidate its position further and using State power it will try to control every sphere of civil society. Political power is not enough for the RSS; its real mission is Hindu hegemony.

APPENDIX

Visit to a RSS Camp

During the Summer of 1995, the *swayamsevaks* of Orissa were participating in three Officers' Training Camps (OTCs): the 1st Year all-Orissa OTC (*Sangh Shiksha Barga*) at Bidyadharpur (Cuttack), the 2nd Year OTC at Brajarajnagar (Sambalpur) and the 3rd Year OTC at Nagpur. (While the numbers of participants were 290, 139 in first two camps respectively, 47 *swayamsevaks* from Orissa went to Nagpur to complete their 3rd year OTC.) I conveyed my desire to visit the Cuttack camp to Bhupendra Kumar Basu, the *prant sanghchalak* of Orissa. He gladly accepted my request and asked me to come with him to the camp on 11 June.

The camp site was a few kilometres away from the main road, the car had to pass through a narrow *kuchcha* road to reach site around 10 a.m. It was an isolated building surrounded by agricultural fields. A *swayamsevak* in uniform opened the locked gate. The organizers greeted us with the traditional *namaskar*. The *sanghachalak* of the Eastern Zone (known as *Agneya Kshetra*), Dr. Subramanyam Shastri, touched the feet of Bose. Though in terms of organizational hierarchy Shastri's position is above Bose, his gesture confirmed how the seniority in age commands respect amongst the RSS functionaries.

The *sarvadhikari* (chief) of the camp was Dr. Dhaneshwar Mohapatra, a retired principal and a known figure in Oriya literature. He admitted that he was only a nominal head. The real head was the *karyavah* (secretary), Gopal Mohapatra, a young Sanskrit lecturer. Mohapatra was well organized and articulate and gave the details of various activities of the camp. The duration of the camp was for 20 days. Each participant paid a fee of Rs 300. The additional expenses would be met with the donations of the well-wishers.

Composition of the Trainees

Shakhas represented:	194
Total participants:	350
Prabasi karyakartas:	22
Mukshya shikshaks:	160
Matriculates (passed + appeared):	46
Secondary (passed + appeared):	72
Graduates:	69

Farmers:	22
Businessmen:	12
School Teachers:	22
College Teachers (Govt. and Private):	7
Service-holders:	29
Pracharaks/Vistaraks:	3
Others:	1

Daily Routine

3-45 a.m.	*Jagarana*
4-45 a.m.	*Sampat-Ekatmata Stotra*
5-05 a.m.–7-30 a.m.:	*Sanghasthana*
7-45 a.m.:	*Jalapana-Snanha*
9-00 a.m.:	*Sampat*
9-15 a.m.–10 a.m.:	*Baithak*
10-15 a.m.–11-15 a.m.:	*Charcha*
11-45 a.m.:	*Bhojana Mantra*
1-45 p.m.:	*Jagarana*
2 p.m.–2-45 p.m.:	*Boudhik Karyakram*
3 p.m.:	*Sampat*
3-15 p.m.–4-15 p.m.:	*Boudhik*
5 p.m.–6-40 p.m.:	*Sanghasthana*
7 p.m.:	*Sampat*
7-45 p.m.–8-45 p.m.:	*Ratri Karyakram*
9-15 p.m.:	*Bhojana Mantra*
10 p.m.:	*Dipa Bisarjana*

The trainees were found to be adhering to the above time schedule punctually. The activities had been designed to teach the participants the games, exercises and songs which form the basis of the *shakha's* programme. But the physical exercises (*sharirik*) were conducted under experienced and efficient instructors and seemed to be more rigorous. Similarly, the intellectual exercise (*boudhik*) was more intense. Everyday there was a *boudhik* session and prominent RSS leaders provided the trainees with a concentrated dose of ideology. These *boudhiks* focused on the ideology of the *Hindu Rashtra*, the need for Hindu unity and contemporary national and international problems. The participants were motivated to learn certain aspects of Indian culture and language. For example, 11 June, the day I visited the camp, was observed as *Sanskruta Divas* (Sanskrit Day). The instructors were teaching every trainee to communicate in Sanskrit only on that day. The trainees were trying their best with broken Sanskrit.

Boudhik (Ideological Discourse)

On that day, Gopal Mohapatra, the *karyavah* of the camp, delivered the *boudhik*. The theme was RSS ideology. The summary of his speech is as follows: It is wrong to perceive the RSS as one of the organizations in the society; actually it has been involved in organizing the society as a whole. It is not a *sanstha* (institution) but a *vyavastha* (system). The RSS worships *pratibha* (talent) not *pratima* (image); it is *tatva nishtha* and *dhaiya nishtha* but not *byakti nishtha*. In other words, the RSS puts premium on ideology and practice, rather than individual leadership. The *swayamsevak* is like a brick and the *adhikari* (officer) a mason. And it is the discretion of the mason to put the brick wherever it would fit in. The RSS is a family and therefore, one finds no *samalochana* (criticism) but only *singhabalokana* (introspection). There is no question of 'I' in the RSS, it has to be sacrificed for the nation. Golwalkar has rightly said *Rashtraya Swaha*. The objective of the RSS is clearly stated in the prayer and the oath, it is *param vaibhav* (pinnacle of glory) of *Hindu Rashtra*. The *swayamsevaks* must become *dhaiya nistha* or to practice the ideology in one's life to achieve this objective. Action, not words, is important. There should be a proper harmony between *achara*, *bichara* and *uchchara* (action, thought and speech).

The most impressive aspect of the camp life was its emphasis on group solidarity and community life. The participants addressed each other as brother (*bhai* or *bhaiya*). They took turns performing all the work in the camp, thus leaving scope for nobody to develop any sense of superiority vis-a-vis other members. More importantly, there was no discrimination between the leaders and the trainee *swayamsevaks*. During the lunch time everybody including the *sanghchalak* of the Eastern Zone and the *prant sanghchalak* of Orissa sat on the floor and took the same food with the trainees.

Bibliography

PRIVATE PAPERS

B.S. Moonje Papers (Nehru Memorial Museum & Library, Delhi).
K.R. Malkani Papers (Nehru Memorial Museum & Library, Delhi).
M.R. Jayakar Papers (National Archives of India, Delhi).
V.D. Savarkar Papers (Nehru Memorial Museum & Library, Delhi).

OFFICIAL RECORDS

Home Department Political Files (National Archives of India, Delhi)
Census of India, 1991.

INTERVIEWS

Baburao Deshpande (*Prant Sampark-Pramukh*, RSS, Orissa), 17 November 1994.

Baburao Paldhikar (first *Prant Pracharak*, RSS, Orissa), 23 November 1994 and 12 June 1995.

Bhupendra Kumar Basu (*Prant Sanghchalak*, RSS, Orissa), 10 and 11 June 1995.

Bishwanath Pandit (Socialist Leader, Orissa), 10 October 1996.

Chandrakant Nath (wholetimer, VKA, Raikia, Phulabani), 30 November 1994.

Damodar Dash (former Organizing Secretary, VHP, Orissa), 8 October 1996.

Debendra Pradhan (former President, BJP, Orissa), 18 February 1997.

Harihara Nanda (former *Prant Pracharak*, RSS, Orissa), 22 November 1994.

Jagabandhu Mishra (ed., *Rashtradeepa*, RSS Weekly), 22 November 1994.

Mukund Deo (ABVKA Activist and Secretary, *Shankaracharya Kanyashram*, Jalaspatta), 1 December 1995.

Pyarelal Khandelwal (*pracharak*, present *prabhari*, BJP, Orissa), 18 February 1997.

Raghunatha Sethi (*pracharak*), 29 November 1994.

Samir Mohanty (BJP Activist), 16 February 1997.

Shyamsundar Mishra (President, Shiksha Vikas Samiti, Orissa), 10 June 1995.

Sudipta Ray (former All-India Secretary, ABVP), 17 February 1997.

PUBLICATIONS OF THE RSS AND ITS AFFILIATES

Advani, L.K., *Why Rathayatra?* (Bangalore: Jagarana Prakashana, 1990).

Aggarwal, S.K., *Dr. Ambedkar on Muslim Fundamentalism* (Delhi: Suruchi Prakashan, 1993).

Agnihotri, Ramashankar, *Dr. Hedgewar: Ek Chamatkar* [in Hindi] (Jaipur: Gyan Ganga Prakashan, n.d.).

Akhil Bharatiya Vanavasi Kalyan Ashram, *Report of Akhil Bharatiya Vanavasi Kalyan Asram, Orissa* (Sundergarh, Orissa: ABVKA, 28 February 1995).

Akhil Bharatiya Vidyarthi Parishad, *Annual Report of the General Secretary of the ABVP presented at 41st National Conference held at Nagpur* [18-21 November 1995] (Mumbai: Central Office, ABVP, n.d.).

Bharatiya Jana Sangh, *Jana Sangh Souvenir* (Delhi: Rakesh Press, 1969).

———, *Democracy With Discipline: Advani-Madhok Correspondence* (Delhi: A Jana Sangh Publication, n.d.).

———, *Presidential Address: Shri L.K. Advani* [18th All India Session, Kanpur, 9, 10, 11 February 1973] (Delhi: n.d.).

Bharatiya Janata Party, *Our Five Commitments* (Delhi: BJP Publication, 1980).

———, *BJP's White Paper on Ayodhya & The Rama Temple Movement* (Delhi: Bharatiya Janata Party Central Office, 1993).

Bhishikar, C.P., *Keshavah Sangha Nirmata* [trans. from Marathi to Hindi by Moreshwar Tapasvi] (New Delhi: Suruchi Prakashan, 1991).

———, *Sangh Vriksh Ke Beej: Dr. Keshavrao Hedgewar* [in Hindi] (Delhi: Suruchi Prakashan, 1994).

Chande, M.B., *Shree Ram Janma Bhoomi* (Nagpur: Shri M.B. Chande, 1992).

Chitaranjan, *Facts About RSS: Mist of Motivated Propaganda Shattered* (Delhi: Suruchi Sahitya, n.d.).

Deendayal Research Institute, *How Others Look at the RSS* (Delhi: Deendayal Research Institute, 1989).

———, *The Russian Revolution & Its Impact on the World: Seminar Papers & Discussions* (Delhi: Deendayal Research Institute, 1988).

Deoras, Balasaheb, *R.S.S. and the Present Controversy* (Delhi: Suruchi Sahitya Prakashan, n.d.).

———, *Hindu Sangathan: The Need Of The Nation* (Delhi: Suruchi Sahitya, n.d.).

———, *Social Equality and Hindu Consolidation* (Delhi: Yugantar Sahitya Prakashan, 1981).

———, *Country's Unity A Must* (Delhi: Suruchi Sahitya Prakashan, 1985).

Devendra Swarup, ed., *Politics of Conversion* (Delhi: Deendayal Research Institute, 1986).

Devi, Savitri, *A Warning to the Hindus* (Meerut: Hindi-Vikas-Peeth, 1989).

Dwivedi, Vireshwar, *Sangh Neeb Me Bisarjeet*, Pratham Pushp [in Hindi] (Lucknow: Lokhit Prakashan, 1989).

———, *Sangh Neeb Me Bisarjeet*, Dwitiya Pushp [in Hindi] (Lucknow: Lokhit Prakashan, 1990).

Golwalkar, M.S., *We or Our Nationhood Defined* (Nagpur: Bharat Publications, 1939, with a foreword by Loknayak M.S. Aney).

———, *Bunch of Thoughts* [1966] (Bangalore: Jagarana Prakashana, 1980).

Golwalkar, M.S., Deendayal Upadhyaya, D.B. Thengadi, *Integral Approach* (Delhi: Suruchi Prakashan, 1991).

Nene, V.V., *Pandit Deendayal Upadhyaya: Ideology and Perception, Part-II, Integral Humanism* [trans. by M.K. Paranjape and D.R. Kulkarni] (Delhi: Suruchi Prakashan, 1991).

Palkar, Narayan Hari, *Dr. Hedgewar* [in Hindi](Prayag: Dr. Surendra Mital, 1962).

———, *Bhagwa Dhwaj* [In Hindi] (Lucknow: Lokhit Prakashana, 1992).

———, ed., *Dr. Hedgewar: Patraroop Vyaktidarshan* [trans. from Marathi to Hindi by Mukund Hambarde] (Indore: Archana Prakashan, 1989).

Parameswaran, P., ed., *Gandhi, Lohia Deendayal* (Delhi: Deendayal Research Institute, 1978).

Raje, Sudhakar, ed., *Pandit Deendayal Upadhyaya: A Profile* (Delhi: Deendayal Research Institute, 1972).

———, *Destination: Nation's Tribute to Deendayal Upadhyaya* (Delhi: Deendayal Research Institute, 1978).

Rao, K. Suryanarayana, *Hindu Rashtra: It is not a mere Slogan but the Vibrant Reality* (Madras: Vigil, 1990).

Rashtriya Swayamsevak Sangh, *Shri Guruji on the Muslim Problem: Dr. Saaiffuddin Jeelany's Interview with Shri Guruji* (Delhi: Suruchi Sahitya, n.d.).

———, *From Red Fort Grounds* [free English-rendering of the speech delivered by Shri M.S. Golwalkar, Sarsanghchalak of RSS, at a public rally on the Red Fort Grounds, Delhi on 14 November 1965] (Delhi: Asia Press, n.d.).

———, *Heralding A New Era: A Bird's Eye View of Dr. Hedgewar Birth Centenary Celebrations* (Bangalore: Jagarana Prakashana, 1989).

———, *Justice on Trial: Historic Document of Guruji-Government Correspondence* (Bangalore: Sharada Press, 1968).

———, *RSS Spearheading National Renaissance* (Bangalore: RSS-Karnatak Prakashan Vibhag, 1985).

———, *Shri Guruji, Man and His Mission: On the Occasion of His 51st Birthday* (Delhi: Bharat Prakashan, 1957).

———, *'Angry Hindhu!'-Yes, Why Not? Why Hindus in the Dock?* (Delhi: Suruchi Prakashan, 1988).

———, *Balasaheb's Speech in Jamshedpur* (Delhi: Suruchi Sahitya, 1981).

———, *Balasaheb Deoras with Delhi Newsmen in The Press Club of India, 12 March 1979* (Delhi: Suruchi Prakashan, n.d.).

———, *My Dear Fellow Sikhs* (Delhi: Suruchi Prakashan, 1987).

———, *Mysore High Court on RSS: A Historic Judgement* (Bangalore: RSS-Karnatak Prakashan Vibhag, 1968).

———, *Pandit Deendayal Upadhyaya: Ideology and Perception*, Vols. I-VI (Delhi: Suruchi Prakashan, 1991).

———, *RSS - A Bird's Eye View* (Bangalore: Prakashan Vibhag, 1978).

———, *RSS: Ready for Selfless Service* (Bangalore: Jagaran Prakashan, 1979).

———, *Sangha Darshan* (Bangalore: Prakashan Vibhag, RSS-Karnatak, 1964).

———, *Shri Balasaheb Deoras Answers Questions* (Bangalore: Sahitya Sindhu, 1984).

———, *Shri Guruji Meets Delhi Newsmen*, 3rd edn. (Delhi: Suruchi Sahitya, n.d.).

———, *The Shah Bano Case: Nation Speaks Out* (Bangalore: Jagarana Prakashana, 1986).

———, *Sarsanghchalak Goes Abroad* [Compiled by Dr. Shankar Tattwawadi] (Delhi: Suruchi Prakashan, 1995).

Rastogi, Gaurinath, *Our Kashmir* (Delhi: Suruchi Prakashan, 1991).

Seshadri, H.V., *Hindus Abroad-The Dilema: Dollar or Dharma?* (Delhi: Suruchi Prakashan, 1990).

———, *The Way* (Delhi: Suruchi Prakashan, 1991).

———, *RSS: A Vision in Action* (Bangalore: Jagarana Prakashana, 1988).

———, ed., *Dr. Hedgewar: The Epoch Maker* (Bangalore: Sahitya Sindhu, 1981).

Seshadri, H.V., K.S. Sudarshan, K. Surya Narain Rao and Balraj Madhok, *Why Hindu Rashtra?* (Delhi: Suruchi Prakashan, 1990).

Singh, Rajendra, *Ever-Vigilant We Have To Be* (Delhi: Suruchi Prakashan, 1994).

———, *Ayodhya Episode: A Turning Point* (Delhi: Suruchi Prakashan, 1993).

Talreja, Kanayalal M., *Pseudo-secularism in India* (Mumbai: Rashtriya Chetna Prakashan, 1996).

Thengadi, Dattopant, *RSS Lights Up—The Path to Eternal Glory* (Bangalore: Jagarana Prakashana, 1979).

Tripathi, Vachnesh and Kaushelendra Kumar, eds., *Dr. Hedgewar: Prerak Jivan Prasang* [in Hindi] (Lucknow: Lokhit Prakashan, 1992).

Upadhyaya, Deendayal, *Integral Humanism* (Delhi: Bharatiya Jana Sangh Central Office, 1965).

Vajpayee, Atal Behari, Lal Krishna Advani, Swami Chinmayanand and Rajendra Singh, *Hindus Betrayed* (Delhi: Suruchi Prakashan, 1993).

Vigil (A Public Opinion Forum), *Hindu Heritage—Assimilative, Not Divisive* (Madras: Vigil, 1993).

NEWSPAPERS AND JOURNALS

Economic and Political Weekly (Bombay)
Frontline (Madras)
Hindu Vishwa (Prayag)
India Today (Delhi)
Mainstream (Delhi)

Organiser (Delhi)
Outlook (Delhi)
Seminar (Delhi)
The Economic Times (Delhi)
The Hindu (Delhi)
The Hindustan Times (Delhi)
The Hitavad (Nagpur)
The Pioneer (Delhi)
The Times of India (Delhi)
The Week (Kochi)

UNPUBLISHED THESES

Flynn, Barbara Wilmot, 'Communalization of Politics: National Political Activity in India, 1926-30', Ph.D. Thesis, Duke University, 1974.

Davey, Hampton Thompson, Jr., 'The Transformation of an Ideological Movement into an Aggregative Party: A Case Study of the Bharatiya Jana Sangh', Ph.D. Thesis, University of California, Los Angeles, 1969.

Venkateswar, Shyama, 'Hindu Nationalism in India: The Impact of Political and Social Realignments', Ph.D. Thesis, University of Columbia, 1997.

BOOKS

Ahmed, Raffiuddin, *The Bengal Muslims 1871-1906: A Quest for Identity* (Delhi: Oxford University Press, 1981).

Ali, M. Athar, *The Mughal Nobility Under Aurangzeb* (Bombay: Asia Publishing House, 1968).

Allen, Douglas, ed., *Religion and Political Conflict in South Asia: India, Pakistan, and Sri Lanka* (Delhi: Oxford University Press, 1993).

Anandhi, S., *Contending Identities: Dalits and Secular Politics in Madras Slums* (Delhi: Indian Social Science Institute, 1995).

Andersen, Walter K. and Shridhar D. Damle, *The Brotherhood in Saffron: The Rashtriya Swayamsevak Sangh and Hindu Revivalism* (Delhi: Vistaar Publications, 1987).

Anderson, Benedict, *Imagined Communities: Reflections on the Origin and Spread of Nationalism* (London: Verso, 1983).

Appadurai, Arjun, *Modernity at Large: Cultural Dimension of Globalization* (Delhi: Oxford University Press, 1997).

Arslan, Mehdi and Janaki Rajan, eds., *Communalism in India: Challenge and Response* (Delhi: Manohar, 1994).

Baig, M.R.A., *The Muslim Dilemma in India* (Delhi: Vikas Publishing House, 1974).

Baird, Robert D., ed., *Religion in Modern India* (Delhi: Manohar, 1989).

Baker, D.E.U., *Changing Political Leadership in an Indian Province: The Central Provinces and Berar 1919-1939* (Delhi: Oxford University Press, 1979).

Barnett, Marguerite Ross, *The Politics of Cultural Nationalism* (Princeton: Princeton University Press, 1976).

Barrier, N.G., ed., *The Census in British India: New Perspective* (Delhi: Manohar, 1981).

Basu, Kaushik and Sanjay Subrahmanyam, eds., *Unravelling the Nation: Sectarian Conflict and India's Secular Identity* (Delhi: Penguin Books, 1996).

Basu, Tapan, Pradip Datta, Sumit Sarkar, Tanika Sarkar and Sambuddha Sen, *Khaki Shorts and Saffron Flags: A Critique of the Hindu Right* (Delhi: Orient Longman, 1993).

Baxter, Craig, *The Jana Sangh: A Biography of an Indian Political Party* (Bombay: Oxford University Press, 1967).

Benavides, Gustavo and M.W. Daly, eds., *Religion and Political Power* (Albany: State University of New York Press, 1989).

Berger, Peter L., *The Social Reality of Religion* (London: Faber and Faber, 1967).

Bhai Paramanand, *Hindu Sangathan* (Lahore: The Hindu Yuvak Sabha, 1936).

Bhambri, C.P., *The Janata Party: A Profile* (Delhi: National Publishing House, 1980).

Biardeau, Madeleine, *Hinduism: The Anthropology of A Civilization* (Delhi: Oxford University Press, 1989).

Bidwai, Praful, Harbans Mukhia and Achin Vanaik, eds., *Religion, Religiosity and Communalism* (Delhi: Manohar, 1996).

Biswas, S.K., *Hindu Raj: Today-Yesterday-Tomorrow* (Bangalore: Orion Books, 1996).

Bjorkman, James Warner, ed., *Fundamentalism, Revivalists and Violence in South Asia* (Delhi: Manohar, 1988).

Bocock, Robert and Kenneth Thompson, eds., *Religion and Ideology: A Reader* (Manchester: Manchester University Press, 1985).

Bokare, M.G., *Swadeshi Economy for War of Economic Imperialism* (Mumbai: Swadeshi Jagaran Manch, 1993).

———, *Hindu Economics [Eternal Economic Order]* (Delhi: Janaki Prakashan, 1993).

Brass, Paul R., ed., *Language, Religion and Politics in North India* (Cambridge: Cambridge University Press, 1974).

Breckenridge, C.A., ed., *Consuming Modernity: Public Culture in a South Asian World* (Menneapolis: University of Minnesota Press, 1995).

Bright, Jagat S., *Guruji Golwalkar & R.S.S.* (Delhi: New India Publishing House, 1950).

Butler, David, Ashok Lahiri and Prannoy Roy, *India Decides: Elections 1952-1995* (Delhi: Books and Things, 1995).

Carr, William, *Hitler: A Study in Personality and Politics* (London: Edward Arnold, 1978).

Chakravarty, Papia, *Hindu Response to Nationalist Ferment* (Calcutta: Subarnarekha, 1992).

Chandra, Bipin, *Communalism in Modern India* (Delhi: Vikas Publishing House, 1987).

Chatterjee, Abhas, *The Concept of Hindu Nation* (Delhi: Voice of India, 1995).

Chatterjee, Partha, *Nationalist Thought and the Colonial World: A Derivative Discourse?* (Delhi: Oxford University Press, 1986).

———, *The Nation and Its Fragments: Colonial and Postcolonial Histories* (Delhi: Oxford University Press, 1995).

Chatterjee, Partha and Gyanendra Pandey, eds., *Subaltern Studies VII: Writings on South Asian History and Society* (Delhi: Oxford University Press, 1993).

Chatterjee, P.C., ed., *Self-Images, Identity and Nationality* (Shimla: Indian Institute of Advanced Studies, 1989).

Cohen, A.P., *The Symbolic Construction of Community* (London: Ellis Harwood Limited, 1985).

Copley, Antony, *Religions in Conflict: Ideology, Cultural Contact and Conversion in Late Colonial India* (Delhi: Oxford University Press, 1997).

Coward, Harold G., ed., *Modern Indian Responses to Religious Pluralism* (Albany: State University of New York, 1987).

Crook, Nigel, ed., *The Transmission of Knowledge in South Asia: Essays on Education, Religion, History, and Politics* (Delhi: Oxford University Press, 1996).

Crossman, Brenda and Ratna Kapoor, *Secularism's Last Sigh?: Hindutva and the (Mis) Rule of Law* (Delhi: Oxford University Press, 1999).

Curran, Jean A., Jr., *Militant Hinduism in Indian Politics: A Study of the R.S.S.* (New York: Institute of Pacific Relations, 1951).

Dalmia, Vasudha and Heinrich von Stietencron, eds., *Representing Hinduism: The Construction of Religious Traditions and National Identity* (Delhi: Sage Publications, 1995).

Dandekar, R.N., *Insights into Hinduism* (Delhi: Ajanta Publications, 1979).

Das, Suranjan, *Communal Riots in Bengal 1905-1947* (Delhi: Oxford University Press, 1991).

Das, Suranjan and Sekhar Bandyopadhyay, eds., *Caste and Communal Politics in South Asia* (Calcutta: K.P. Bagchi & Company, 1993).

Das, Veena, *Critical Events: An Anthropological Perspective on Contemporary India* (Delhi: Oxford University Press, 1995).

———, ed., *Mirrors of Violence: Communities, Riots and Survivors in South Asia* (Delhi: Oxford University Press, 1990).

Deshmukh, Nana, *RSS Victim of Slander: A Multidimensional Study of RSS, Jana Sangh, Janata Party and the Present Political Crisis* (Delhi: Vision Books, 1979).

Dhooria, Ram Lall, *I was a Swayamsevak: An Inside View of the RSS* (Delhi: Sampradayikta Virodhi Committee, n.d.).

Dube, Leela et al., eds., *Visibility and Power: Essays on Women in Society and Development* (Delhi: Oxford University Press, 1986).

Eaton, Richard, *The Rise of Islam and the Bengal Frontier: 1204-1760* (Berkeley: University of California Press, 1993).

Elenjimittam, Anthony, *Philosophy and Action of the R.S.S. for the Hind Swaraj* (Bombay: Laxmi Publications, 1951).

Elst, Koenraad, *Negationism in India: Concealing the Record of Islam* (New Delhi: Voice of India, 1992).

———, *Ramjanambhoomi vs. Babri Masjid: A Case Study in Hindu-Muslim Conflict* (New Delhi: Voice of India, 1990).

———, *Dr. Ambedkar: A True Aryan* (New Delhi: Voice of India, 1993).

Embree, Ainslie T., *Utopias in Conflict: Religion and Nationalism in Modern India* (Delhi: Oxford University Press, 1990).

Engineer, Asghar Ali, ed., *Communal Riots in Post-Independence India* (New Delhi: Sangam Books, 1985).

———, *Politics of Confrontation: The Babri Masjid-Ramjanambhoomi Controversy Runs Riot* (Delhi: Ajanta, 1992).

Fernandes, Walter K., ed., *The Indigenous Question: Search For An Identity* (Delhi: Indian Social Institute, 1993).

Frawley, David, *The Myth of the Aryan Invasion of India* (Delhi: Voice of India, 1995).

Freitag, Sandria B., *Collective Action and Community: Public Arenas and the Emergence of Communalism in North India* (Delhi: Oxford University Press, 1990).

Gandhi, M.K., *The Essence of Hinduism* (Ahmedabad: Navjivan Trust, 1987).

Gangadharan, K.K., *Sociology of Revivalism: A Study of Indianisation, Sanskritisation and Golwalkarism* (Delhi: Kalamkar, 1970).

Geertz, Clifford, *The Interpretation of Cultures* (New York: Basic Books, 1973).

Gellner, Ernest, ed., *Culture, Identity and Politics* (London: Cambridge University Press, 1987).

Ghose, Rajeshwari, ed., *In Quest of A Secular Symbol: Ayodhya and After* (Perth: Indian Ocean Centre and South Asian Research Unit, Curtin University of Technology, 1996).

Ghosh, Partha S., *BJP and the Evolution of Hindu Nationalism: From Periphery to Centre* (Delhi: Manohar, 1999).

Ghurye, G.S., *Indian Sadhus* (Bombay: Popular Prakashan, 1964).

Goel, Sitaram, ed., *Time for Stock Taking: Whither Sangh Parivar?* (Delhi: Voice of India, 1997).

Gold, Daniel, *The Lord as Guru: Hindi Sants in North Indian Tradition* (New York: Oxford University Press, 1987).

Gopal, S., ed., *Anatomy of Confrontation: The Babri Masjid-Ramjanmabhumi Dispute* (Delhi: Viking, 1991).

Gore, M.S., *The Social Context of an Ideology: Ambedkar's Political and Social Thought* (Delhi: Sage Publications, 1993).

Goyal, D.R., *Rashtriya Swayamsevak Sangh* (Delhi: Radha Krishna Prakashan, 1979).

Graham, Bruce D., *Hindu Nationalism and Indian Politics: The Origins and Development of the Bharatiya Jana Sangh* (Cambridge: Cambridge University Press, 1990).

Gupta, Dipankar, *The Context of Ethnicity: Sikh Identity in a Comparative Perspective* (Delhi: Oxford University Press, 1996).

———, *Rivalry & Brotherhood: Politics in the Life of Farmers in Northern India* (Delhi: Oxford University Press, 1997).

Gupta, Patha Sarathi, ed., *Towards Freedom: Documents on the Movement for Independence in India 1943-1944*, Part III (Delhi: Oxford University Press, 1997).

Halbfass, Wilhelm, *Tradition and Reflection: Explorations in Indian Thought* (Albany: State University of New York Press, 1991).

Hansen, Thomas Blom, *The Saffron Wave: Democracy and Hindu Nationalism in Modern India* (Delhi: Oxford University Press, 1999).

Hasan, Mushirul, *Nationalism and Communal Politics in India 1885-1930* (Delhi: Manohar, 1991).

Hawley, John Stratton, ed., *Saints and Virtues* (Berkeley: University of California Press, 1987).

———, *Fundamentalism and Gender* (New York: Oxford University Press, 1994).

———, *Sati, the Blessing and the Curse: The Burning of Wives in India* (New York: Oxford University Press, 1994).

Heimsath, Charles, *Indian Nationalism and Hindu Social Reform* (Princeton: Princeton University Press, 1964).

Hutchinson, John and Anthony D. Smith, eds., *Nationalism* (Oxford: Oxford University Press, 1994).

Ilaiah, Kancha, *Why I am not a Hindu: A Sudra Critique of Hindutva Philosophy Culture and Political Economy* (Calcutta: Samya, 1996).

Jaffrelot, Christophe, *The Hindu Nationalist Movement and Indian Politics 1925 to the 1990s: Strategies of Identity-Building, Implantation and Mobilisation [with special reference to Central India]* (Delhi: Viking Penguin India, 1996).

Jain, Girilal, *The Hindu Phenomenon* (Delhi: UBS Publishers' Distributors Ltd., 1994).

Jayaprasad, K., *R.S.S. and Hindu Nationalism: Inroads in a Leftist Stronghold* (Delhi: Deep & Deep, 1991).

Jenks, Chris, *Culture* (London: Routledge, 1993).

Jhangiani, Motilal A., *Jana Sangh and Swatantra: A Profile of the Rightist Parties in India* (Bombay: Manaktalas, 1967).

Jog, B.N., *Threat of Islam: Indian Dimensions* (Bombay: Unnati Prakashan, 1994).

Jones, Kenneth W., *Arya Dharm: Hindu Consciousness in Nineteenth Century Punjab* (Delhi: Manohar, 1976).

Jordens, J.T.F., *Dayananda Saraswati: His Life and Ideas* (Delhi: Oxford University Press, 1981).

———, *Swami Shradhanand: His Life and Causes* (Delhi: Oxford University Press, 1981).

Joshi, Barbara, *Untouchable! Voices of Dalit Liberation* (London: Zed Books, 1984).

Joshi, Shashi and Bhagwan Josh, *Struggle for Hegemony in India 1920-47: Culture, Community and Power*, Vol. III: *1941-47* (Delhi: Sage Publications, 1994).

Joshi, Subhadra, *RSS: Is it a Cultural Organisation?* (Delhi: Sampradayikta Virodhi Committee, 1966).

———, *RSS: Is it a Political Organisation?* (Delhi: Sampradayikta Virodhi Committee, n.d.).

———, ed., *RSS: A Danger to Democracy* (Delhi: Sampradayikta Virodhi Committee, 1967).

Juergensmeyer, Mark, *Religious Nationalism Confronts the Secular State* (Delhi: Oxford University Press, 1995).

Kakar, Sudhir, *The Inner World: A Psychoanalytic Study of Childhood and Society in India* (Delhi: Oxford University Press, 1981).

———, *The Colours of Violence* (Delhi: Viking, 1995).

Kamenka, Eugene, ed., *Community as a Social Ideal* (London: Edward Arnold, 1982).

Karmarkar, D.P., *Bal Gangadhar Tilak: A Study* (Bombay: Popular Book Depot, 1956).

Karunakaran, K.P., *Continuity and Change in Indian Politics* (Delhi: People's Publishing House, 1964).

Keer, Dhananjay, *Veer Savarkar* (Bombay: Popular Prakashan, 1966).

Khan, Rasheeduddin, *Bewildered India: Identity, Pluralism, Discord* (Delhi: Har Anand Publications, 1994).

Khare, R.S., *Cultural Diversity and Social Discontent: Anthropological Studies on Contemporary India* (Delhi: Sage Publications, 1998).

Kinsley, David R., *Hinduism: A Cultural Perspective* (New Jersey: Prentice Hall, 1993).

Klostermaiere, Klaus K., *A Survey of Hinduism* (New York: State University of New York Press, 1989).

Kohli, Atul, *Democracy and Discontent: India's Growing Crisis of Governability* (Cambridge: Cambridge University Press, 1991).

Kopf, David, *British Orientalism and the Bengal Renaissance* (Berkeley: University of California Press, 1969).

———, *The Brahmo Samaj and the Shaping of the Modern Indian Mind* (Princeton: Princeton University Press, 1979).

Kothari, Rajni, *Politics in India* (Delhi: Orient Longman, 1970).

Krishna Iyer, V.R., *Religion and Politics* (Delhi: Konark Publishers, 1991).

Laclau, Ernesto, ed., *The Making of Political Identities* (London: Verso, 1994).

Lal Chand, R.B., *Self Abnegation in Politics* (Lahore: The Central Hindu Yuvak Sabha, 1938).

Lele, Jayant K., *Hindutva: The Emergence of the Right* (Madras: Earthworm Books, 1995).

Leslie, Julia, ed., *Roles and Rituals for Hindu Women* (London: Pinter Publishers, 1991).

Limaye, Madhu, *Janata Party Experiment: An Insider's Account of Opposition Politics 1975-1977*, Vols. I and II (Delhi: B.R. Publishing Corporation, 1994).

———, *Religious Bigotry: A Threat to Ordered State* (Delhi: Ajanta Publications, 1994).

Llewellyn, J.E., *The Arya Samaj as a Fundamentalist Movement: A Study in Comparative Fundamentalism* (Delhi: Manohar, 1993).

Lorenzen, David N., *Bhakti Religion in North India: Community Identity and Political Action* (Albany: State University of New York Press, 1995).

Ludden, David, ed., *Making India Hindu: Religion, Community and the Politics of Democracy in India* (Delhi: Oxford University Press, 1996).

MacLellan, David, *Ideology* (Milton Keynes: Open University Press, 1986).

Madan, T.N., ed., *Religion in India* (Delhi: Oxford University Press, 1991).

———, *Modern Myths, Locked Minds: Secularism and Fundamentalism in India* (Delhi: Oxford University Press, 1997).

Madhok, Balraj, *R.S.S. and Politics* (Delhi: Hindu World Publications, 1980).

———, *Indianisation? What, Why and How* (Delhi: S. Chand, 1970).

Mahendra, K.L., *Defeat the R.S.S. Fascist Designs* (Delhi: Communist Party of India Publication, 1973).

Malaviya, H.D., *The Danger of Right Reaction* (Delhi: A Socialist Congressman Publication, 1965).

Malik, Yogendra K. and V.B. Singh, *Hindu Nationalists in India: The Rise of the Bharatiya Janata Party* (Delhi: Vistaar Publications, 1995).

Malkani, K.R., *The RSS Story* (Delhi: Impex India, 1980).

———, *The Politics Of Ayodhya and Hindu-Muslim Relations* (Delhi: Har Anand Publications, 1993).

Manning, D.J. and T.J. Robinson, *The Place of Ideology in Political Life* (London: Croom Helm, 1985).

Manuel, Peter, *Cassette Culture: Popular Music and Technology in North India* (Chicago: University of Chicago Press, 1993).

Marty, Martin E. and R. Scott Appleby, eds., *Fundamentalisms Observed*, Vol. 1 (Chicago: University of Chicago Press, 1991).

———, *Fundamentalisms and Society*, Vol. 2 (Chicago: University of Chicago Press, 1992).

———, *Fundamentalisms and the State: Remaking Polities, Economies and Militance*, Vol. 3 (Chicago: University of Chicago Press, 1993).

———, *Accounting for Fundamentalisms: The Dynamic Character of Movements*, Vol. 4 (Chicago: University of Chicago Press, 1994).

———, *Fundamentalisms Comprehended*, Vol. 5 (Chicago: University of Chicago Press, 1995).

Mathew, Philip and Ajit Muricken, eds., *Religion, Ideology and Counter-Culture* (Bangalore: Horizon Books, 1987).

Mckean, Lise, *Divine Enterprise: Gurus and the Hindu Nationalist Movement* (Chicago: University of Chicago Press, 1996).

Merkl, Peter H. and Ninian Smart, eds., *Religion and Politics in the Modern World* (New York: New York University Press, 1983).

Minault, Gail, *The Khilafat Movement: Religious Symbolism and Political Mobilization in India* (Delhi: Oxford University Press, 1982).

Mishra, Dina Nath, *R.S.S.: Myth and Reality* (Delhi: Vikas Publishing House, 1980).

Mishra, Girish, *RSS Shadow over Benaras Hindu University* (Delhi: Sampradayikta Virodhi Committee, n.d.).

Moghadam, Valentine M., *Identity Politics and Women: Cultural Reassertions and Feminisms in International Perspective* (Oxford: Westview, 1994).

Mookerji, Radha Kumud, *Nationalism in Hindu Culture* (Delhi: S. Chand & Co., 1957).

Mukhopadhya, Nilanjan, *The Demolition: India at the Crossroads* (Delhi: Indus, 1994).

Naik, Pradeep, *The Politics of Ayodhya Dispute: Rise of Communalism and Future Voting Behaviour* (Delhi: Commonwealth Publishers, 1993).

Namboodripad, E.M.S., *The B.J.P.-R.S.S.: In the Service of Right Reaction* (Delhi: NBC, 1990).

Nandy, Ashis, *The Intimate Enemy: Loss and Recovery of Self Under Colonialism* (Delhi: Oxford University Press, 1983).

———, *At the Edge of Psychology: Essays in Politics and Culture* (Delhi: Oxford University Press, 1993 rep.).

Nandy, Ashis, Shikha Trivedy, Shail Mayaram, Achyut Yagnik, *Creating a Nationality: The Ramjanmabhoomi Movement and Fear of the Self* (Delhi: Oxford University Press, 1995).

Nisbet, Robert A., *Community and Power* (Oxford: Oxford University Press, 1968).

Oberoi, Harjot, *The Construction of Religious Boundaries: Culture, Identity and Diversity in Sikh Tradition* (Delhi: Oxford University Press, 1994).

Oddie, G.A., ed., *Religion in South Asia* (Delhi: Manohar, 1991).

Omvedt, Gail, *Cultural Revolt in a Colonial Society: The Non-Brahman Movement in Western India 1873-1930* (Bombay: Scientific Socialist Education Trust, 1976).

———, *Dalit Visions: The Anti-Caste Movement and the Construction of an Indian Identity* (Delhi: Orient Longman, 1995).

Pande, B.N., *Islam and Indian Culture* (Patna: Khuda Bakhsh Oriental Public Library, 1986).

Pandey, Gyanendra, *The Construction of Communalism in Colonial North India* (Delhi: Oxford University Press, 1990).

———, ed., *Hindus and Others: The Question of Identity in India Today* (Delhi: Viking, 1993).

Pandian, Jacob, *The Making of India and Indian Traditions* (New Jersey: Prentice Hall, 1995).

Panikkar, K.N., *Against Lord and State: Religion and Peasant Uprisings in Malabar, 1836-1921* (Delhi: Oxford University Press, 1989).

———, ed., *Communalism in India: History, Politics and Culture* (Delhi: Manohar, 1991).

———, ed., *The Concerned Indian's Guide to Communalism* (Delhi: Viking, 1999).

Pantham, Thomas and Kenneth L. Deutsch, eds., *Political Thought in Modern India* (Delhi: Sage Publications, 1986).

Pearson, Anne Mackenzie, *'Because It Gives Me Peace of Mind': Ritual Fasts in the Religious Lives of Hindu Women* (Albany: SUNY Press, 1996).

Prakash, Indra, *A Review of the History and Work of Hindu Mahasabha and the Hindu Sangathan Movement* (Delhi: Akhil Bharat Hindu Mahasabha, 1952).

Pramod Kumar, *Polluting Sacred Faith: A Study of Communalism and Violence in India* (Delhi: Ajanta Publications, 1992).

Puri, Geeta, *Bharatiya Jana Sangh Organisation and Ideology, Delhi: A Case Study* (Delhi: Sterling Publishers, 1980).

Purohit, B.R., *Hindu Revivalism and Indian Nationalism* (Sagar: Sathi Prakashan, 1965).

Rajaram, Navaratna S., *Aryan Invasion of India: The Myth and the Truth* (Delhi: Voice of India, 1993).

Ram Nath, *Dalit-Muslim Unity: Why and How?* (Bangalore: Dalit Sahitya Academy, 1995).

Raychaudhury, Tapan, *Europe Reconsidered: Perceptions of the West in Nineteenth Century Bengal* (Delhi: Oxford University Press, 1988).

Richman, Paula, ed., *Many Ramayanas: The Diversity of Narrative Tradition in South Asia* (Delhi: Oxford University Press, 1992).

Robb, Peter, ed., *Society and Ideology: Essays in South Asian History* (Delhi: Oxford University Press, 1993).

———, *The Concept of Race in South Asia* (Delhi: Oxford University Press, 1995).

Robinson, Francis, *Sepratism Among Indian Muslims: The Politics of the United Provinces' Muslims 1860-1923* (Delhi: Oxford University Press, 1993).

Sahai Govind, *R.S.S. Ideology, Technique Propaganda* (Allahabad, 1948).

Sarkar, Sumit, *Writing Social History* (Delhi: Oxford University Press, 1997).

Savarkar, V.D., *Who is A Hindu? Hindutva* (Poona: S.P. Gokhale, 1949).

Selected Writings on Communalism (Delhi: People's Publishing House, 1994).

Seliger, Martin, *Ideology and Politics* (London: George Allen & Unwin, 1976).
Sen, Amiya P., *Hindu Revivalism in Bengal 1872-1905: Some Essays in Interpretation* (Delhi: Oxford University Press, 1993).
Sethna, K.D., *The Problem of Aryan Origins: From an Indian point of View* (Delhi: Voice of India, 1992).
Shah, Ghanshyam, *Protest Movements in Two Indian States: A Study of the Gujarat and Bihar Movements* (Delhi: Ajanta Publications, 1977).
Sharma, Arvind, ed., *Today's Woman in World Religions* (Albany: State University of New York Press, 1994).
Sharma, R.S., *Communal History and Ram's Ayodhya* (Delhi: People's Publishing House, 1990).
Sharma, R.S., M. Athar Ali, D.N. Jha, Suraj Bhan, *Ramjanmabhumi-Baburi Masjid: A Historians' Report to the Nation* (Delhi: People's Publishing House, 1991).
Shourie, Arun, *Religion in Politics* (Delhi: Roll Books International, 1987).
Shourie, Arun and Jay Dubashi, *Hindu Temples: What Happened to Them—A Preliminary Survey* (Delhi: Voice of India, 1990).
Smith, Donald Eugene, *India as a Secular State* (Princeton: Princeton University Press, 1963).
Smith, W. C., *The Meaning and End of Religion: A New Approach to the Religious Traditions of Mankind* (New York: Macmillan, 1962).
Sontheimer, Gunther-D. and Hermann Kulke, eds., *Hinduism Reconsidered* (Delhi: Manohar, 1989).
Srivastava, Sushil, *The Disputed Mosque: A Historical Inquiry* (Delhi: Vistaar Publications, 1991).
Sutton, Amos, *Orissa and Its Evangelization* (Derby, England, 1850).
Swaro, Dasarathi, *The Christian Missionaries in Orissa: Their Impact on Nineteenth Century Society* (Calcutta: Punthi Pustak, 1990).
Swarup, Hem Lata and Sarojini Bisaria, eds., *Women, Politics and Religion* (Etawah: A.C. Brothers, 1991).
Talageri, Shrikant G., *Aryan Invasion Theory: A Reappraisal* (Delhi: Voice of India, 1993).
Talreja, Kanayalal M., *Pseudo-secularism in India* (Mumbai: Rashtriya Chetna Prakashan, 1996).
Talwar, Veer Bharat, *Jharkhand ke Adivasi aur RSS* [in Hindi](Chhaibasa: St. Martin Printer, n.d.).
Taneja, Nalini, *BJP's Assault on Education and Educational Institutions* (Delhi: CPI [M] Publication, 1999).
Thompson, Kenneth, *Belief and Ideology* (London: Taristock Publications, 1986).
Thursby, G.R., *Hindu-Muslim Relations in British India: A Study of Controversy, Conflict and Communal Movements in Northern India 1923-1928* (Leiden: E.J. Brill, 1975).
Tripathi, Amales, *The Extremist Challenge: India between 1890 and 1910* (Calcutta: Orient Longman, 1967).

van der Veer, Peter, *Religious Nationalism: Hindus and Muslims in India* (Delhi: Oxford University Press, 1996).

Vyas, H.K., *Vishwa Hindu Parishad: The R.S.S. Broad Outfit for Spreading Militant Aggressive Hindu Communal Poison* (Delhi: Communist Party Publication, 1983).

Weber, Max, *The Religion of India* (New York: The Free Press, 1958).

Wolpert, Stanley, *Tilak and Gokhale: Revolution and Reform in the Making of Modern India* (Berkeley: University of California Press, 1962).

Wood, C., *The Moplah Rebellion and its Genesis* (Delhi: People's Publishing House, 1987).

Yechuri, Sitaram, *What is Hindu Rashtra?: On Golwalkar's Fascistic Ideology and the Saffron Brigade's Practice* (Madras: Frontline Publication, 1993).

———, *Pseudo Hinduism Exposed: Saffron Brigade's Myth and Reality* (Delhi: CPI[M] Publication, 1993).

Zakaria, Rafiq, *The Widening Divide: An Insight into Hindu-Muslim Relations* (Delhi: Viking, 1995).

Zavos, John, *The Emergence of Hindu Nationalism in India* (Delhi: Oxford University Press, 2000).

Zelliot, Eleanor, *From Untouchable to Dalit: Essays on the Ambedkar Movement* (Delhi: Manohar, 1992).

Zelliot, Eleanor and Maxine Bernsten, eds., *The Experience of Hinduism: Essays on Religion in Maharashtra* (Albany: State University of New York Press, 1988).

ARTICLES

Ahmed, Aijaz, 'Culture, Community, Nation: On the Ruins of Ayodhya', *Social Scientist*, 21 (7-8), July-August 1993, pp. 17-48.

Alam, Javed, 'Composite Culture and Communal Consciousness: The Ittehadul Muslimeen in Hyderabad', in Vasudha Dalmia and Heinrich von Stietencron, eds., *Representing Hinduism: The Construction of Religious Traditions and National Identity* (Delhi: Sage Publications, 1995), pp. 338-57.

Aloysius, G, 'Trajectory of Hindutva', *Economic and Political Weekly*, XXIX (24), 11 June 1994, pp. 1450-2.

Andersen, Walter, 'The Rashtriya Swayamsevak Sangh', *Economic and Political Weekly*, VII (11-14), 11, 18, 25 March and 1 April 1972.

Bakker, Hans, 'Ayodhya: A Hindu Jerusalem: An Investigation of "Holy War" as a Religious Idea in the Light of Communal Unrest in India', *Numen*, 38 (1), June 1991, pp. 80-109.

Banerjee, Sumanta, '"Hindutva": Ideology and Social Psychology', *Economic and Political Weekly*, XXVI (3), 19 January 1991, pp. 97-101.

Bayly, C.A., 'The Pre-history of "Communalism"? Religious Conflict in India, 1700-1860', *Modern Asian Studies*, 19 (2), 1985, pp. 177-203.

Bayly, Susan, 'Fundamentalism: A Historian's View of India after Ayodhya', *The Cambridge Review*, 114 (2322), October 1993, pp. 99-106.

Bhargava, Rajeev, 'Giving Secularism its Due', *Economic and Political Weekly*, XXIX (28), 9 July 1994, pp. 1784-91.

Bharucha, Rustom, 'In the Name of the Secular: Cultural Interactions and Interventions', *Economic and Political Weekly*, XXIX (45-6), 5 and 12 November 1994, pp. 2925-34.

———, 'Somebody's Other: Disorientations in the Cultural Politics of our Times', *Economic and Political Weekly*, XXIX (3), 15 January 1994, pp. 105-10.

Bhattacharya, Neeladri, 'Myth, History and the Politics of Ramjanmabhumi', in S. Gopal, ed., *Anatomy of Confrontation: The Babri Masjid Ramjanmabhumi Dispute* (Delhi: Viking, 1991), pp. 122-40.

Bilgrami, Akeel, 'Two Concepts of Secularism: Reason, Modernity and Archimedean Ideal', *Economic and Political Weekly*, XXIX (28), 9 July 1994, pp. 1749-61.

Bosch, Lourens P. Van Den, 'Burning Question: Sati and Sati Temples as the Focus of Political Interest', *Numen* 37 (2), December 1990, pp. 174-94.

Breman, Jan, 'Anti-Muslim Pogrom in Surat', *Economic and Political Weekly*, XXVIII (16), 17 April 1993, pp. 737-41.

Casolari, Marzia, 'Hindutva's Foreign Tie-up in the 1930s: Archival Evidence', *Economic and Political Weekly*, XXXV (4), 22 January 2000, pp. 218-28.

Chakrabarty, Bidyut, 'India's Secularism: Tolerance and Coercion', in Bidyut Chakrabarty, ed., *Secularism and Indian Polity* (Delhi: Segment Book Distributors, 1990), pp. 93-106.

Chakravarti, Uma and Kumkum Roy, 'In Search of Our Past: A Review of the Limitations and Possibilities of Historiography of Women in Early India', *Economic and Political Weekly*, XXIII (18), 1988, pp. WS 2-10.

Chakravarty, Gargi, 'BJP-RSS and Distortion of History: Myths and Realities of History', in *Selected Writings on Communalism* (Delhi: People's Publishing House, 1994), pp. 161-80.

Chandra, Sudhir, 'Of Communal Consciousness and Communal Violence: Impressions from Post-riot Surat', *Economic and Political Weekly*, XXVIII (36), 4 September 1993, pp. 1883-7.

Chatterjee, Partha, 'Secularism and Toleration', *Economic and Political Weekly*, XXIX (28), 9 July 1994, pp. 1768-77.

Chatterjee, Manini, 'The BJP: Political Mobilization for Hindutva', *South Asia Bulletin*, XIV (1), 1994, pp. 14-23.

Chaturvedi, Jayati and Gyaneshwar Chaturvedi, 'Dharma Yudh: Communal Violence, Riots and Public Space in Ayodhya and Agra City, 1990 and 1992', in Paul Brass, ed., *Riots and Pogroms* (Houndmills: Macmillan Press, 1996), pp. 177-200.

Chhachhi, Amrita, 'The State, Religious Fundamentalism and Women: Trends in South Asia', *Economic and Political Weekly*, XXIV (11), 18 March 1989, pp. 567-78.

Chiriyankandath, James, 'Tricolour and Saffron: Congress and the neo-Hindu Challenge', in Subrata K. Mitra and James Chiriyankandath, eds., *Electoral Politics in India: A Changing Landscape* (Delhi: Segment Books, 1992), pp. 55-80.

Choudhary, Kameshwar, 'BJP's Changing View of Hindu-Muslim Relations', *Economic and Political Weekly*, XXVI (23), 17 August 1991, pp. 1901-4.

Choudhury, Arundhati Roy, 'Search for a Tribal Identity: The Dominant and the Subaltern', in Walter Fernandes, ed., *The Indigenous Question: Search for an Identity* (Delhi: Indian Social Institute, 1993), pp. 9-22.

Chousalkar, S., 'Neo Hindu Nationalism', *Social Science Probings*, 5 (1-4), March-December 1988, pp. 118-30.

Datta, Pradip Kumar, 'VHP's Ram at Ayodhya: Reincarnation through Ideology and Organisation', *Economic and Political Weekly*, XXVI (44), 2 November 1991, pp. 2517-26.

———, '"Dying Hindus": Production of Hindu Communal Common Sense in Early 20th Century Bengal', *Economic and Political Weekly*, XXVIII (25), 19 June 1993, pp.1305-19.

Davis, Richard H., 'The Iconography of Rama's Chariot', in David Ludden, ed., *Making India Hindu: Religion, Community and the Politics of Democracy in India* (Delhi: Oxford University Press, 1996), pp. 27-54.

Deshpande, G.P., 'The Plural Tradition', *Seminar*, 365, January 1990, pp. 23-5.

Deshpande, S.H., 'My days in the RSS', *Quest*, 96, July-August 1975, pp. 19-30.

———, 'RSS and the Muslims: No Escape from Secularism', *The Times of India*, 25 May 1994.

Devalle, Susana B.C., 'Social Identities, Hindu Fundamentalism, and Politics in India', in David N. Lorenzen, ed., *Bhakti Religion in North India: Community Identity and Political Action* (Albany: State University of New York Press, 1995), pp. 306-22.

Dharma Kumar, 'Left Secularists and Communalism', *Economic and Political Weekly*, XXIX (28), 9 July 1994, pp. 1803-9.

Dube, Leela, 'The Symbolism of Biological Reproduction and Sexual Relations in Reproduction', in Leela Dube et al., eds., *Visibility and Power: Essays on Women in Society and Development* (Delhi: Oxford University Press, 1986), pp. 22-53.

Embree, Ainslie T., 'The Function of the Rashtriya Swayamsevak Sangh: To Define the Hindu Nation', in Martin E. Marty and R. Scott Appleby, eds., *Accounting for Fundamentalisms: The Dynamic character of Movements*, Vol. 4 (Chicago: University of Chicago Press, 1994), pp. 617-68.

Fox, Richard G., 'Gandhian Socialism and Hindu Nationalism: Cultural

Domination in the World System', *Journal of Commonwealth and Comparative Politics*, 25 (3), November 1987, pp. 233-47.

Frietag, Sandria B., 'Sacred Symbol as Mobilizing Ideology: The North Indian Search for a "Hindu" Community', *Comparative Studies in Society and History*, 22 (4), 1980, pp. 597-625.

Frykenberg, Robert Eric, 'The Emergence of Modern "Hinduism" as a Concept and as an Institution: A Reappraisal With Special Reference to South India', in Gunther-D. Sontheimer and Hermann Kulke, eds., *Hinduism Reconsidered* (Delhi: Manohar, 1989), pp. 29-49.

———, 'Hindu Fundamentalism and the Structural Stability of India', in Martin E. Marty and R. Scott Appleby, eds., *Fundamentalisms and the State: Remaking Polities, Economies and Militance*, Vol. 3 (Chicago: University of Chicago Press, 1993), pp. 233-55.

Gold, Daniel, 'Rational Action and Uncontrolled Violence: Explaining Hindu Communalism', *Religion*, 21, 1991, pp. 357-70.

———, 'Organized Hinduisms: From Vedic Truth to Hindu Nation', in Martin E. Marty and R. Scott Appleby, eds., *Fundamentalisms Observed*, Vol. 1 (Chicago: University of Chicago Press, 1991), pp. 531-93.

Halbfass, Wilhelm, 'Practical Vedanta', in Vasudha Dalmia and Heinrich von Stietencron, eds., *Representing Hinduism: the Construction of Religious Traditions and National Identity* (Delhi: Sage Publications, 1995), pp. 211-23.

Harvey, Mark J., 'The Secular as Sacred? The Religio-Political Rationalization of B.G. Tilak', *Modern Asian Studies*, 20 (2), 1986, pp. 321-31.

Hasan, Zoya, 'Changing Orientation of the State and the Emergence of Majoritarianism in the 1980s', in K.N. Panikkar, ed., *Communalism in India: History, Politics and Culture* (Delhi: Manohar, 1991), pp. 142-52.

Hatcher, Brian A. '"The cosmos is one family" (*vasudhaiva kutumbakam*): Problematic mantra of Hindu humanism', *Contributions to Indian Sociology*, 28 (1), 1994, pp. 149-62.

Heuze, Gerard, 'Shiv Sena and National Hinduism', *Economic and Political Weekly*, XXVII (41), 10 October 1992, pp. 2253-63.

Hutchinson, John, 'Cultural Nationalism and Moral Regeneration', in John Hutchinson and Anthony D. Smith, eds., *Nationalism* (Oxford: Oxford University Press, 1994), pp. 122-31.

Inden, Ronald, 'Orientalist Constructions of India', *Modern Asian Studies*, 20 (3), 1986, pp. 401-46.

Jaffrelot, Christophe, 'Hindu Nationalism: Strategic Syncretism in Ideolgy Building', *Economic and Political Weekly*, XXVIII (12-13), 20-7 March 1993, pp. 517-24.

Jeffery, Roger and Patricia Jeffery, 'The Bijnor Riots, October 1990: Collapse of a Mythical Special Relationships?', *Economic and Political Weekly*, XXIX (10), 5 March 1994, pp. 551-8.

Jha, Ajit Kumar, 'Hindutva Swadeshi Waves of Economic Nationalism', *The Times of India*, 6 September 1995.

Jones, Kenneth W., 'Religious Identity and the Indian Census', in N.G. Barrier, ed., *The Census of British India: New Perspective* (Delhi: Manohar, 1981), pp. 73-101.

———, 'Politicized Hinduism: The Ideology and Program of the Hindu Mahasabha', in Robert D. Baird, ed., *Religion in Modern India* (Delhi: Manohar, 1989), pp. 239-74.

Joseph, Sarah, 'Identity, Culture and Community', *Economic and Political Weekly*, XXVIII (17), 24 April 1993, pp. 807-9.

Kapur, Anuradha, 'Deity to Crusader: The Changing Iconography of Ram', in Gyanendra Pandey, ed., *Hindus and Others: The Question of Identity in India Today* (Delhi: Viking, 1993), pp. 74-109.

Kapoor, Ratna and Brenda Crossman, 'Communalising Gender/Engendering Community: Women, Legal Discourse and Saffron Agenda', *Economic and Political Weekly*, XXVIII (17), 24 April 1993, pp. WS 35-44.

Kaviraj, Sudipta, 'The Imaginary Institution of India', in Partha Chatterjee and Gyanendra Pandey, eds., *Subaltern Studies VII: Writings on South Asian History and Society* (Delhi: Oxford University Press, 1993), pp. 1-39.

Khan, Rasheeduddin, 'Prejudice, Myth and History', *Mainstream*, 31 (41), 21 August 1993, pp. 11-12 and 21.

Kishwar, Madhu, 'Religion at the Service of Nationalism: An Analysis of Sangh Parivar Politics', *Manushi*, 76, May-June 1993, pp. 2-20.

Kothari, Rajni, 'The Congress System in India', *Asian Survey*, 4 (12), December 1964, pp. 1161-73.

———, 'Hindutva in Perspective', *Mainstream*, Annual, 1993, pp. 27-30.

Madan, T.N., 'Secularism in its Place', *The Journal of Asian Studies*, 46 (4), November 1987, pp. 747-58.

Malkani, K.R., 'Hindu Perception of Muslim and Christian Rule in India', *Mainstream*, 31 (28), 22 May 1993, pp. 4 and 35.

Minz, Nirmal, 'Identity of Tribals in India', in Walter Fernandes, ed., *The Indigenous Question: Search for an Identity* (Delhi: Indian Social Institute, 1993), pp. 23-32.

Mitra, Subrata Kumar, 'Desecularising the State: Religion and Politics in India after Independence', *Comparative Studies in Society and History*, 33 (4), October 1991, pp. 755-77.

Muralidharan, Sukumar, 'Mandal, Mandir aur Masjid: "Hindu" Communalism and the Crisis of the State', in K.N. Panikkar, ed., *Communalism in India: History, Politics and Culture* (Delhi: Manohar, 1991), pp. 196-218.

Nandy, Ashis, 'Culture, State, and the Recovery of Religious Tolerance', *Economic and Political Weekly*, XIV (49), 8 December 1984, pp. 2079-83.

———, 'An Anti-Secularist Manifesto', *Seminar*, 314, October 1985, pp.14-24.

———, 'The Politics of Secularism and the Recovery of Religious Tolerance', *Alternatives*, XIII (2), April 1988, pp. 177-94.

———, 'The Fear of Gandhi: Nathuram Godse & His Successors', *The Times of India*, 27 April 1994.

———, 'Three Propositions', *Seminar*, 402, February 1993, pp. 15-17.

Noorani, A.G., 'History of the BJP (1980-1990)', *Mainstream*, 29 (23), 30 March 1991, pp. 7-12.

———, 'BJP: Child of RSS and Heir to Hindu Mahasabha', *Mainstream*, 29 (40), 27 July 1991, pp.16-19.

O'Hanlon, Rosalind, 'Historical Approaches to Communalism: Perspectives from Western India', in Peter Robb, ed., *Society and Ideology* (Delhi: Oxford University Press, 1992), pp. 247-66.

Omvedt, Gail, 'Hinduism and Politics', *Economic and Political Weekly*, XXV (14), 7 April 1990, pp. 723-9.

———, 'Of Brahmins, Sacred and Socialist', *Economic and Political Weekly*, XXVIII (44), 30 October 1993, pp. 2402-4.

Pandey, Gyanendra, 'Hindus and Others: The Militant Hindu Construction', *Economic and Political Weekly*, XXVI (52), 28 December 1991, pp. 2997-3009.

———, 'In Defence of Fragment: Writing about Hindu-Muslim Riots in India Today', *Economic and Political Weekly*, XXVI (11 and 12), 1991, pp. 559-72.

———, 'Modes of History Writing: New Hindu History of Ayodhya', *Economic and Political Weekly*, XXIX (25), 18 June 1994, pp. 1523-8.

———, 'The Appeal of Hindu History', in Vasudha Dalmia and H. von Stietencron, eds., *Representing Hinduism: The Construction of Religious Traditions and National Identity* (Delhi: Sage Publications, 1995), pp. 369-88.

Pollock, Sheldon, 'Ramayana and Political Imagination in India', *Journal of Asian Studies*, 52 (2), May 1993, pp. 261-97.

Raghavan, T.C.A., 'Origins and Development of Hindu Mahasabha Ideology: The Call of V.D. Savarkar and Bhai Parmanand', *Economic and Political Weekly*, XVIII (15), 9 April 1983, pp. 595-600.

Rajagopal, Arvind, 'Ram Janmabhoomi, Consumer Identity and Image-Based Politics', *Economic and Political Weekly*, XXIX (27), 2 July 1994, pp. 1659-68.

Rudd, Arild Engelsmen, 'Contradictions and Ambivalence in the Hindu Nationalist Discourse in West Bengal', in Stein Tonnesson and Hans Antlov, eds., *Asian Forms of the Nation* (Surrey: Curzon Press, 1996), pp. 150-80.

Rudolph, Lloyd. I., 'The Media and Cultural Politics', in Subrata K. Mitra and James Chiriyankandath, eds., *Electoral Politics in India: A Changing Landscape* (Delhi: Segment Books, 1992), pp. 81-98.

Rudolph, L.I. and S.H. Rudolph, 'Rethinking Secularism: Genesis and

Implications of the Textbook Controversy, 1977-79', *Pacific Affairs*, 56 (1), Spring 1983, pp. 15-37.

Sahgal, Nayantara, 'The Making of Mrs. Gandhi', *South Asian Review*, 8 (3), 8 April 1975, pp. 189-210.

Sarkar, Sumit, 'The Fascism of the Sangh Parivar', *Economic and Political Weekly*, XXVIII (5), 30 January 1993, pp. 163-7.

———, 'Roots of Secularism', *The Times of India*, 26 March 1993.

———, 'Hindutva and the Question of Conversions', in K.N. Panikkar, ed., *The Concerned Indian's Guide to Communalism* (Delhi: Viking, 1999).

Sarkar, Tanika, 'The Woman as Communal Subject: Rashtrasevika Samiti and Ram Janmabhoomi Movement', *Economic and Political Weekly*, XXVI (35), 31 August 1991, pp. 2057-62.

———, 'Imagining a Hindu Nation: Hindu and Muslim in Bankimchandra's Later Writings', *Economic and Political Weekly*, XXIX (39), 24 September 1994, pp. 2553-64.

———, 'Educating the Children of the Hindu Rashtra: Notes on the RSS Schools', *South Asia Bulletin*, XIV (2), 1994, pp. 10-15.

Saxena, Kiran, 'The Hindu Trade Union Movement in India: The Bharatiya Mazdoor Sangh', *Asian Survey*, XXXIII (7), July 1993, pp. 685-96.

Sen, Amartya, 'Secularism and Its Discontents', in Kaushik Basu and Sanjay Subrahmanyam, eds., *Unravelling the Nation: Sectarian Conflict and India's Secular Identity* (Delhi: Penguin Books, 1996), pp. 11-43.

Shah, Ghanshyam, 'Identity, Communal Consciousness and Politics', *Economic and Political Weekly*, XXIX (19), 7 May 1994, pp. 1133-40.

Shakir, Moin, 'Rise of Fundamentalism: An Enquiry into Its Causes', *Radical Humanist*, 50 (5), August 1986.

Shivanandan, S., 'Mandal, Mandir and Masjid: Dubious Role of Media', *Mainstream*, 28 (52), 20 October 1990, pp. 8-13 and 35.

Sikand, Yoginder, 'Manusmriti versus Constitution of India', *Mainstream*, 31 (23), 17 April 1993, pp. 15-18.

Simeon, Dilip, 'Communalism in Modern India', *Mainstream*, 25 (13), 13 December 1986, pp. 7-17.

Stewart, Tony K., 'Satya Pir: Muslim Holy Man and Hindu God', in Donald S. Lopez, Jr., ed., *Religions of India in Practice* (New Jersey: Princeton University Press, 1995), pp. 578-97.

Thakur, Ramesh, 'Ayodhya and the Politics of India's Secularism: A Double-Standards Discourse', *Asian Survey*, 33 (7), July 1993, pp. 645-64.

Thapar, Romila, 'Syndicated Moksha?' *Seminar*, 313, September 1985, pp. 14-22.

———,'The Ramayana Syndrome', *Seminar*, 353, January 1989, pp. 71-5.

———, 'Imagined Religious Communities? Ancient History and the Modern Search for a Hindu Identity', *Modern Asian Studies*, 23(2), 1989, pp. 209-31.

———, 'The Politics of Religious Communities', *Seminar*, 365, January 1990, pp. 27-32.

Upadhyaya, Prakash Chandra, 'The Politics of Indian Secularism', *Modern Asian Studies*, 26 (4), 1992, pp. 815-53.

van der Veer, Peter, 'Hindu Nationalism and the Discourse of Modernity: The Vishwa Hindu Parishad', in Martin E. Marty and R. Scott Appleby, eds., *Accounting for Fundamentalisms: The Dynamic Character of Movements*, Vol. 4 (Chicago: University of Chicago Press, 1994), pp. 653-68.

Vanaik, Achin, 'Situating Threat of Hindu Nationalism: Problems with Fascist Paradigm', *Economic and Political Weekly*, XXIX (28), 9 July 1994, pp. 1729-48.

Varshney, Ashutosh, 'Contested Meanings: Indian National Unity, Hindu Nationalism, and the Politics of Anxiety', *Daedalus*, 122, 1993, pp. 227-61.

Yang, Anand A., 'Sacred Symbol and Sacred Space in Rural India: Community Mobilization in the "Anti-Cow Killing" Riots of 1893', *Comparative Studies in Society and History*, 22 (4), 1980, pp. 576-96.

Index